ATLA BIBLIOGRAPHY SERIES
edited by Dr. Kenneth E. Rowe

1. *A Guide to the Study of the Holiness Movement,* by Charles Edwin Jones. 1974.
2. *Thomas Merton: A Bibliography,* by Marquita E. Breit. 1974.
3. *The Sermon on the Mount: A History of Interpretation and Bibliography,* by Warren S. Kissinger. 1975.
4. *The Parables of Jesus: A History of Interpretation and Bibliography,* by Warren S. Kissinger. 1979.
5. *Homosexuality and the Judeo-Christian Tradition: An Annotated Bibliography,* by Thom Horner. 1981.
6. *A Guide to the Study of the Pentecostal Movement,* by Charles Edwin Jones. 1983.
7. *The Genesis of Modern Process Thought: A Historical Outline with Bibliography,* by George R. Lucas, Jr. 1983.
8. *A Presbyterian Bibliography,* by Harold B. Prince. 1983.
9. *Paul Tillich: A Comprehensive Bibliography . . .,* by Richard C. Crossman. 1983.
10. *A Bibliography of the Samaritans,* by Alan David Crown. 1984 (see no. 32).
11. *An Annotated and Classified Bibliography of English Literature Pertaining to the Ethiopian Orthodox Church,* by Jon Bonk. 1984.
12. *International Meditation Bibliography, 1950 to 1982,* by Howard R. Jarrell. 1984.
13. *Rabindranath Tagore: A Bibliography,* by Katherine Henn. 1985.
14. *Research in Ritual Studies: A Programmatic Essay and Bibliography,* by Ronald L. Grimes, 1985.
15. *Protestant Theological Education in America,* by Heather F. Day. 1985.
16. *Unconscious: A Guide to Sources,* by Natalino Caputi. 1985.
17. *The New Testament Apocrypha and Pseudepigrapha,* by James H. Charlesworth. 1987.
18. *Black Holiness,* by Charles Edwin Jones. 1987.

19. *A Bibliography on Ancient Ephesus,* by Richard Oster. 1987.
20. *Jerusalem, the Holy City: A Bibliography,* by James D. Purvis. 1988; Vol. II, 1991.
21. *An Index to English Periodical Literature on the Old Testament and Ancient Near Eastern Studies,* by William G. Hupper. Vol. I, 1987; Vol. II, 1988; Vol. III, 1990; Vol. IV, 1990; Vol. V, 1992.
22. *John and Charles Wesley: A Bibliography,* by Betty M. Jarboe. 1987.
23. *A Scholar's Guide to Academic Journals in Religion,* by James Dawsey. 1988.
24. *The Oxford Movement and Its Leaders: A Bibliography of Secondary and Lesser Primary Sources,* by Lawrence N. Crumb. 1988; Supplement, 1993.
25. *A Bibliography of Christian Worship,* by Bard Thompson. 1989.
26. *The Disciples and American Culture: A Bibliography of Works by Disciples of Christ Members, 1866–1984,* by Leslie R. Galbraith and Heather F. Day. 1990.
27. *The Yogacara School of Buddhism: A Bibliography,* by John Powers. 1991.
28. *The Doctrine of the Holy Spirit: A Bibliography Showing Its Chronological Development* (2 vols.), by Esther Dech Schandorff. 1993.
29. *Rediscovery of Creation: A Bibliographical Study of the Church's Response to the Environmental Crisis,* by Joseph K. Sheldon. 1992.
30. *The Charismatic Movement: A Guide to the Study of Neo- Pentecostalism with Emphasis on Anglo-American Sources,* by Charles Edwin Jones. 1993.
31. *Cities and Churches: An International Bibliography* (3 vols.), by Loyde H. Hartley. 1992.
32. *A Bibliography of the Samaritans,* 2nd ed., by Alan David Crown. 1993.

LINGVARVM

duodecim characteri.
BVS DIFFERENTIVM ALPHA.
betvm, introdvctio, ac legendi
modus longè facilimus . Linguarum
nomina sequens proximè
pagella offeret.

Guilielmi Postelli Barentonij diligentia.

אמלרבדיז בּיני
סדכין חפם רבי
בעטיסה׳ אלדי׳ אכיל
רב בחגדולת דסק
חהתרוב הלאצ׳רֹת
ךוששיפושש וסשו:

ΔΥΧΘΡΑΝ ΕΠΙΘΥΜΕΙΣΘΑΙ ΠΟΛΥ.
IN MAGNIS VOLVISSE SAT EST.

Cum priuilegio.

Prostant Parisiis apud Dionysium Lescuier , sub porcelli
signo, vico Hilario, è regione diui Hilarij.

A BIBLIOGRAPHY OF THE SAMARITANS

Second Edition

by
Alan David Crown

ATLA Bibliography Series, No. 32

The American Theological Library Association and
The Scarecrow Press, Inc.
Metuchen, N.J., & London
1993

Also by Alan David Crown from Scarecrow Press

A Bibliography of the Samaritans, 1984

Frontispiece: The first printed Samaritan font

British Library Catologuing-in-Publication data available

Library of Congress Cataloging-in-publication Data

Crown, Alan David
  A Bibliography of the Samaritans / by Alan David Crown. — 2nd ed.
    p.   cm.— (ATLA bibliography series ; no.32
  Includes index
  ISBN 0--8108-2646-1 (acid-free paper)
  1. Samaritans—Bibliography. I. Title II. Series
  Z3479. S24C76 1993
  [DS 129]
  016.909'04922—dc20   92-42799

1-12-96

To Sorrell
who shared the research and the problems

CONTENTS

EDITOR'S FOREWORD

Since 1974 the American Theological Library Association, through its Publications Section, has undertaken responsibility for publishing a series of bibliographies. The series is designed to stimulate and encourage the preparation of reliable bibliographies and guides to the literature on religious studies in all of its scope and variety. Compilers are free to define their field, make their own selections and work out internal organization as the unique demands of the subject indicate. We are pleased to publish a revised and updated version of number 10 in our series, *A Bibliography of the Samaritans*, first published in 1984, compiled by Alan D. Crown.

Alan David Crown took his undergraduate training at the Universities of Leeds and Birmingham in his native England and earned a Ph.D at the University of Sydney. Currently Professor (Personal Chair) and Head of the Department of Semitic Studies at the University of Sydney, he also directs the university's Archive of Australian Judaica project. Professor Crown has held visiting professorships at several leading universities in England, Israel and the United States. He has authored, edited or translated more than twenty books and has published more than fifty scholarly articles.

Kenneth E. Rowe
Series Editor
Drew University Library
Madison, NJ 07940 USA

PREFACE

A belated review of the first edition of this bibliography drew attention to the rapid strides that were being made in the study of the Samaritans and expressed the hope that a new edition would soon be forthcoming. The editor has long been aware of the need for a second edition, not merely because the field of Samaritan studies has been so active in recent years, especially since the establishment of the *Société d'Études Samaritaines*, but also because of deficiencies in the first edition. Despite the friendliness of most of the reviews, the author was aware of the errors that had entered the text in several stages of processing. (It should be remembered that the problems of bibliography are such that one of the harshest of the reviews was replete with a whole crop of errors of its own, which were not in the original text.) Since it became apparent that many scholars were relying on the bibliography as a prime source of information and, indeed, so were catalogers and booksellers, it also became imperative to ensure that the text be as correct as possible. There was a need, too, to extend coverage of the literature on the connection between the New Testament and the Samaritans and to increase the entries given to reviews of the major works in the field.

In so far as possible, these tasks have been done, with the help of the excellent library at the Annenberg Research Center in Philadelphia and that of the library of the Oxford Centre for Postgraduate Hebrew Studies.

To minimize the possibility of errors entering the text during processing and to permit constant updating of the text with automatic indexing, the editor retyped the whole text on the word processor, using the *Pro-Cite* bibliographic database which has its own way of prompting the writer to prevent the omission of data, and then each entry was again checked against original sources. Finally, my loyal wife, Sadie Crown, to whom this book is dedicated, again devoted many long hours to reading the printouts and marking anomalies. In this edition I was also helped by my students Sr. Antoinette Collins and Elizabeth Owen, who both checked data and offered additional entries that had been missed. I am especially indebted to Ms. Owen for her constant scrutiny of new material, especially in the field of New Testament – Samaritan studies. She drew my attention to quite a few valuable new references.

Doubtless there are still problems, though the problems pointed up by reviewers were sometimes unreal—for example, differing canons of transcription of Hebrew names may give the impression of an omission when the work is in fact noted in the text, e.g., Balkind/Belkind. One deficiency concerns diacritical marks on Semitic names. So far as the postscript font allowed, the marks were inserted, but most postscript fonts do not yet provide for ease of transcribing names that have complicated diacritical markings.

The parameters of extent that were set for the first edition have been retained for the second, though somewhat more extensive reference is made to the connection between New Testament scholarship and Samaritan studies, reflecting the resurgence of interest in this field. Despite Samaritan claims to be descended from the Israelites, the *Bnai Yisrael,* the distinctive lines of Samaritanism do not appear until late in the Biblical period. Thus 2 Kings 17 was taken as the *terminus a quo* for the Samaritan bibliographer. However, because the historical geography of any site has a legacy from the past, as well as an accommodation with the present, that temporal parameter was disregarded in respect of references to Shechem and Samaria, the cities most closely identified with the origins of the Samaritans. As in the previous edition, only the more important references in the prolific writings of pilgrims and travellers are presented here, with some few others that serendipity brought to hand.

For the sake of catalogers of the rarer works, greater attention was paid to the number of editions available of each work. Moreover, a few comments were appended to some of the rarer works to give an indication of their focus. By and large, however, the user will still need to refer to the indexing system to gain insight into content of items listed. The indexing system has been slightly extended as almost all users have noted that this was a most important feature of the work, which saved them considerable labor. A short title index has been added as an additional finding aid.

As in the first edition, when possible, rare items have been annotated with the name of the holding library. The dimensions, in centimeters, have been retained for some of the publications of the Samaritan community, especially for those which appeared without any indication of place of publication or publisher. This system has been used by some libraries as an effective means of distinguishing between different editions of the Samaritans' publications. Whenever possible, at least one entry for an author of several works has been given using the full name. For the rest, initials only are provided or the usual —————————.

The system of transliterating Hebrew titles has been abandoned in favor of translation except for those works that are so well-known by their Hebrew name as to be unrecognizable in a translated form.

Alan David Crown
Sydney, 1993

ABBREVIATIONS

A. and S.	*Antiquity and Survival*
A. Seign.	*Assemblées du Seigneur, Paris*
A. zur T.	*Arbeiten zur Theologie*
AAJR	*American Academy of Jewish Research*
AASOR	*Annual of the American School of Oriental Research*
AAT	*Altestamentliche Abhandlungen (series)*
A-B	*Aleph Beth – Samaritan News*
ABBL	*Allgemeine Bibliothek der Biblischen Literatur*
Abt.	*Abteilung*
ACIO	*Actes du Congrès International des Orientalistes*
ADAJ	*Annual of the Department of Antiquity of Jordan*
AEPHE	*Annuaire de l'École Pratique des Hautes Études*
AIBL	*Comptes Rendus de l'Académie des Inscriptions et Belles-Lettres*
AION	*Annali del'Instituto Orientale di Napoli*
AJA	*American Journal of Archaeology*
AJBA	*Australian Journal of Biblical Archaeology*
AJHG	*American Journal of Human Genetics*
AJPA	*American Journal of Physical Anthropology*
AJSL	*American Journal of Semitic Languages*
AJT	*American Journal of Theology*
AKM	*Abhandlungen für die Kunde des Morgenlandes*
Allg. Ev. Luth. K.Z.	*Allgemeine Evangelische Lutheranische Kirchenzeitung*

ALUOS	Annual of the Leeds University Oriental Society
AN	Abr Nahrain
An. Bib.	Analecta Biblica
Anz. Akad. Wiss. Wien	Anzeiger der Akademie der Wissenschaft (Wien)
AOAT	Alter Orient und Altes Testament
AOL	Archives de l'Orient Latin
Ar. Or./ AO	Archiv orientalni
Arb.	Arbeiter
ASTI	Annual of the Swedish Theological Institute
ATR	Anglican Theological Review
AZJ	Allegmeine Zeitung des Judentums
BA	The Biblical Archaeologist
BAEO	Boletín de la Asociación Española de Orientalistas
BAIAS	Bulletin of the Anglo-Israel Archaeological Society
BAR	Biblical Archaeology Review
BASOR	Bulletin of the American Schools of Oriental Research
BeO	Bibbia et Orientia
BGBE	Beiträge zur Geschichte der Biblischen Exegese
Bi. Ki.	Bibel und Kirche
Bib.	Biblica
BIES	Bulletin of the Israel Exploration Society
Bijdr.	Bijdragen. Tijdschcrift voor Philosofie en Theologie
BJPES	Bulletin of the Jewish Palestine Exploration Society
BJRL	Bulletin of the John Rylands Library
BL	Bibel und Leben
BL (with call number)	British Library

BM	*Beth Mikra*
BO	*Bibliotheca Orientalis*
BR	*Bulletin Rabinowitz (Hebrew University Synagogue Bulletin)*
BS	*Bibliotheca Sacra*
BSJ	*Baker Street Journal*
BSt	*Biblische Studien*
BT	*Bible Today*
BTS	*Bible et Terre Sainte*
BVC	*Bible et Vie Chrétienne*
BW	*The Biblical World*
BZ	*Biblische Zeitschrift*
BZAW	*Beiheft, Zeitschrift für die Altestamentliche Wissenschaft*
CB	*Cultura Bíblica*
CBQ	*Catholic Biblical Quarterly*
CCAR	*Central Conference of American Rabbis, Journal*
CCER	*Cahiers du Cercle Ernest Renan*
CNI	*Christian News from Israel*
CNL	*Classici e neolatini*
CNT	*Coniectanea Neotestamentica*
CRB	*Chiers Revue Biblique*
DB	*Dictionnaire de la Bible (F. Vigouroux)*
DHL	*Das Heilige Land*
Div.	*Divinitas*
DL	*Deutsche Literaturzeitung*
DPV	*(See ZDPV) Deutschen Palästina-Verein (Zeitschrift)*
DVJ	*Deutsche Vierteljahrsschrift für Englische Theologische Forschung*
E	*The Expositor*

E. et T.	*Église et Théologie*
EAEHL	*Encyclopaedia of Archaeological Excavations in the Holy Land* (Hebrew and English editions)
EB	*Estudios Bíblicos*
EBB	*Elenchus Bibliographicus Biblicus*
EE	*Estudios Eclesiásticos*
EI	*Eretz Israel*
EJ	*Encyclopaedia Judaica*
EM	*Encyclopaedia Miqrait*
EPHE	*École Pratique des Hautes Études*
Ephem. Theol. Lov.	*Ephemeridea Theologicae Lovanienses*
EQ	*Evangelical Quarterly*
ER	*Ecumenical Review*
ERE	*Encyclopaedia of Religion and Ethics (James Hastings)*
ET	*Expository Times*
ETR	*Études Théologiques et Religieuses*
GGA	*Göttingische Gelehrte Anzeiger*
GGN	*Göttingische Gelehrte Nachrichten*
GUL	*Geist und Leben – Zeitschrift für Aszese und Mystik*
HJ	*Heythrop Journal*
HTR	*Harvard Theological Review*
HUCA	*Hebrew Union College Annual*
IAP	*Israel Annual of Psychiatry*
IASH	*Israel Academy of Sciences and Humanities*
IDB	*Interpreter's Dictionary of the Bible*
IEJ	*Israel Exploration Journal*
IES	*Israel Exploration Society*

IJES	Israel Journal of Earth Sciences
IJMES	International Journal of Middle East Studies
IJUT	Institutum Judaicum der Universität Tübingen
ILN	Illustrated London News
ILR	Israel Law Review
Inter.	Interpretation
IOS	Israel Oriental Studies
JA	Journal Asiatique
JANES	Journal of Ancient Near Eastern Society (Columbia University)
JAOS	Journal of the American Oriental Society
JBL	Journal of Biblical Literature
JC	Jewish Chronicle
JEH (J. Eccl. H.)	Journal of Ecclesiastical History
JEOL	Jaarbericht van het Vooraziatisch Egyptisch Genootschap ex Oriente Lux
JETS	Journal of the Evangelical Theological Society
JJ	Jerusalem Jahrbuch
JJS	Journal of Jewish Studies
JJSS	Journal of Jewish Social Studies
JLB	Jüdisches Literaturblatt
JNSL	Journal of Northwest Semitic Languages
JPES	Journal of the Jewish Palestine Exploration Society
JPOS	Journal of the Palestine Oriental Society
JQ	Jewish Quarterly
JQR	Jewish Quarterly Review
JRAS	Journal of the Royal Asiatic Society
JSJ	Journal for the Study of Judaism

JSNT	*Journal for the Study of the New Testament*
JSOT	*Journal for the Study of the Old Testament*
JSS	*Journal of Semitic Studies*
JTS	*Journal of Theological Studies*
JTVI	*Journal of the Transactions of the Victoria Institute*
JZWL	*Jüdische Zeitschrift für Wissenschaft und Leben*
KD	*Kerygma und Dogma*
Kornfeld	*Studien Zum Pentateuch: Walter Kornfeld zum 60 Geburtstag*
Lo. Ph.	*Lore and Philosophy (Journal of Jewish)*
LQHR	*London Quarterly and Holborn Review*
Louv. Stud.	*Louvain Studies*
LOT	*Literary and Oral Tradition* (Ben-Hayyim)
LUOS	*Leeds University Oriental Society*
LZ	*Literarisches Zentralblatt für Deutschland*
MES	*Middle Eastern Studies*
MGWJ	*Monatsschrift für Geschichte und Wissenschaft des Judenthums*
MHa	*Museum Ha'aretz*
MNDPV	*Mitteilungen und Nachrichten des Deutschen Palästina-Vereins*
MThS/MTS	*Münchener Theologische Studien*
MWJ	*Magazin für die Wissenschaft des Judentum, Berlin*
NAPC	*Nouvelles Annales de Philosophie Catholique*
NKGW	*Nachrichten Koeniglich Gesellschaft der Wissenschaft zu Göttingen*
NT	*Novum Testamentum*
NTAb	*New Testament Abstracts*
NTS	*New Testament Studies*
NTSup	*Novum Testamentum, Supplementary Volume*

NTT	*Nederlands Theologische Tijdschrift*
OGL	*Osterreich in Geschichte und Literatur*
OLZ	*Orientalische Literaturzeitung*
Or. Ant./OA	*Oriens Antiquus*
Oriens Christ.	*Oriens Christianus*
OTS	*Oudtestamentische Studiën*
PAAJR	*Proceedings of the American Academy for Jewish Research*
PE	*Politique Étrangère*
PEFQS	*Palestine Exploration Fund Quarterly Statement*
PEQ	*Palestine Exploration Quarterly*
PG	*Patriologia Graeca (Migne)*
PJB	*Palästinajahrbuch*
PL	*Patriologia Latina (Migne)*
PO	*Patriologia Orientalis*
PPTS	*Palestine Pilgrim Text Society*
PRE	*Protestant Realencyklopädie*
Pr. T.	*Present Tense*
PS	*Palestinskii Sbornik*
PSBA	*Proceedings of the Society of Biblical Archaeology*
QDAP	*Quarterly of the Department of Antiquities in Palestine*
QS	*(Q) Kiryath Sepher (Hebrew)*
R. Ex.	*Review and Expositor*
RAO	*Recueil d'Archéologie Orientale*
RB	*Revue Biblique*
RB (Holding Library)	Fisher Library, University of Sydney
RBiCalz	*Revista Bíblica Rafael Calzada, Argentina*

RBMC	*Repertorium für Biblische und Morgenländische Literatur*
RC	*Revue Critique*
RCB	*Revista de Cultura Bíblica*
REJ	*Revue des Études Juives*
RFR	*Rivista di Filologia Romanza*
RHC	*Recueil des Historiens des Croisades*
RHLR	*Revue de l'Histoire et de la Littérature Réligieuse*
RHR	*Revue de l'Histoire des Religions*
Rivist. Bib.	*Rivista Biblica*
RMI	*Rassegna Mensil di Israel*
ROL	*Revue de l'Orient Latin*
RQ	*Revue de Qumran*
RSO	*Rivista degli Studi Orientali*
RSR	*Revue des Sciences Religieuses.* Strasbourg
RTR	*Reformed Theological Review*
RUO	*Review of University of Ottawa/Revue de l'Université d'Ottawa*
SBFLA	*Studii Biblici Franciscani Liber Annuus*
SD	*Sacra Dottrina*
SDB	*Supplément au Dictionnaire de la Bible*
SES	*Lettre annuelle de Société des Études Samaritaines*
SHR	*Studies in the History of Religions*
SJT	*Scottish Journal of Theology*
SNVAO	*Skrifter Ugutt Av Det Norske Videnskaps Akademie i Oslo*
SPAW	*Sitzungsbericht der Preusisch. Akkad. Wissenschaft*
SPTROL	*Statuts 1879 Société pour la Publication de Textes Relatifs de l'Orient Latin*
Stuttg. Bibelst.	*Stuttgarter Bibelstudien*

SVT	*Supplement to Vetus Testamentum (see also VTS)*
T. und G.	*Theologie und Glaube*
TAIA	*Tel Aviv Institute of Archaeology*
TAS	*Thesaurus Antiquitates Sacra*
TGUOS	*Transactions of the Glasgow University Oriental Society*
TJ	*Theological Journal*
TLB	*Theologisches Literaturblatt*
TLS	*Times Literary Supplement*
TLZ	*Theologische Literaturzeitung*
TR	*Theologische Rundschau*
TS (F)	*Terre Sainte (French edition)*
TT or *Th. To.*	*Theology Today*
TTZ	*Trierer Theologische Zeitschrift*
TWNT	*Theologisches Wörterbuch zum Neuen Testament*
TZ	*Theologische Zeitschrift*
UNT	*Untersuchungen zum Neuen Testament*
VC	*Vigilae Christianae*
VDI	*Vestnik Drevnej Istorii (Moscow)*
VT	*Vetus Testamentum*
VTS	*Vetus Testamentum Supplementary Volume*
WCJS	*World Congress of Jewish Studies*
Wright	G.E.Wright, *The Mighty Acts of God*
WTJ	*Westminster Theological Journal*
WZKM	*Wiener Zeitschrift für die Kunde des Morgenländes*
ZA	*Zeitschrift für Assyriologie*
ZAW	*Zeitschrift für die alttestamentliche Wissenschaft*
ZDMG	*Zeitschrift der Deutschen Morgenländischen Gesellschaft*

ZDPV   *Zeitschrift des Deutschen Palästina Vereins*

ZHB   *Zeitschrift für Hebraïsche Bibliographie*

ZNW   *Zeitschrift für die neutestamentliche Wissenschaft und die Kunde
              der älteren Kirche*

ZRGG   *Zeitschrift für Religions und Geistesgeschichte*

ZTK   *Zeitschrift für Theologie und Kirche*

ZWT   *Zeitschrift für Wissenschaftliche Theologie*

A

1. **Abbot, Ezra.** "Samaritan Pentateuch." In *Smith's Dictionary*. New York, 1872. 2803-2817.
   [2300].

2. **Abbott, Thomas Kingsmill.** *Catalogue of the Manuscripts in the Library of Trinity College, Dublin.* Dublin & London: Hodges, Figgis & Co., Longmans, Green & Co., 1900. [P. 402, no.1498, Samaritan Pentateuch of 1287H].
   [101/ 103].

3. **Abdel-al, D. M.** A Comparative Study of the Unedited Works of Abu'l-Hasan al-Suri Yusuf ibn Salamah. Leeds University: Ph.D. thesis, 1958.
   [1106/ 2200/ 2203/ 3002].

4. **Abel, Félix-Marie.** "Alexandre le Grand en Syrie et en Palestine." *RB* 44 (1935): 42-61.
   [804].

5. ——————. *Géographie de la Palestine.* Paris: J. Gabalda, 1933-1938.
   [400].

6. ——————. *Histoire de la Palestine depuis la conquête d'Alexandre jusqu'à l'invasion Arabe.* Paris: J. Gabalda, 1952.
   [800/ 804/ 809].

7. ——————. Reviewer. **S. Saller,** "The Memorial of Moses on Mt. Nebo." *RB* 53 (1946): 452-456.
   [107 /409/ 3008].

8. ——————. "Naplouse, essai de topographie." *RB* 32 (1923): 120-132, 4 figs., plate III 5, IV. [A survey of Neapolis and its plan as it appears on the Madeba map].
   [408/ 600/ 808].

9. ——————. "Notre exploration à Naplouse." *RB* 31 (1922): 89-99, figs. 1-3, pl. 3-5.
   [400/ 401/ 408].

10. ——————. "Nouvelle inscription de la Ve légion Macédonique (répression en 67)." *RB* 35 (1926): 421-424. 2 figs.
    [303.4/ 808.1/ 2508].

11. ——————. "Le puits de Jacob et l'église Saint Sauveur." *RB* 42 (1933): 384-402. 2 figs.
    [401/ 407/ 602].

12. **Abel, F. M.,and C. Clermont-Ganneau.** "Inscription samaritaine de Gaza et inscriptions grecques de Bersabée." *RB* 3 (1906): 84-91. [The article cites Abel as the author but is signed Clermont-Ganneau].
    [2500/ 2508].

13. **Aberbach, M.** "The Conflicting Accounts of Josephus and Tacitus Concerning
    Cumanus' and Felix's Terms of Office." *JQR* 40 (1949): 1-14.
    [303.5/ 807].

14. **Abu Salih, al-Armani. B. T. A.** Evetts, editor, *The Churches and Monasteries of
    Egypt.* Anecdota Oxoniensia, Semitic Series 7. Oxford: OUP, 1895.
    [Samaritans in Egypt and their cemetery].
    [305.3/ 305.6/ 505 / 1203].

15. **Abu'l Fedae. J. B. Koehler,** editor, *Tabula Syriae cum excerpto Geographico ex ibn
    Ol Wardii Geographia et Historia Naturali.* Lipsae, 1767 & 1768.
    [307.1/ 408].

16. **Abu'l Fida.** "Resumé de l'histoire des croisades tiré des annales d'Abu'l-Fidâ."
    RHC, Historiens Orientaux 1 (1872): 52-56, 141.
    [307.2/ 809/ 810].

17. **Abu'l-Fath ben Abu'l Hasan as-Samiri.** Eduard Vilmar, editor, *Annales samaritani
    quos ad fidem codicum manuscriptorum Berolinensium, Bodlejani, Parisini editit et
    prolegomenis instruxit Eduardus Vilmar.* Gotha: F. A. Perthes, 1865. [For a new
    text see Paul Stenhouse].
    [1601].

18. —————. "Excerpta Chronici Abu'l Fath Samaritani e Codice Arabico Don
    Roberto Huntington Angli." *Helsinki* 33 (n.d.): 63-76.
    [1601].

19. **Abu'l-Hama.** "Les livres des deux jardins; histoire des deux règnes, celui de Nour
    ed-Din et celui de Salah ed-Din." *RHC, Historiens Orientaux* 4 (1898): 52-416.
    [809/ 810].

20. **Ackroyd, Peter R.** *Exile and Restoration; a Study of Hebrew Thought of the Sixth
    Century B.C.* London, 1968.
    [303.5/ 801/ 802].

21. —————. "Samaria." In **D. Winton-Thomas,** editor, *Archaeology and Old
    Testament Study.* Oxford: OUP, 1967. 343-354.
    [410].

22. **Acoluthi, Andreae.** *De Aquis Amaris Zelotypiae Philologema.* Lipsae, 1682. Typis
    Justini Brandl.
    [105/ 2300/ 2600].

23. **Adelphi, N.** "Gli ultimi Samaritani." *L'Illustrazione Italiana* 12 (1955).
    [200/ 903].

24. **Adler, Elkan N.** *Catalogue of the Hebrew Manuscripts in the Collection of Elkan
    Nathan Adler.* Cambridge: CUP, 1921. [See pp. 154-156 for the listing of
    Samaritan manuscripts in the collection].
    [101/ 103].

25. —————. *The Itinerary of Benjamin of Tudela.* London: OUP, 1907.
    [304.4].

26. ——————. *Jewish Travellers*. London: Routledge, 1930.
    [304.4].

27. ——————. "On the Samaritan Book of Joshua." *JRAS* 1143-1147 (October, 1908):
    [1604/ 1605].

28. **Adler, E. N. and M. Seligsohn.** "Une nouvelle chronique samaritaine." *REJ* 44, 45, 46 (1902-1903): 188-222 (44); 70-98, 160, 223-254 (45); 123-146 (46). Reprinted, Paris, 1903.
    [1600/ 1602].

29. **Adler, J. G. C.** *Abulfedae Annales Muslemici Arabice et Latine.* Hafniae, 1786.
    [307].

30. **Adler, M.** "The Emperor Julian and the Jews." *JQR* 5 (1893): 591-691.
    [808].

31. **Akaviah, A. A.** "The Secret of the Samaritan Calendar." (Hebrew) *Melilah* III-IV (1950): 328-347. [Last pages not numbered].
    [1400].

32. **Aland, K. and F. L. Cross.** "Problems of the Septuagint." In *Studia Patristica I.* Berlin, 1957. 331-333.
    [2400].

33. **Al-Biruni.** *Kitab Tahdiel al-Amakin (The Determination of the Co-ordinates of Cities).* Beirut, 1967.
    [307.1/ 400/ 809].

34. **Albright, William Foxwell.** "The Beit-el-Ma Inscription." *BASOR* 84 (1941): 4. [A commentary on the article by I. Ben-Zvi].
    [2500/ 2503].

35. ——————. *From the Stone Age to Christianity.* Baltimore: Johns Hopkins University, 1946.
    [801].

36. ——————. "Simon Magus as the Great Power of God." In **J. Munck,** editor, *The Acts of the Apostles.* The Anchor Bible, 31, appendix VII. New York, 1967. 305-308.
    [1502.1/ 1506/ 1506.2].

37. **Alexandre, (Noel) Natalis.** "De Samaritanis." In *Selecta Historia Ecclesiastica Veteris Testamentum.* VI. Paris: A. Dezallier, 1699. [British Library fol. 4533 h.2].
    [200].

38. **Alishan, P. Léonce.** "Deux descriptions arméniennes des Lieux saints de Palestine." *AOL* 2 (1884): 394-403. [Nicolas évêque d'Acquirmann: Les SS Lieux de Jerusalem, 1483].
    [305.2/ 401].

39. **Allan, Nigel.** "Catalogue of the Hebrew Manuscripts in the Welcome Institute, London." *JJS* 27.2 (1982): 193-221. [P. 215 catalogues a fragment of a Samaritan Pentateuch].
[101/ 103/ 2300].

40. **Allegro, J. M. and A. A. Anderson.** *Qumran Cave 4.* Discoveries in the Judean Desert of Jordan V. Oxford: OUP, 1968. 3-5 (plate i), 57-58 (plate xxi).
[4Q158+Q186].
[1005/ 2307].

41. **Allony, N.** *List of Manuscripts, etc., Acquired in Europe After the Second World War.* Jerusalem: Reuben Mass, 1968. 26-30.
[101/ 103].

42. **Allony, N. and E. Kupfer.** *Institute of Hebrew Manuscripts, List of Photocopies II (Belgium, Denmark, Netherlands, Spain, Switzerland).* Jerusalem: Reuben Mass, 1964.
[101/ 103].

43. **Allony, N. and D. S. Loewinger.** *The Institute of Hebrew Manuscripts. List of the Photocopies in the Institute, pt.1. Hebrew Manuscripts in the Libraries of Austria and Germany.* Jerusalem: Ministry for Education and Culture, 1957.
[Supplement to *Bahinukh Uvatarbut*].
[101/ 103].

44. —————. *Institute of Hebrew Manuscripts, part 3. Hebrew Manuscripts in the Vatican.* Jerusalem: Reuben Mass, 1968.
[101/ 103].

45. **Almkvist, Herman.** "Ein samaritanischer Brief an König Oscar in Faksimile herausgegeben und übersetzt...mit einer Schrifttafel von Julius Euting." *Skrifter utgifna af Kongl. Humanistika Vetenskapssamfundet i Uppsala* 2 (1897): 10 pp, 2 pls. Facsimiles. [Manchester, R 126840].
[1700/ 2501].

46. **Alon, Gedaliahu.** "The Jews in Their Land in the Talmudic Age." **Gershon Levi,** translator, 2 vols. Jerusalem: Magnes Press, 1980 & 1985. 562-566, 603-607.
[807].

47. —————. "The Origins of the Samaritans in Halakhic Tradition." (Hebrew) *Tarbiz* 18 (1946/7): 146-156. [Reprinted in *Researches in Israelite History* (Hebrew) vol. 2 Tel Aviv (1958) pp. 1-14. For the English version see the next entry].
[304.1/ 801.1/ 1003.4/ 1106].

48. —————. "The Origins of the Samaritans in the Halakhic Tradition." In *Jews, Judaism and the Classical World.* Jerusalem: Magnes Press, 1977. 352-377.
[1003.4].

49. **Alperovitch, D. J.** "Deep Soils in the Samaritan Desert." *IJES* 24 (1945): 57-68.
[400.1].

50. **Alt, Albrecht.** "Das Institut im Jahr 1924." *PJ* 21 (1925): 5-18.
[400].

51. —————. "Das Institut im Jahr 1933." *PJ* 30 (1934): 5-31. [2 plates, pp. 16-17.
On the Samaritan inscriptions at Gaza].
[2500/ 2508].

52. —————. "Die Rolle Samarias bei Entstehung des Judentums." In *Festschrift
Otto Procksh.* Leipzig, 1934. 5-28. [Reprinted in *Kl. Schriften II* (Munich;
1953) pp. 316-337].
[801].

53. —————. "Die Wallfahrt von Sichem nach Bethel." *Bulmerincq-Gedenkschrift
(1938). 218-230 = Kleine Schriften I.* 1953. 79-88.
[400/ 408].

54. —————. "Ein Ritt durch Palästina im Jahre 1869. Reise briefe von Albert
Socin." *ZDPV* 60 (1937): 1-132.
[200/ 308/ 1404].

55. —————. "Der Stadstaat Samaria." *Berichte über die Verhandlungen der
Sächsischen Akademie der Wissenschaften zu Leipzig, Philologisch-historische
Klasse= Kleine Schriften III. 258-302* 101.pt. 5 (1954):
[801].

56. —————. "Zu den samaritanischen Dekaloginschriften." *VT* 2 (1952): 273-
276.
[2500/ 2504].

57. —————. "Zur Geschichte der Grenze Zwischen Judaia und Samaria." *PJ* 31
(1935): 94-111. [= *Kl. Schriften II,* Munich (1953) pp.346-362].
[801].

58. —————. "Zwei samaritanische Inschriften." *ZDPV* 48 (1925): 398-400.
Illustrations.
[2500/ 2504].

59. **Alting, Jacob.** *Fundamenta punctationis linguae sanctae. Synopsis institutionum
Chaldaearum et Syrarum. Edition sexta. Simili institutionum Samaritanorum.*
Francofurti ad Moenum, 1701. [Nine editions known, 1717-1746].
[105/ 2600].

60. **Amaduzzi, G. C.** *Alphabetum Hebraicum Addito Samaritano Rabbinico cum
Oratione Dominicali.* Romae, 1771.
[105].

61. **Ambal (Sverre),** Pseudonym? *Levit och Präst. Goda och onder Människov. Ett
Psykologist och Socialt Studium.* Motala, 1944.
[1302].

62. **Amelotti, R. D.** *Monumenta epistolica ...qui scripterunt de antiquitatibus ecclesiae
Orientalis. Quibus praefixa est Jo. Morini vita.* Lugduni Batavorum, 1698.
[301/ 1700/ 2300].

63. **Amico, Fra Bernadino**, translated by Theophilus Bellorini and E. Hoade. *Plans of the Sacred Edifices of the Holy Land.* Jerusalem: Franciscan Press, 1953.
    [407/ 602].

64. **Amram b. Ishaq, the Priest.** *The History and Religion of the Samaritans.* Nablus & Jerusalem: Greek Convent Press, n.d. [The Jerusalem edition was printed at the Greek Convent Press].
    [200/ 800/1000].

65. —————. *Mt. Gerizim, the One True Sanctuary.* Nablus & Jerusalem: Greek Convent Press, n.d. [The Jerusalem edition was printed at the Greek Convent Press].
    [401/ 406].

66. —————. *The Samaritan History. A Portion of Abu'l Fath's Chronicle of 1355.* Nablus, n.d.
    [800/ 1600/ 1601].

67. **Anders G.** "Die Falschen Samariter." In **W. Jens**, *Der Barmherzige Samariter.* Stuttgart, 1973. 125-134.
    [1003/ 1003.1].

68. **Anderson, Robert T.** "Clustering Samaritan Hebrew Pentateuchal Manuscripts." In **Rothschild and Sixdenier**, editors, *Études samaritaines.* Louvain-Paris: Peeters, 1988. 57-66.
    [103/ 2300].

69. —————. "Columned Letters and Words in Samaritan Manuscripts." *Proceedings of the Eastern Great Lakes and Midwest Society of Biblical Literature* (November, 1985).
    [103].

70. —————. "Craft and Function in Samaritan Hebrew Manuscript Decoration." *Hebrew Studies* 33 (1992): 37-49.
    [103/ 2300/ 3100].

71. —————. "The Elusive Samaritan Temple." *BA* 54 (June, 1991): 104-107.
    [604/ 800/ 1305].

72. —————. "Jean Morin as a Prime Catalyst in Modern Textual Criticism." In **Michael Haykin**, editor, *For a Testimony: Essays in Honor of John H. Wilson.* Toronto: Central Baptist Seminary and Bible College, 1989.
    [106/ 2300].

73. —————. "Josephus' Account of Temple Building: History, Literature or Politics?" *Proceedings of the Eastern Great Lakes and Midwest Biblical Societies* 9 (1989): 246-257.
    [303.5].

74. —————. "Mount Gerizim: Navel of the World." *BA* 43.4 (1980): 217-221.
    [200/ 406].

75. —————. "The Museum Trail: The Michigan State University Samaritan Collection." *BA* 47.1 (1984): 41-43.
[103].

76. —————. "Le pentateuque samaritain Chamberlain-Warren, CW 2473." *RB* 77 (1970): 68-75.
[103/ 2300].

77. —————. "Le pentateuque samaritain Chamberlain-Warren, CW 2478A." *RB* 77 (1970): 550-560.
[103/ 2300].

78. —————. "Le pentateuque samaritain Chamberlain-Warren, CW 2484." *RB* 79 (1972): 368-380.
[103/ 2300].

79. —————. "Samaritan History During the Renaissance." In **A. D. Crown,** editor, *The Samaritans.* Tübingen: J. C. B. Mohr, 1989. 95-112.
[812].

80. —————. "Samaritan Pentateuch: General Account." In **A. D. Crown,** editor, *The Samaritans.* Tübingen: J. C. B. Mohr, 1989. 390-396.
[2300].

81. —————. "Samaritans." In **Mircea Eliade,** editor, *Encyclopaedia of Religion.* Chicago: University of Chicago Press, 1987. 13: 33-36.
[200/ 201/ 202].

82. —————. "Samaritans." In **G. W. Bromiley,** editor, *International Standard Bible Encyclopaedia.* Grand Rapids, Michigan: Eerdmans, 1988. 4: 303-308.
[200/ 201/ 202].

83. —————. "Seventeenth Century European Responses to the Samaritan Pentateuch." *Proceedings of the Eastern Great Lakes and Midwest Society of Biblical Literature* (November, 1984).
[106/ 1700/ 2205/ 2300].

84. —————. *Studies in Samaritan Manuscripts and Artifacts—The Chamberlain-Warren Collection.* 99pp + plates: ASOR Monographs, 1978.
[101/ 103/ 1550/ 2300/ 2501/ 2502].

85. —————. "Temple and Tabernacle as Symbols in Jewish-Samaritan Conflict." *Proceedings of the Eastern Great Lakes and Midwest Society of Biblical Literature* 8 (1988): 23-34.
[604/ 800/ 1003/ 1305].

86. **Andreas, Cesareae.** "Commentary on the Apocalypse." *PG* 106 371, 372, 373, 374.
[305/ 305.4].

87. **Ankori, Zvi.** *Karaites in Byzantium; The Formative Years, 970-1100.* New York: Columbia University Press, 1959. 2nd edn. AMS Press, New York, 1968.
[811/ 1004].

88. **Anon.** *The Account of the Samaritans in a letter to J. M.* London, 1714.
[Bodleian, 1419e 167 (i)].
[200].

89. ——————.*Alphabeta linguarum praecipuarum hodiernarum sequuntur
samaritanae...* 1825. [BL C.126.h.3.(11)].
[105].

90. ——————. *Alphabetum Hebraicum addito Samaritano et Rabbinico.* Rome:
Propaganda Fidé, 1771. [Bodleian].
[105/ 2501].

91. ——————. *Alphabetum Linguarum Orientalium atque Aliarum Linguarum.*
Rome, 1636. [Title page is missing but the catalogue gives the date as 1636.
Bodleian Library].
[105/ 2501].

92. ——————. "Archaeological Survey of Israel." *RB* 76 (1969): 411. [Short report in
French on a survey in the Samaria region].
[400/ 400.3/ 600].

93. ——————. *Begin/Genesis. (The Hebrew Text in the Samaritan Recension and the
Samaritan Character).* Jerusalem, 1864. [Quarto. Lithographed].
[2300].

94. ——————. Reviewer. **Alan David Crown,** "Bibliography of the Samaritans."
Theology Digest (Spring, 1986): 168.
[100/ 107].

95. ——————. Reviewer. **M. Heidenheim,** "Bibliotheca Samaritana I. (Die
samaritanische Pentateuch version und samaritanischer Text der Genesis)." *REJ*
9 (1884): 125.
[107/ 2300].

96. ——————. Reviewer. **M. Heidenheim,** "Bibliotheca Samaritana." *AJSL* 7
(1886): 117-118.
[107/ 2300].

97. ——————. *The Book of Joyous Occasions (Circumcision).* Holon: Samaritan
community, 1964. 2 volumes. See also R.(atson) Tsedaka, *The Book of Joyous
Occasions,* Holon; 383 pp.
[1204/ 2103].

98. ——————. "Commemoratium De Casis dei vel Monasteries." *SPTROL* (1879):
304-305.
[306.2/ 400].

99. ——————. "Development of the Hebrew Script." (Hebrew) *Ha'aretz* (17/9/76):
15. [Includes an illustration of the Samaritan script].
[2501].

100. —————. "Die Samaritaner. Eine historische Skizze." *Der Israelit* Mainz, 3rd year (1862): 209-211, 217-219.
[800/ 801].

101. —————. "Dositheans." In *Dictionary of Sects, Heresies, Ecclesiastical Parties and Schools of Religious Thought.* London, 1892. 200, 201.
[1503].

102. —————. (Samaritan High Priest). *Exodus, the Ten Commandments—Samaritan text.* Nablus: Samaritan Community, n.d. (before 1968). Bought in Nablus in 1968.
[1103/ 2300].

103. —————. "Extrait d'une lettre écrite de Wolfenbuttel à Mr. Reeland...sur les médailles Juives avec les caractères Samaritains." *Histoire critique de la République des Lettres.* vol II, Utrecht, 1713. 65-95.
[800/ 2501].

104. —————. "Finnes det en fremtia lor Samaritanerne?" *Varm Land* (31/12/1980):
[903].

105. —————. *Guide-book to Palestine.* London, 1894.
[400].

106. —————. "History and Religion of the Samaritans." *Review of Reviews* 35 (February, 1907): 238-239.
[107/ 200/ 800].

107. —————. "Israel and the Resources of the West Bank; from a Report by the Economics Department of the Royal Scientific Society of Jordan." *JPS* 8.4 (1979): 94-104.
[903].

108. —————. "Itinéraire de Bordeaux à Jerusalem." *Revue Archéologique* n.s. 10 (1864): 98-112.
[400].

109. —————. *Itinerarium à Burdigala Hierusalem Usque c. 333.* Paris: *SPTROL,* 1879.
[306.2/ 400/ 406/ 408/ 412].

110. —————. *Itinerarium St. Willibrand.* Paris: *SPTROL,* 1879. 293f.
[400/ 408/ 412].

111. —————. "Kfar Bilu Inscription—Notes and News—Epigraphy." *IEJ* 4 (1954): 129.
[2501/ 2509].

112. —————. *L'Art du livre à l'imprimerie nationale; des origines à nos jours.* Paris: Bibliothèque Nationale, 1951. [Especially pp. 42-49].
[100/ 105].

113. —————. *Liturgy for the Mo'ed of Succoth: Evening and Morning.* Samaritan print, n.d. Holon? [No publication data in the work].
[1409/ 2102].

114. —————. "Nablus, Der samaritanischen Pentateuch und die Samaritaner in dem alten Sichem." *Der Orient* 41 (1844): 313-314.
[200/ 2300].

115. —————. Reviewer. L. A. Frankl, "Nach Jerusalem." *The North American Review* 95 (1862): 331-354.
[107].

116. —————. "Notes and News." *PEFQS* (1904): 3.
[200].

117. —————. *Orientalischer Kirchen-Staat...Persianischer, Samaritanischer.* Gotha, 1699. 12º.
[200].

118. —————. "Passover, Samaritan Style. Sacrificial Lambs at Nablus." *Jewish Observer* 17 (April 19th 1968): 8.
[1303/ 1404].

119. —————. Review notice. A. F. von Gall, "Pentateuque Samaritain." *RB* 4 (1907): 314.
[103/ 107/ 2300].

120. —————. *Peregrinato Sanctae Paulae.* Paris: *SPTROL,* 1879. [Especially pp. 37-39].
[306.2/ 400/ 401/ 406/ 408/ 412].

121. —————. "Religion of the Samaritans", "Samaritans", "Samaritan Pentateuch." In *Biblical Encyclopedia and Scriptural Dictionary.* Chicago, 1909. Vol.3.
[200/ 201].

122. —————. "Samaria." *History for Ready Reference.* New York, 1901. Vol. 4.
[200/ 201].

123. —————. "Samaria and the Samaritans." In *Religious Encyclopedia.* New York, 1891. Vol. 4.
[200/ 201].

124. —————. "Samaria", "Samaritan Language and Literature", "Samaritans." In *The Encyclopaedia Americana.* New York, Chicago, Washington, 1954.
[200/ 201/ 1550/ 2300/ 2600].

125. —————. "Samaria", "Samaritan Pentateuch." In *The Illustrated Chambers' Encyclopaedia.* London, 1935. Vol. 9.
[200/ 201/ 2300].

126. —————. Reviewer. Leo Haefeli, "Samaria und Peraea bei Flavius Josephus." *RB* 11 (1914): 156.
[107/ 303.5/ 800].

127. —————. "Le Samarie." *BTS* 184 (Sept.—Oct. 1976).
     [408/ 412/ 801].

128. —————. "Samaritaine", "Samaritain." In *Grand Dictionnaire Universel*. Paris,
     1875. Vol.19.
     [200/ 201].

129. —————. Reviewer. **O. T. Crane**, "The Samaritan Chronicle." *The New York
     Evangelist* (June 12, 1890).
     [107/ 1600/ 1604].

130. —————. "Samaritan Paschal Sacrifice." *Israel Digest* 11 (April 18th 1968): 8.
     [1303/ 1404].

131. —————. "The Samaritan Stone at Gaza." *PEFQS* (1873):157.
     [2508].

132. —————. "A Samaritan Stone Plaque." *Jerusalem Post* (Sunday, Feb. 7th,
     1954): 3, cols. 7-8.
     [2500/ 2503/ 2514].

133. —————. "Samaritanische Pentateuchrolle moderne Abschrift auf Papier."
     *Orientalia Hamburgensia; Festgabe den Teilnehmern am 4 Deutschen
     Orientalistenag.* Hamburg, 1926.
     [103/ 2300].

134. —————. "Samaritano", "Samaritanos." *Enciclopaedia Universal Ilustrada.*
     Madrid, n.d. col. 53.
     [200/ 201].

135. —————. "Samaritans." In *Harmsworth's Universal Encyclopaedia*. London, n.d.
     Vol.8.
     [200/ 201].

136. —————. "Samaritans." In *The Encyclopaedia Britannica*. Cambridge, 1911.
     Vol. 24.
     [200/ 201].

137. —————. "The Samaritans." *Time* 73 (April 27, 1959): p. 58.
     [200].

138. —————. "The Samaritans." *Religious Life and Communities.* Jerusalem: Keter
     Books, 1974. (Israel Pocket Library): 61-73.
     [200/ 201/ 1000/ 1001/ 2900].

139. —————. "The Samaritans Form the World's Smallest Sect." *World Over* 26 (1
     January 1965): 15.
     [903].

140. —————. "The Samaritans in 1978." *A–B Samaritan News.* 22/2/79, 31.
     [903].

141. —————. "The Samaritans in 1979." *A–B Samaritan News*. 10/4/80, 36.
      [903].

142. —————. *Specimens of a Polyglott of the Old Testament. Containing the Hebrew
      and Samaritan texts with the Greek...Syriac...etc.* London, 1655? [BL 675.1.1].
      [2300].

143. —————. *Specimens of Type Faces.* Leiden: E. J. Brill, 1970. [See especially
      p.142].
      [105].

144. —————. "The Travels of an Unknown Pupil of Nachmanides in the
      Fourteenth Century." (Hebrew) in A. Ya'ari, editor, *Masa'ot Eretz Yisrael.*
      Ramat Gan, 1967. 81-97. [Describes the sacred sites at Shechem with some
      observations on the Samaritans].
      [200/ 304.4/ 401/ 408].

145   —————. *The Travels of Certain Englishmen into Africa, Asia, Samaria, etc.*
      London, 1609.
      [306.3/ 400/ 401].

146. —————. (Adam). *Alfabeto del protoparente Adamo I (-III. Alfabeto Hebreo.
      Alfabeto Hebreo Rabbinico. Lettere Alfabeto Samaritano).* Rome, 1770. 8ᵛᵒ. [
      British Library 58.b.31 (1)].
      [105].

147. **Antoine, P.** "Garizim." *DB* Suppl. III (1938): 535-561.
      [200/ 201/ 406].

148. **Antonius Martyr.** "Locus Transmarinis Sacris, c. 636." *SPTROL.* Paris, 1879.
      119-121. [Mentions the Basilica of St. John].
      [306.2/ 408].

149. —————. "Perambulatio Locorum Sanctorum c. 570." *SPTROL.* Paris, 1879.
      92-96.
      [306.2/ 400/ 401/ 403].

150. **Anver, M.** "Then Joshua Built an Altar to the Lord God of Israel on Mt. Ebal."
      (Hebrew) *BM* 101.2 (Jan-March, 1985): 345-353.
      [404/ 801].

151. **Appel, Meier.** Quaestiones de rebus Samaritanorum sub imperio Romanorum
      peractis.Vratislavae and Breslau: W. Friederich: 1874. [Inaugural dissertation,
      University of Breslau; 97 pp. Reprinted, Göttingen, 1874].
      [807/ 1002].

152. —————. "Über die Samaritaner." *Jüdische Lit. Blätter* 7 (1878): 14-18.
      [202].

153. **Applebaum, S., S. Dar and Z. Safrai.** "The Towers of Samaria." *PEQ* 110 (1978):
      91-100.
      [400/ 801].

154. **Applebaum, Shimon.** *Jews and Greeks in Ancient Cyrene.* Leiden: E. J. Brill, 1979.
Studies in Judaism in Late Antiquity no. 28.
[506/ 804/ 806].

155. **Aptowitzer, V.** *Parteipolitik der Hasmonäerzeit im Rabbinischen und
Pseudoepigraphischen Schriftum.* Wien: Alexander Kohut Memorial Foundation
V, 1927.
[304/ 304.1/ 304.2/ 805].

156. **Aquensis, Alberti.** *Historia Hierosolymitana, RHC 4.* Paris, 1879.
[306.2/ 810].

157. **Ararat, Nisan.** "Ezra, His Deeds in the Biblical and Post-Biblical Sources." *BM*
52.1 (1972): 85-101(Hebrew); 130-132 (English). [Ezra's struggle with the
Samaritans].
[801/ 802].

158. **Archer, G. L. Jnr.** "Old Testament History and Recent Archaeology from the
Exile to Malachi." *BS* 127.508 (1970): 291-298.
[600/ 1305].

159. **Arculf, Bishop.** "Relatio de Locis Sanctis (written by his scribe Adamnan)."
SPTROL. Paris, 1879. 180-182. [See also the version of Arculf in T. Wright,
Early Travels in Palestine London, 1848].
[306.2/ 401/ 600/ 1301].

160. **Argyle, A. W.** "A Note on John 4:35 (ετι) τετραμηνοσ εστιν χω θεριμοσ
ερχεται." *ET* 82 (1971): 247-248.
[1003.1/ 1502.1].

161. **Assemanus, Josephus Simonius.** *Bibliotheca orientalis Clementino-Vaticana in quo
manuscriptos codices...Bibliothecae Vaticanae addictos.* Romae, 1719-1728.
[Reprinted, Hildesheim 1975].
[101/ 103/ 105].

162. **Assemanus, Josephus Simonius and Stephanus Evodius Assemanus.** *Bibliothecae
Apostolicae Vaticanae codicum manuscriptorum catalogus...codices ebraicos et
samaritanos.* Rome, 1756. New edition, Paris, 1926-1929.
[101/ 103/ 105].

163. **Astley, H. D.** "Date of the Samaritan Pentateuch." *Thinker* (July, 1892 and
October 1899): 6, 299-308.
[2300].

164. **Astour, M. C.** "The Origin of the Samaritans. A Critical Examination of the
Evidence." In *The First International Symposium on Palestine Antiquities.* Beirut,
1981. Unpublished.
[801.1].

165. **Auld, A. G.** *Joshua, Moses and the Land.* Edinburgh: T & T Clark, 1980.
[1604].

166. **Aune, David E.** Reviewer. **Rita Egger,** "Josephus Flavius und die Samaritaner."
CBQ 50.4 (October 1986): 715.
[107/ 303.5].

167. **Auvray, P.** "Jean Morin, 1591-1659." *RB* 66 (1959): 397-414. [Includes a full list
of Morin's Samaritan works].
[100/ 1003/ 1700].

168. **Avigad, Nachman.** "Excavations at Samaria." (Hebrew) *EM* 8 (1982): 148-162.
[401/ 600].

169. ——————. "Shomron." (Hebrew) *EAEHL* (1970): 527-538.
[410].

170. **Aviram, J.,** editor. (Hebrew) *Eretz Shomron.* Jerusalem: IES, 1973.
[400/ 400.1/ 400.2/ 400.3/ 400.4].

171. **Avi-Yonah, Michael.** "Ancient Synagogues." *Ariel* 32 (1973): 29-43. [Notes on
the Samaritan synagogues at Sha'albim and Beth Shean].
[600/ 1304].

172. ——————. *Gazetteer of Roman Palestine.* Jerusalem: Institute of Archaeology,
Hebrew University, 1976. [First appeared in *QDAP*].
[400/ 806/ 808].

173. ——————. "Geschichte der Juden im Zeitalter des Talmud in den Tagen von
Rom und Byzanz." *Studia Judaica* 2 (1962).
[807/ 808].

174. ——————. *The Jews of Palestine: A Political History from the Bar Kochba War to
the Arab Conquest.* Oxford: OUP, 1976. 241-245. [A section on the Samaritan
revolts].
[807/ 808].

175. ——————. *The Madaba Mosaic Map.* Jerusalem: IES, 1954. [A section on
Neapolis and Samaria].
[400/ 408].

176. ——————. "A New Dating of the Roman Road from Scythopolis to Neapolis."
IEJ 16 (1966): 75-76.
[400.2/ 808].

177. ——————. "Places of Worship in the Roman and Byzantine Periods." In *The
Holy Land. New Light on the Prehistory and Early History of Israel.* The Hague
and Jerusalem: Hebrew University, Dept. of Antiquities and IES, 1957.
Antiquity and Survival II: 262-272 figs. 1-14.
[600/ 1304].

178. ——————. "'Samaria' and 'Marissa' of *Antiquities* xiii 275." (Hebrew) *Yediot*
16.3 29-31.
[303.5/ 410/ 600].

179. —————. "The Samaritan Revolts Against the Byzantine Empire." (Hebrew) *EI* 4 (1956): 127-132. English summary p.ix.
[808.1].

180. —————. "The Samaritans in the Roman and Byzantine Periods." (Hebrew) in J. Aviram, editor, *Eretz Shomron.* Jerusalem: IES, 1973. 34-37.
[807/ 808].

181. —————. "The Second Temple (332 B.C.-A.D. 70) Jews, Romans and Byzantines (70-640)." In M. Avi-Yonah, editor, *A History of the Holy Land.* Jerusalem: Macmillan, 1969. 109-184.
[808].

182. Ayalon, Etan. "The 'Samaritan' olive oil press." M. Heltzer and D. Eitam, editors, *Olive Oil in Antiquity; Israel and Neighbouring Countries from Neolith to Early Arab Period.* Haifa: University of Haifa, 1987. 5-10. [Conference, Haifa, 1987].
[600].

B

183. **Baars, W.** Reviewer. **E. Robertson,** "Catalogue of the Manuscripts in the John Rylands Library, Manchester; vol.2, the Gaster Manuscripts." *VT* 13 (1963): 98.
[101/ 103/ 107].

184. **Bacchi Della Lega, Alberto,** editor. **Niccolo da Poggibonsi,** *Libro D'Oltramare di Fra Nicolo da Poggibonsi.* Bologna, 1881. [Reprinted Bologna 1968. See below for a new edition by B. Bagatti].
[306.2/ 408/ 412].

185. **Bacher, Wilhelm.** "Comment on Margoliouth's 'An Early copy of a Samaritan Hebrew Manuscript'." *JQR* 16 (1904): 602.
[103/ 107].

186. —————. "Étude critique sur quelques traditions étranges relatives à Rabbi Meir." *REJ* 5-6 (1882): 178-187. [Continuation in vol. 6, p. 159. Deals with the discussion between Rabbi Meir and the Samaritans].
[304/ 304.2/ 1003.4].

187. —————. Reviewer. **A. Merx,** "Der Messias oder Ta'eb der Samaritaner." *OLZ* 13 (1910): 315-319.
[107/ 1105/ 1107].

188. —————. "Qirqisani the Qaraite and his work on the Jewish Sects." *JQR* 7 (1897): 687-710.
[304.3/ 1500/ 1503].

189. —————. Reviewer. **A. E. Cowley,** "The Samaritan Liturgy." *TLZ* 35 (1910): 680-682.
[107/ 1550/ 2100].

190. —————. Reviewer. **A. E. Cowley,** "The Samaritan Liturgy." *Athenaeum* 1 (1910): 486-487.
[107/ 1550/ 2100].

191. —————. "The Supposed Inscription upon 'Joshua the Robber'." *JQR* 3 (1891): 354-357.
[1605].

192. **Bachiènne, W. A.** *Historische un geographische Beschreibung von Palästina.* Cleve, 1773. Vol. 3.
[400].

193. **Bader, G.** "Sie Shomronim." (Yiddish) in *Our Spiritual Heroes (The Lives and Works of Our Rabbinical Teachers).* New York: Moinester, 1934. Vol. 7.
[200/ 800].

194. **Baensch-Drugulin, Johannes.** *Marksteine aus der Welt Litteratur.* Leipzig, 1902. 78-88. [A history of the Samaritan fount; see Merx and Crown].
[105].

195. **Bagatti, Bellarmino.** "Nuovi Apporti Archeologici sul pozzo di Giacobbe in Samaria." *SBLFA* 16 (1965): 127-164. [A Samaritan-Christian sarcophagus]. [401/ 407/ 600].

196. ——————. "Phasqa (on Mt.Nebo)." *SDB* 40 (1965): 1129-1132. [See also fig. 714]. [409/ 600/ 1404].

197. ——————. "Ricordi di S. Giovanni Battista in Samaria." *Euntes Docete* 25 (1972): 294-298. [306/ 1002/ 1502].

198. ——————, editor. **Niccolo da Poggibonsi,** *A Voyage Beyond the Sea.* Jerusalem: Franciscan Press, 1945. [306/ 306.2].

199. **Bagster, Samuel.** *Biblia Hebraica ad editionem Hooghtiam.* London, 1831; reprinted 1838 & 1853. [Contains a register of Samaritan variant readings]. [105/ 2300].

200. ——————. *Biblia Sacra Polyglotta...* London, 1821: reprinted 1829, 1831. [All copies of the 1821 edition were burned. The work contains the Kennicott text of the Samaritan Pentateuch in an appendix and an introduction by Samuel Lee. The 1821 edition was preceded by two editions of a *Prospectus of a Polyglott Bible,* 1816]. [105/ 2300].

201. **Baguley, E.** A Critical Edition with Translation of the Hebrew text of the Malef and a Comparison of its Teachings with those in the Samaritan Liturgy. Leeds: Doctoral thesis, University of Leeds, 1961. [1100/ 2100].

202. ——————. A Critical Study and Translation of the Samaritan New Year Liturgy with a Comparison with the Corresponding Jewish Rite. Leeds: Master of Arts thesis, University of Leeds, 1956. [1003.4/ 1403/ 2102].

203. **Baier, Werner.** "Liturgie und Kult in der frühjüdischen und frühchristlichen Umwelt, vi. Samaritaner." *Archiv für Liturgiewissenschaft* 13 (1971): 291f. [1300/ 2100].

204. ——————. "Der Garizim. Bibelkundliches zum heiligen Berg der Samaritaner." *DHL* 10.2 (1970): 38-47. [401/ 406].

205. **Bailey, Albert E.** "The Samaritan Passover." *Biblical World* 34 (1909): 8-14. [1404].

206. **Bailey, H. J.** "The Waters of Jacob's Well." *PEFQS* (1897): 196. [407].

207. **Bailey, J. A.** "The Traditions Common to the Gospels of Luke and John." *NTSup* 7 (1963): 103-114.
      [1003.1/ 1502/ 1502.1].

208. **Baillet, Maurice.** Reviewer. H. Shehadeh, "The Arabic Translation of the Samaritan Pentateuch." *RB* 88 (1981): 598-602.
      [107/ 2302].

209. —————. La Bible, les manuscrits de la mer Morte et les Samaritains. Rapport de synthèse pour le Doctorat d'État ès lettres sur travaux. (Typescript) Lyons, 1984.
      [200/ 100/ 2300/ 2307].

210. —————. Reviewer. "Le calendrier samaritain." (A review of Sylvia Powels, *Der Kalender der Samaritaner*) *RB* 85 (1978): 481-499. [Abstracted in *Religion Index One*, Chicago, 1980, p.451].
      [107/ 1400].

211. —————. "Commandements et lois (Farâ'id et Tûrot) dans quatres manuscrits samaritains." In **Rothschild and Sixdenier**, editors, *Études samaritaines.* Louvain-Paris, 1988. 259-270. [Abstracted in *SES, Lettre annuelle* 1, 1985-86, p. 9].
      [1100/ 1106].

212. —————. "Corrections a l'édition de Von Gall on Pentateuque samaritain (der hebraïsche Pentateuch der Samaritaner, 1914-1918)." In *Von Kanaan bis Kerala. Festschrift für J. P. M. van der Ploeg.* Alter Orient und altes Testament, band 211. Neukirchen-Vluyen, 1982. 23-35.
      [107/ 2300].

213. —————. "Deux inscriptions samaritaines de la région de Naplouse." *RB* 71 (1964): 57-72. Plates I & II.
      [2500/ 2510/ 2504].

214. —————. "Esséniens et Samaritains." *Le Monde de la Bible* 4 (1978): 28-30. New edn. 1985 pp. 26-28.
      [1500/ 1505].

215. —————. "Une feuille du Pentateuque samaritain à l'Abbaye de Beuron." *RB* 70 (1963): 225-242. Plates III-IV.
      [103/ 2300].

216. —————. Reviewer. **Rudolph Macuch**, "Grammatik des samaritanischen Aramäisch." *Biblica* 66.2 (1985): 284-290.
      [107/ 1900/ 2800].

217. —————. Reviewer. **H. Pohl**, "Kitab al-Mirat." *RB* 84 (1977): 113-122.
      [107/ 2204].

218. —————. "Les divers états du Pentateuque samaritain." *Mémorial Jean Carmignac=RQ* 13.1-4 (1988): 531-545.
      [2300/ 2302/ 2309/ 2400/ 2401].

219. ————. "Les Samaritains." *BTS* 28 (April 1960): 1, 4-18.
[200].

220. ————. "Les Samaritains." *Amicalement Vôtre* 6 (février-mars, 1989): 2-8.
[200].

221. ————. Reviewer. **Z. Ben-Hayyim**, "The Literary and Oral Tradition of Hebrew and Aramaic Among the Samaritans, vol. III part II: The Recitation of Prayers and Hymns." *RB* 75 (1968): 286-293. "Vol. IV: The Words of the Pentateuch, vol.V: Grammar of the Pentateuch." *RB* 91.4 (1984): 606-611.
[107/ 2100/ 2300/ 2602].

222. ————. Reviewer. **L.Vilsker**, "Manuel d'Araméen Samaritain." *JNES* 42.4 (1983): 295-297.
[107/ 2800].

223. ————. "Un nouveau fragment du Pentateuque samaritain." *RB* 67 (1960): 49-57. Plates I & II.
[103/ 2300].

224. ————. "La Pâque chez les samaritains." *La Croix du Dimanche* no. 3378 (1960 68e année): 6.
[1303/ 1404].

225. ————. "La Pâque samaritaine en 1986." *Le Monde de la Bible* 43 (Mars-Avril, 1986): 12-13, 27-33. [With 12 photographs].
[1303/ 1404].

226. ————. "Le Pentateuque d'Israel Nassi." *BTS* 184 (1976): 7f.
[103/ 2300].

227. ————. Reviewer. **S. Lowy**, "Principles of Samaritan Bible Exegesis." *RB* 86 (1979): 594-606.
[107/ 2300/ 2305].

228. ————. "Quelques manuscrits samaritains." *Semitica* 26 (1976): 143-166.
[103/ 2300].

229. ————. Reviewer. "La récitation de la loi chez les Samaritains, d'après Z. Ben-Hayyim." (Review, Ben-Hayyim, *The Literary...* vol. 3 part 1) *RB* 69 (1962): 570-587.
[107/ 2300/ 2308].

230. ————. Reviewer. **J. Macdonald**, "The Samaritan Chronicle No. II (*Sefer Ha-Yamim*). From Joshua to Nebuchadnezzar." *RB* 77 (1970): 592-603.
[107/ 1603].

231. ————. Reviewer. **J. Cohen**, "A Samaritan Chronicle." *RB* 90.2 (1983): 271-281.
[107/ 1603/ 3003].

232. ————. "Le texte samaritain de l'Exode dans les manuscrits de Qumran." In **A. Caquot and M. Philonenko**, editors, *Hommages à André Dupont-Sommer.*

Paris: Librairie d'Amerique et d'Orient Adrien-Maisonneuve, 1971. 363-381.
[103/ 1005/ 2300].

233. ――――――. "Trois inscriptions samaritaines au musée de l'École Biblique de
Jerusalem." *RB* 86.4 (1979): 583-593. Plates xxix-xxxi.
[2500/ 2501].

234. **Baillet, Maurice, J. T. Milik and R. de Vaux.** *Les 'petites grottes' de Qumran.*
Discoveries in the Judaean Desert of Jordan. III. Oxford: OUP, 1962. 2 parts.
[600/ 1005].

235. **Bakon, Shimon.** "The Fall of Samaria —Biblical Historiosophy on Trial." *Dor le
Dor* 17.1 (1988): 26-33.
[800/ 801/ 801.1].

236. **Balague, M.** "Hacia la religión del espíritu. Dialogo de Jesus con la Samaritana."
RBiCalz 21 (1959): 211-222. [See also, *Cultura Biblica* 18 (1961):151-166 and
NTAb 6 (1962) n. 810].
[407/ 1003.1/ 1502.1].

237. **Baldi, D.** "Samaritani." *Enciclopaedia Cattolica.* Vaticano, 1954. 10: cols. 1734-
1736.
[200].

238. **Baldrici.** "Historia Jerosolimitana." In *RHC, Historiens Occidentaux.* Paris, 1879.
Vol.4.
[306.2/ 401].

239. **Balkind, I.** (Hebrew) *The Samaritans.* Tel Aviv, 1928. [Library of Congress].
[200].

240. **Baltensz, Frans.** *Samaritane...des Evangelist Johanne.* Dordrecht, 1648. [Another
edition at Utrecht].
[1003.1/ 1502.1].

241. **Bandini, Angelo Maria.** *La Stamperia Mediceo-Orientale.* Firenze, 1848.
[105].

242. **Baneth, H.** Des Samaritaners Marqah an die 22 Buchstaben den Grundstock der
hebräischen Sprache anknüpfende Abhandlung.Halle: University of Halle
Inaugural dissertation, 1888.Reprinted, Berlin, 1888.
[1803/ 2600/ 2800].

243. ――――――. Reviewer. "Des Samaritaners Marqah Erzählung über den Tod
Moses." *Monatsblatt für vergangenheit und gegenweit des Judentums* (1891).
[107/ 1803].

244. **Bannister, J. T.** *A Survey of the Holy Land.* Bath, S.D. 184? Other editions.
[200/ 500].

245. **Barag, D.** "Shaalbim." *EAEHL.* English edition. Vol. 4.
[411.1/ 600/ 1304].

246. **Baramki, D. C.** *The Coin Collection of the American University of Beirut Museum — Palestine and Phoenicia.* Beirut: American University of Beirut, 1974. 6-30. [The coins show scenes of Mt. Gerizim and the temple sacra]. [406/ 603/ 604].

247. **Bar-Asher, M.** "L'Hébreu Michinique et la tradition samaritaine de l'Hébreu." In A.Tal & M Florentin, editors, *Proceedings of the First International Congress of the Société d'Études Samaritaines.* Tel Aviv: Chaim Rosenberg School for Jewish Studies, University of Tel Aviv, 1991. 315-330. [The article also appeared in the abstracts printed before the Congress]. [2600].

248. —————. "The Samaritan Targum to the Torah." (Hebrew) *Leshonenu* 45 (1980): 61-72. [2401].

249. **Bargès, L. Abbé J. J. L.** "Les Samaritains de Naplouse, épisode d'un pèlerinage dans les lieux saints." *Revue de l'Orient* 1 (1855): 81-90. [Reprinted, Paris, 1855 by Imprimerie polyglotte Édouard Blot in a limited edition of 200 copies; 127 pp]. [200/ 306.2/ 408].

250. —————. *Notice sur deux fragments d'un Pentateuque Hébreu-samaritain.* Paris: Imprimerie polyglotte Édouard Blot, 1865. 91pp. [103/ 2300].

251. **Barkai, Rachel.** "Four Samaritan Sarcophagi of the Roman Period." (Hebrew) *EI* 19 (1987): 6-18. [600/ 1203].

252. —————. "A Roman Period Samaritan Burial from Taluze." *BAIAS* 7 (1987-1988): 8-20. [600].

253. —————. "Samaritan Ossuaries from the Roman Period." (Hebrew) in Z.Ehrlich, editor, *Samaria and Benjamin.* 1987. 211-220. [600/ 1203].

254. —————. *Samaritan Sarcofagi of the Roman Period from the Land of Israel.*(Hebrew) MA Dissertation, Jerusalem: Hebrew University, 1983. [600].

255. —————. "Samaritan Sarcofagi of the Roman Period from the Land of Israel." In A. Tal & M. Florentin, editors, *Proceedings of the First International Congress of the Société d'Études Samaritaines.* Tel Aviv: Chaim Rosenberg School for Jewish Studies, University of Tel Aviv, 1991. 83-99. [600].

256. —————. "Samaritan Sarcophagi of the Roman Period in Eretz Israel." (Hebrew) *Cathedra* (1990): 63-73. [On the size of the Samaritan population in Israel]. [600].

257. **Barnard, L. W.** "Saint Stephen and Early Alexandrian Christianity." *NTS* 7 (1960): 31-45.
[1003.1/ 1502.2].

258. **Baron, Caesar.** "Samaritani curtam insensi inter se hostes" and "Samaritanorum contentio de templu primatu." In *Ingeus Ecclesiasticorum annalium opus.* 1. Rome, 1591.
[105/ 200].

259. **Baron, Salo W.** *A Social and Religious History of the Jews.* New York: Columbia University Press, 1957. Vol. 2, pp. 81-87 and 193-196 with additional notes.
[200/ 800].

260. **Baron, Salo W. and Joseph L. Blau.** *Judaism, Post-Biblical and Talmudic Period.* Indianapolis and New York: Bobbs-Merrill / The Library of Liberal Arts, 1954. [See chapter III "The Samaritans" pp. 67-71 (= *Massekhet Kuthim*)].
[304.2/ 2205].

261. **Baronian, Rev S. and F. C. Conybeare.** "MS Marshall (Or) 83 pt.1 Samaritan Alphabet." In *Catalogue of the Armenian Manuscripts in the Bodleian Library.* Oxford: OUP, 1918. 92.
[105].

262. **Barr, James.** Reviewer. S. Lowy, "Principles of Samaritan Bible Exegesis." *JTL* 29 (1978): 551-552.
[107/ 2305].

263. **Barrett, C. K.** "Stephen and the Son of Man." In *Apophoreta, Festschrift für E.Haenchen.* Berlin, 1964. 32-38.
[1502.2].

264. ————. "The Samaritan Woman." In *The Gospel According to St. John.* London, 1955. 190-204. [See also the 1978 edn. pp. 228-243].
[1502.1].

265. **Barthelemy, D. Iacobi.** "De Numis Hebr. Samaritanis." In F. P. Bayer, *Numorum Hebraeo-Samaritanorum Vindiciae.* Valentiae Edetanorum, 1790. I-XVII (=211-228).
[600/ 603].

266. **Bartlett, J. R.** Reviewer. A. D. Crown, "The Samaritans." *SOTS Book List* (1990): 131-132.
[107/ 200].

267. **Bartoloccius de Celleno, Julius.** "Dissertatio de Samaritanis." (Hebrew and Latin) in *Bibliotheca magna Rabbinica...de scriptoribus et scriptis Hebraicis, ordine alphabetico.* Rome, 1675-1695. 5 vols: vol. 4. Reprinted by Gregg reprints, 1968.
[200/ 2300].

268. **Barton, G.** "Altar (Semitic)." In *ERE* 1908. 1: 350-354.
[1303].

269. ——————. Reviewer. **J. A. Montgomery**, "The Samaritans." *BW* 32 (1908):
216-218.
[107/ 200].

270. ——————. Reviewer. **J. A. Montgomery**, "The Samaritans." *RB* 5 (1908): 308.
[107/ 200].

271. ——————. "Semites." In *ERE* 1920. 11: 378-384.
[200].

272. **Barton, William E.** "The Samaritan Messiah. Further Comments of the Samaritan
High Priest." *Open Court* 21 (1908): 528-538. [Illustrated. See also entries for
Jacob ben Aaron].
[1107].

273. ——————. "The Samaritan Passover." *Open Court* 22 (1909): 193-215.
Illustrations.
[1303/ 1404].

274. ——————. "The Samaritan Pentateuch." *BS* 60 (1903): 601-632. [Reprinted as
The Samaritan Pentateuch. The Story of Survival Among the Sects. Oberlin,Ohio:
1903; 42 pp. Also known in the form of a paper read before the Chicago
Society of Biblical Research, 1912, entitled, "The Samaritan Theory of the
Unity of the Pentateuch"].
[103/ 2300].

275. ——————. "The War and the Samaritan Colony." *BS* 78.309 (1921): 1-22.
[Read as a paper before the Chicago Society of Biblical Research, March 1920.
The text includes census figures and letters exchanged between Barton and the
Samaritan High Priests].
[813.1/ 903].

276. **Basil of Caesarea. Migne,** "Commentary on Isaiah." *PG* 30: 455-458, 479-482.
[305/ 305.4].

277. **Basnage, Jacques Sieux de Beauval.** "Dissertation sur l'antiquité de la monnaye et
des médailles des Juifs sur la préférence des caractères samaritains aux Hébreux
par Mr. B." *Histoires des ouvrages des Sçavans.* Rotterdam, January, 1709. 32-72.
[603/ 2501].

278. ——————. "L'histoire des sectes." In *Histoire des Juifs depuis Jésus-Christ jusqu'à
présent.* La Haye, 1716. Vol. 2: 1-318. [Second French edition. An English
edition appeared in 1708].
[800].

279. **Basola, Moses.** "Travels of Moses of Basola." (Hebrew) in **A Ya'ari,** *Travellers in
the Holy Land.* Ramat Gan, 1967. 125-264.
[304.4/ 401/ 412/ 1400].

280. **Basset, René,** editor. "Synaxaire Arabe Jacobite (Rédaction copte)." *PO* 1 (1907).
[Samaritans at Caesarea, Simon Magus, the Diaspora in Istanbul].
[305.3/ 403.1/ 502/ 1506.2].

281. **Baumgarten, Joseph M.** Reviewer. **I. R. M. Boid**, "Principles of Samaritan Halachah." *JQR* 82.3-4 (1992): 496-497.

282. **Baumstark, Anton.** "Jüdischer und christlicher Gebetstypus im Koran." *Islam* 16 (1927): 229-248.
[1003.3/ 1003.4/ 2100].

283. ——————. "Neue orientalische Problem biblischer Textgeschichte." *ZDMG* 89 (1935): 89-118.
[2300].

284. **Bayer, Franciscus Perez.** "Confutacion de la diatribe 'de numis hebraicis' de D. Olao Gerhardo Tychsen." In *Legitimidad de las monedas hebraeo-samaritanas.* Valencia, 1793. 4.
[603/ 2501].

285. ——————. "Iacobi Barthelemii...de Numis hebr. samaritanis litterae." Appendix, in *Numorum Hebraeo-Samaritanorum vindiciae.* Valentiae Edetanorum, 1790.
[603/ 2501].

286. **Beausobre, I. de and Jacques Lenfant.** *Le nouveau testament de notre seigneur Jésus Christ.* Lausanne, 1735-36. Preface; 26-35, 173-175.
[1003.1/ 1502/ 1502.1].

287. **Beazley, C. R.** "Early Christian Geography." *Transactions of the Royal Historical Society* 10 (1896): 85-109.
[400/ 401/ 1002].

288. **Becking, William.** *The Fall of Samaria.* Leiden: Brill, 1992.
[801/801.1].

289. **Bede, The Venerable.** "De Locis Sanctis." *SPTROL* (1879): 210f.
[306.2/ 407/ 600/ 1301].

290. **Beer, B.** "Samaria", "Samariter", "Samaritaner." In *PRE, Zweite Reihe (R-Z).* , 1920. 1: cols. 2102-2110.
[200/ 201].

291. ——————. "Zur dem Aufsatze des Oberrab. Zipser in Bezug auf die Samaritaner." *Ben Chananja* 2nd year (Szgedin, 1859): 519-520.
[1302/ 1800].

292. **Bell, H. I. and B. R. Rees.** "A Repudium from Hermopolis." *Eos* 48.1 (1956): 175-179. [=*Symbolae Raphaeli Taubenschag Dedicatae*].
[303.2/ 1205].

293. **Belleville, Linda M.** "Samaritan Documents." = section 6 Pt.1 in *Reflections of Glory: Paul's Polemica; Use of the Moses-Doxa Tradition in 2 Corinthians 3. 1-18. JSNT* Supplement Series 52. Sheffield: Sheffield Academic Press, 1991. 48-52.
[3008].

294. **Bellorini, T. and E. Hoade,** editors. *Plans of the Sacred Edifices of the Holy Land (1609).* Jerusalem: Franciscan Press, 1953.
[401/ 408/ 412].

295. —————, editors. *Visit to the Holy Places of Egypt, Sinai, Palestine and Syria in 1394 by Frescobaldi, Gucci and Sigoli.* Jerusalem: Franciscan Press, 1948.
[306/ 306.3/ 401/ 902].

296. **Beltz, W.** "Samaritanertum und Gnosis." In **K. W. Tröger,** editor, *Gnosis und Neues Testament.* Gütersloh, 1973. 89-95. Studien aus Religionswissenschaft und Theologie.
[1002/ 1503/ 1506].

297. **Ben Ami, Z.** "End of a 3, 000 Year Feud." *Jewish Digest* 11 (March, 1966): 23-24.
[903/ 1003.4].

298. **Ben Arieh, Y.** "The Uniqueness of the Settlement in Samaria." (Hebrew) in **J. Aviram,** editor, *Eretz Shomron.* Jerusalem: IES, 1973. 121-138.
[400/400.3].

299. **Ben Dor.** "A Hebrew Seal from Samaria." *QDAP* 12 (1946): 77-83.
[607].

300. **Ben Hananiah, J.** "The Samaritans in World War II." *BJPES* 11 (1944-1945): 57-63.
[813.2].

301. **Ben-Hayyim, Ze'ev.** "An Additional Study on Chronology in Language." (Hebrew) in *Studies in the Bible and the Biblical World: Essays in Honour of I. A. Zeligman.* Jerusalem: Elhanan Rubenstein, 1983. 1: 25-41.
[2600].

302. —————. "Allocution de clôture (de la Table Ronde)." In **Rothschild and Sixdenier,** editors, *Études samaritaines.* Louvain-Paris, 1988. 293-296.
[107].

303. —————. "The Asatir with Translation and Commentary." (Hebrew) *Tarbiz* 14 & 15 (1943): 14: 104-125; 174-190. 15: 44, 71-87, 128.
[1801].

304. —————. "Baqqasha of Saadia Gaon—A Samaritan Prayer." *Jerusalem Studies in Arabic and Islam* 9 (1987): 161-182.
[2100].

305. —————. "Between Hebrew and Hebrew." (Hebrew) *Leshonenu la'am* 20.9-10 (1969): 252-271.
[2600/ 2602].

306. —————. "A Bibliography of Ze'ev Ben-Hayyim's Writings." (Hebrew) *Leshonenu* 32 (Tevet, 1967): 1-13. [See also the supplement to *Leshonenu* 42, (1978) pp. 5-8 and "Bibliography " in Halkin, *Hebrew Language Studies* pp.1-25].
[100].

307. —————. Reviewer. **G. Margoliouth,** "Catalogue of the Hebrew and Samaritan Manuscripts in the British Museum." *JSS* 12 (1967): 326-327. [101/ 103/ 107].

308. —————. Reviewer. **E. Robertson,** "Catalogue of the Samaritan Manuscripts in the John Rylands Library, vol. II." *JSS* 14.1 (1969): 143-148. [101/ 103/ 107].

309. —————. "Comments and Corrections on the Asatir." (Hebrew) *Tarbiz* 15 (1943): 128. [1801].

310. —————. "Comments on a Samaritan Lamp from the Beth Shean Region." (Hebrew) *Yediot* 19 (1954): 106. [600/ 605].

311. —————. "The Contribution of I. Ben-Zvi to Samaritan Research." (Hebrew) *Sefunot* 8.Memorial volume for Ben Zvi (1964): 15-18. [Reprinted in a German version in Dexinger and Pummer, *Die Samaritaner* 274-280]. [106].

312. —————. "The Contribution of the Samaritan Inheritance to Research into the History of Hebrew." *Proceedings of the Israel Academy of Sciences and Humanities* 3 (1968): 162-174 (English version). 63-71 (Hebrew version). [Reprinted in both languages, 1968, 13 pp. and in Dexinger and Pummer, *Die Samaritaner*, 324-330]. [106/ 2600].

313. —————. "The Currency of a Lost Blessing." (Hebrew) in *Scholarship and Community in Medieval Jewish History*. Essays in Honour of Hayyim Hillel Ben-Sasson. Jerusalem: The Zalman Shazar Centre, 1989. 9-17. [804/ 2100].

314. —————. "Deuteronomy 32 in Samaritan Hebrew." (Hebrew) *Leshonenu* 15 (1946): 75-86. [2300].

315. —————. "Einige Bemerkungen zur samaritanischen Liturgie." *ZDPV* 86 (1970): 87-89. [2100].

316. —————. "Epilogue." (Hebrew) in **A. Tal & M. Florentin,** editors, *Proceedings of the First International Congress of the Société d'Études Samaritaines.* Tel Aviv: Chaim Rosenberg School for Jewish Studies, University of Tel Aviv, 1991. 19*. [106].

317. —————. "On the Essay of Raphael Weiss." (Hebrew) *Leshonenu* 39 (1975): 51-54. [107].

318. —————. Reviewer. **John Macdonald,** "Former Prophets in a Samaritan Version?= *Samaritan Chronicle II*." (Hebrew) *Leshonenu* 35 (1971): 292-302. [107/ 1603].

319. —————. M.A. Friedman, "A Fragment of the Memar Marqah in an Unknown Version." (Hebrew) *Teudah, Researches in Talmudic Literature* 3 (1983): 121-137. [An English summary, p. xiii, and a facsimile of JNUL MS 8° 47].
[103/ 1803].

320. —————. (Hebrew) *From the Samaritan Liturgy—Seminar Material.* Jerusalem: Academon, Hebrew University, 1965.
[2100].

321. —————. "Gerizim and Mount Gerizim." (Hebrew) in *EM* 1953. 2: 554-558. Also in the third edn. 1973.
[201/ 406].

322. —————. "Hebrew According to the Samaritan Pronunciation." (Hebrew) *Leshonenu* 12 (1943-4): 45-60, 112-126.
[2600/ 2604].

323. —————. "The Helpers of Death." (Hebrew) *Leshonenu La'am* 18 (1967): 135-137. [English summary 176-177].
[2603].

324. —————. "Introduction." (Hebrew) in **R. Tsedaka,** editor, *The Five Books of the Torah, Samaritan-Jewish Version.* Tel Aviv, 1962.
[2300].

325. —————. Reviewer. **H. Pohl,** "The *Kitab al Mirat.*" *OLZ* 74.2 (1979): 130-134.
[107/ 2204].

326. —————. "The Language of Tibåt Marqe and its Time." In **A. Tal & M. Florentin,** editors, *Proceedings of the First International Congress of the Société d'Études Samaritaines.* Tel Aviv: Chaim Rosenberg School for Jewish Studies, University of Tel Aviv, 1991. 331-346.
[2800].

327. —————. *The Literary and Oral Tradition of Hebrew and Aramaic Among the Samaritans. I Introduction—The Grammatical Writings. II The masoretical and Lexicographical Writings III/1 Recitation of the Law. III/2 The Recitation of Prayers and Hymns. IV The Words of the Pentateuch. V Grammar of the Pentateuch.* Jerusalem: Academy of the Hebrew Language, I-II 1957. III/1 & 2 1968 IV-V 1977. [The introduction was reprinted in *A–B Samaritan News*, 234 1/5/79 and an English version of the final conclusions of the series was printed in A. D. Crown, *The Samaritans,* Tübingen, 1989].
[1900/ 2100/ 2300/ 2306.1/ 2308/ 2600/ 2602/ 2607].

328. —————. Reviewer. **John Macdonald,** "Memar Marqah." *BO* 23. 3-4 (1966): 185-191.
[107/ 1803].

329. —————. "Method in Research in Samaritan Language." (Hebrew) *A–B Samaritan News* 249/250 (16/12/1979): 25-27.
[106/ 2600].

330. —————. "Mono and Bi-Syllabic Middle Guttural Nouns in Samaritan
Hebrew." *JANES* 11 (1979): 19-29. Near Eastern Studies in Memory of M. M.
Bravman.
[2600].

331. —————. "Observations et réponses à propos de l'article précédent." In
Rothschild and Sixdenier, editors, *Études samaritaines.* Louvain-Paris, 1988.
107-108.
[1004].

332. —————. "Observations on the Hebrew and Aramaic Lexicon from Samaritan
Tradition." *VT Supplement* 16 (1967): 12-24.
[2600/ 2603/ 2800].

333. —————. "On the Pronunciation of the Tetragrammaton by the Samaritans."
(Hebrew) *EI* 3 (1954): 147-154.
[2604/ 2605].

334. —————. "Samaritan." In **F. Rosenthal,** editor, *An Aramaic Handbook.* Part
II/1 & II/2. Wiesbaden: Harrassowitz, 1968.
[2600/ 2800].

335. —————. "Samaritan Hebrew—an Evaluation." In **A. D. Crown,** editor, *The
Samaritans.* Tübingen: J.C.B.Mohr, 1989. 517-530.
[2600].

336. —————. "A Samaritan Inscription of the XIth century." (Hebrew) *Yediot* 12
(1946): 74-82. [Reprinted in the *BIES Reader A,* Jerusalem, 1965, pp. 238-
246].
[2500/ 2514].

337. —————. "On the Samaritan Inscription from Yavneh." (Hebrew) *Yediot* 14
(1948): 49-50.
[2515].

338. —————. Reviewer. **J. D. Purvis,** "The Samaritan Pentateuch and the Origin
of the Samaritan Sect." *Biblica* 52 (1971): 253-255.
[107/ 2300].

339. —————. "Samaritan Piyyutim for Festivals." (Hebrew) *Tarbiz* 10 (1938): 190-
200, 333-374.
[2100/ 2102].

340. —————. "A Samaritan Poem of the Fourth Century." (Hebrew) *EI* 4 (1956):
119-127. An English summary, p. viii.
[1550/ 2100/ 2102.2].

341. —————. "The Samaritan Punctuation, Especially its Three Patachs." (Hebrew)
in *J. M. Epstein Jubilee Volume.* Jerusalem: Magnes Press, 1950. 215-224. On
the occasion of his seventieth birthday.
[2600/ 2607].

342. —————. "The Samaritan Tradition and its Use for Research into Hebrew and Aramaic." (Hebrew) *Leshonenu* 17 (1950): 133-138. [This paper was also delivered as a lecture at the World Congress of Jewish Studies, 1946. See the *Proceedings*, vol. 1, Jerusalem (1951) pp.146-153].
[106].

343. —————. "The Samaritan Tradition and its Relationship to the Hebrew of the Language of the Dead Sea Scrolls." (Hebrew) *Leshonenu* 22 (1958): 223-245. [An English version appears in *Scripta Hierosolymitana* 4 (1958) pp. 200-214].
[2600/ 2600.1].

344. —————. "The Samaritan Vowel System and its Graphic Representation." *AO* 22 (1954): 515-530.
[2600/ 2601/ 2607].

345. —————. (Hebrew) *Selected Problems in Hebrew Linguistics—Questions of Hebrew Morphology in Samaritan Sources.* Jerusalem: Akademon, 1957. 1. Extracts from the *Sepher Hamaslul* 2. Extracts from the *Principles of Reading of Abu Said.*
[1900/ 2600/ 2603.1].

346. —————. (Hebrew) *Selections from the Samaritan Liturgy; Seminar material on Problems in Palestinian Aramaic.* Jerusalem: Akademon, Hebrew University, 1963 (1964/1965). Transcribed by I. Tsedaka.
[2100/ 2800].

347. —————. Reviewer. **R. Macuch,** "Some Problems of a Grammar of Samaritan Hebrew (=*Grammatik des samaritanischen Hebräisch*)." *Biblica* 52.2 (1971): 229-252.
[107/ 2600/ 2602].

348. —————. "Studies in Palestinian Aramaic and Samaritan Poetry." (Hebrew) in **S. Abramson and A. Mirsky,** editors, *Hayyim (Jefim) Schirmann Jubilee Volume.* Jerusalem: Schocken, 1970. 39-68.
[2100/ 2800].

349. —————. *Studies in the Traditions of the Hebrew Language.* Madrid–Barcelona, 1954. See especially pp.1-150.
[2600].

350. —————. "On the Study of the Samaritan Language." (Hebrew) *Tarbiz* 10 (1939): 81-89, 113.
[106/ 2600].

351. —————. "Thoughts on the Hebrew Vowel System." (Hebrew with an English summary.) In **Y. Avishur and J. Blau,** editors, *Studies in the Bible and the Ancient Near East.* Jerusalem, 1978. 95-105.
[1004].

352. —————. *Tibât Marqe: A Collection of Samaritan Midrashim.* Jerusalem: Israel Academy of Sciences and Humanities, 1988.
[1803].

353. —————. "Towards a New Edition of Tibåt Marqe." In **Rothschild and Sixdenier**, editors, *Études samaritaines.* Louvain-Paris, 1988. 161-179. [1803].

354. —————. "La tradition samaritaine et sa parenté avec les autres traditions de la langue hébraïque." *Mélanges de Philosophie et Littérature Juives* 3-5 (1958-1962): 89-128. [See *Leshonenu* 22]. [2600].

355. —————. "Traditions in the Hebrew Language with Special Reference to the Dead Sea Scrolls." In C. **Rabin** and Y. **Yadin**, editors, *Scripta Hierosolymitana IV: Aspects of the Dead Sea Scrolls.* Jerusalem: Magnes Press, 1958. 200-214. [1005/ 2600/ 2600.1].

356. —————. "Two Notes (Additions to *Leshonenu La'am* 20, 1969, pp. 252-271)." (Hebrew) *Leshonenu La'am* 21 (1970): 78. [2600].

357. —————. "The Verb Tenses in Biblical Hebrew and the Samaritan Tradition." (Hebrew) in *Festschrift for Dov Sadan's 70th Birthday.* Jerusalem and Tel Aviv, 1977. 66-86. [2600/ 2602].

358. —————. "On the Vocalization of the Samaritan, Especially its Three Patachs." (Hebrew) *Tarbiz* 20 (1949-1950): 215-224. [2600/ 2607].

359. —————. "Whence the *Knst myh* Samaritan Synagogue?" (Hebrew) *EI* 14 (1978): 188-190. [English summary, p. 130]. [600/ 1304].

360. **Benjamin of Tudela.** "The Travels of Benjamin of Tudela in the Land of Israel and in Russia." (Hebrew) in A. **Ya'ari**, editor, *Masa'ot Eretz Israel.* Ramat Gan, 1976. 31-47. [See also the edition by E. N. Adler]. [304.4/ 400/ 401/ 408].

361. **Bennet, Thomas.** *Hebrew Grammar.* London, 1732. [Reprinted, Bristol, (or London) 1795. This edition included a "Breve consilium de studio praecipuarum... orientalium scilicet Hebraeae, Chaldaeae, Syricae, Samaritanae et Arabice, institiuendo et perficiendo."]. [2600].

362. **Benoit, P.** "Le travail d'édition des fragments manuscrits de Qumran." *RB* 63 (1956): 54-60. [106/ 1005/ 2300].

363. **Benoit, P.** and **T. J. Milik.** *Discoveries in the Judaean Desert II: Les Grottes de Murabba'at.* Oxford: OUP, 1961. [600/ 1005/ 2300].

364. **Ben-Pazzi, Y.** "Samaritans in the Tents of Shem." (Hebrew) *Ziyyon* 1897. (Galicia) (1): 19-20. [2600].

365. **Benvenisti, M.** *The Crusaders in the Holy Land.* Jerusalem, 1970.
[810].

366. **Ben-Yessak, A.** "The Samaritan High Priest Dead at 92." *A–B* 256 (16/3/1980): 19-20.
[200/ 1302/ 3000].

367. **Ben-Zvi, Izhak.** "The Abisha Scroll." (Hebrew) *EI* 5 (1958): 240-252. English summary p. 97.
[103/ 2300/ 2301].

368. ————. "Abraham b. Marhib the Samaritan." (Hebrew) *Supplement to Davar* Heshvan, 1929.1032 [An obituary].
[3000].

369. ————. "Apropos of the Samaritan Inscription of Beit-el-Ma." (Hebrew) *Yediot* 3.4 (1935): 131-133. [Reprinted in *Yediot Reader A,* (1965) 229-231].
[2500/ 2503].

370. ————. "The Book of Joshua from the Samaritan Point of View." (Hebrew) *El Ha'ayin* 1 (1958): 34 pp. [The volume has several pages of discussion from participants at the President's seminar].
[1604/ 1605].

371. ————. "The Book of Joshua from the Samaritan Point of View." (Hebrew) in **C. Rabin,** editor, *Studies in the Book of Joshua.* Jerusalem, 1960. 127-163.
[1604/ 1605].

372. ————. "Dahr ben Amr and the Shechemites." (Hebrew) *Zion (Reader)* 6 (1934): 139-148.
[813/ 903].

373. ————. *Eretz Israel Veyishuveha.* Jerusalem: Yad Itzhak Ben-Zvi, 1955 & 1968.
[200].

374. ————. "The Foundations of Samaritan Chronology." (Hebrew) *Sura* 3 (1958): 24-35.
[700].

375. ————. "From the Samaritan Genizot." (Hebrew) *Sinai* 9, 10, 11, 12, 13, 14 (1941-1944): 9: 323-333. 10: 100-106; 216-222. 11: 156-162. 12: 410-417. 13: 245-266; 308-316. 14:17-20. [1. Synagogues or churches. 2. Dates and Tashqils. 3. Pentateuchs].
[103/ 700/ 1301/ 1304/ 1400/ 2300].

376. ————. "A Greco-Samaritan Inscription from Lydda." (Hebrew) *Yediot* 8 (1940): 18-20.
[2500/ 2515].

377. ————. "A Lamp with a Samaritan Inscription 'There Is None like unto Thee, O God of Jeshurun'." *IEJ* 11 (1961): 139-142.
[605/ 2500].

378. ————. "Les Samaritains." In **Eduard de Minuit,** *Les Tribus dispersées.* Paris,
1959. Chapter 11, 185-191.
[200/ 800].

379. ————. "On the Mount of Blessing—The Samaritan Passover Sacrifice."
(Hebrew) *Hatoran* 3 (1917): 15-17.
[406/ 1303/ 1404].

380. ————. "New Finds at Shechem." (Hebrew) *Yediot* 3 (1925): 1-6.
[412/ 600].

381. ————. "An Old Samaritan Synagogue in Sha'alavim." (Hebrew) *Devar
Yerushalayim* 51 (1947): [See also *Ha'olam,* year 3 (41) nos. 1-2 (1948)].
[411.1/ 1304].

382. ————. "The Origin of the Samaritans and their Tribal Divisions." In E.
Mills, *Census of Palestine.* Alexandria, 1931-1933. 1: 86-90. [See also the
Hebrew version in *Hapo'el Hatsair,* 26th year, no. 31:1 (Sivan, 1931). Reprinted
in English in Dexinger and Pummer, *Die Samaritaner* 187-197 and in the
microfiche edn. of IDC, Leiden].
[801.1/ 2904/ 2902].

383. ————. "Pinhasia." (Hebrew) *QS* 7 (1930-31): 570-573.
[103/ 2300].

384. ————. "Rabbi Nathan of Safed's Description of the Lives of the
Samaritans." (Hebrew) *Anthology of the Jews of Spain.* Jerusalem, 1964. 5.
[304.4/ 902].

385. ————. "On the Ruins of Samaria." (Hebrew) *Ahdut* 18 (1910): [Reprinted,
Collected Works, vol. 1, pp. 54-67].
[410/ 600].

386. ————. "Samaritan Arsuf." (Hebrew) *Yediot* 1.2 (1933): 24-26. [Reprinted,
Sefer Hashomronim].
[401/ 401.1].

387. ————. "The Samaritan Book of Joshua and its Recent Forgery." (Hebrew)
Knesset 10 (1945): 130-153.
[1605].

388. ————. "The Samaritan Diaspora of the Judaean Coast." (Hebrew) *Yediot* 19
(1954-55): 125-128.
[400/ 500].

389. ————. "Samaritan History in the Nineteenth Century." (Hebrew) *Ha'olam*
38-39 (33rd year, 1945):
[813/ 813.1].

390. ————. "A Samaritan Inscription from Kafr Khalil." (Hebrew) *JPOS* 10
(1930): 222-226. [Reprinted in *Ha'olam* 27th Ellul (1930) 18: 38. 181-184 and
in *Sefer Hashomronim,* 165-168].
[2500/ 2510].

391. —————. "A Samaritan Inscription of the Fifth Century AH." (Hebrew) *BJPES* 2, Mazie volume (1934): 108-112. [= *Sefer Hashomronim:* 168-172]. [2500/ 2508.1].

392. —————. "A Samaritan Inscription from Beit-el-Ma." (Hebrew) *Yediot* 3 (1935): 131-133. [2500/ 2503].

393. —————. "A Samaritan Inscription of the Ayubbid Period from Beit Chanin." (Hebrew) *Yediot* 12 (1946): 82-84. [2500/ 2502].

394. —————. "Samaritan Inscriptions from Yavneh." (Hebrew) *Yediot* 13 (1946): 166-168. [2500/ 2515].

395. —————. "A Samaritan Inscription from Kfar Bilu." (Hebrew) *Yediot* 18 (1952): 223-229. [2500/ 2509].

396. —————. "Samaritan Inscriptions on a Lamp from Beth Shean." (Hebrew) *Yediot* 19 (1954): 105. [411/ 605/ 2501/ 2503.1/ 2504].

397. —————. "A Samaritan Pentateuch Manuscript." (Hebrew) *Jerusalem (Luncz Memorial Volume)* (1927): 91-304. [Reprinted, *Sefer Hashomronim*]. [103/ 2300].

398. —————. "Samaritan Script in Gaonic Writings." (Hebrew) *Yediot* 7 (1939): 30-33. 1 plate. [304/ 2501].

399. —————. "The Samaritan Settlement in Transjordania." (Hebrew) *Yediot* 1.4 (1934): 17-20. [Reprinted: *Sefer Hashomronim,* 118-121]. [508].

400. —————. "The Samaritan Version of the Ten Lost Tribes." (Hebrew) *Ha'olam* 25th year. 27, 29, 39 (1940): [801.2].

401. —————. "Samaritan Villages in Samaria and Judaea." In **A. Shmueli, D. Grossman and R. Zeevy,** editors, *Judaea and Samaria. Studies in Settlement Geography.* Jerusalem, 1977. 103-117. [400.3].

402. —————. "Samaritans and Jews." (Hebrew) *Davar* (3 Tammuz 1931): no. 2166. [Reprinted as "Karaites and Samaritans" in *Collected Works,* 5, 97-105]. [1004].

403. —————. "The Samaritans in Jaffa." (Hebrew) *Davar* no. 2780 (21 Tammuz 1933). [Reprinted in *Sefer Hashomronim*]. [400/ 500].

404. —————. "The Samaritans in the Beth Shean District." (Hebrew) in *The Seventeenth Archaeological Convention Proceedings.* Jerusalem: IES, 1961. 74-79.
[411/ 500/ 808].

405. —————. *Sefer Hashomronim (The Book of the Samaritans).* Tel Aviv: Shtibel, 1935. Revised editions, Yad Izhak Ben-Zvi, 1970, 1977.
[200/ 202].

406. —————. "'There is None like the God of Jeshurun'." *Yediot* 25.4 (1960): 247-254.
[600/ 605/ 2500].

407. —————. "Three Samaritan Torah Scrolls." (Hebrew) *Journal of the Jewish Palestine Exploration Society (Mazie Memorial Volume)* (1934): 113-116.
[103/ 2300].

408. **Ben-Zvi, Izhak and W. F. Albright.** "The Beit-el-Ma Samaritan Inscription." *BASOR* 84 (1941): 2-4. [Page 4 is a comment by Albright].
[2500/ 2503].

409. **Ben-Zvi, Izhak and I. Ben-Ze'ev.** "Samaritan Origins and the Arabic Writings of their Sages." (Hebrew) *Knesset* 4 (1938): 321-327.
[801.1/ 1600/ 1800].

410. **Ben-Zvi, Rachel.** "With the Samaritans at Mt. Gerizim." (Hebrew) *Davar* (15 Sivan 1967): A Yiddish version appeared in *Kiryath Sepher,* 1972, p. 280.
[200].

411. **Berens, Balthasar.** *Gentis Samaritanae historiam et ceremonias...proponit B. Berens.* Halae Magdeburgicae, 1694. [Typography by I Stegmann].
[200/ 800].

412. **Berger, Philippe.** "Alphabet samaritain" and "Alphabet des siècles du temple." *Histoire de l'écriture dans l'antiquité.* Paris, 1891. 197-204. 2nd ed. 1892.
[2501].

413. —————. *Deux inscriptions funéraires de Naplouse.* Paris, 1898.
[2500].

414. —————. *Répertoire d'épigraphie semitique.* Paris, 1900, 1907-1914. 1 & 2: nos. 437, 678. No. 437 is reprinted in AIBL 1903, p. 92.
[2500/ 2501/ 2506].

415. **Bergmeier, R.** "Zur Frühdatierung samaritanischer Theologumena." *JSJ* 5.2 (1974): 121-153.
[1000].

416. **Bergmeier, Roland.** Reviewer. Fossum, "The Name of God and the Angel of the Lord." *TLZ* 111.11 (1986): 815-817.
[107/ 1101].

417. **Berliner, A.** Reviewer. **Leopold Wreschner,** "Samaritanische Traditionen." *LZ* 40 (1889): 739ff.
[107/ 800/ 1550].

418. —————. Reviewer. **Adolph Brüll,** "Zur Geschichte und Literatur der Samaritaner." *MWJ* 3 (1876): 166.
[107/ 800/ 1550].

419. **Berliner, Ruhamman.** "Eastern Samaria—Not Desert but a Flourishing Border Area." (Hebrew) *Teva va'aretz* 20 (1977): 156-160.
[400/ 400.1/ 400.3].

420. **Bernard, Edward.** *Catalogi librorum manuscriptorum Angliae et Hiberniae in unum collecti, cum indice alphabetico.* Oxford, 1697. 2 parts. [Typography by Humphrey Wanley].
[101/ 103/ 105].

421. —————. "Chronologiae Samaritanae synopsis...ex manuscriptis eruta et Oxonio Transmissa." *Acta Eruditorum* (1691): 167-193. [A summary of the content of the Huntington manuscript of Abu'l Fath in Bodley].
[103/ 1601].

422. —————. *Orbis eruditi literaturam à charactere Samaritico hunc in modum favente Deo deduxit E. Bernardus.* Oxford, 1689. [Reprinted 1700 under the same title edited by John Owen; reprinted London, 1759. Contains a large number of related alphabets. Bodleian, 1881 c 7 (123)].
[105/ 2501].

423. —————. *Orbis eruditi literatura à charactere Samaritico deducta.* Oxford, 1759.
[105/ 2501].

424. —————. *Tabulam hanc a se restauratum et supplementis quibusdam egregiis humanissime sibi subministratis auctam, Musei Britannici curatoribus...Carolus Morton.* London, 1759. [Holding library: Bodleian].
[105/ 2501].

425. **Bernard, J. H.** *Guide Book to Palestine.* London: Palestine Pilgrims Text Society, 1894.
[400/ 800].

426. **Bernheimer, Carolo.** *Codices Hebraici Bibliothecae Ambrosianae.* Florence, 1933. 179-180.
[101/ 103].

427. **Bertinoro, Obadiah b. Abraham.** "Letters." (Hebrew) in **Abraham Ya'ari,** editor, *Letters from the Land of Israel.* Tel Aviv, 1963. 94-141.
[304.4/ 400/ 505/ 811/ 1400].

428. **Besant, W.** "On the Amwas Inscription." (A letter) *The Athenaeum* (1881): 780, 814.
[2500/ 2502].

429. **Beveridge, William.** *De Linguarum Orientalium, Praesertim Hebraicae, Chaldaicae, Syriacae, Arabicae et Samaritanae Praesantia.* London, 1658. Printer, Thomas Roycroft. [Bodleian, Or. f.5].
[2500/ 2600].

430. **Beyer, G.** "Neapolis (Nablus) und sein gebiet in der Kreuzfahrezeit." *ZDPV* 63 (1940): 155-209. [Reprinted, Lichtenstein, 1972].
[400/ 408/ 810].

431. **Beynon, Elias.** *Eliae Beynon dess Jüngern...Barmhertziger Samariter...* Nürnberg: J. Hoffmann, 1696. [Other editions, Geneva, 1673 "Le Samaritain charitable...", Stockholm, 1709 "Den Barmhertigen Samariten."].
[1502.3].

432. **Beyschlag, K.** *Simon Magus und die christliche Gnosis.* WUNT 16. Tübingen, 1974.
[1502/ 1506/ 1506.2].

433. —————. "Zur Simon-Magus-Fräge." *ZTK* 68 (1971): 395-426.
[1506/ 1506.2].

434. **Bickerman, Elias.** "Un document relatif à la persécution d'Antiochus IV Epiphane." *RHR* 115 (1938): 118-223. [For the German version see Bikerman, 1973. He argues the authenticity of the Samaritan petition quoted by Josephus].
[303.5/ 804].

435. —————. *Studies in Jewish and Christian History.* Leiden: E. J. Brill, 1980-1986. Vol.2:105-135, vol.3: 270-281. [Reprints earlier articles. See especially the section on the Samaritan Gods on Mt. Gerizim in "Anonymous Gods"].
[200/ 800/ 1110].

436. **Bihler, Johann.** "Der Stephanusbericht APG. 6, 8-15 und 7, 54 - 8, 2." *BZ* N.F. 3 (1959): 252-270.
[1502/ 1502.2].

437. —————. "Der Stephanusgeschichte im Zusammenhäng der Apostelgeschichte." *MTS 1 Historische Abteilung* 30 Bd. (1963): [Appeared first as a doctoral dissertation, Munich, 1957].
[1502/ 1502.2].

438. **Bikerman, Elias.** "Ein Dokument zur Verfolgung Antiochos IV Epiphanes." In **A. Schalit,** editor, *Zur Josephus Forschung.* Darmstadt, 1973. 241-277.
[303.5/ 804].

439. **Bin Gorion-Berdichevski, Micha Joseph.** "Judah and Israel." (Hebrew) *A–B* (1965): 11-28, 31-68, 108-117.
[801].

440. —————. *Sinai und Garizim.* Berlin, 1926. [The book was abstracted under the same title, in Hebrew in *A–B Samaritan News* in 1962].
[800].

441. **Binder, H.** "Das Gleichnis vom barmherzigen Samariter." *TZ* 15 (1959): 176-194. [1003.1/ 1502.3].

442. **Bin-Nun, Joel.** "My Holy Place Which is in Shiloh." (Hebrew) in Z. Ehrlich, editor, *Samaria and Benjamin.* Jerusalem, 1987. 102-106. [401].

443. **Biran, A.** "Mount Gerizim." *CNI* 20.3-4 (1969): 44-45. [406].

444. **Birnbaum, Philip.** "The Samaritans." (Hebrew) in *Plitat Soferim.* 1971. 317-320. [200].

445. **Birnbaum, Solomon.** *The Hebrew Scripts.* Leiden: Brill, 1971. 2 volumes. [2501].

446. ──────. "The Leviticus Fragments from the Cache in the Judaean Desert." *BASOR* 118 (April 1950): 20-27. [1005/ 2307].

447. ──────. *The Qumran [Dead Sea] Scrolls and Palaeography.* New Haven, Connecticut, 1952. [1005/ 2501].

448. **Biser, E.** "Wer ist mein Nächster? Zu Lk.10, 29." *GUL* 48.6 (1975): 406-414. [1502/ 1502.3].

449. **Bishop, Eric F.** "People on the Road to Jericho: the Good Samaritan and Others." *EQ* 42 (1970): 2-6. [1003/ 1502.3].

450. ──────. "Some Relationships of Samaritanism with Judaism, Islam and Christianity." *The Moslem World* 37 (1947): 11-33. [1003.1/ 1003.3/ 1003.4].

451. **Björnstahl, Jacob Jonas.** "Über die samaritanische handschrift in der Barberinischen Bibliothek: II Von der samaritanischen Triglotte." *RBML* 3 (1778): 84-102. [103/ 2300/ 2302/ 2401].

452. **Blaiklock, E. M. B.** "Samaria", "Samaritans." In *Zondervan Pictorial Bible Dictionary.* Grand Rapids, Michigan: Eerdmans, 1963. 744-747. Numerous reprints. [200/ 201].

453. **Blake, H.** "Samaritans and Jews: Reconciliation of an Old Feud." *Hadassah Magazine* 55 (1974): 10-11. [1003.4].

454. ──────. "Samaritans and Jews." *Jewish Digest* 20 (1975): 68-73. [1003.4].

455. **Blanchino, Joseph.** *Evangeliarum quadruplex Latinae versionis antiquae.* Rome, 1749. Vol. II part 2 facing p. dciv. [The author is also identified as Giuseppe Bianchini].
[1003.1].

456. **Blau, J.** Reviewer. A. Murtonen, "Hebrew in its West Semitic Setting." *AN* 26 (1988): 122-126.
[107/ 2600].

457. **Blau, O.** "Der Dekalog in einer samaritanischen Inschrift aus dem Tempel des Garizim." *ZDMG* 13 (1859): 275-281. [Cf. vol. 14 (1860) 632-634].
[805/ 1103/ 1305/ 2504].

458. **Blayney, Benjamin.** *Pentateuchus Hebraeo-Samaritanus charactere Hebraeo-Chaldaico editus cura et studio B. Blayney.* Oxford, 1790. [Reprint of Kennicott's edition and comments].
[2300].

459. **Bleek, F.** *Einleitung in das Alte Testament.* Berlin, 1870. See p. 758f. [Ed. Kamphausen (another edition ed.Wellhausen, 1878)].
[2300].

460. **Bleich, J.** "Judaea and Samaria; Settlement and Return." *Tradition* 18.1 (1979): 44-78.
[813/ 2904].

461. **Bligh, J.** "Jesus in Samaria." *HJ* 3 (1962): 329-346.
[806/ 1003.1/ 1502].

462. **Bliss, F. J.** *The Development of Palestine Exploration.* New York, 1907.
[400/ 600].

463. **Bloch, Josef Samuel.** Die samaritanisch-arabische Pentateuchübersetzung, Deuteronomium I-XI mit Einleitung und Noten.Berlin, Poppelauer's Buchhandlung: Kaiser-Wilhelms-Universtät zu Strassburg, 1901. [On manuscripts in Berlin, Gotha, Kiel, Leiden and Paris. He deals with theories relating to the Samaritan Arabic Pentateuch and its translation].
[103/ 2300/ 2302].

464. **Blochet, E.** *Catalogue des Manuscrits Arabes: des Nouvelles Acquisitions, 1884-1925.* Paris: Bibliothèque Nationale, 1925. 73-74.
[101/ 103].

465. **Blunt, J. H.** "Dositheans." In *Dictionary of Sects, Heresies, Ecclesiastical Parties.* London, 1874. 134-135.
[1503].

466. **Blyth, Estelle.** "The Samaritans." *The Near East: Jewish Missionary Intelligence* 13 (1923): 73-75. Illustrated.
[200].

467. —————. "The Samaritans." *Asiatic Review* 43.155 (January 1947): 256-262.
[200].

468. **Boberg, Andreas.** On the Language and Script of the Samaritans. (Sive de lingua et literis Samaritanorum, dissertatio philologica, cujus partem priorem...placido honorum examini... submittit Magnus Ericander). (Hebrew and Latin) Uppsala: Uppsala, 1733. Typis Wernerianis, 68 pp.
[2500/ 2600].

469. —————. (Hebrew) *On the Samaritan Language and Pentateuch. (Sive de lingua et pentateucho Samaritanorum)*. Stockholmiae, 1734. Hebrew.
[2300/ 2500/ 2600].

470. **Bochart, Samuel.** *Opera Omnia.* Trajecti ad Rhenum & Lugduni Batavorum, 1712-13.
[800/ 1100].

471. **Bockel, P.** "Jésus au puits de Jacob." *BTS* 184 (1976): 20-21.
[407/ 1003.1/ 1502.1].

472. **Boers, Hendrikus.** *Neither on This Mountain nor in Jerusalem: A Study of John 4.* Atlanta: Scholars Press, 1988. [Has a good bibliography on John 4].
[1502.1].

473. **Bogaert, P. M.** Reviewer. **L.Vilsker,** "Manuel d'Araméen Samaritain." *Muséon* 95 (1982): 394f.
[107/ 2800].

474. **Bogle, A. N.** "Gerizim." In **J. D. Hastings,** *Dictionary of Christ and the Gospels.* Edinburgh: T & T Clark, 1906. Vol.1: 644-645.
[200/ 201/ 406].

475. **Boher, D.** "Les Samaritains, derniers prophètes du XXe siècle." *Sciences et Voyages* 33 (January, 1968): 44-48.
[200].

476. —————. "Les Samaritains ont retrouvé Israël." *Tant qu'il fait jour* (Sept./Oct. 1969): 4f.
[200].

477. **Bôhl, F. M. Th. de Liagre.** *De Opgraving van Sichem, Bericht over de voorjaarscampagne en de zomercampagne in 1926.* Zeist, 1927. [BL 7703 e 20].
[411/ 503].

478. —————. "Sichem Keilschrifttafeln." *ZDPV* 49 (1926): 321-327. Plates 44-46.
[801].

479. —————. "De geschiednis der stad Sichem en de Opgravingen Aldar." *Mededeelingen der Koninklijke Akademie van Wetenschappen te Amsterdam, Afdeeling Letterkunde* 62 (1926): 1-19. Series B.
[600].

480. **Böhmer, Julius.** "Samaria." *Studierstube* (1908): 544-546.
[410/ 801].

481. Bóid, I. R. M. *Principles of Samaritan Halachah.* Studies in Judaism in Late
     Antiquity. Leiden: E. J. Brill, 1989.
     [1106/ 2200].

482. —————. "The Samaritan Halachah." In A. D. Crown, editor, *The Samaritans.*
     Tübingen: Mohr, 1989. 624-649.
     [1100/ 1106/ 2200/ 2202/ 2203/ 2204].

483. —————. "Use, Authority and Exegesis of Mikra in the Samaritan Tradition."
     In Mulder and Sysling, editors, *Mikra.* Assen/Maastricht/Philadelphia: Van
     Gorcum/Fortress, 1988. 379-420.
     [2300/ 2305].

484. —————. Principles of Samaritan Halachah. (Ph. D thesis) Sydney: University
     of Sydney, 1982.
     [1106/ 2200].

485. Boismard, M.-E. "Aenon, prés de Salem (Jean III, 23)." *RB* 80.2 (1973): 218-229.
     [401.2/ 1502.1].

486. —————. *Môise ou Jésus. Essai de christologie Johannique.* Bibliotheca
     Ephemeridum Theologicarum Lovaniensum 84. Louvain: Leuven University
     Press/Peeters, 1988.
     [1502.1].

487. Boissy, Louis Michel de and Jacques Basnage. *Dissertations critiques pour servir
     d'éclaircissemens à l'histoire des Juifs.* Paris, 1785. Vol. 1, 246-282.
     [800/ 801].

488. Boling, Robert G. "Bronze Age Buildings at the Shechem High Place." *BA* 32.4
     (1969): 81-103.
     [412/ 600].

489. —————. "Short Report on the Excavations at Tananir (Mt. Gerizim), 1968."
     (French, untitled) *RB* 76.3 (1969): 419-421. Plates XX-XXI.
     [600/ 801].

490. Bonné, B., A. Adam, Y. Askenazi, et al. "A Preliminary Report on Some
     Genetical Characteristics in the Samaritan Population." *AJPA* 23 (1965): 397-
     400.
     [2900/ 2901].

491. Bonné, Batsheva. "Are There Hebrews Left?" *AJPA* 24.2 (1966): 135-145.
     [2900/ 2901].

492. —————. "Genes and Phenotypes in the Samaritan Isolate." *AJPA* 24.1 (1966):
     1-20.
     [2900/ 2901].

493. —————. A Genetic View of the Samaritan Isolate. (Ph.D thesis) Boston,
     unpublished: University of Boston, 1965.
     [2900/ 2901].

494. ————. "Merits and Difficulties in Studies of Middle Eastern Isolates." *Israel Journal of Medical Science* 9.9-10 (1973): 1291-1298.
[2900/ 2901].

495. ————. "The Samaritan Isolate." In E. **Goldschmidt**, editor, *The Genetics of Migrant and Isolate Populations.* New York: Williams and Wilkins, 1963. 354-364.
[2900/ 2901].

496. ————. "The Samaritans: A Demographic Study." *Human Biology* 35 (1963): 61-89.
[2900/ 2901].

497. ————. "The Samaritans; A Living Ancient Isolate: A Follow Up Study with Particular Reference to the HLA System." In A. W. **Eriksson**, editor, *Population, Genetic Studies on Isolates.* London: Academic Press Inc., 1977.
[2900/ 2901].

498. ————. "The Samaritans; A Living Isolate." In A. W. **Eriksson**, editor, *Population Structure and Genetic Disorders.* (Proceedings of the 7th Sigfred Juselius Foundation Symposia). London, 1980. 27-41.
[2900/ 2901].

499. ————. "Twenty Years of Friendship and Research." (Hebrew) *A–B* 249-250 (16/12/1979): 53-56.
[2900/ 2901].

500. ————. "Were the Samaritans Really Good?" *Proceedings of the 33rd Meeting of the American Association of Physical Anthropology* (1964). [Abstracted in the *American Journal of Physical Anthropology* 22 (1964): 503].
[2900/ 2901].

501. **Bonné, Batsheva and D. F. Roberts.** "Reproduction and Inbreeding Among the Samaritans." *Social Biology* 20 (1973): 64-70.
[2900/ 2901].

502. **Bonneau, N. R.** "The Woman at the Well. John 4 and Genesis 24." *BT* 67 (1973): 1252-1259.
[1003.1/ 1502.1].

503. **Bonner, C.** *Studies in Magical Amulets.* Ann Arbor, Michigan: University of Michigan, 1950.
[601].

504. **Boraas, R. S.** Judges ix and Tell Balatah. Drew University: Doctoral dissertation, 1965.
[412].

505. **Borisov, A.** "The Firkowitz Collection in Leningrad." *A–B* 196/197 (1977): 20-23/19-20.
[103].

506. —————. "Sobranie samaritjanskikh rukpisej A. Firkovica." *PS* 15.78 (1966): 60-73.
     [103].

507. **Bornhäuser, Karl.** "Die Samariter die N.T." *ZSTh* 9 (1932): 552-556.
     [1002/ 1003.1/ 1502].

508. **Bose, Johann Andreas.** "De Pentateucho Samaritano." In *Schediasma de Comparanda Notitia scriptorum ecclesiasticorum.* Jena, 1673: reprinted 1686.
     [2300].

509. **Botha, J. Eugene.** *Jesus and the Samaritan Woman.* Brill: Leiden, 1992. *NT*Supp. 65.
     [1003.1/1502.1].

510. **Botha, J. Eugene.** "Reader 'entrapment' as literary device in John 4:1-42." *Neotestamentica* 24 (1990): 37-47.
     [1502.1].

511. **Boujo, J.** Les samaritains d'après la Bible et les oeuvres juives postbibliques. (Thèse de IIIᵉ cycle soutenue à la Sorbonne-Paris) Paris: Sorbonne, 1975.
     [801/ 802].

512. **Bousset, D. W.** "Das chronologische System des biblischen Geschichtsbücher." *ZAW* 20 (1900): 136-147.
     [700].

513. **Bousset, D. W. and H. Gressmann.** "Die Religion des Judentums in späthellenistischen Zeitalter." *UNT* 21.3:A (1926):
     [804/ 805/ 1003].

514. **Bouwman, Gijs.** "Samaria im lukanischen Doppelwerk." In **Albert Fuchs,** editor, *Theologie aus dem Norden.* A band 2. Linz: Studien zum neuen Testament und seiner Umwelt, 1977. 118-141.
     [1003.1/ 1502.4].

515. **Bouyer, L.** "La Samaritaine." *Le quatrième Evangile.* Paris, 1955. 98-110. 2nd edn.
     [1003.1/ 1502.1].

516. **Bowman, John.** "Banu Isra'il in the Qur'an." *Islamic Studies* 2.4 (1963): 447-455.
     [1003.3].

517. —————. Reviewer. **J. van Goudoever,** "Biblical Calendars." *VT* 15.1 (1965): 120-126.
     [107/ 1400].

518. —————. "Contact Between Samaritan Sects and Qumran?" *VT* 7 (1957): 184-189.
     [1005/ 1500].

519. —————. "Did the Qumran Sect Burn the Red Heifer?" *RQ* 1.1 (1958): 73-84.
     [*NTAb* 3 (1958) no.750].
     [1005/ 1109/ 1109.1].

520. —————. "The Doctrine of Creation, the Fall of Man and Original Sin in Samaritan and Pauline Theology." *RTR* 19.3 (1960): 65-72. [1003.1/ 1102].

521. —————. "Early Samaritan Eschatology." *JJS* 6.2 (1955): 63-73. [1105].

522. —————. "The Exegesis of the Pentateuch Among the Samaritans and Among the Rabbis." *OTS* 8 (1950): 220-262. [2305].

523. —————. "Ezekiel and the Zadokite Priesthood." *TGUOS* 16 (1955-1956): 1-14. [1302].

524. —————. "La genealogjoj de la Cefpastroj en la hebrea kaj la samariana tradicjoj." *Biblia Revuo* 5 (1966): 1-16. [700].

525. —————. "The Gospel of Barnabas and the Samaritans." *AN* 30 (1992): 20-33. [1502.5].

526. —————. *The Hebrew Text of a Samaritan Allegory by Phinehas on the Taheb.* Leeds: LUOS, 1955. [1107].

527. —————. "The History of the Samaritans." *AN* 18 1978/9 (1980): 76-115. [800].

528. —————. "The Identity and Date of the Unnamed Feast in John 5:1." In **H. Goedicke,** editor, *Near Eastern Studies in Honor of William Foxwell Albright.* Baltimore and London: Johns Hopkins, 1971. 43-56. [1400/ 1502.1].

529. —————. "The Importance of Samaritan Researches." *ALUOS* 2 (1960): 43-54. [106].

530. —————. "The Importance of the Moon in Hebrew and Samaritan Festival Observances." *ACIO* Moscow, 1960:1 (1962): 360-362. [1400/ 1402].

531. —————. "An Interesting Leningrad Samaritan Manuscript." *AN* 1 (1959): 73-78. [103].

532. —————. "Is the Samaritan Calendar the Old Zadokite One?" *PEQ* 91 (1959): 23-27. [1400].

533. —————. "The Leeds Samaritan Decalogue Inscription." *Proceedings of the Leeds Philosophical Society* 1 (1951): 567-575. [1103/ 2504].

534. ————. "The Malef." *AN* 20 (1981): 1-19.
[2206].

535. ————. "Modern Samaritan Sabbath Morning and Afternoon Services: Ancient Survival." *Proceedings of the 23rd International Congress of Orientalists, 1954* (1956): 86-87.
[2100].

536. ————. "The Parable of the Good Samaritan." *ET* 59.6 & 9 (1948): 151-153; 248-249.
[1502.3].

537. ————. "Phylacteries." *TGUOS* 15 (1953-54): 54-55.
[1211].

538. ————. "Phylacteries." *Texte und untersuchungen zur Geschichte du altchristlichen Literatur* 73 (1959): 523-538.
[1211].

539. ————. "Pilgrimage to Mount Gerizim." *EI* 7 (1963): 17-28.
[406/ 1400/ 1404/ 1407/ 1409].

540. ————. "Samaria in Lucas—Handelingen." *Bijdr* .34 (1973).
[*NTAb*18(1973) no.128].
[410/ 1003.1/ 1502].

541. ————. *Samaritan Documents Relating to their History, Religion and Life.* Pittsburgh, 1977.
[200/ 800/ 1100/ 1300/ 1500/ 2900].

542. ————. "Samaritan Law and Liturgy." *BJRL* 40 (1958): 315-327.
[2100/ 2104/ 2308].

543. ————. *Samaritan Problem.* (English Version). Pittsburgh Theological Monographs, 54. Pittsburgh, 1976.
[1500/ 1503].

544. ————. "Samaritan Remnant." *JC* (21/1/1955): 19, 34.
[200/ 2904].

545. ————. "Samaritan Studies. I) The Fourth Gospel and the Samaritans, II) Faith in Samaritan Thought, III) Samaritan Law and Liturgy." *BJRL* 40.2 (1958): 298-327. [N⁰· I was read at the September meeting of the Society for New Testament Studies, Bangor, 1955].
[1003.1/ 1102/ 1502.1/ 2100].

546. ————. "The Samaritan Ten Words of Creation and their Ten Commandments According to the Malef." *AN* 21 (1983): 1-9.
[1103/ 2206].

547. ————. *Samaritanische Probleme. Studien zum Verhaltnis von Samaritanertum, Judentum und Urchristentum.* Stuttgart, 1967. Franz Delitzsch-Vorlesungen.
[1500/ 1503].

548.   ————. "Samaritans." In C. Roth, editor, *Standard Jewish Encyclopaedia.*
        New York, 1959. Col.1647.
        [200].

549.   ————. "Samaritans." In J. D. Hastings, editor, *Dictionary of the Bible.*
        Edinburgh: T & T Clark, 1963. 880. 2nd edition.
        [200].

550.   ————. "Samaritans." In *Chambers Encyclopaedia.* London, 1973. New,
        revised edn. 180.
        [201].

551.   ————. "The Samaritans and the Book of Deuteronomy." *TGUOS* 17
        (1957-1958): 9-18.
        [1001/ 1105/ 1107].

552.   ————. "The Significance of Teshuvah." *AN* 15 (1975): 27-34.
        [1111].

553.   ————. *Transcript of the Original Text of the Samaritan Chronicle Tolidah.*
        Leeds: LUOS, 1954.
        [1607].

554.   ————. "The Unknown Feast of John 5:1 and Esther and Purim." In *The
        Fourth Gospel and the Jews: A Study in Rabbi Akiba, Esther and the Gospel of
        John.* Pittsburgh Theological Monograph Series 8. Pittsburgh, 1975. 111-132.
        [1003.1/ 1502.1].

555.   ————. "Word and Worship in Middle Eastern Religions." *JANES* 5 (1973):
        35-44.
        [1210].

556.   **Bowman, John and S.Talmon.** "Samaritan Decalogue Inscriptions." *BJRL* 31
        (1950/51): 211-236.
        [1103/ 2504].

557.   ————. "Samaritan Decalogue ineditas." *Boletín de la Asociación Española de
        Orientalistas* 6 (1970): 109-115.
        [1103].

558.   **Bowring, John.** *Samaria and the Samaritans: A Sketch.* London: Edward T.
        Whitfield, 1861. 16pp.
        [202].

559.   **Boys, D. J.** "The Creed and Hymns of the Samaritan Liturgy." *London Quarterly
        and Holborn Review* 186 (1961): 32-37.
        [1100/ 2100].

560.   ————. A Critical Edition and Translation of the Samaritan Festival Liturgy
        for Hag-haShabhu'ot with Special Reference to the Use of the Law. (Doctoral
        thesis): University of Leeds, 1956.
        [1407/ 2102].

561. ——————. "The Samaritans and Their Liturgy." *London Quarterly and Holborn Review* 183 (1958): 284f.
[202/ 1100/ 2100].

562. **Braitl, N.** Reviewer. H. Baneth, "Memar Marqah." *Central Anzeiger f. Jüdischen Lit.* 1 (1890): 38.
[107/ 1803].

563. **Braslavi, Joseph.** "The Tomb of Joseph in Shechem and the Mound of Pinhas." (Hebrew) *Mahanaim* (Tammuz, 1966): 78-85. [Reprinted in *A-B* 236-237(1979)].
[407.1/ 409.1].

564. **Bratianu, G. I.** *Études byzantines d'histoire économique et sociale.* Paris, 1938. [Section on the Samaritans].
[200/ 808/ 808.1].

565. **Braun, F. M.** "Avoir soif et boir (Jn 4, 10-14; 7, 37-39)." In **A. Descamps and A. de Halleux,** *Mélanges bibliques en hommage au R. P. Béda Rigaux.* Gembloux: Duculot, 1970. 247-258.
[1502.1].

566. **Bricout, J.** "Samarie", "Samaritains." In *Dictionnaire pratique des connaissances religieuses.* Paris. 6: 195-198.
[200/ 201].

567. **Brigham, C. H.** "The History and Literature of the Samaritans." *Unitarian Review* 4 (1877): 141f.
[200/ 800/ 1100].

568. **Bright, John.** "The Date of Ezra's Mission to Jerusalem." In **M. Haran,** editor, *Studies in Bible and the Jewish Religion Dedicated to Yehezkel Kaufman on the Occasion of his Seventieth Birthday.* Jerusalem: Magnes Press, 1960. 70-87.
[802].

569. **Brindle, Wayne A.** "The Origin and History of the Samaritans." *Grace Theological Journal* 5.1 (1984): 47-75.
[801.1].

570. **Brinker, R.** "The Samaritans and the Text of Deuteronomy." In *Sanctuaries and Legislation in Early Israel.* Manchester: University Press, 1946. 212-228.
[2205].

571. **Brisman, S.** *A History and Guide to Judaic Bibliography.* New York: Ktav, 1977.
[100].

572. **Broadie, Alexander.** *A Samaritan Philosophy: A Study of the Hellenistic Cutural Ethos of the Memar Marqah.* Leiden: E. J. Brill, 1981. Studia Post-Biblica, 31.
[1803/ 2000].

573. **Broadribb, Donald.** *Bibliography of the Samaritans.* Leiden: E. J. Brill, 1964. [Supplement to *Abr Nahrain* 1].
[100].

574. **Brock, Sebastian P.** Reviewer. A. Tal, "The Samaritan Targum of the Pentateuch, Pt.III—Introduction." *Orientalia* 55 (1986): 447.
[107/ 2401].

575. **Brockelmann, Carl.** *Grundriss der vergleichenden grammatik der semitischen Sprachen.* Hildesheim: Georg Olms, 1961. [Original edn. Berlin & New York 1907-1913].
[2600].

576. **Brockelmann, Carl.** *Katalog der orientalischen Handschriften der Stadtbibliothek zu Hamburg.* Hamburg, 1908. [MSS nos. 334-335].
[103/ 105].

577. **Brodsky, Harold.** "Three Capitals on the Hills of Ephraim." *Bible Review* 5.1 (1989): 38-44. [On Shechem, Tirzah and Samaria].
[410/ 412/ 1001].

578. **Brønno, E.** "Samaritan Hebrew and Origen's Secunda." *JSS* 13 (1968): 192-201.
[2600].

579. **Brooke, George J.** Reviewer. J. Sanderson, "An Exodus Scroll from Qumran: 4QPaleoExod^m and the Samaritan Tradition." *JTS* 39 (1988): 183-187.
[107/ 2307].

580. —————. Reviewer. **Rita Egger**, "Josephus Flavius und die Samaritaner." *JSS* 37.1 (1992): 109-112.
[303.5].

581. **Brooks, E. W.** "The Chronological Canon of James of Edessa." *ZDMG* 53 (1899): 261-327. [See p. 319 no. 207, 4280].
[700].

582. **Brown, Sarah Graham-.** "The Political Economy of the Jabal Nablus." In **R. Owen**, editor, *Studies in the Economic and Social History of Palestine in the Nineteenth and Twentieth Centuries.* Oxford, 1982. 88-176.
[400].

583. **Brown, Solomon.** A Critical Edition and Translation of the Ancient Samaritan Defter (i.e. Liturgy) and a Comparison of it with Early Jewish Liturgy. (Doctoral thesis): University of Leeds, 1955.
[1210/ 2102.1].

584. **Browne, Edward Granville.** *A Handlist of the Muhammedan Manuscripts Preserved in the Library of the University of Cambridge.* Cambridge: CUP, 1900. 30, 353-355.
[101/ 103].

585. —————. *A Supplementary Handlist of the Muhammedan Manuscripts Preserved in the Library of the University and Colleges of Cambridge.* Cambridge: CUP, 1922. 167, 314, 319. Mss listed are Christ College Dd 5.13(a) Liturgy : 1014 (a) Heb.Dd 5.12 Samaritan and Hebrew Prayers (1774).
[101/ 103].

586. **Bruce, Frederick F.** *The Books and the Parchments.* New Jersey, 1950.
     [2300/ 2307].

587. —————. "Gerizim." *Illustrated Bible Dictionary* 1 (1986): 553-554.
     [406].

588. **Brüll, Adolf.** *Das samaritanische Targum zum Pentateuch.* Frankfurt, 1873-1876.
     [Reprinted Georg Olms, 1971, including "Kritische Studien über Oxforder
     Manuscript Fragmente", and "Zur Geschichte und Literatur der Samaritaner
     nebst Varientum zum buch Genesis"].
     [2401].

589. —————. *Zur Geschichte und Literatur der Samaritaner.* Frankfurt, 1876.
     [800/ 1550].

590. **Bruneau, P.** "Les Israelites de Délos et la Juiverie Déliènne." *Bulletin de
     Correspondence Hellenique* 106 (1982): 466-504.
     [504].

591. **Bruners, W.** "Die Reinigung der zehn Aussätzigen und die Heilung des
     Samariters. Lk.17, 11-19: Ein Beitrag zur lukanischen Interpretation der
     Reinigung von Aussätzigen." *Forschung zur Bibel* 23 (1977).
     [1003.1/ 1502.4].

592. **Brunet, Pierre Gustave.** "Dictionnaire de bibliographie et de bibliologie.
     Supplément contenant: première partie: Bible hébraïques, samaritaines.." In J.
     P. Migne, *Troisième et dernière Encyclopédie théologique.* Paris, 1855-1866. 44:
     [201].

593. **Brunot, A.** "A travers la Samarie." *BTS* 184 (1976): 8-17.
     [410].

594. **Bruns, Paul Jacob.** *De Eo Quod Praestandum Restat in Letteris Orientalibus.*
     Helmstadt, 1781.
     [105/ 2501].

595. —————. *Epistolam Samaritanam Sichemitarum tertiam ad Jobum Ludolfum.*
     Helmstadt, 1781. [Reprinted in *RBML* (1783) part 13, 277-292].
     [1703].

596. —————. "Über die Samariter." *Beiträge zur Philosophie und Geschichte der
     Religion und Sittenlebre of C. F. Stäudlin* 1 (1797): 78-97.
     [200].

597. **Buchanan, G. G.** "The Derivation of Ebal." *Academy* 49.1259 (June 20 1896):
     510.
     [404].

598. **Buchanan, George W.** "The Samaritan Origin of the Gospel of John." In J.
     Neusner, editor, *Religion in Antiquity.* Essays in Memory of E. T.
     Goodenough, Leiden: E. J. Brill, 1968. 149-175.
     [1502.1].

599. **Bucher, Samuel F.** *Prolegomena ad Thesaurus Orientis sive compendiosa et facilis methodus linguarum hebraeae...Samaritanae...* Frankfurt and Leipzig, 1725. [British Library 622 g 28].
[2600].

600. **Büchler, Adolph.** "The Samaritan Participation in the Bar Cochba Revolt." (Hebrew) in **A. Oppenheimer,** editor, *The Bar Kochva Revolt.* Jerusalem, 1950. 115-121. A Hebrew reprint of the original Hungarian (see no. 519 in the first edition of the bibliography).
[808].

601. —————. "Les Dosithéens dans le Midrasch. L'interdit prononcé contre les samaritains dans les Pirké de R. Eliézer XXXVIII et Tanhuma Vayeshev 3." *REJ* 42, 43 (1901 & 1902): 220-231, 50-71.
[304/ 1503].

602. —————. "On the Provisioning of Jerusalem in the Years 60-70 CE." In *Studies in Jewish History.* Oxford, 1956. 99-125.
[806/ 1003.4/ 1601].

603. —————. "La Relation de Josèphe concernant Alexandre le Grand." *REJ* 36 (1897): 1-26.
[303.5/ 804/ 1003.4].

604. —————. "A Szamaritanusoh resvetele a Bar Kockba fel Kesleben (The Participation of the Samaritans in the Bar Kochba Revolt)." (Hungarian) *Magyar-Zsidó Szemle* 14 (1897): 36-47. [Reprinted in a Hebrew version in A. Oppenheimer, ed.*The Bar Kochba Revolt* Jerusalem, 1980 (= Issues in Jewish History 10) 115-121].
[808].

605. **Buckingham, James Silk.** "Shechem or Neapolis, Mt. Ebal and Gerizim and the Wells of Samaria." In *Travels in Palestine.* London, 1822. Vol. II: 421-463. [A German edition, *Reisen durch Syrien und Palästina,* 1827].
[308].

606. **Budge, E. A. Wallis.** *Amulets and Superstitions.* London, 1930. 258-272. [Reprinted, 1970, 1978].
[601/ 1100].

607. —————. *Amulets and Talismans.* New York, 1961. 258-271; plates XX & XXI.
[601].

608. —————. *The Book of the Bee.* Oxford, 1886. Vol. 1, part II.
[300].

609. —————. *Miscellaneous Coptic Texts in the Dialect of Upper Egypt.* London, 1915. [See especially the Discourse of Cyril, Archbishop of Jerusalem on the discovery of the cross and on the baptism of Isaac the Samaritan].
[305/ 305.3].

610. **Buhl, Franz.** *Canon and Text of the Old Testament.* Edinburgh, 1892. Translated by John MacPherson.
[2300].

611. **Bull, R. J., J. A. Callaway, E. F. Campbell Jnr, et al.** "The Fifth Campaign at Balâtah (Shechem)." *BASOR* 180 (1965): 7-41.
[412/ 801/ 803].

612. **Bull, Robert J.** "An Archeological Context for Understanding John 4:20." *BA* 38 (1975): 54-59.
[600/ 1003.1/ 1502.1].

613. ————. "An Archeological Footnote to 'Our Fathers Worshipped on This Mountain' (John iv:20)." *NTS* 23 (1977): 460-462.
[600/ 1003.1/ 1502.1].

614. ————. "Er Râs,Tell (Mt Gerizim)." In **Michael Avi-Yonah and Ephraim Stern,** eds., *EAEHL.* Jerusalem–Englewood Cliffs, NJ–Oxford: IES–Massada Press–Prentice Hall–OUP, 1978. 4: 1015-1022. [Reprinted in Dexinger and Pummer, *Die Samaritaner,* 419-427].
[406/ 412/ 415].

615. ————. "The Excavation of Tell-er Ras on Gerizim (1964 and 1966)." *BA* 31 (1968): 58-72. [Figs. 11-18].
[406/ 600].

616. ————. "Excavation of the Temples at Shechem." *Drew Gateway* 32 (Spring, 1962): 156-165.
[412/ 415/ 801/ 1305].

617. ————. "A Note on Theodotus' Description of Shechem." *HTR* 60 (1967): 221-227.
[412/ 2005].

618. ————. "A Preliminary Excavation of an Hadrianic Temple at Tell er-Râs on Mt. Gerizim." *AJA* 71 (1967): 387-393. Plates 109-111.
[406/ 412/ 415/ 801].

619. ————. "A Reexamination of the Shechem Temple." *BA* 23 (1960): 110-119. Figs 5-7.
[412/ 600/ 1305].

620. ————. "Tell er-Râs (Gerizim)." *RB* 75.2 (1968): 238-243.
[406/ 412/ 415].

621. ————. "A Tripartite Sundial from Tell er-Râs on Mount Gerizim." *BASOR* 219 (October 1975): 29-37.
[406/ 412/ 415/ 600].

622. **Bull, Robert J. and E. F. Campbell.** "The Sixth (1966) Campaign at Balâtah (Shechem)." *BASOR* 190 (1968): 2-41. 17 figures.
[412/ 600].

623. **Bull, Robert J. and G. E. Wright.** "Newly Discovered Temples on Mount Gerizim in Jordan." *HTR* 58 (1965): 234-237.
[406/ 600/ 1305].

624. **Burgess, Thomas Bishop of St. David's.** *The Samaritan and Syriack Alphabets with a Praxis to Each.* London, 1814.
[105/ 2500/ 2501].

625. **Burkitt, F. C.** "Hebrew Papyrus of the Ten Commandments." *JQR* 15 (1903): 392-408.
[1103/ 2300].

626. **Burrows, Millar.** *More Light on the Dead Sea Scrolls.* London, 1958.
[2300/ 2307].

627. ——————. "Orthography, Morphology and Syntax of the St. Mark's Isaiah Manuscript." *JBL* 68 (1940): 195-212.
[2300/ 2307/ 2501].

628. **Burton, Henry.** "Christ and the Samaritans." *Expositor* 6 (1877): 186-196.
[1003.1/ 1502].

629. **Buschan, G.** Reviewer. H. M. Huxley, "Zur Anthropologie der Samaritaner." *Zentralblatt für Anthropologie* 11 (1906): 335.
[107/ 2901].

630. **Busman(us), Johann E.** "De Antiquis Hebraeorum literis ab Esdra in Assyriacas mutatis." Helmstadt, 1675.
[2501].

631. **Butler, E. M.** *The Fortunes of Faust.* Cambridge, 1952.
[1506.2].

632. ——————. *The Myth of the Magus.* Cambridge, 1948.
[1506.2].

633. **Buxtorf, Johannes (the younger).** "Dissertatio de Literarum Hebraicarum Genuina Antiquitate." In **Blasio Ugolini,** *Thesaurus Antiquitatum Sacrum Complectens.* Venice, 1765. 28: 970-1086.
[105/ 800/ 2501].

634. ——————. *Exercitationes Anticritica seu vindiciae veritatis Hebraicae; adversus Ludovici Cappelli criticam.* Basilae, 1653.
[105/ 2500].

C

635. **Caetani, Leone.** *Annali dell' Islam.* Milano, 1910. 10 vols.
     [809/ 1003.3].

636. **Cahen, Samuel.** "Notice sur les samaritains." In *La Bible, traduction nouvelle avec l'hébreu...et les principales variantes de la version des Septant et du text samaritain.* Paris, 1831-1851. Vol. 5. [BL 01903.a.1].
     [2300/ 2400].

637. **Cahill, Joseph P.** "Narrative Art in John 4." *Religious Studies Bulletin* 2.2 (1982): 41-47.
     [1502.1].

638. **Caldwell, T. A.** "Dositheos Samaritanus." *Kairos* 4 (1962): 105-117.
     [1500/ 1503/ 1504].

639. —————. "The Samaritans." In *The New Catholic Encyclopaedia.* 12: 1009-1010.
     [200/ 201].

640. **Callaway, Phillip R.** Reviewer. Judith E. Sanderson, "An Exodus Scroll from Qumran: 4QPaleoExod^m and the Samaritan Tradition." *Hebrew Studies* 30 (1989): 186-192.
     [2300/ 2307/ 2309.1].

641. **Callebaut, Paul Jacques.** *Les derniers Samaritains.* Paris: Asfar, 1990. 96 pp. + ill.
     [200].

642. **Calmès, P. Th.** Reviewer. F. Vigouroux, "La Sainte Bible." *RB* 9 (1900): 301-303.
     [107/ 2300].

643. **Calmet, Augustin.** "Samaritains", "Samarie ", "Samaritaine", "Pentateuque Samaritain." In *Dictionnaire historique, critique, géographique, chronologique et littéral de la Bible.* 4 vols. Paris, 1846. 4: cols. 262-286. [Several English versions of the first edition of this work].
     [201/ 202].

644. **Campbell Jr.,Edward F.** "Excavations at Shechem." *BA* 23 (1960): 101-110. Figs.1-4.
     [412/ 600/ 801].

645. —————. "Jewish Shrines of the Hellenistic and Roman Periods." In F. M. Cross, editor, *Symposia Celebrating the 75th Anniversary of the Founding of the American School of Oriental Research, 1900-1975.* 159-167.
     [406/ 412/ 800/ 804/ 806/ 807/ 1305].

646. —————. "The Shechem Area Survey." *BASOR* 190 (1968): 19-41.
     [400/ 412].

647. —————. *Shechem II: Portrait of a Hill Country Vale. The Shechem Regional Survey.* Atlanta: Scholars Press, 1991. American Schools of Oriental Research. [406/ 412/ 600/ 801].

648. —————. "Shechem in the Amarna Archive" and "Two Cuneiform Tablets from Shechem." In G. E. Wright, *Shechem, The Biography of A Biblical City.* New York and Toronto: McGraw-Hill, 1965. 191-213. [412/ 801].

649. —————. "Untitled, Short Report on Excavations at Tell Balatah (Shechem)." *IEJ* 18 (1968): 192-193. [406/ 412/ 600/ 801].

650. Campbell Jr.,Edward F., G. E. Wright, G. E. Wright, et al. "The Eighth Campaign at Balatah (Shechem)." *BASOR* 204 (1971): 2-17. 8 figs. [412/ 600].

651. —————. "Excavations at Shechem, 1956-1969." (Hebrew) *Qadmoniot* 3 (1970): 126-133. Figures, plate 3. [412/ 600/ 801].

652. Campbell Jr.,Edward F. and J. F. Ross. "The Excavations of Shechem and the Biblical Tradition." *BA* 26.1 (1963): 2-27. [412/ 600/ 801].

653. Campbell Jr.,Edward F., Lawrence E.Toombs and G. E.Wright. "The Fourth Campaign at Balatah (Shechem)." *BASOR* 169 (1963): 1-60. Figs. 1-26. [412/ 600].

654. Campbell Jr.,Edward F. and G. E.Wright. "Tribal League Shrines in Amman and Shechem." *BA* 23 (1969): 104-116. Figs. 17-22. [801/ 1001/ 1305].

655. Campbell Jr.,Edward F., J. F. Ross and G. E. Wright. "The Fifth Campaign at Balatah (Shechem)." *BASOR* 180 (1965): 7-41. Figs. 1-20. [412/ 600].

656. Campbell, K. M. "The New Jerusalem in Matthew 5:14." *SJT* 31 (1978): 335-363. [1003.1].

657. Camus, L. abbaye, E. Le. *Notre voyage aux pays bibliques.* Paris, 1890. 2nd edn. Bruxelles, Paris, 1895. [308].

658. Canfil, David K. "Samaritan Delegation in Europe." *A–B* 269/270 (8/10/1980): 43-44. [903/ 3011].

659. —————. "Samaritans, Through a Glass Darkly." *A–B* 251-253 (1/1/1980-1/2/1980). [200].

660. —————. "Tamir 'Chatam Torah'." *A–B* 264-265 (15/7/1980): 37.
     [2300/ 2308].

661. —————. "Thoughts on the Samaritan Social Dimension." *A–B* 250 (1979):
     53-56.
     [903].

662. **Cantwell, L.** "Immortal Longings in Sermone Humili: A Study of John 4:5-26."
     SJT 36 (1983): 73-86.
     [1002/ 1502.1].

663. **Cappell, Louis Ludovici.** *Arcanum Punctuationis Revelatum.* Lugduni Batavorum,
     1624.
     [2601].

664. **Carel, Zvi.** "The Samaritan Passover." In *Mishna with a New Commentary.*
     Lemberg, 1925. Part 3: *Pesahim*: 50-51.
     [304.1/ 1404].

665. **Carlinius, Dominicus.** *Dominici Carlinii dissertatio nomica seu commentarius ad
     Novellam Imp.*

666. —————. *Dominici Carlinii...commentarius ad Novellam Imp. Theodosii junioris
     titulo III. de Judaeis Samaritanis haereticis et paganis...* Veronae, 1752. 42 pp: 4°.
     [808].

667. **Carmichael, Callum M.** "Marriage and the Samaritan Woman." *NTS* 26 (April,
     1980): 332-346.
     [1502.1].

668. **Carpzov, Johann Gottlob.** *Critica Sacra Veteris Testamenti.* Lipsae, 1728. Pt.I:
     [2300].

669. **Carrett, Susan R.** "Simon Magus." In *The Demise of the Devil: Magic and the
     Demonic in Luke's Writings.* Minneapolis: Fortress, 1989. 61-78, 139-148.
     [1506.2].

670. **Casey, Robert J.** "The Doomed Samaritans: A Saddened People Walking with the
     Death Warrant in Their Hands." *Asia* (1937): 114-119, 160-162. Illustrations.
     [903/ 2904].

671. **Casey, Robert P.** "Simon Magus." In **F. J. Foakes Jackson and Kirsopp Lake,**
     editors, *The Beginnings of Christianity, Pt. 1 The Acts of the Apostles.* Vol. 5,
     Additional Notes to the Commentary by Kirsopp Lake and H. J. Cadbury.
     London, 1933. 151-163.
     [1506.2].

672. **Casley, David.** *A Catalogue of the Harleian Manuscripts in the British Museum.*
     London, 1908. [Samaritan items are listed in vol. 3].
     [101].

673. **Castell, Edmund.** "Animadversiones Samariticae in Pentateuchum." In **Brian
     Walton,** editor, *Biblia Sacra Polyglotta.* London, 1657. Volume 6, section 4: 1-

19.
[801/ 2300].

674. —————. *Catalogus Codicum Manuscriptorum Bibliothecae Regiae.* Paris, 1739.
Volume 1.
[101/ 103].

675. —————. *Catalogus Librorum tam impressorum quam manuscriptorum
Bibliothecae publicae Universitatis Lugduno-Batavae.* Lugduni apud Batavos,
1716.
[101/ 103].

676. —————. *Edmundi Castelli Lexicon syriacum ex ejus Lexico heptaglotto seorsim
typis describi curavit, atque sua adnotata adiecit Joannes David Michaelis.*
Göttingae, 1788.
[2501/ 2600].

677. —————. *Edmundi Castelli Lexicon hebraicum ex ejus Lexico heptaglotto seorsim
typis descriptum adnotatis in margine vocum numeris ex Joannis Davidis Michaelis
Supplementis ad lexica hebraica.* Göttingae and Lipsae, 1790-1792. Ed. J. F. L.
Trier.
[2500/ 2600].

678. —————. *Lexicon Heptaglotton, Hebraicum, Chaldaicum, Syriacum,
Samaritanum, Aethiopicum, Arabicum conjunctim; et Persicum separatim. Opus
non tantum ad Biblia Polyglotta Londinensia tantum.* London: Thomas
Roycroft, 1669. 2 vols. 3 parts: [Reprinted with a different title page, 1669.
Reissued, 1686. Reprinted Gräz, 1970].
[2300/ 2600].

679. —————. *Lexicon linguarum orientalium.* London, 1658. [A Prospectus of the
Lexicon Heptaglotton].
[2500/ 2600].

680. —————. *Sol Angliae Oriens auspiciis Caroli II, regum gloriosissimi.* London,
1660. [Poems in Hebrew, Chaldee, Syriac, Samaritan, Ethiopic, Arabic, Persian
and Greek with Latin translations].
[105/ 2101/ 2500/ 2600].

681. **Castellino, G. R.** "Il Sacerdote e il Levita nella del buon samaritano." *Divinitas* 9.1
(1965): 134-140. [*NTAb* 10 (1965) no.151].
[1502.3].

682. **Castley, D.** *A Catalogue of the Harleian Manuscripts in the British Museum, vol. iii.*
London, 1808.
[101].

683. **Cathcart, Kevin J. and John F. Healey.** *Back to the Sources. Biblical and Near
Eastern Studies in Honour of Dermot Ryan.* Dublin: Glendale Press, 1989.
[Includes a description of the Chester Beatty Samaritan Manuscripts. 129-163].
[103].

684. **Cedrenus, George.** "Compendium Historiarum." *PG* 121: 211-214, 219-222, 359-362.
[305/ 305.4].

685. **Cellarius [Keller], Christophorius.** *Collectanea historiae Samaritanae quibus praeter res geographicas tam politia huius gentis, quam religio et res literaria explicantur.* Cizae: Typis Fridem, 1688. [Reprinted in B. Ugolini, *Thesaurus* Venice, 1759; 22 cols. 603-648].
[200/ 401/ 800/ 1000/ 1550].

686. **Cellarius [Keller], Christophorius.** *Epistolae Samaritanae Sichemitarum ad Iobum Ludolfum cum eiusdem Lat. versione et annotationibus; acc. versio Lat. persimilium literarum a Sichemitis had ita pridem ad Anglos datarum.* Cizae, 1688. [BL 219. f8 (13)].
[1703].

687. —————. *Excercitatio gentis Samaritanae historiam et caerimonias ost ejusdem auctoris. Collectanea historiae Samaritanae magis illustrans.* Halle, 1707.
[800/ 1000/ 1506.2].

688. —————. *Historia gentis et religionis Samaritanae.* Halle: 1699,
[200/ 800/ 1000].

689. —————. *Horae Samaritanae, hoc est excerpta Pentateuchi Samaritanae versionis, cum latina interpretatione nova, et annotationibus perpetuiss, etiam grammatica samaritana...et glossarium.* Cizae: I. Bielckii, 1682. [Typis Martin Jacquetti. A second edn. Frankfurt and Jena, 1795].
[800/ 2300/ 2603].

690. —————. *Notitiae Orbis Antiqui sive Geographiae Plenioris.* Tomus alter. Lipsae, 1706. [A second edn. Lipsae, 1773].
[400/ 401].

691. —————. *Philogicarum Incubrationum sylloge, hoc est praecipuarum linguarum orientis, Ebraicae, Chaldaicae, Syrae, Samaritanae et Arabicae grammatica praecepta.* Jenae, 1683.
[2600/ 2602].

692. **Celleno, P. D. I. B. de.** "De Samaritanis de illarum lingua, charactere et Pentateuchi antiquitate." In *Bibliotheca Magna Rabbinica.* Rome, 1693. Part 4: 171-187. [Font of the Propaganda Fide].
[2300/ 2501].

693. **Cellesi, L.** "Samaritana." *Bullettino senese di Storia Patria* 1.NS (1937): 117-147.
[200].

694. **Celsius, Olaf.** *Dissertatio philologica natales linguae literarumque samaritanarum exhibens...* Uppsala, 1717.
[2501/ 2600].

695. **Celsius, Olaf.** *De Templo Samaritanorum in Garizim.* Uppsala, 1722.
[1305].

696. **Cerfaux, Lucien.** "La gnose simonienne." In *Recueil Lucien Cerfaux*. Gembloux, 1954. 1: 189-258. [Reprinted from *RSR* 15 & 16 (1925/1926) 489-511; 5f, 265f, 481f].
[1506.2].

697. —————. "Simon le magicien à Samarie." In *Recueil Lucien Cerfaux*. Gembloux, 1954. 1: 259-262. [Reprinted from *RSR* 27 (1937) 615-617].
[1506.2].

698. —————. "Trois réhabilitations dans l'Évangile." In *Recueil Lucien Cerfaux*. Gembloux, 1954. 2: 51-59.
[1502].

699. **Chabot, J.-B.**, editor. *Chronique de Michel le Syrien, patriarche jacobite d'Antioche, 166-1199.* Paris, 1900. [Deals with the slaughter of Samaritans during the Moslem invasion].
[305.6/ 809].

700. —————. "Pierre l'Iberian évêque monophysite de Mayouma (Gaza) à la fin de Ve siècle d'après une récent publication." *ROL* 3 (1895): 367-397.
[305/ 305.5].

701. —————. *Répertoire d'épigraphie sémitique.* Paris, 1908-1918. 3 volumes: nos. 366, 437, 678, 1900.
[2500].

702. **Chang, Choon Shik.** Samaritan Origins and Identity in the Light of Recent Scholarship. (Ph.D. dissertation): University of Sydney, 1990.
[801.1].

703. —————. A Survey of Samaritan Studies from 1950-1982.(Master's thesis) Drew University: 1984.
[101/ 202].

704. **Chappuis, J.-M.** "Jesus and the Samaritan Woman: The Variable Geometry of Communications." *ER* 34 (January, 1982): 8-34.
[1502.1].

705. —————. *Jésus et la Samaritaine. La géométrie variable de la communication.* Génève: Labor et Fides, 1982. II 63 pp.
[1502.1].

706. **Charles, R. H.** *Apocrypha and Pseudepigrapha of the Old Testament.* Oxford: OUP, 1913, new edition 1963. 2 vols.
[302.1/ 302.2].

707. **Charlesworth, James H.**, editor. *The Old Testament Pseudepigrapha.* London: Darton, Longman and Todd, 1985. 785-793, 803-819, 883-886, 873-879. [Essays by Doran, Fallon and Robertson include studies of the Samaritan Hellenistic writers under their individual names].
[2000/2002/2003/2004/2005/].

708. **Cheyne, T. K.** "The Derivation of 'Ebal' and 'Janoah'." *The Academy* 50.261 (1896): 16.
[404].

709. ————. "A Forgotten Kingdom in a Prophecy of Balaam." *The Expositor* 3, series 5 (1896): 77-80.
[801].

710. **Chiskiel, I.** "Die Secten der Samaritaner." *Der Israelitische Volkslehrer* 10 (1860): 246-251.
[1500].

711. **Christian, A.** *Débuts de l'imprimerie en France: l'Imprimerie Nationale, l'Hôtel de Rohan.* Paris, 1905. [Samaritan typefaces].
[105].

712. **Christie, W. M.** "Samaria", "Samaritans." In **J. D. Hastings,** editor, *Dictionary of Christ and the Gospels.* Edinburgh: T & T Clark, 1906. Vol. 2: 557-560.
[201].

713. **Chrysostom, John (Spuria).** "Contra Judaeos et Gentiles, quod Christus sit Deus." In **Migne,** *PG.* 48: 829, 830.
[305.4/ 1003.1].

714. ————. "Homilia de Anathemate." In **Migne,** *PG.* 48: 947, 948.
[305/ 305.4/ 1003.1].

715. ————. "Homilies on John." In **Migne,** *PG.* 59: 477-485.
[305/ 305.4/ 1502.1].

716. ————. "In Duodecim Apostolos Sermo: In Sanctum Thomana Apostolum Sermo." In **Migne,** *PG.* 59 & 60: 497-500, 485-486.
[305/ 305.4].

717. ————. "In Petrum et Paulum, Sermo." In **Migne,** *PG.* 59: 493, 494.
[305/ 305.4/ 1003.1].

718. ————. "De Lazaro Concio." In **Migne,** *PG.* 48: 1029, 1030.
[305/ 305.4].

719. ————. "Orationes viii adversus Judaeos." In **Migne,** *PG.* 48: 931, 932.
[305/ 305.4/ 1003.1].

720. ————. "Synopsis Scripturae Sacrae." In **Migne,** *PG.* 56: 335, 336.
[305/ 305.4].

721. **Churbell, T.** "The Conjugation of the Qal in Samaritan Hebrew." *Mesorot* 1 (1984): 135-151.
[1001].

722. **Churgin, P.** "The Samaritan Schism." (Hebrew) *Horeb* 1 (1934): 127-150.
[801.1/ 802].

723. **Clamer, Christa.** "Burial Cave Near Nablus (Tell Balata)." *IEJ* 27.1 (1977): 48.
    [600/ 1203].

724. **Clarke, A.** *A Bibliographical Dictionary.* London, 1802. [A study of the Samaritan Polyglot].
    [100/ 105/ 2300].

725. **Clarke, E. G.** Reviewer. James Purvis, "The Samaritan Pentateuch and the Origin of the Samaritan Sect." *JNES* 30 (1971): 144-146.
    [107/ 801.1/ 2300].

726. **Clement 1st, Pope.** *Recognitions: PL.* 1: cols. 1235-1238.
    [305/ 305.5/ 808/ 1500].

727. **Clerc, David Le.** *Quaestiones sacrae in quibus sulta Scripturae loca.* Amsterdam, 1685.
    [2300].

728. **Clermont-Ganneau, Charles Simon.** "1900 (Sam.)—Inscription samaritaine de Gaza." *Répertoire d'épigraphie Sémitique* 3 & 4 (1916): 368. [A reprint of *AIBL* (1905) p. 539 and *RAO* 7, (1905) p. 183].
    [2500/ 2508].

729. —————. "678 (Sam.)—Second Inscription of Gaza." In J.-B. Chabot, editor, *Répertoire d'épigraphie Sémitique*, 1907-1914. 2. [A reprint of RAO 7 (1905) p. *184 and Arch.* Researches 1, p. 328].
    [2500/ 2508].

730. —————. *Archaeological Researches in Palestine During the Years 1873-1874.* London: PEF Publications, 1896 & 1899. Vol.2.
    [106/ 600].

731. —————. "Extrait d'une lettre de M. C. G. relative aux résultats de ses excursions." *AIBL* 9. Series 4 (1881): 186.
    [308/ 600].

732. —————. "Inscription samaritaine de Gaza et inscriptions grecques de Bersabée." *RAO* 6 (1905): 183-190.
    [2508].

733. —————. "Itinéraire d'un pélerin français du XIVe siècle de Damas à Naplouse." *RAO* 3 (1899): 259-264.
    [306.2/ 400/ 408].

734. —————. "Jésus dans la tradition samaritaine." *RAO* 7 (1907): 40.
    [1003.1].

735. —————. "Les samaritains à Yabneh." *RAO* 2 (1898): 219-220.
    [416/ 600/ 2515].

736. —————. *Mission en Palestine et en Phénicie entreprise en 1881.* Paris: Imprimerie Nationale, 1884. See p. 105.
    [600].

737. ——————. "Une nouvelle chronique samaritaine." *Journal des Savants* 2 (1904): 34ff. [Reprinted in *RAO* 6 (1904) 83-105].
      [1600/ 1602/ 1607].

738. ——————. "Premiers rapports sur une mission en Palestine et en Phénicie, entreprise en 1881." *Archives des missions scientifiques et littéraires* 9.Series 3 (1882): 277-321. [Discusses Emmaus and Nablus].
      [404.1/ 408/ 2502].

739. **Clifton, Bishop of**. Editor, *Saewulf.* Palestine Pilgrim's Text Society. London, 1896.
      [306.2/ 400].

740. **Clodius, Christianus Conradus**. *De Nummorum Ebraicorum inscriptionibus Samaritanis.* Helmstadii, 1712. 23 pp.
      [600/ 603/ 2501].

741. **Cogan, M.** "'For we, like you, worship your God'; Three Biblical Portrayals of Samaritan Origins." *VT* 38.3 (1988): 286-292.
      [801.1].

742. ——————. "Israel in Exile—the View of a Josianic Historian." *JBL* 91.1 (1978): 40-44.
      [802].

743. **Coggins, Richard J.** *Samaritans and Jews: The Origins of the Samaritans Reconsidered.* Oxford: Blackwell, 1975.
      [800/ 801.1].

744. ——————. "The Samaritans and Northern Israelite Tradition." In **A. Tal & M. Florentin**, editors, *Proceedings of the First International Congress of the Société d'Études Samaritaines.* Tel Aviv: Chaim Rosenberg School for Jewish Studies, University of Tel Aviv, 1991. 99-108.
      [801/ 801.1].

745. ——————. Reviewer. **N. Schur**, "History of the Samaritans." *SOTS Book List* (1990): 41.
      [107/ 800].

746. ——————. "The Samaritans in Josephus." In **Louis Feldman and Gohei Hata**, editors, *Josephus, Judaism and Christianity.* Wayne State University, 1987. 257-273.
      [303.5].

747. ——————. Reviewer. **A. D. Crown**, "Bibliography of the Samaritans." *JTS* 37.1 (1986): 298.
      [100/ 107].

748. ——————. Reviewer. **J. P.Rothschild, G. D. Sixdenier**, "Études samaritaines: Pentateuque et Targum, exégèse et philologie." *SOTS Book List* (1990): 142.
      [107/ 200].

749. —————. Reviewer. J. Sanderson, "An Exodus Scroll from Qumran. 4Q Paleo Exodus^m and the Samaritan Tradition." *JSS* 33.2 (1988): 132-133. [107/ 2300/ 2307].

750. —————. Reviewer. H. G. Kippenberg, "Garizim und Synagoge." *JSS* 17 (1972): 262. [107/ 800/ 1000/ 1500].

751. —————. Reviewer. J. Fossum, "The Name of God and the Angel of the Lord." *SOTS Booklist* (1986): 119. [107/ 1100/ 1101/ 1110].

752. —————. "The Old Testament and Samaritan Origins." *ASTI* 6 (1967-68): 35-48. [800/ 801.1].

753. —————. Reviewer. J. D. Purvis, "Samaritan Pentateuch." *JSS* 14 (1969): 273-275. [107/ 2300].

754. —————. Reviewer. J. Bowman, "Samaritanische Probleme." *JSS* 13 (1968): 276. [107/ 1500].

755. —————. Reviewer. R. Pummer, "The Samaritans." *JSS* 34.2 (1989): 212-213. [107/ 200/ 202].

756. —————. "The Samaritans and Acts." *NTS* 28.3 (1982): 423-424. [1502.2].

757. **Cohen, Atef Naji-Yusef Abu-el-Hasan.** *Brief Theoretical Points of View About the Samaritan Sect of Nablus.* Nablus: Samaritan Community, n.d. [200/ 800/ 1000].

758. **Cohen, B. and B. Lewis.** *Population and Revenue in the Towns of Palestine in the Sixteenth Century.* Princeton, 1978. [See especially pp. 144-155 (Nablus)]. [408/ 903/ 2904].

759. **Cohen, D.** Declension of the Lamed Yad Verbs in the Samaritan Targum.(Ph.D. thesis in Hebrew) Jerusalem: Hebrew University, 1973. [2600/ 2602].

760. **Cohen, D. and Ruth Targovnik-Katz.** "Explorations in the Music of the Samaritans: An Illustration of the Utility of Graphic Notation." (Hebrew) *Yediot Hamachon Ha'Israeli Lemusika Datit* 3 (1962): 102-113. [3300].

761. **Cohen, J. M.** "A Samaritan Authentication of the Rabbinic Interpretation of *kephi tahrâ.*" *VT* 24 (1974): 361-366. [2305].

762. —————. *A Samaritan Chronicle. A Source Critical Analysis of the Life and Times of the Great Samaritan Reformer, Baba Rabbah.* Leiden: E. J. Brill, 1981. Studia

Post-Biblica 30.
[1603/ 3003].

763. **Cohen, Menahem.** Orthographic Systems in Ancient Massorah Codices. (Ph.D. thesis, Hebrew) Jerusalem: Hebrew University,
[2306.1/ 2603.1].

764. —————. "The Orthography of the Samaritan Pentateuch." (Hebrew) *BM* 64.1 (1974/5): 54-70. [An English summary, pp. 173-174].
[2306.1/ 2603.1].

765. —————. "The Orthography of the Samaritan Pentateuch, its Place in the History of Orthography." (Hebrew) *BM* 66.3 (1976): 361-391. [An English summary on p. 489].
[2300/ 2603.1].

766. —————. "Reply to B.Tsedaka's Review—'Samaritan Writing'." *A–B* 166 (1976): 10-11.
[2603.1].

767. **Cohen, S. &. Katz, Ruth.** "Explorations in the Music of the Samaritans." *Ethnomusicology* 4 (1960): 2f.
[3300].

768. **Cohen-Zedek, J.** "Die Samariter." *Katholischer Digest* 8 (1949): 50-54. Illustrated.
[200].

769. —————. "La Samarianoj." *Malgranda Revuo* 1 (1948): 1-7. Illustrated.
[200/ 202].

770. **Cohn, J.** Reviewer. E. Munk, "Des Samaritaners Marqah." *JLB* 20 (1891): 32-34.
[107/ 1803].

771. **Cohn, Naphtali.** Die Vorschriften betreffend die Zarâath nach dem Kitâb al-Kâfi. (Inaugural dissertation) Kirchain, NL: University of Erlangen, 1898.
[1106/ 1109.1].

772. —————. *Die Zarâath Gesetze der Bibel nach dem Kitab al-Kâfi des Jusuf ibn Salamah. Ein Beiträg zur Pentateuchexegese und Dogmatik der Samaritaner.* Frankfurt a. M, 1899. 54 + xviii pp. [A reprint of his inaugural dissertation under a different title].
[1106/ 1109.1].

773. **Coleman-Norton, P. R.** *Roman State and Christian Church.* London, 1966. 3 vols.
[305.4/ 305.5].

774. **Collin, Friederich E.** *Quator prima capita Geneseos Samaritana ex Waltoni Bibliis polyglottis descripta et glossario harmonico ornata.* Francofurti ad M., 1704.
[105/ 2300/ 2400].

775. **Collins, John J.** "The Epic of Theodotus and the Hellenism of the Hasmoneans." *HTR* 73 (1980): 91-104.
[2005].

776. **Collins, Mary F.** Reviewer. J. S. Isser, "The Dositheans." *CBQ* 40.1 (1978): 126-127.
[107/ 1503].

777. —————. "The Hidden Vessels in Samaritan Tradition." *JSJ* 3 (1972/3): 97-116.
[1105/ 1600/ 1800].

778. **Colman, L.** "The Samaritans, Ancient and Modern." *Princeton Review* 38 (1866): 195f.
[200/ 800/ 813].

779. **Colpe, Carsten.** "Das Samaritanische Pinchas-Grab in Awerta und die Beziehungen zwischen itadir-und Georgs-Legende." *ZDPV* 85.2 (1969): 162-196.
[402/ 1104/ 1800].

780. —————. Reviewer. **John Macdonald**, "Memar Marqah." *ZDMG* 115 (1965): 200-204.
[107/ 1803].

781. —————. "Samaria." In *Die Religion in Geschichte und Gegenwart.* Tübingen, 1961. Vol. 5: 1350-1355.
[410].

782. **Compain, M.** "Samarie une terre d'évangélisation." *BTS* 184 (1976): 18-19.
[1502/ 1502.1].

783. **Conder, Claude R.** *The City of Jerusalem—1220 AD.* London, 1887. 233f.
[500].

784. —————. Editor, *Ernoul's Account of Palestine.* London: Palestine Pilgrim Text Society, 1896. 6: 60-64. [See also the version edited by Ish Shalom].
[306.2/ 400].

785. —————. "The Mountains of Judah and Ephraim." In C. Wilson, *Picturesque Palestine.* London, Melbourne and Sydney, n.d. Cap. 2: vol. 1.
[108/ 308].

786. —————. "Notes on New Discoveries." *PEFQS* 41 (1909): 266-275. [On the Book of Joshua].
[600/ 1605].

787. —————. *Palestine.* London, 1891.
[200].

788. —————. "Reports." *PEFQS* (1881): 199-201.
[600].

789. —————. "Samaritan Customs." *PEFQS* (1887): 233-236.
[1100/ 1200].

790. —————. "The Samaritan Temple." *PEFQS* 19 (1885): 19.
     [1305].

791. —————. "Samaritan Topography." *PEFQS* (1876): 182-197. Special papers
     (1881) 216-231.
     [400/ 400.4].

792. —————. *Tent Work in Palestine.* London, 1878. 2 vols.
     [200/ 500/ 800].

793. —————. Reviewer. A. S. Yahuda, "Zum samaritanischen Josua. Eine
     Erklärung." *PEFQS* 41 (1909): 272.
     [107/ 1605].

794. **Conder, Claude R. and H. H. Kitchener.** *The Survey of Western Palestine.*
     Memoirs of the Topography, Orthography, Hydrography and Archaeology.
     London, 1882. Vol. 2, Samaria. [Plates facing 204, 206].
     [400/ 410].

795. **Cookman. F. S.** What Was the Yahveh Cult of the Early Samaritans.(Ph.D.
     dissertation) New York: New York University, 1899.
     [1001].

796. **Cormack, G.** Reviewer. James A. Montgomery, "The Samaritans." *PEFQS* 39
     (1907): 311-313.
     [100/ 200].

797. **Cosmos** (an Egyptian monk). Translated by J. W. McCindle, *The Christian*
     Topography. London: 1907. [See also *PG* 88: 315-318 "Cosmos
     Indicopleustes"].
     [305.3/ 400/ 800].

798. **Couring, H.** "Paradoxa de Numaiis Hebraeorum." In B. Ugolini, editor,
     Thesaurus. Venice, 1765. 28: cols. 490-585.
     [603/ 2501].

799. **Courtois, H.** *Les samaritains moderns.* Toulouse, 1848. 40pp.
     [200/ 813].

800. **Couryer, B.** Reviewer. F. Perez-Castro, "Sefer Abisha." *RB* 69 (1962): 157-158.
     [107/ 2301].

801. **Covell, John,** Chaplain to British Consul at Constantinople. "Some Account of the
     Jewes, Karaims and Rabanaims." (Manuscript of 1677) *BL Add 22911.* [Ff
     781-782 describe the contemporary Samaritans on Gerizim.].
     [200].

802. **Cowley, Arthur E.** "Description of Four Samaritan Manuscripts Belonging to the
     Palestine Exploration Fund." *PEFQS* (1904): 67-78.
     [103].

803. —————. "Notes on *JQR* XIV pages 26 sqq." *JQR* 14 (1902): 352-353. [On the article by J. Skinner].
[103/ 107].

804. —————. "Samaria", "Samaritans." In **T. K. Cheyne & J. S. Black,** *Encyclopaedia Biblica.* London, 1903. 4: [Various impressions].
[200/ 201/ 410].

805. —————. "The Samaritan Doctrine of the Messiah." *The Expositor* 5th series, 7 (1895): 161-174.
[1107].

806. —————. *The Samaritan Liturgy.* Oxford: OUP, 1909. 2 vols.
[2100].

807. —————. "The Samaritan Liturgy and the Reading of the Law." *JQR* 7 (1895): 121-140.
[2100/ 2308].

808. —————. "Samaritana I: Samaritan Dealings with Jews. II: An Alleged Copy of the Samaritan Pentateuch." *JQR* 16 (1904): 474-484. [I= letters from the Cairo Geniza].
[1003.4/ 2300].

809. —————. "Samaritans." In *Encyclopaedia Britannica.* 11th edition.
[201].

810. —————. "Samaritans", "Samaritan Version of the Pentateuch." In **I. Singer,** editor, *Jewish Encyclopaedia.* New York & London: Funk & Wagnalls, 1901-1906. 10: 669-681.
[200/ 201/ 2300].

811. —————. "Some Remarks on Samaritan Literature and Religion." *JQR* 8 (1896): 562-575.
[1000/ 1100/ 1550].

812. —————. "A Supposed Early Copy of the Samaritan Pentateuch." *PEFQS* (1904): 394-396. Illustrated.
[2300].

813. **Crane, Oliver T.** *The Samaritan Chronicle or the Book of Joshua, the Son of Nun.* New York: John Alden, 1890. [Translation of the Scaliger codex].
[1604].

814. **Cranfield, C. E. B.** "The Good Samaritan." *TT* 11 (1954): 368-372.
[1502.3].

815. **Crespy, G.** "The Parable of the Good Samaritan. An Essay in Structural Research." *Semeia* 2 (1974): 27-50. Translated by T. Kirby.
[1502.3].

816. —————. "La parabole dit 'le bon Samaritain'; Recherches structurales." *ETR* 48 (1973): 61-79.
[1502.3].

817. **Créten, J.** "La pâque des samaritains." *RB* 31 (1922): 432-442. [4 figs.].
[1404].

818. **Crinesius, M. Christopher.** *Discursus de Confusione Linguarum.* Noribergae: Simon Halbmayer, 1629. 144 pp.
[2600].

819. —————. *Lingua Samaritica ex scriptura sacra...fideliter eruta.* Altdorf: Balthasaris Scherefi, n.d. [See the Bodley handlist for the date of 1628].
[2300/ 2600].

820. **Crone, Patricia.** "Islam, Judeo-Christianity and Byzantine Iconoclasm." *Jerusalem Studies in Arabic and Islam* 2 (1980): 59-95.
[809/ 1501].

821. **Crone, Patricia and Michael Cook.** *Hagarism, the Making of the Islamic World.* Cambridge: CUP, 1977.
[305.1/ 1003.3].

822. **Cross, Frank M.** *The Ancient Library of Qumran and Modern Biblical Studies.* Revised edn. New York, 1961.
[600/ 2300].

823. —————. "Aspects of the Samaritan and Jewish History in Late Persian and Hellenistic Times." *HTR* 59.3 (1966): 201-211. [Reprinted in Dexinger and Pummer, *Die Samaritaner,* 312-323].
[802/ 802.1/ 803/ 804].

824. —————. "The Contribution of the Qumran Discoveries to the Study of the Biblical Text." *IEJ* 14 (1966): 81-95.
[1005].

825. —————. "The Development of the Jewish Scripts." In **G. E. Wright,** editor, *The Bible and the Ancient Near East: Essays in Honor of William Foxwell Albright.* New York, 1961. 133-202.
[2501].

826. —————. "The Discovery of the Samaria Papyri." *BA* 26 (1963): 110-121 (figs. 1-5). [Reprinted in *Biblical Archaeologist Reader* 3 1970: 227-239].
[303.3].

827. —————. "The Discovery of the Samaria Papyri." *CNI* 14.3-4 (1963): 24-35.
[303.3].

828. —————. "Historical Importance of the Samaria Papyri." *BAR* 4.1 (1978): 25-27.
[303.3/ 804].

829. ————. "The History of the Biblical Text in the Light of the Discoveries in the Judaean Desert." *HTR* 57.4 (October, 1964): 281-299.
[1005/ 2300].

830. ————. "The Papyri and Their Historical Implications." In **P. W. & N. Lapp**, editors, *Discoveries in the Wadi ed-Daliyeh*. Cambridge, Massachusetts: AASOR, 1974. Monograph series, vol. 41: 17-19.
[303.3/ 804].

831. ————. "Papyri of the Fourth Century B.C. from Daliyeh." In **David N. Freedman & Jonas C. Greenfield**, editors, *New Directions in Biblical Archaeology*. New York: Doubleday, 1969. 41-62.
[303.3].

832. ————. "A Reconstruction of the Judaean Restoration." *JBL* 94 (1975): 4-18. [Reprinted in *Interpretation* (1975) 29:187-201].
[802/ 802.1].

833. ————. "Report on the Biblical Fragments of Cave Four in Wadi Qumran." *BASOR* 141 (1956): 9-13.
[600/ 1005].

834. ————. "A Report on the Samaria Papyri." In **John A. Emerton**, editor, *Congress Volume: Jerusalem 1986. VT* Supp. 40. Leiden: Brill, 1988. 17-26.
[303.3].

835. ————. "Samaria Papyrus 1: An Aramaic Slave Conveyance of 335 BCE Found in the Wâdi ed-Dâliyeh." *EI* 18 (1985): 7-17.
[303.1].

836. ————. "Samaritans." (Hebrew) in *EM* 1981. 8: 164-173.
[200/ 201/2300].

837. **Crossan, J. D.** "Comments on the Article of D. Patte and Reply to the Preceding Note." *Semeia* 2 (1974): 121-128.
[1502/ 1502.1/ 1502.2].

838. ————. "The Good Samaritan: Towards a Genetic Definition of Parable." *Semeia* 2 (1974): 82-112. [*NTab* 19(1975) no. 981].
[108/ 1502.3].

839. ————. "Parable and Example in the Teaching of Jesus." *Semeia* 1 (1974): 63-104. [See also *NTS* 18 (1971-72): 285-307].
[1502/ 1502.1/ 1502.2].

840. **Crowfoot, J. W.** *Early Churches in Palestine*. London, 1941. [See especially fig. 6, p. 37, pp. 92-94 plates 8b, 27a-b, 30d].
[1301/ 1502].

841. ————. "Excavation in Samaria." *PEFQS* (1934): 10-14.
[410/ 600].

842. —————. "Report of the 1935 Samaria Excavations." *PEFQS* (1935): 182-194.
[410/ 600].

843. —————. "Samaria: Interim Report on the Work in 1933." *PEFQS* (1933): 129-136.
[410/ 600].

844. —————. "Work of the Joint Expedition to Samaria-Sebustiya." *PEFQS* (1931& 1932): 139-142 & 63-70.
[410/ 600].

845. **Crowfoot, J. W. with Crowfoot, G. M.** *Samaria–Sebaste.* London, 1938. Vol. 2. Ivories from Samaria.
[410/ 600/ 606.1].

846. —————. *Samaria-Sebaste.* London, 1957. Vol. 3. The Objects from Samaria.
[410/ 600/ 601/ 603/ 607].

847. **Crowfoot, J. W., E. L. Sukenik and K. Kenyon.** *Samaria-Sebaste.* London, 1942. Vol. 1. (Reports of the Work of the Joint Expedition).
[410/ 600/ 606.1].

848. **Crown, Alan D.** "The Abisha Scroll of the Samaritans." *BJRL* 58.1 (1975): 36-65.
[2301].

849. —————. "The Abisha Scroll—3,000 Years Old?" *Bible Review* 7.5 (1991): 12-21; 39.
[2301].

850. —————. "The Biblical Samaritans in the Present Day." *BAIAS* 7 (1987-8): 40-49.
[200/ 800].

851. —————. "The Byzantine and Moslem Period." In **A. D. Crown,** editor, *The Samaritans.* Tübingen: Mohr, 1989. 55-81.
[800/ 808/ 809].

852. —————. "A Chronological Survey of Style and Format in Samaritan Binding." In **Rothschild and Sixdenier,** editors, *Études samaritaines.* Louvain-Paris, 1988. 67-81.
[103].

853. —————. Reviewer. **J. M. Cohen,** "Cohen's Samaritan Chronicle." *JQR* 75.4 (1985): 402-405.
[107/ 1600].

854. —————. A Critical Edition and Translation of the Samaritan Burial Service with a Comparative Study of the Related Jewish Liturgies. (M.A. dissertation) Leeds: University of Leeds, 1958.
[1003.4/ 2100/ 2103].

855. —————. A Critical Re-evaluation of the Samaritan Sepher Yehoshua. (Doctoral dissertation) Sydney: University of Sydney, 1966. [1604/ 1605].

856. —————. "The Date and Authenticity of the Samaritan Hebrew Book of Joshua as Seen in its Territorial Allotments." *PEQ* 96 (1964): 79-100. [Reprinted in Dexinger and Pummer, *Die Samaritaner*, 281-311]. [1605].

857. —————. *Dated Samaritan Manuscripts: Some Codicological Implications.* Sydney: Dept. of Semitic Studies, University of Sydney, 1986. [A limited edition of 100 copies produced for a seminar at the Smithsonian Institution Library, Washington]. [103].

858. —————. "Dositheans, Resurrection and a Messianic Joshua." *Antichthon* 1.1 (1967): 70-85. [1105/ 1107/ 1503/ 3006.1].

859. —————. Reviewer. **Sylvia Powels,** "Der Kalender der Samaritaner." *JSS* 26.1 (1981): 130-134. [107/ 1400].

860. —————. Reviewer. **L. H. Vilsker,** "Manuel d'araméen samaritain." *JSS* 28.1 (1983). [107/ 2800].

861. —————. "Manuscripts and Cast Type: The Cutting of the Samaritan Fonts." *BJRUL* 72.1 (1990):87-130 [103].

862. —————. "The Morphology of Paper in Samaritan Manuscripts: A Diachronic Profile." *BJRUL* 71.1 (1989): 71-93. [103].

863. —————. "New Light on the Inter-relationships of Samaritan Chronicles from some Manuscripts in the John Rylands Library." *BJRL* 54:2 & 55:1 (1972): 282-313; 86-111. [Reprinted, separatum, 58 pp]. [1600].

864. —————. "New Ways in Samaritan Epigraphy and Palaeography." *A–B* 8.200 (15/2/ 1977): 37-38. [A Hebrew version appeared on pp. 34-36]. [2501].

865. —————. "Problems in Epigraphy and Palaeography: The Nature of the Evidence in Samaritan Sources." *BJRL* 62.1 (1979): 37-60. [2501].

866. —————. "Qumran or the Samaritans: Which has the Closer Relationship with Early Christianity?" Division A. Jerusalem, 1990. 221-228. [Paper delivered at the 10th World Congress of Jewish Studies, Jerusalem, 1989]. [1003.1/ 1005].

867. —————. "Redating the Schism Between the Judaeans and the Samaritans."
     JQR 82.1-2 (1991): 17-50.
     [801.1].

868. —————. "The Samaritan Diaspora." In **A. D. Crown,** editor, *The Samaritans.*
     Tübingen: J.C.B.Mohr, 1989. 195-217.
     [500].

869. —————. "The Samaritan Diaspora to the End of the Byzantine Era." *AJBA*
     2.3 (1974-5): 107-123. [Abstracted in *NTAb* 21(1977) no.267].
     [500/ 808].

870. —————. "Samaritan Literature and its Manuscripts." *BJRUL.* Spring (1994):
     [In press].
     [103/ 1550].

871. —————. "Samaritan Majuscule Palaeography: Eleventh to the Twentieth
     Century." *BJRL* 60:2 & 60:3 (1978): I, 434f. II, 29-55. [Reprinted seperatum
     BJRL and in *A–B* 261, 266-268, 271-275 (1980)].
     [2501].

872. —————. "Samaritan Manuscripts." In **M. B. Parkes,** *Medieval Manuscripts of
     Keble College, Oxford.* London: Scolar Press, 1979.
     [101/ 103].

873. —————. Reviewer. **R. T. Anderson,** "Samaritan Manuscripts and Artefacts:
     The Chamberlain Warren Collection." *JSS* 26.2 (1981): 316-317.
     [101/ 103/ 107].

874. —————. "Samaritan Minuscule Palaeography." *BJRL* 63.2 (1980): 330-368.
     [2501].

875. —————. "Samaritan Religion in the Fourth Century." *NTT* 41.1 (1986): 29-
     47.
     [808/ 1000].

876. —————. Reviewer. **R. Pummer,** "The Samaritans." *JRH* 15.1 (1988): 145-
     146.
     [107/ 200/ 1400].

877. —————. Reviewer. **R. Pummer,** "The Samaritans." *JQR* 79.2-3 (1988-1989):
     231-234.
     [107/ 200/ 1400].

878. —————, editor. *The Samaritans.* Tübingen: J. C. B. Mohr, 1989.
     [200].

879. —————. "The Samaritans in 1984." *Yod (= Revue des études hébraïques et
     Juives modernes et contemporaines)* 20 (1984): 8-31. [French summary p. 8].
     [1500].

880. —————. "Samaritans in the Byzantine Orbit." *BJRUL* 69.1 (1986): 96-138.
     [808].

881. ——————. "Second Thoughts on the Age of the Anonymous Portions of the Samaritan Burial Liturgy." In E. C. B. MacLaurin, editor, *Essays in Honour of G. W. Thatcher.* Sydney: Sydney University Press, 1967. 63-83. [2103].

882. ——————. "Some Traces of Heterodox Theology in the Samaritan Book of Joshua." *BJRL* 10.1 (1967): 179-198. [1100/ 1604/ 1605].

883. ——————. "Studies in Samaritan Scribal Practices and Manuscript History, General Introduction. I. Manuscript Prices and Values." *BJRUL* 65.2 (1983): 72-94. [103].

884. ——————. "Studies in Samaritan Scribal Practices and Manuscript History II. The Rate of Writing of Samaritan Scribes." *BJRUL* 66. 2 (1984): 97-124. [103].

885. ——————. "Studies in Samaritan Scribal Practices and Manuscript History III. Columnar Writing and the Samaritan Massorah." *BJRUL* 67.1 (1984): 349-381. [103].

886. ——————. "Studies in Samaritan Scribal Practices and Manuscript History IV. An Index of Scribes, Witnesses, Owners and Others Mentioned in Samaritan Manuscripts, with a Key to the Principal Families Therein." *BJRUL* 68.2 (Spring, 1986): 317-372. [103/ 3000].

887. ——————. "Studies in Samaritan Scribal Practices and Manuscript History V. Samaritan Bindings: A Chronological Survey with Special Reference to Nag Hammadi Techniques." *BJRUL* 69.2 (Spring, 1987): 425-491. [103].

888. ——————. Reviewer. F. Dexinger, "Der Taheb." *JQR* 80.1-2 (1989): 139-141. [1107].

889. ——————. "Theology, Eschatology and Law in Samaritan Funeral Rites and Liturgy." *TGUOS* 23 (1972): 86-101. [1100/ 1105/ 1203/ 2103].

890. ——————. Reviewer. Z. Ben-Hayyim, "Tibât Marqe." *JQR* 82.3-4 (1992): 515-518. [107/ 1803].

891. ——————. "An Unpublished Fragment of a Samaritan Torah Scroll." *BJRL* 64.2 (1982): 386-406. [103/ 2309.1].

892. Crown, Alan D., R. Pummer and A. Tal, editors. *Companion to Samaritan Studies.* Tübingen: Mohr, 1992-3. [200].

893. **Crown, Alan David.** "A Profile of Paper in Samaritan Manuscripts." In **A. Tal &
     M. Florentin,** editors, *Proceedings of the First International Congress of the
     Société d'Études Samaritaines.* Tel Aviv: Chaim Rosenberg School for Jewish
     Studies, University of Tel Aviv, 1991. 205-224.
     [103].

894. **Cullman, Oscar.** *Des sources de l'évangile à la formation de la théologie chrétienne.*
     Neuchatel, 1969.
     [1502.1].

895. ——————. "La Preghiera nell' evangelo di Giovanni, trad di Erica e Luca
     Negro." *Protestantesimo* 36.1 (1981): 1-20.
     [1502.1].

896. ——————. "Samaria and the Origins of the Christian Mission." In **J. B.
     Higgins,** editor, *The Early Church.* London, 1956. 183-192.
     [1003.1/ 1502/ 1502.1/ 1502.2].

897. ——————. "La Samarie et les origines de la mission chrétienne." *AEH* (1953-4):
     3-12.
     [1003.1/ 1502/ 1502.1/ 1502.2].

898. ——————. "Von Jesus zum Stephanuskreis und zum Johannesevangelium." In **E.
     E. Ellis and E. Grässer,** eds., *Jesus und Paulus: Festschrift für Werner Georg
     Kümmel zum 70 Geburtstag.* Göttingen, 1975. 44-56. [Reprinted in Dexinger
     and Pummer, *Die Samaritaner,* 393-407].
     [1003.1/1502.1].

899. **Cumont, F.** *Die orientalischen Religionem im romischen Heidentum.* Leipzig, 1910.
     [Numerous editions and translations in German, French and English].
     [1002].

900. **Cureton, W.** *Book of Religious and Philosophical Sects by Muhammad Shahrastani.*
     London: Society for the Publication of Oriental Texts, 1842, 1846. 2 vols.
     [305.1/ 1003.3/ 1500].

901. **Curtiss, S. I.** "The Samaritan Passover." In *Primitive Semitic Religion Today.*
     Chicago, 1902. 264-265. [=Appendix F].
     [1400/1404].

902. ——————. "Survival of Ancient Semitic Religion in Syrian Centres of Moslem
     and Christian Influence." *The Expositor* 11.Series 6 (1905): 415-431.
     [1003.1/ 1003.3].

903. **Curzon, Robert.** *Catalogue of Material for Writing on Early Tablets and Stones, Rolls
     and Other Manuscripts and Oriental Manuscript Books in the Library of the Hon.
     Robert Curzon at Parham in the County of Sussex.* London, 1849.
     [101].

904. ——————. "On Two Tablets of the Law in Samaritan Characters." *Proceedings of
     the Archaeological Institute of Great Britain and Ireland* (1853): 27f.
     [1103/ 2501].

905. **Cyril of Alexandria.** "Commentary of John." *PG* 73 287-306, 311-322, 331-339, 439-446, 907-910.
[305/ 1502.1].

906. —————. "Commentary on Amos." *PG* 71 471-478, 491-494.
[305].

907. —————. "Commentary on Hosea." *PG* 71 45-48, 275-282.
[305].

908. —————. "Commentary on Isaiah." *PG* 70 423-426.
[305].

909. —————. "Commentary on John." *PG* 77 919-922.
[305/ 1502.1].

910. —————. "Commentary on Micah." *PG* 71 747-754.
[305].

D

911. **Da Sylveira, João.** "De Samaritan lectione." In *Opuscula Varia et Primum.* Leiden, 1697, 1700, 1725. [Held, BL fol. 1846 m.14].
     [2300].

912. **Dagonet, Ph.** *Selon saint Jean une femme de Samarie.* Paris: Éditions du Cerf, 1979.
     [1003.1/ 1502/ 1502.1].

913. **Dalley, Stephanie.** "Foreign Chariotry and Cavalry in the Armies of Tiglath Pileser III and Sargon II." *Iraq* 47 (1985): 31-38. [Units from Samaria].
     [801/ 801.2].

914. **Dalman, Gustaf.** "Das samaritanische Passah im Verhältnis zum jüdischen." *PJB* 8th year (1912): 123-138.
     [1003.4/ 1404].

915. —————. "Epigraphisches und Pseudepigraphisches." *MNDPV* 10 (1903): 29-30.
     [2501].

916. —————. *Grammatik des Jüdisch-Palästinischen Aramäisch.* Leipzig, 1894. [Reprinted, Darmstadt, 1960].
     [2800].

917. —————. "Nochmals der samaritanische Joshua." *TLZ* (1908): column 665.
     [1604/ 1605].

918. —————. Reviewer. **A. S. Yahuda,** "Zum samaritanischen Joshua. Eine Erklärung." *Serubbabel* (1908): 553-565.
     [107/ 1604/ 1605].

919. —————. Reviewer. **A. S.Yahuda,** "Zum samaritanischen Joshua: Eine Erklärung." *Christliche Welt* 22 (1908): 868-870.
     [107/ 1604/ 1605].

920. —————. "Zum samaritanischen Joshua." *TLZ* (26 Sept.1908): column 553.
     [1604/ 1605].

921. **Damati, Emanuel.** "Askar—Notes and News." *IEJ* 22 (1972): 14.
     [413/ 600].

922. —————. "A Roman Mausoleum at Askar." (Hebrew) *Qadmoniot* 6 (1973): 118-120.
     [413/ 600/ 1203].

923. **Dan, Yaron.** "Circus Factions (Blues and Greens in Byzantine Palestine)." *Cathedra* 4 (1977): 133-146. [Reprinted in *Jerusalem Cathedra* (1981) 1:105-119. On the Samaritans in Caesarea].
     [403.1/ 808].

924. —————. "Information About Acre in a Greek Work of the Seventh Century." In *Studies in the History of the Jewish People—The Land of Israel.* Haifa: University of Haifa Press, 1972. 2: 53-62.
[305.4/ 808.1].

925. —————. "Notices of Jewish and Samaritan Relations in the Late Byzantine Period." (Hebrew) *Zion* 46.2 (1981): 67-76. [English summary, p. ix].
[808/ 1003.4].

926. Daniel, C. "Les Esséniens et l'arrière-fond historique de la parable du bon Samaritain." *NT* 11 (1969): 71-104.
[1502.3].

927. Daniel, Richard. *Daniels Copy-Book: or a Compendium of the most unusual hands...Samaritan...together with sundry portraitures.* London: Mathew Collins & Francis Cossinet, 1664.
[105].

928. Daniel, W. "A Journal or Account of William Daniel, his late Expedition or Undertaking to Go from London to Surrat." In *The Red Sea and Adjacent Countries at the Close of the Seventeenth Century.* Hakluyt Society Series,. London, 1949. 65f.
[308].

929. Daniélou, Jean. "Le bon samaritain." In *Mélanges bibliques rédigés en l'honneur d'André Robert.* Paris: Bloud & Gay, 1967. 457-465.
[1502.3].

930. Daniels, Peter T. "A Calligraphic Approach to Aramaic Palaeography." *JNES* 43.1 (1984): 55-69.
[2501.1].

931. Daoust, J. "La Samarie." *BTS* 184 (1976): 3-5.
[410].

932. Dar, Shimon. "Archaeological Evidence on the Samaritan Revolts of the Byzantine Period." (Hebrew) in Jacoby and Tsafrir, editors, *Jews, Samaritans and Christians in Byzantine Palestine.* Jerusalem: Yad I Ben-Zvi, 1988. 228-237:
[600/ 808.1].

933. —————. *Landscape and Pattern: An Archaeological Survey of Samaria 800 BCE-636 CE With a Historical Commentary by Shimon Applebaum.* 2 vols. series 308(i). Oxford: BAR International, 1986. [Reviewed by W. R. Kotter, *BASOR* 284 Nov. 1991 91-92].
[400.3/ 600/ 801/ 804/ 806/ 808].

934. —————. "Three Menorot From Western Samaria." *IEJ* 34.2-3 (1984): 177-179.
[605].

935. Dar, Shimon and Z. Safrai, editors. *Samaria Studies.* Tel Aviv: Kibbutz Hameuhad, 1989.
[400/ 600/ 800].

936. Dar, Shimon, Y. Tepper and Z. Safrai. *Um Rihan, A City of the Mishnaic Period.* Tel Aviv: Kibbutz Hameuhad, 1986.
[600].

937. Darlow, T. H. and H. F. Moule. *Historical Catalogue of the Printed Editions of Holy Scripture in the Library of the British and Foreign Bible Society.* London, 1903-1911. 2 volumes. [Pt. 2, polyglot bibles: p. 81 Samaritan-Arabic].
[105/ 2300/ 2302].

938. Dauani, Paulus Mussa. "Etwas über die Samariter." *Palästina Mitt. des Evang. Karmelvereins* 4 (1916): 30f., 43f.
[200].

939. Daube, David. "Jesus and the Samaritan Woman: the Meaning of συγχράομαι." *JBL* 69 (1950): 137-147.
[1502/ 1502.1].

940. ————. "The Samaritan Woman." In *The New Testament and Rabbinic Judaism.* London: University of London/Athlone Press, 1956. 373-382. [Jordan Lectures, 1952].
[1502/ 1502.1].

941. ————. "Zum frühtalmudischen Rechtspraxis." *ZAW* 2 (1932): 148-159.
[304.2/ 1106].

942. Davidson, S. "Samaritans", "Samaritan Pentateuch." In S. **Fallows**, editor, *The Popular and Critical Bible Encyclopedia and Scriptural Dictionary.* Chicago, 1909. Vol. 3.
[201].

943. Davies, G. Reviewer. A. D.Crown, "Studies in Samaritan Scribal Practices III." *ZAW* 99.3 (1987): 434.
[103/ 107].

944. ————. Reviewer. A. D. Crown, "Studies in Scribal Practices IV: Index of Scribes." *ZAW* 100.1 (1988): 121.
[107].

945. Davila, James Rohr. Unpublished Pentateuchal Manuscripts from Cave IV, Qumran 4Q Genesis[(A)].(Ph.D.) Harvard University: 1988.
[2307].

946. de Diego, J. R. "¿Quién es mi prójimo?" *EE* 41 (1966): 93-107. [Reprinted in *NTAb* 11(1966) n⁰. 263].
[1502].

947. de Jonge, H. J. "The Story of the New Testament." In T. H. L. Scheurleer et al., *Leiden University in the Seventeenth Century.* Leiden: Brill, 1975. 65-110.
[1002].

948. **de Jonge, M.** "Jesus as Prophet and King in the Fourth Gospel." *ETL* 49 (1973): 160-171. [Argues against a Qumran parallel to NT].
[1502.1].

949. **de la Potterie, I.** "Gv. 4, 5-42: Gesù e i samaritani." *La Parola per l'assemblea festiva* 13 (1972): 36-30.
[1502.1].

950. —————. "'Nous adorons, nous, ce que connaissons, car le salut vient des Juifs'. Histoire de l'exégèse et interprétation de Jn. 4, 22." *Biblica* 64 (1983): 74-115.
[1502.1].

951. **de Montmollin, E.** *Des samaritaines et de l'origine de leur secte.* Neuchatel, 1951.
[200/ 800].

952. **de Muis, Simeon.** *Assertatio Altera.* Paris, 1634.
[2300].

953. —————. *Assertatio veritatis hebraicae adversus exercitationes ecclesiastias in utrumque Samaritanorum Pentateuchum Ioannis Morini, autore Simeone de Muis.* Paris, 1631.
[2300].

954. —————. *Castigatio animadversionum Morini Blesensis (in censuram exercitationum ecclesiasticarum ad Pentateuchum Samaritanum).* Paris, 1639.
[2300].

955. —————. "Censura in aliquot capita exercitationum in utrumque Samaritanorum Pentateuchum." In *Opera Omnia.* Paris, 1650. Vol. 2: 159-258.
[2300].

956. **de Muralt, Eduard.** *Essai de Chronographie Byzantine.* Paris, 1963.
[808/ 808.1].

957. **de Nicola, A.** "La Pasqua dei Samaritani." *BeO* 13 (1971-72): 49-56.
[1404].

958. **de Robert, Philippe.** "La naissance des études samaritaines en Europe aux XVIe et XVIIe siècles." In **Rothschild and Sixdenier**, editors, *Études samaritaines.* Louvain-Paris, 1988. 15-26.
[106/ 1700].

959. —————. "Aspects de l'exégèse samaritaine." *ETR* 62 (1987): 551-554. [Review article of S. Lowy and A. Tal].
[107/ 2305/ 2401].

960. —————. "Les samaritains et le nouveau testament." *ETR* 45.2 (1970): 179-184.
[806/ 1003.1/ 1502].

961. —————. Reviewer. **J. Macdonald**, "The Samaritan Chronicle II." *ETR* 46 (1971): 91-92.
[107/ 1603].

962. —————. Reviewer. A. D. Crown, "The Samaritans." *Revue d'histoire et de philosophie religieuses* 70.2 (1990): 253.
[107/ 200].

963. de Robert, Philippe, R. Goetschel and P. Maraval. "La fin de Moïse. Le récit de Deutéronome. Les traditions samaritaines. Les traditions juives. Les traditions patristiques. L'énigme de la sépulture de Moïse." *Le Monde de la Bible* 44 (1986): 21-29.
[3008].

964. De Rossi, [Giovanni] Joanne Bernardo. *Carmina Orientalia Heb...Samar.* Augustae Taurinorum: Typographia Regia, 1768.
[105].

965. —————. *De Hebraici Typographie origine ac primitiis seu antiquis ac rarissimis Hebraicorum librorum editionibus seculi XV disquisitio historico-critica.* Parmae, 1776.
[105].

966. —————. *In Nuptiis Augustorum Principum Ferdinandi Borbonii et Amaliae Austriacae Poema Anatolico-Polyglottum.* Parmae: Ex Regia Typographia, 1799. 12. [An engraved Samaritan type face].
[105].

967. —————. *Specimen varium lectionum sacri textus. Appendix de celeberrimo Samaritano, codice triplato Bibliothecae Barberinae.* Rome & Tübingen, 1782, 1783. 165-228.
[103/ 2300].

968. —————. *Variae Lectiones Veteris Testamenti Librorum.* Parmae, 1784. [Reprinted, Amsterdam 1969, 2 vols.].
[2300].

969. de Sacy, M. le Baron Silvestre. "1. Notices et extraits de divers manuscrits arabes et autres (tome XI) 2. Correspondance de samaritains de Naplouse pendant les années 1808 et suivants (tome XII)." *Notices et extraits des manuscrits de la bibliothèque royale et autres bibliothèques* (Paris, 1829). [The offprints appeared in monographic form before the source was printed].
[103/ 1700/ 1701/ 2302].

970. —————. *Chrestomathie Arabe.* Paris, 1806. New edition, Paris, 1862.
[307.2/ 1550/ 1600].

971. —————. "Litterae samaritanorum ad Josephum Scaligerum datae." *RBML* 13 (1783): 257-277.
[1705].

972. —————. "Mémoire sur la version arabe des livres de Moïse a l'usage des samaritaines et sur les manuscrits de cette version." *Mémoires de l'Académie des Inscriptions et Belles-Lettres* 49 (1808): 1-149, 783-786.
[103/ 2302].

973. —————. "Mémoire sur l'état actuel des samaritains." *Annales des voyages, de la géographie et de l'histoire* 19.55 (1812): 5-71. [A German translation appeared in *Theologische Nachtrichten*, 2 (Oct. 1813): 356-405: see also *Archive für alte und neue Kirchengeschichte* 1. 3 (1814): 40-86. All the material in these items is subsumed into his later works].
[813/ 903].

974. —————. "Recherches sur les restes des samaritains." *Annales de Philosophie Chrétienne* 4 (1832): 244-262, 321-341. [Includes a preface, pp. 241-243, probably written by Bonnetty and the author's "Mémoire sur l'état actuel."].
[813/ 903].

975. —————. "Über den gegenwärtigen Zustand der Samaritaner." *Archive für alte und neue Kirchengeschichte* 1.40-86 (1814):
[813/ 903].

976. —————. "De versione Samaritano-Arabica Librorum Mosis...commentatio." *Allgemeine Bibliothek de Biblischen Literatur* 10 (1800): 1-176.
[2302].

977. de Sandoli, S. "La Signoria di Nablus." *Corpus Inscriptionum Crucesignatorion Terrae Sanctae.* Jerusalem, 1974. 1099-1201.
[810].

978. de Saulcy, F. *Narrative of a Journey Round the Dead Sea and in the Bible Lands in 1850 and 1851.* London, 1854. Vol.2:306-350.
[308/ 400].

979. —————. *Voyage en Terre Sainte.* Paris, 1865. Vol. 2.
[308/ 400].

980. de Sénarclens, P. "La politique israélienne dans les territoires occupés." *PE* 44.2 (1979): 189-212.
[903].

981. de Slane, M. G. *Catalogue des manuscrits Arabes.* Paris: Imprimerie Nationale, 1883-1895.
[101/ 103].

982. —————. "Untitled note on Borés impending visit to the Samaritans." *JA* Ve series (1838): 111-112.
[308].

983. de Vaux, Roland. Reviewer. E. Robertson, "Catalogue of the Samaritan Manuscripts in the John Rylands Library—vol.1." *RB* 48 (1939): 450-451.
[101/ 107].

984. —————. Reviewer. F. Diening, "Das Hebräische bei den Samaritanern." *RB* 48 (1939): 470.
[107/ 2600].

985. De Vogüe, Melchior. "Nouvelle inscription samaritaine d'Amwas." *RB* 5 (1896): 432-434. [Reprinted in Chabot, *Répertoire d'épigraphie sémitique*, I no. 366]. [2502].

986. Deaut, Roger le. "Manuscrits du targum samaritain et du targums juifs." In Rothschild and Sixdenier, editors, *Etudes samaritaines.* Louvain-Paris, 1988. 109-121. [103/ 2401].

987. ——————. Reviewer. J. Macdonald, "Memar Marqah." *Biblica* 46 (1965): 84-87. [107/ 1803].

988. ——————. Reviewer. A. Tal, "The Samaritan Targum." *Biblica* 63.4 (1982): 579-582. [107/ 2401].

989. Decroix, J. "La longue histoire des Samaritains; peuple fidèle et tourmenté." *BTS* 121 (1970): 16-17. [200/ 800].

990. Degon, A. "Samaritains d'aujourd'hui." *Le Pèlerin* .4948 (2/10/1977): 36f. [200/ 813/ 903].

991. ——————. "La tradition samaritaine." *Le Spectacle du Monde* (November, 1977): 81-84. [200].

992. Dehan, Emanuel. *A History of Jacob's Well in Shechem (Nablus) and the City of Samaria (Sebaste).* Tel Aviv, 1977. [A guidebook sold at Jacob's Well: 48 pp.]. [407].

993. Dehn, G. *Jesus und die Samariter. Eine Auslegung von Johannes 4,1-43.* Neukirchen: BSt.13, 1956. [1502.1].

994. Deissman, Gustav A. *Forschungen und Funde im Serai. Mit einem Verzeichnis der nichtislamischen Handschriften im Topkapi Serai zu Istanbul.* Berlin & Leipzig, 1933. 123-135. [See also nos. 102-112, 128-135]. [101/ 103].

995. Deist, F. E. "The Samaritan Pentateuch." In *Towards the Text of the Old Testament.* Pretoria, 1978. Chapter 3: 110-125. [Translated by W. K. Winckler]. [2300].

996. del Valle, C. "Los Samaritanos." *Tierra Santa* 480 (1969): 18-24. [200].

997. Delcor, Mathias. "La Correspondance des savants européens, enquête de manuscrits, avec les Samaritains du XVIe au XIXe siècle." In Rothschild and Sixdenier, editors, *Études samaritaines.* Louvain-Paris, 1988. 27-43. [1700].

998. —————. "La divinité Ashima de Samarie en 2R17,30 et ses survivances." In **A. Tal & M. Florentin,** editors, *Proceedings of the First International Congress of the Société d'Études Samaritaines.* Tel Aviv: Chaim Rosenberg School for Jewish Studies, University of Tel Aviv, 1991. 33-48.
[1110].

999. —————. "Hinweise auf das samaritanische Schisma im Alten Testament." *ZAW* 74.3 (1962): 281-291. [Reprinted in Dexinger and Pummer, *Die Samaritaner* 250-262].
[801.1/ 802].

1000. —————. Reviewer. **A.D.Crown,** "The Samaritans." *Bulletin de Littérature Ecclesiastique* 91.4 (1990): 287-288.
[107/ 200].

1001. —————. "Vom Sichem der hellenistischen Epoche zum Sychar des Neuen Testament." *ZDPV* 78 (1962): 34-48. Reprinted in *Religion d'Israel et Proche Orient,* (Brill, 1976) 389-404.
[412/ 413/ 804].

1002. **Delitzsch, Franz.** "Ueber den Jahve-Namen." *ZAW* 3 (1883): 280-298.
[1110].

1003. **Delitzsch, Friederich Julius.** *Die Lese und Schreibfehler im Alten Testament.* Berlin & Leipzig, 1920.
[2300].

1004. **Della Lega, Alberto.** *Libro d'Oltramare di Fra Nicolo da Poggibonsi.* Bologna, 1968. Vols. 1 & 2.
[306.2/ 408/ 503].

1005. **Della Valle, Pietro.** *Les fameux voyages de Pietro della Valle.* Paris, 1670. Volume 1. [Another edn. containing the Samaritan material: George Bull, ed. *The Journeys of Pietro della Valle: The Pilgrim,* London: The Folio Society, 1989].
[306.3/ 1704].

1006. —————. *Viaggio in Levante.* Venezia, 1667. [Most English editions omit the Samaritan material, but see the translation by Hoven and the French edition (preceding entry); there are numerous other editions and translations].
[306.3/ 1704].

1007. **Demombynes, Gaudefroy.** *Les institutions Fatimides en Égypte.* Algiers, 1957. [On Qalqashandi].
[307].

1008. —————. *Le Syrie a l'époque des Mamelouks, d'après les autres Arabes.* Paris, 1923. Volumes 5-15: [Qalqashandi].
[307].

1009. **Demsky, Aaron.** "The Permitted Villages of Sebaste in the Rehov Mosaic." *IEJ* 29 (1979): 182-193.
[303.1/ 304/ 400].

1010. **Denis, A. M.** *Fragmenta Pseudepigraphorum quad Supersunt Graeca.* Leiden: Brill, 1970.
[305.4/ 805/ 2309/ 2400].

1011. —————. *Introduction aux pseudépigraphes grecs d'ancien testament.* Leiden: Brill, 1970.
[305.4/ 805/ 2309/ 2400].

1012. **Derenbourg, J.** "Essai de restitution de ancienne rédaction de Massekhet Kippourim." *REJ* 6 (1882): 41-80. [Blessings on Mt. Gerizim].
[304/ 406].

1013. —————. Reviewer. J. Bargès, "Les samaritains de Naplouse." *Archives Israélites* 16 (1855): 531-535.
[107/ 200].

1014. **Derrett, John Duncan M.** "Law in the New Testament: Fresh Light on the Parable of the Good Samaritan." *NTS* 11.1 (1964): 23-37. [Abstracted, *NTAb* 9(1964) no.566].
[1502.3].

1015. —————. "The Samaritan Woman's Pitcher." *The Downside Review* 102 (1984): 252-261. [Has a very useful bibliography of John 4].
[1502.1].

1016. —————. "The Samaritan Woman's Purity (John 4:4-52)." *EQ* 60.4 (1988): 291-296.
[1502.1].

1017. —————. "The Son of Man Standing (Acts 7:55-56)." *BEO* 156.11 (1978): 71-84.
[1003.1].

1018. **Dessau, H.** "Samaritaner bei den Scriptores historiae Augustae." In *Janus: Arbeiten zur alten und Byzantinischen Geschichte.* Vienna: Festschrift Lehmann-Haupt sechzigen Geburtstag, 1921. 124-124.
[303.4/ 804].

1019. **Deus, B.** "Das Osterfest auf dem Berg Garizim." *DHL* 96 (1964): 15-18.
[1404].

1020. **Deutsch, Emanuel O. M.** "The Samaritan Pentateuch." In W. Smith, *A Dictionary of the Bible.* London, 1863. Vol. 3.
[201/ 2300].

1021. —————. "On the Samaritan Pentateuch." In *Literary Remains of the Late Emanuel Deutsch.* London, 1874. 404-439.
[103/ 2300].

1022. —————. Reviewer. L.Wreschner, "Samaritanische Traditionen." *JLB* 18 (1889): 12.
[107/ 1100/ 3009].

1023. **Dever, William G.** "Excavations at Shechem and Mt. Gerizim." In *Eretz Shomron.* Jerusalem, 1973. 8-10.
[412/ 600].

1024. —————. "Shechem (Balata)." *IEJ* 23.4 (1973): 243-244.
[412/ 600].

1025. **Devreese, R.** "La fin ineditée d'une lettre de Sainte Maxime: un baptême forcé de Juifs et de Samaritaines à Carthage, en 632." *Revue des Sciences Religieuses* 17 (1937): 25-35.
[305.4/ 808/ 1003.1].

1026. **Dexinger, Ferdinand.** "Der Ursprung der Samaritaner im Spiegel der frühen Quellen." In **F. Dexinger and R. Pummer**, eds., *Die Samaritaner.* Darmstadt: Wissenschaftliche Buchgesellschaft, 1992. 67-140.
[801.1].

1027. —————. "Das Gerizimgebot im Dekalog der Samaritaner." In **G. Braulik,** editor, *Studien zum Pentateuch, Walter Kornfeld zum 60 Geburstag.* Wien, 1977. 111-133.
[1103].

1028. —————. "Der Dekalog im Judentum." *Bibel und Liturgie* 59 (1986): 86-93.
[1103].

1029. —————. "Die frühesten Samaritanischen Belege de Taheb-Vorstellung." *Kairos* 26.3-4 (1984): 224-252.
[1100/ 1105/ 1107].

1030. —————. "Die Funde von Gehinnom." *Bibel und Liturgie* 59 (1986): 259-261.
[1100/ 1105/ 1105.1/ 1107].

1031. —————. "Die Sektenproblematik im Judentum." *Kairos* 21.4 (1979): 273-287.
[Especially 283-286].
[1003.4/ 1500].

1032. —————. "Die Taheb-Vorstellung als politische Utopie." *Numen* 37.1 (1990): 1-23.
[1107].

1033. —————. Reviewer. **H. Kippenberg,** "Garizim und Synagoge." *WZKM* 68 (1976): 226-229.
[107/ 200/ 1000].

1034. —————. "Josephus Ant 18, 85-87 und der samaritanische Taheb." In **A. Tal & M. Florentin,** editors, *Proceedings of the First International Congress of the Société d'Études Samaritaines.* Tel Aviv: Chaim Rosenberg School for Jewish Studies, University of Tel Aviv, 1991. 49-60.
[1107].

1035. —————. "Limits of Tolerance in Judaism: the Samaritan Example." In **E. P. Sanders,** editor, *Jewish and Christian Self-Definition.* Philadelphia: Fortress

Press, 1981. Vol. 2: 88-114.
[806/ 1001/ 1002/ 1003.4].

1036. ——————. "Der 'Prophet wie Mose' in Qumran und bei den Samaritanern." In
A. Caquot, S. Légasse and M. Tardieu, editors, *Mélanges bibliques et orientaux
en l'honneur de M. Mathias Delcor.* Neukirchen-Vluyn: Butzon and Bercker,
1985. Alter Orient und Altes Testament 215: 97-111.
[1105/ 3008].

1037. ——————. "Samaritan Eschatology." In A. D. Crown, editor, *The Samaritans.*
Tübingen: Mohr, 1989. 266-292.
[1105/ 1107].

1038. ——————. "Samaritaner." In Drehsen, Häring, Kuschel, et al., editors,
Wörterbuch des Christentums. Gütersloh: Gerd Mohn, 1988.
[200].

1039. ——————. *Der Taheb. Die "Messianische" Gestalt bei den Samaritanern.* Wien,
1978.
[1105/ 1107].

1040. ——————. *Der Taheb, Ein "messianischer" Heilsbringer der Samaritaner.*
Salzburg: Otto Müller, 1986. [="Der Taheb", Kairos (1985) 1-173].
[1100/ 1105/ 1107].

1041. ——————. "The Taheb in Samaritan Tradition." *A–B* 195 (1977): 10-11.
[1105/ 1107].

1042. **Dexinger, Ferdinand and R. Pummer,** editors. *Die Samaritaner.* (Weger der
Forschung, 604). Darmstadt: Wissenschaftliche Buchgesellscaft, 1992. 477 +
viii. [A reprint of eight articles by others and some original contributions (listed
separately) except for the foreword: vii-viii and bibliography: 431-455].
[200].

1043. **di Modena, Leon.** "Touchant les samaritains." In *Cérémonies et Coutumes.* 2nd.
Paris, 1681. Supplement, 182-224. [Numerous editions in various languages.
See especially, R.Simon].
[200/ 903].

1044. **di Nola, Alfonso M.** "Samaritani." In *Enciclopedia delle Religioni.* Rome, 1973.
Vol.5: 778-794.
[200/ 201].

1045. **di Segni, Leah.** "The Church of Mary Theotokos on Mount Gerizim—The
Inscriptions." In *Christian Archaeology in the Holy Land, New Discoveries—
Archaeological Essays in Honour of Virgilio C. Corbo.* Jerusalem, 1990. Collectio
Maior XXXVI: 343-350.
[1301].

1046. ——————. "Scythopolis (Bet Shean) During the Samaritan Rebellion of 529
C.E." (Hebrew) in Tsafrai//Jacoby, *Jews, Samaritans and Christians in Byzantine
Palestine.* Jerusalem, 1988. 217-227.
[808/ 808.1].

1047. **Díaz, José Ramón.** "Arameo Samaritano." *EB* 18 (1959): 171-182.
[2800].

1048. —————. "Ediciones Fuentes del Targum Samaritano." *EB* 15 (1956): 105-
108.
[2401].

1049. —————. "Las Fuentes del Targum Samaritano Publicadas." *EB* 18.2 (1959):
183-197.
[2401].

1050. —————. "Las versiones Árabes del Pentateuco entre los Samaritanos." *EB* 18
(1959): 229-301.
[2300/ 2302].

1051 —————. "Los Fragmentos del Targum Samaritano Publicadas." *EB* 16
(1957): 297-300.
[2401].

1052. —————. "Notes Arameo-Samaritano." *EB* 18 (1959): 171-182.
[2800].

1053. —————. "Targum Samaritano." *Enciclopedia de la Biblia* 6 (1965): 881-884.
[2401].

1054. **Diening, F.** *Das Hebräische bei den Samaritanern. Ein Beitrag zur vormasoretischen
Grammatik des Hebräischen.* Stuttgart: Bonner Orientalische Studien, 1938.
[2600].

1055. **Díez Macho, A.** "Arameo-Samaritano." In *Enciclopedia de la Biblia.* Vol.5, 1965.
cols. 816-818.
[2800].

1056. —————. "La Legenda Hablada por Jesucristo." *OA* 11 (1963): 103-106.
[1800].

1057. **Díez Merino, Luis.** "El Arameo-Samaritano; estudios y textos." *EB* 40.3/4
(1982): 221-276.
[2800].

1058. —————. Reviewer. A. Tal, "The Samaritan Targum of the Pentateuch 1-3."
Aula Orientalis 1 (1983): 134-136.
[107/ 2401].

1059. —————. Reviewer. A. Tal, "The Samaritan Targum of the Pentateuch, 3."
(English and Hebrew) *EB* 42.1/2 (1984): 217-222.
[107/ 2401].

1060. **L. Dindorf,** editor, *Chronicon Paschale ad exemplar Vaticanum.* Bonnae, 1832. [The
Alexandrian chronicle].
[305.4/ 808].

86   Bibliography of the Samaritans

1061. **Dion, P. E. and Reinhard Pummer.** "A Note on the 'Samaritan Christian Synagogue'in Ramat Aviv." *JSJ* 11.2 (1980): 217-222.
[1304/ 1502].

1062. **Diringer, David.** *The Alphabet, a Key to the History of Mankind.* London, 1949. [See especially 242-243 and figs. 119-120].
[105/ 2501].

1063. ——————. "Early Hebrew Script v. Square Hebrew Script." In **D. Winton-Thomas,** editor, *Essays and Studies Presented to S. A. Cook.* Cambridge: Cambridge Oriental Series, 1950. 35-49.
[2501].

1064. **Dix, G. H.** "The Messiah ben Joseph." *JTS* 27 (1926): 130-143.
[1107].

1065. **Dobrowsky, Josephus.** *De Antiquis Hebraeorum Characteribus Dissertatio.* 55 pp. Prague, 1783. [There is a Czech version of this work, *Disertace o starych hebrejskych znacich (pisma), v nichz obzvlaste se obhajuje vernost Origenova a Jeronymova svedectvim Josefa Flavia,* in Miloslav Kanak, *Z nabozenskeho odkazu Josefa Dobrovskeho,* Prague, 1954].
[105/ 2501].

1066. **Dodd, C. H.** *The Interpretation of the Fourth Gospel.* Cambridge: CUP, 1960.
[1502.1].

1067. **Döderlein, Johann Christoph.** *Pentateuchus ad fidem recensionis Masoreticae, cum varietate lectionis Samaritanae et aliorum codicum Hebraeorum.* Halae and Berolini, 1818.
[2300].

1068. **Doikos, D.** "The Samaritan Schism." (Greek) *Gregorios Palamas* 57 (1974): 3-21.
[200/ 801.1].

1069. **Donaldson, T. L.** "Joseph's Tomb in Shechem." *TSBA* 2 (1873): 80-82.
[407.1].

1070. ——————. "Moses Typography and the Sectarian Nature of Early Christian Anti-Judaism: A Study in Acts 7." *JSNT* 12 (1981): 27-52.
[1502.2].

1071. **Doran, Robert.** "2 Maccabees 6: 2 and the Samaritan Question." *HTR* 76.4 (1983): 481-485.
[302.1/ 805].

1072. **Dorsey, David.** "Lateral and Local Roads of Samaria." In *The Roads and Highways of Ancient Israel.* Baltimore and London: Johns Hopkins University Press, 1991. 163-180.
[400.2/ 412].

1073. ——————. "Shechem and the Road Network of Central Samaria." *BASOR* 268 (November 1987): 57-70.
[400.2/ 412].

1074. **Downey, Glanville.** "Who Is My Neighbour? The Greek and Roman Answer." *ATR* 47 (1965): 3-15.
[808/ 1502.2].

1075. **Drabkin, Abraham.** *Fragmenta commentarii ad Pentateuchum Samaritano-Arabici sex, nunc primum edita atque illustrata.* Lipsae: William Drugulin, 1875. 60 pp. Inaugural dissertation, University of Leipzig.
[2302].

1076. **Drach, Paul L. B.** "Nouveaux documents sur les restes des samaritains." *Annales de Philosophie Chrétienne* (November, 1853): 361-363. Plate 82.
[903].

1077. **Drake, C. F. Tyrwhitt.** "Reports." *PEFQS* (1872): 174-193. [Includes notes by J. F. Kraus on a Samaritan manuscript known as the 'Fire tried'].
[103/ 2300].

1078. **Drane, J. W.** "Simon the Samaritan and the Lucan Concept of Salvation History." *EQ* 47.3 (1975): 131-137. [*NTAb* 20 (1978) no. 156].
[1502/ 1506.2].

1079. **Dresde, Fridericus W.** *De usu Pentateuchi Samaritani ad emendandam lectionem Hebr.* Vitebsk, 1782. 2 volumes.
[2300].

1080. **Dressler, L.** "The Blood Group Distribution Among the Jews in Israel." *Proceedings of the Fourth International Congress of Blood Transfusion.* 1951. 388-389.
[3500].

1081. **Dreyfus, J.** *Type Specimen Facsimiles.* London, 1963. [Two type specimen sheets show a Samaritan font].
[105].

1082. **Driver, G. R.** *The Judaean Scrolls.* Oxford & London: Blackwell, 1965. [Especially 78-80].
[1005].

1083. —————. Reviewer. J. Bowman, "Samaritanische Probleme." *JTS* 20 (1969): 267-269.
[107/ 1500].

1084. **Drori, M.** "Second Municipal Elections in Judaea and Samaria under Israel Administration:Legislative Changes." *ILR* 12.4 (1977): 526-540.
[813/ 903].

1085. **Drusius, Joannes the Elder.** *Alphabetum Hebraicum Vetus, Interpretatione Connexionesque nominum alphabeti ex Hieronymo et Eusebio.* Frankerae, 1587.
[105/ 2501].

1086. —————. "Praeteritorum libri 1." In J. Pearson, *Critici Sacri.* London, 1660.
[1200].

1087. —————. *De Sectis iudaicis commentarii.* Arnhemiae, 1619. [BL 1017 f.10].
[200/ 1500].

1088. **Du Buit, M.** "Le bon samaritain." *BTS* 184 (1976): 19-20.
[1502.3].

1089. —————. "The Good Samaritan." *A–B Samaritan News* 175 (1976): 11-12.
[1502.3].

1090. **Du Pin, L. E.** "Du Pentateuch Samaritain." In *Dissertation préliminaire ou prolégomènes sur la Bible.* 2nd. Paris, 1701. 1: 526-551.
[2300].

1091. **Duff, Douglas V.** "Ichabod: The Glory Has Departed." *Dublin Review* (October, 1933): 231-243.
[801.1].

1092. **Dugmore, Clifford W.** "Two Samaritan MSS in the Library of Queen's College, Cambridge." *JTS* 36 (1935): 131-146. [1 plate].
[101/ 103].

1093. **Dulière, W. L.** "La seconde circoncision pratiquée entre Juifs et Samaritains." *L'Antiquité Classique* 36.2 (1967): 553-565.
[1003.4/ 1204].

1094. **Dunn, J. D. G.** "They Believed Philip Preaching (Acts 8:12): A Reply." *Irish Biblical Studies* 1 (July, 1979): 177-183.
[1502.2].

1095. **Duret, Claude.** *L'histoire des langues de cet univers samaritaine, etc.* Cologny, 1613. Second edn., Yverdon, 1619.
[2600].

1096. **Durrell, David.** *The Hebrew Text of the Parallel Prophecies of Jacob and Moses...to Which are Added the Samaritan Arabic Version of those Passages and Part of Another Arabic Version Made from the Samaritan text...*Oxford: Clarendon Press, 1763.
[2300/ 2302].

1097. **Dussaud, R.** "Ecriture hebraïque et samaritaine." In C. Fossey, *Notices sur les caractères étrangers anciens et modernes.* Paris, 1948. 81-87. [Published for the 21st Congress of Orientalists].
[2501.1].

1098. —————. "Samarie au temps d'Achab." *Syria* 6 (1925): 314-338.
[801].

1099. **Duval, R.** Reviewer. E. Munk, "Des Samaritaners Marqah." *RC* 33 (1892): 221.
[107/ 1803].

1100. —————. Reviewer. J. H. Petermann, K. Vollers, "Pentateuchus Samaritanus ad Fidem Librorum." *RC* 32 (1891): 252-255.
[107/ 2300].

E

1101. **Ebertus, Theodorus.** *De Litteris Hebraicus.* Leipzig, 1664.
[2501].

1102. **Ecchellensis, Abraham.** *Chronicon Orientale Latinitate Donatum...Accessit Supplementum Historiae Orientalis ab eodem concinnatum.* Paris, 1651. [See also the Venice ed. 1729. Other editions known. Reprinted in *Corpus Scriptorum Christianorum Orientalium*].
[305.5/ 700].

1103. —————. "Prefatio ad Eutychi origines Ecclesiae Alexandriae h.e. contextionem gemmorum sive Eutychii Patriarchae Alexandrini Annales." *PL* 57 (1863).
[305.5/ 700].

1104. —————. *Tractatus continens Catalogum Librorum Chaldaeorum tam Ecclesiasticorum, quam profanorum Auctore Hebediesu Metropolita Sobensi.* Rome, 1653. [Especially p. 161f].
[105/ 2401/ 2501].

1105. **Eckstein, Adolf.** *Geschichte und Bedeutung der stadt Sichem.* Berlin: Itzkowski, 1886.
[412/ 801].

1106. **Edelstein, Judah.** "The Samaritan Complication in Research in Biblical Historiography." (Hebrew) *BM* 18-19.3-4 (1964): 135-153.
[801/ 801.1].

1107. **Edzardi, Sebastian.** *Jacobii Patriarchi de Shiloh Vaticinium a depravatiore Johannis Clerici in Pentateuchi Commentatoris.* London, 1673.
[2300].

1108. **Efrat, Elisha.** "Changes in the Settlement Pattern of Judaea and Samaria During Jordanian Rule." *MES* 13.1 (1977): 97-111.
[400.3].

1109. —————. *Judaea, Samaria and Gaza.* Jerusalem, 1982.
[400].

1110. **Egger, Rita.** "Josephus Flavius and the Samaritans." In **A. Tal & M. Florentin**, editors, *Proceedings of the First International Congress of the Société d'Études Samaritaines.* Tel Aviv: Chaim Rosenberg School for Jewish Studies, University of Tel Aviv, 1991. 109-114.
[303.5].

1111. —————. *Josephus Flavius und die Samaritaner: eine terminologische Untersuchung zur Identitätsklarung der Samaritaner.* Novum Testamentum. Freiburg und Göttingen: Universitätsverlag, Freiburg, 1986.
[303.5].

1112. **Ehrlich, Zev H.** "Samaria —Three Divisions That Are One." (Hebrew) in
Z.Ehrlich, editor, *Samaria and Benjamin.* Jerusalem, 1987. 221-223.
[400].

1113. —————, editor. (Hebrew) *Samaria and Benjamin— a Collection of Researches
on Historical Geography.* Jerusalem: The Society for the Protection of Nature,
1987.
[400/ 800].

1114. —————. "A Samaritan Source for Information About Ophrah, Near
Shechem." (Hebrew) *Cathedra* 28 (1983): 151-154.
[309.1/ 400].

1115. —————. "The Tomb of Joseph and the Covering Structure." (Hebrew) in Z.
Ehrlich, editor, *Samaria and Benjamin.* Jerusalem, 1987. 153-162.
[407.1/ 602].

1116. **Eichholz, Georg.** "Vom barmherzigen Samariter." In *Gleichnisse der Evangelien.
Form ueberlieferung Auslegung.* 1971. 148-178.
[1502.3].

1117. **Eichhorn, Johann Gottfried**, editor. *Allgemeine Bibliothek der Biblischen
Literatur.* Leipzig, 1787-1801. [Numerous articles on the Samaritans in this
journal are cited by Eichhorn's name].
[104].

1118. —————. *Einleitung ins Alte Testament.* Leipzig, 1787. [A number of other
editions from both Leipzig and Göttingen, 1780-1783, 1790, 1823 some with
the title *Einleitung in das Alte Testament.* Note the version printed in
translation for private circulation, *Introduction to the Study of the Old
Testament,* translated by G. T. Gollop, London, 1888].
[2300].

1119. —————. (Arabic & Latin) *Monumenta antiquissimae historiae Arabum (post
Albertum Schultensium).* Gothae, 1775.
[1003.3].

1120. —————, editor. *Repertorium für Biblische und Morgenländische Literatur.*
[Numerous articles on the Samaritans in this journal are cited by Eichhorn's
name].
[104].

1121. **Eilmer, George Christian.** *Samaritanismus: Neuer Samaritanischer Religions.*
Königsberg, 1708. [Lund University Library].
[1000].

1122. **Eisler, R.** "The Sadoqite Book of the New Covenant, its Date and Origins." In **B.
Schindler,** editor, *Occident and Orient: Essays in Honour of Haham Dr M.
Gaster's 80th Birthday.* London, 1936. 110-143.
[1003.4/ 1500].

1123. **Eissfeldt, Otto.** *Einleitung in das Alte Testament.* Tübingen, 1934. [Another
edition, 1976. An English edn., *The Old Testament an Introduction,* Blackwell,

Oxford, 1974].
[2300].

1124. **Elderen, B. van.** "Another Look at the Parable of the Good Samaritan." In James I.Cook, editor, *Saved by Hope*. Grand Rapids: Eerdmans, 1978. 109-119.
[1502.3].

1125. **Elhorst, H. J.** "De Messias der Samaritanen." *Theologisch Tijdschrift* 9 (1910): 533-545.
[1107].

1126. **Eliash, M.** "The Cuthites and Psalm 74." *JPOS* 5.1 (1925): 58-60.
[801.1].

1127. **Eligius.** "Homilies IX: 'de Vulnerato Samaritano'." *PL* 87: 627-630.
[305].

1128. **Ellis, Alexander George and E. Edwards.** *A Descriptive List of the Arabic Manuscripts Acquired by the Trustees of the British Museum Since 1894.* London, 1912. [Catalogues Or. 7562, bilingual Samaritan Pentateuch, c. 1200].
[101/ 103].

1129. **Ellis, Earle E.** Reviewer. J. Sanderson, "An Exodus Scroll from Qumran. 4Q Palaeo Ex^m and Samaritan Tradition." *Journal of Theology* 30 (1988): 44.
[107/ 1005/ 2307].

1130. **Ellis, Sir Henry,** editor. *The Pilgrimage of Sir Richard Guylforde to the Holy Land.* London: (Camden Society edition), 1851. [Other edns.].
[306.3].

1131. **Elmaliah, A.** "The Legal and Religious Status of the Samaritans in the Land of Israel." In *Encyclopaedia Judaica (yearbook).* Jerusalem, 1974. 4-6.
[813/ 903/ 1003.4].

1132. **Emerton, John.** Reviewer. Judith E. Sanderson, "4Q Paleo Exodus^m and the Samaritan Tradition." *VT* 37 (1987): 501.
[107/ 2307].

1133. —————. "The Site of Salem, the City of Melchizedek (Gen. xiv:18)." In John Emerton, editor, *Studies in the Pentateuch. SVT 41.* Leiden: Brill, 1990. 45-71.
[410.1].

1134. **Emmerich, L.** Das Siegeslied (Exodus cap.15) eine Schrifterklärung des Samaritaners Marqah.(Inaugural dissertation) Berlin: University of Giessen, 1897. [Printed by H. Izkowski: Chicago Oriental Institute Library BS 1248 M9M4].
[1803].

1135. **Engle, Anita.** "Galilee as a Centre of Glassmaking in the Roman Period." In *Readings in Glass History.* Jerusalem: Phoenix Books, 1973. 35-50. [Samaritan glassmakers].
[606.1/ 806].

1136. **Enslin, Morton S.** "Luke and the Samaritans." *HTR* 36 (1943): 277-297.
[1502.4].

1137. ────. "The Samaritan Ministry and Mission." *HUCA* 51 (1980): 29-38.
[1502].

1138. **Enslin, W.** "Theodoros." In *PRE.* 1934. II (R-Z) Fünfter Band, column 1905 f.
[Sinos dux Palaestinae 529 den Aufsland der Samaritaner].
[305.4/ 808].

1139. **Epiphanius, (Dubia aut Spuria).** "Liber de Vitis Prophetarum." *PG* 43: 411-418.
[305].

1140. ────. "Libri de Duodecim gemmis." *PG* 43: 351-356.
[305/ 305.4].

1141. ────. "Panarium- Against Heresies." *PG* 41: 219-238.
[1500/ 1503].

1142. **Epstein, Abraham.** *Eldad Hadani.* Pressburg, 1891. [A comparison of Samaritan
and Falasha halacha].
[1003.2/ 1106].

1143. ────. "A Hebrew Papyrus." *Beiträge zur Jüdischen Alterthumskunde* 1
(1887): 116-118. [A Samaritan papyrus].
[309.1].

1144. **Ericander, Magnus.** *Al Leshon Ukhetav Hashomronim. Sive de Lingua et Literis
Samaritanorum.* Upsaliae, 1733. [A dissertation of Uppsala University, 65 pp.
Chicago Oriental Institute library, PS 5271 E8].
[2501/ 2600].

1145. **Eshel, Hanan.** "The Prayer of Joseph, a Papyrus from Massada and the Samaritan
Temple on ARGARIZIN." *Zion* 56 (1991): 125-132.
[English summary: xii].
[1005/1305/3006.2].

1146. **Eulenstein, R.** " 'Und wer ist mein Nächster' Lk. 10, 25-37 in der Sicht eines
klassischen Philologen." *T und G* 67.2 (1977): 127-145.
[1502.4].

1147. **Eusebius of Caesaria.** "Ecclesiastical History." *PG.* 20: Cols. 383-386.
[305.4/ 808].

1148. ────. (Hebrew) **A. Z. Melammed,** editor, *Eusebius' Onomasticon.*
Jerusalem, 1950. [Melammed's translation was originally published in *Tarbiz*
19.2.3.4 (1948); **20**.2 (1949) 21.2 (1950)].
[305.4/ 400].

1149. **Euting, J.** "Epigraphische Miscellen." *SPAW* (1885): 679.
[2502].

1150. **Eutychius of Alexandria.** *Annales Latini.* PG. 3: cols. 955-958.
       [305/ 800].

1151. **Everts, William W.** "The Date of the Samaritan Pentateuch." *Homiletic Review* 56
       (1908): 193-196.
       [2300].

1152. **Ewald, G. H. A. von.** *Geschichte des Volkes Israel.* Göttingen, 1864-66. [English
       editions. See especially, 3:724f, 4:129f, 197f].
       [801.1].

1153. **Ewing, William.** Reviewer. **J. E. H. Thompson,** "The Samaritan Pentateuch and
       Higher Criticism (= a review of *The Samaritans, Their Testimony to the Religion
       of Israel.*" *The Expositor* (December, 1919): 451-469.
       [107/ 2300].

1154. ——————. "The Samaritans and Their Sacred Law. The Antiquity of the Five
       Books of Moses." *BS* 79 (1922): 418-451.
       [2300].

1155. **Eybers, I. H.** "Relations Between the Jews and the Samaritans in the Persian
       Period." In *Die OudeTestamentiese Werkgemeenskap van Suid-Afrika:Biblical
       Essays.* Proceedings of the Ninth Meeting held at the University of Stellenbosch
       (26-29 July 1966). Potchefstroom: Potchefstroom Herald, 1966. 72-89.
       [803].

F

1156. **Faber, Io Erhard and Lederer Guil. Ludov.** *Exercitatio Theologica de Calumnia Samaritanismi Christo Servatori a Iudaeis olim adspersa ad illustrationem Ioh. VIII, 48.* Tübingae, 1754.
[1502.1].

1157. **Fabricius, Johann Albert.** *Bibliotheca graeca, sive notitia scriptorum.* Hamburg, 1704-1728. 3 vols. [Several editions].
[2309/ 2400].

1158. ————. "Liber Josuae quem jactant Samaritani." *Codex Pseudepigraphus Veteris Testamenti Collectus Castigatus Testimonisque, Censuris Animadversionibus Illustratus.* Hamburg & Lipsiae: Christiani Liebezeit, 1713, 1722, 1723. 876-888. [Bodley Douce F. 406, 7].
[1604].

1159. **Fabricius, Johann the Younger.** *Muhammidis Testamentum sive Pacta cum Christianis in Oriente inita.* Rostochii, 1638.
[1003.1].

1160. **Fabricy, Gabriel.** *Des titres primitifs de la révélation...comparé avec les manuscrits hébreux et les anciennes versions...* Rome, 1772. 1: 373-385.
[1003.1/ 1100].

1161. **Falconer, R. A.** "Is Second Peter a Genuine Epistle to the Churches of Samaria." *The Expositor* 5.6th series (1902): 459-472.
[1003/ 1003.1/ 1502.2].

1162. **Falk, Z. W.** "Sectarian Halakha —The Samaritans." Chapter II, in *Introduction to the Jewish Law of the Second Commonwealth.* Leiden: Brill, 1972.
[1106].

1163. **Farkas, J.** "Discussions." (Hebrew) in **M. Klein and D. Dar,** editors, *The Blau Festschrift.* Budapest, 1926. 224-230.
[800].

1164. **Farmer, L.** *We Saw the Holy City.* London, 1944. Chapter 10.
[308].

1165. **Fassberg, Steven Ellis.** A Grammar of the Palestinian Targum Fragments from the Cairo Geniza (Aramaic).(Ph.D.) Boston: Harvard University, 1984.
[2800].

1166. **Federici, M.** "La Liturgia samaritana." *Revista storio-critica delle scienze teologiche* (1910): 600-607.
[2100].

1167. **Feldman, Louis H.** "Josephus' Portrait of Moses." *JQR* 82.3-4 (1992): 285-328.
[3008].

1168. —————. "Prolegomenon." In **M.R.James**, *The Biblical Antiquities of Philo*. 2nd. New York, 1971. vii-clxix.
[303/ 303.1].

1169. —————. "Religious Movements: the Samaritans: Josephus as a Source." In *Josephus and Modern Scholarship (1937- 1980)*. Berlin & New York: Walter de Gruyter, 1984. 528-541.
[303.5].

1170. —————. "Selected Literature on the Samaritans (Ant. xviii 29-30, 85-87 etc.)." In *Josephus, Jewish Antiquities*. Loeb Classical Library 9. London, 1965. 565. Appendix F.
[303.5].

1171. **Feldman, Louis H. and Gohei Hata**, editors. *Josephus, Judaism and Christianity*. Wayne State University Press, 1987. 257-273.
[303/ 303.1].

1172. **Felix, R., M. Amit, H. Birenboim, et al.** "A Psychological Comparative Study of the Samaritan Community, Shechem (Nablus) and Holon: I: General Survey." *IAP* 8.2 (1970): 123-136. [Part II: Felix, Amit, Bar-Yoseph & Wintner, *IAP* 9.2 (August 1971): 117-131].
[200/ 903/ 2904].

1173. **Ferrari, Bartolommeo.** *La Mission di Mosè, con una dissertazione sul Pentateuco Samaritano*. Milano, 1799. 8°. [A note on the Samaritan pentateuch by G.Almanzi].
[2300].

1174. **Fetellus.** *Description of the Holy Land*. London, 1896.
[306].

1175. **Février, J. G.** "Littérature samaritaine." In "Histoire des littératures, I", *Encyclopédie de la Pléiade*. Paris: Gallimard, 1955. 658-664.
[1550].

1176. **Ffoulkes, E. S.** "Gerizim." In **Wm.Smith**, *Dictionary of the Bible*. London: 1863. 1.
[406].

1177. **Field, F.** *Origenis Hexapla*. Oxford, 1875. 1: LXXXII-LXXXIV; 7-330. [Reprinted, Hildesheim, 1964].
[305.4/ 2400/ 2400.1].

1178. **Figueras, P.** "Dos inscripciones samaritanas inéditas." *BAEO* 6 (1970): 109-115.
[2500].

1179. **Finegan, J.** *The Archeology of the New Testament*. Princeton, 1969. 34-42. [Figs. 41-50].
[600/ 807].

1180. **Finkel, Joshua.** "Jewish, Christian and Samaritan Influences on Arabia." In *The Macdonald Presentation Volume*. Princeton, 1933. 147-166.
[1003.2].

1181. **Finkelstein, Louis.** *The Pharisees: the Sociological Background of their Faith.*
Philadelphia, 1938. II: 546-569.
[1003.1/ 1003.4].

1182. **Finn, James.** "The Samaritans in 1850." *PEFQS* 32 (1911). [Deals with the
Passover of 1850].
[903/ 1404].

1183. **Fischel, H. A.** "Jewish Gnosticism in the Fourth Gospel." *JBL* 65 (1946): 157-174.
[1502.1/ 1506].

1184. **Fischer, K.** "Verspengte Wächter mosaischen Glaubens." *Pogrom* 14.102-103
(1983): 47. [Study of the Samaritans today].
[813].

1185. **Fischer, O.** "Die Chronologie des Priesterkodex und ihre Umgestaltungen." *ZAW*
31 (1911): 241-255.
[700/ 1302/ 1600].

1186. **Fisk, George.** *A Pastor's Memorial of Egypt, the Dead Sea, the Wilderness of Sin.*
London, 1845. 3rd edn.
[306.3].

1187. **Fitzgerald, M.** "A Find of Stone Seats at Nablus." *PEFQS* (1929): 104-110. [Plate
17].
[600/ 606.1].

1188. **Fitzmyer, J.** "Further Light on Melchizedek from Qumran Cave 11." *JBL* 86
(1969): 25-41.
[2006].

1189. —————. "Now this Melchizedek: Hebrews 7:1." *CBQ* 25 (1963): 305-321.
[1003.1/ 2006].

1190. **Flavigny, Valerianus de.** *Epistola in qua de ingenti Bibliorum opera quod nuper
Lutetiae Parisiorum Hebraica, Graece... Samaritane.* Paris, 1646.
[2300].

1191. **Fleischhacker, A.** Der Tod Moses nach der Sage.(Doctoral dissertation) Halle:
University of Halle, 1888.
[1800/ 1801/ 3008].

1192. **Fleischmann, Paul.** "Von den Samaritern." *Orient im Bild* 7 (1934): 7.
[102/ 200/ 903].

1193. **Fleury, Claude. Adam Clarke,** editor, *The Manners of the Ancient Israelites with a
Short Account of the Ancient and Modern Samaritans.* 3rd edition. London,
1805. [1st edn. Paris, 1681; 2nd edn. 1780, also republished as part of the
Opuscules. 2nd English edn. 1809].
[800/ 903].

1194. **Florentin, Moshe.** Kavim beMaarachat Hapoal ha'Aramit Hashomronit–Iyyun
Diachroni al-pi Hachomer shebeTargum Hashomroni laTorah.(Hebrew) Tel

Aviv: Tel Aviv University, 1982. [Not for sale; contact author].
[2800].

1195. —————. "On the Lexical Character of the Late Samaritan (Hebrew)."
(Hebrew) in **A. Tal & M. Florentin**, editors, *Proceedings of the First
International Congress of the Société d'Études Samaritaines.* Tel Aviv: Chaim
Rosenberg School for Jewish Studies, University of Tel Aviv, 1991. 7*-12*.
[2603].

1196. —————. "The Object Suffixes in Samaritan Aramaic and the Modes of Their
Attachment to the Verb." *Abr Nahrain* 29 (1991): 67-82.
[2800].

1197. **Florentin, Moshe and A. Tal**, editors. *Proceedings of the First International
Congress of the Société d'Études Samaritaines. Tel Aviv.* Tel Aviv: Chaim
Rosenberg School for Jewish Studies, University of Tel Aviv, 1991.
[200].

1198. **Flusser, David**. "The Great Goddess of Samaria." *IEJ* 25.1 (1975): 13-20.
[801].

1199. **Fo'ad, Hassanein (Fu 'ad Hasanein Ali)**. "Beiträge zur Kenntnis der hebräisch-
samaritanischen Sprache." *Bulletin of the Faculty of Arts, Cairo* 8, 9 (1946-
1947): 19-37:17-84.
[2600].

1200. —————. "The Hebrew of the Samaritans." *Bulletin of the Faculty of Arts, Cairo*
6 (1942): 55-71. [Reprinted, 1953].
[2600].

1201. **Foerster, Werner**. "Die 'ersten Gnostiker' Simon und Menander." In **U. Bianchi**,
editor, *Le origini dello Gnosticismo*. Studies in the History of Religion. Leiden:
Brill, 1967. 12: 190-196.
[1506/ 1506.1/ 1506.2].

1202. —————. Reviewer. **Joachim Jeremias**, "Die Passahfeier der Samaritaner."
ZDPV 56 (1933): 196-198.
[107/ 1404].

1203. —————. "Stephanus und die Urgemeinde." In **Karl Janssen**, editor, *Dienst
unter dem Wort. Eine Festgabe für Prof. D. Dr Helmuth Schreiner zum 60
Geburtstag am 2 März 1953*. Gütersloh: Bertelsmann, 1953. 9-30.
[1502.2].

1204. **Fohrer, Georg**. "Die israelitischen Propheten in den Samaritanischen Chronik II."
In Memoriam Paul Kahle. Berlin: BZAW, 1968. 103: 129-137.
[1603].

1205. —————. Reviewer. **J.A. Montgomery**, "The Samaritans." *ZAW* 81 (1969):
139. [2nd edn].
[107/ 200].

1206. **Ford, J. Massyngbaerde** /Massingberd-. "Can We Exclude Samaritan Influence from Qumran?" *RQ* 6 (1967): 109-129.
[1005].

1207. —————. "Jesus' Peaceable Approach to the Hated Samaritans." In *My Enemy is My Guest: Jesus and Violence in Luke.* Maryknoll, New York: Orbis Books, 1984. 79-95.
[1003.1/ 1502.4].

1208. **Fossum, Jarl.** "Gen.1, 26 and 2, 7 in Judaism, Samaritanism and Gnosticism." *JSJ* 16.2 (1985): 202-239.
[1003.4/ 1506/ 2305].

1209. —————. "Gnosticism and Samaritan Judaism." In **W. Haasse,** editor, *Religion. Gnostizismus und Verwandtes.* Tübingen: 1981.
[1506].

1210. —————. "Kyrios Jesus as the Angel of the Lord in Jude 5-7." *NTS* 33 (1987): 226-243.
[1101/ 1105].

1211. —————. *The Name of God and the Angel of the Lord. Samaritan and Jewish Concepts of Intermediation and the Origin of Gnosticism.* Tübingen: J.C.B.Mohr (Paul Siebeck), 1985. [Abstract: *NTAb* 30:2 (1986) p.247 & *Theology Digest* 33:2 (1986) p. 270a].
[1101/ 1104/ 1506].

1212. —————. "Reminisenser av det 'kongliche mönstret' i samaritanismen." *Religion och Bibel* [1983-1984] 42-43 (1985): 45-62.
[1105/ 3008].

1213. —————. "Samaritan Demiurgical Traditions and the Alleged Dove Cult of the Samaritans." In **R. van den Broek & M.J. Vermaseren,** editors, *Studies in Gnosticism and Hellenistic Religions Presented to Gilles Quispel on the Occasion of his 65th Birthday.* Leiden: Brill, 1981. 143-160.
[1002/ 1102].

1214. —————. "Samaritan Sects and Movements." In **Alan D. Crown,** editor, *The Samaritans.* Tübingen: Mohr, 1989. 293-389.
[1500/ 1503/ 1504].

1215. **Foster, W.** *The Travels of John Sanderson in the Levant, 1534-1602.* London, 1931.
[308].

1216. **Foucher, A.** "La Samarie et les Origines de la Mission chrétienne." *AEPHE* (1953): 2-99.
[1002].

1217. **Fournier, Le Jeune.** *Manuel Typographique.* Paris, 1766. [See especially, p. 242-248].
[105].

1218. **Fowler, M. D.** "A Closer Look at the Temple of El-Berith at Shechem." *PEQ* 115.1 (1983): 49-53.
[412/ 1305].

1219. **Fraenkel, Siegmund.** Reviewer. A. S. Yahuda, "Das Buch Josua bei den Samaritanern (=Zum Samaritanischen Josua. Eine Erklärung)." *TLZ* 33 (1908): columns 481-483.
[107/ 1604/ 1605].

1220. ——————. "Miscellen zum Koran, §3 Der Sâmirî." *ZDMG* 56 (1902): 73f.
[307/ 1003.3].

1221. **Fraine, J. de.** *Atlas Historico y Cultural de la Biblia.* Madrid, 1963.
[200].

1222. **Frankel, Zechariah.** *Historisch-kritische Studien zu der Septuaginta nebst beiträgen zu den Targumim.* Vorstudien zu der Septuaginta. Leipzig: F. C. W. Vogel, 1841. Bd.I, abt.7.
[2300/ 2305/ 2400].

1223. ——————. *Über den Einfluss der palästinnischen Exegese auf die alexandrinische Hermeneutik.* Leipzig: J. A. Barth, 1851.
[2300/ 2305/ 2400].

1224. **Frankl, Ludwig August.** *Nach Jerusalem.* Leipzig, 1858. [Several editions. See especially pp. 441, 516].
[309/ 903].

1225. **Franklin, G. E.** *Palestine Depicted and Described.* London, 1911.
[102/ 308].

1226. **Fraser, James G.** The British Museum MS Or. 5034 of the Samaritan Defter.Melbourne: M. A. Dissertation, 1965.
[103/ 2102.1].

1227. ——————. "A Checklist of Samaritan Manuscripts Known to Have Entered Europe Before AD 1700." *AN* 21 (1983): 10-27.
[103].

1228. ——————. "Documents from a Samaritan Genizah in Damascus." *PEQ* (1971): 85-92.
[103/ 503].

1229. ——————. "The First Attempt at Collating the Text of a Samaritan Pentateuch." *Harvard Library Bulletin* 19.2 (1971): 160-164.
[103/ 2300].

1230. ——————. "Guillaume Postel and Samaritan Studies." In *Postello, Venezia e il suo mondo, a cura di M.L.Kunz.* Firenze, 1988. 99-117.
[105].

1231. —————. The History of the Defter of the Samaritan Liturgy. (Ph.D. dissertation) Melbourne: University of Melbourne, 1970. [103/ 2100/ 2102.1].

1232. —————. "Marginalia of the Bibliothèque Nationale MS Samaritain 2." *AN* 11 (1971): 105-109. [103/ 2300].

1233. —————. "A Prelude to the Samaritan Pentateuch Texts of the Paris Polyglot Bible." In J. D. Martin & P. R. Davies, *A Word in Season: Essays in Honour of William McKane.* Sheffield: JSOT supplement, 1986. 42: 223-247. [103/ 2300].

1234. —————. "Ussher's Sixth Copy of the Samaritan Pentateuch." *VT* 21.1 (1971): 100-102. [103/ 2300].

1235. **Freed, Edwin D.** "Did John Write His Gospel Partly to Win Samaritan Converts?" *NT* 12.3 (1970): 241-256. [*NTAb* 15 (1970-1971) no.554]. [1502.1].

1236. —————. "Egó Emi in John 1:20 & 4:25." *CBQ* 41 (1979): 288-291. [1502.1].

1237. —————. "The Manner of Worship in John 4, 23." In Festschrift for R. T. Stamm, **J. M. Meyers** et. al., editor, *Search the Scriptures.* Leiden: Brill, 1969. 33-48. [1502.1].

1238. —————. "Samaritan Influence in the Gospel of John." *CBQ* 30.4 (1968): 580-587. [*NTAb* 13 (1968) no.609]. [1502.1].

1239. **Freedman, Albert.** "Blood Groups Could be a Vital Clue to Our History." *Australian Jewish Times* (14 February 1985). [3500].

1240. **Freedman, D. N., G. A. Herion and D. F. Graf and J. D. Pleins,** editors. The following articles should be noted. "Aenon" I.87 (J. A. Pattengale) "Daliyeh, Wadi-El" II 3-4 (F. M. Cross) "Gerizim, Mount" II 993 (J. K. Lott) "Jacob's Well" III 608 (Z. Stefanovic) "Salem" V 905 (M. C. Astour) "Samaria" V 914-921 (J. D. Purvis) "Samaria-Archaeological Survey of the Region" V 926-931 (S. Dar) "Samaria Papyri" V 931-932 (D. M. Gropp) "Samaritan Pentateuch" V 932-940 (B. K. Waltke) "Samaritans" V 940-947 (R. T. Anderson) "Sanballat" V 973-975 (H. G. Williamson) "Shechem" V 1174-1186 (L. E. Toombs)." In *The Anchor Bible Dictionary.* 5 vols. London, New York: Doubleday, 1992. [201/ 303.3/ 400 / 401.2 / 406 / 407 / 410 / 412 / 600 / 801 / 802.1 /2300].

1241. **Freedman, D. N. and K. A. Mathews.** *The Paleo-Hebrew Leviticus Scroll (11QpalaeoLev).* Winona Lake, Indiana: AASOR/Eisenbrauns, 1985. [103/2307/2309].

1242. **Frentzken, Joannes Daniel.** Disputatio Philologica prima et secunda de causis odii, Judaeos inter aque Samaritanos. (Doctoral dissertation) Trajecti ad Rhenum: University of Utrecht, 1725. [BL T. 2184(16)]. [1003.4/ 2600].

1243. **Freudenthal, Jacob.** *Hellenistische Studien: Alexander Polyhistor und die von ihm erhalten Reste jüdischer und samaritanischer Geschichtswerke.* Breslau: Jüdische-theologisches Seminar, 1875. [Reprinted from the Jahresbericht des jüdische-theologischen Seminars, 1874-1875]. [2000/ 2001/ 2002/ 2003/ 2005].

1244. **Frick, C.** Reviewer. A.Wirth, "Aus orientalischen Chroniken." *GGA* 157 (1895): 940-947. [107/ 1600].

1245. **Frickel, J. H.** "'Die Apophasis Megale' in Hyppolyt's Refutatio (VI: 9-18)." *Analecta Orientalia Christiana* 182 (1968). [1506.2].

1246. ——————. "'Die Apophasis Megale' eine Grundschrift de Gnosis?" In U. Bianchi, editor, *Le Origini dello Gnosticismo.* Studies in the History of Religion 12. Leiden: Brill, 1967. 197-202. [1506/ 1506.2].

1247. **Friederich, Gerhard.** *Wer ist Jesus? Die Verkündigung des vierten Evangelisten dargestellt an Johannes 4, 4-42.* Biblisches Seminar. Stuttgart: Calwer Verlag, 1967. [1502.1].

1248. **Friederich, Joan Christoph.** *Discussionem de christologia Samaritanorum liber. Accedit appendicula de Columba dea Samaritanum.* Lipsae, 1821. [1003.1/ 1502].

1249. **Friedlander, G.** *Pirke de Rabbi Eliezer.* London, 1916. [Reprinted New York, 1971]. [304].

1250. **Friedman, Mordechai A.** *Jewish Marriage in Palestine: A Cairo Genizah Study.* Tel Aviv & New York: Jewish Theological Seminary, 1980. [2 vols.]. [1205/1208].

1251. **Fritz, Johann Friederich.** *Orientalisch und occidentalischer Sprachmeister...hundert Alphabete nebst ihrer Aussprache...auch einigen Tabulis Polyglottis.* Leipzig, 1748. [105/ 2501].

1252. **Frommberger, G.** De Simone Mago. (Doctoral dissertation) Breslau: University of Breslau, 1886. [1506.2].

1253. **Frondel, Ericus.** *Dissertation philologica natales linguae literarumque Samaritanarum.* Upsalis: Wernerianis, 1717. 56 pp. 8°. [Frondel's *Response,* to the discussion of his dissertation was published in 1774 in J.Oelrichs *Daniae ac*

Sveciae litteratae opuscula, vol.2].
[2600].

1254. **Frumkin, A.** "Truly water was unknown in Samaria." (Hebrew) *Teva Va'aretz* 20 (1977): 172-177.
[400.5].

1255. **Fulco, W. J. and F. Zayadine.** "Coins from Samaria-Sebastiya." *ADAJ* 25 (1981): 197-225.
[410/ 603].

1256. **Funk, Robert W.** "The Good Samaritan as a Metaphor." *Semeia* 2 (1974): 74-81.
[*NTAb* 19(1975) no. 982].
[1502.3].

1257. ——————. "How Do You Read? A Sermon on Luke 10: 25-37." *Interpretation* 18 (1964): 56-61.
[1502.4].

1258. ——————. "The Old Testament in Parable. A Study of Luke 10: 25-37." *Encounter* 26.2 (1965): 251-267. [Reprinted as "Language, Hermeneutic and Word of God" in *The Problem of Language in the New Testament and Contemporary Theology*, 1966:199-222].
[1502.4].

1259. **Furness, J. M.** "Fresh Light on Luke 10:25-37." *ET* 80.6 (1969): 182f.
[1502.4].

1260. **Fürst, Julius.** "Judischer Bevolker in Nablus." *Der Orient. Berichte, Studien und Kritiken für jüdische Geschichte und Literatur* 1 (1840): 1-3.
[801.1/ 1003].

1261. ——————. "Zur Differenz Zwischen Juden und Samaritanern." *ZDMG* 35 (1881): 132-138. [*The American Journal of Philology* 2 (1881) p.381 carries a report of the article].
[1003.4].

G

1262. **Gabay, A.** "Les samaritains." *A–B* no.202.(15/1/78) [200/ 903].

1263. —————. "Les samaritains, vestiges et dépérissement d'une secte." *Information Juive* no. 277 (December, 1977): 5-7. [200/ 903].

1264. **Gafni, Yeshayahu.** Relations Between Jews and Samaritans in Talmudic and Mishnaic Times. (Hebrew, M. A. dissertation) Jerusalem: Hebrew University, 1969. [304/ 807/ 808/ 1003.4].

1265. —————. "The Samaritans and Their Dwelling Places." (Hebrew) In **S. Dar &** **Y. Roth,** editors, *Eretz Shomron.* Tel Aviv, 1971. 166-181. [400.3].

1266. **Gagnier, J.** "Epistola de Nummis Samaritanis." In **B. Ugolini,** editor, *Thesaurus.* Venice, 1765. Vol. 28: 1283-1286. [603/ 2501].

1267. —————. "Lettre sur les médailles samaritaines expliquées par M. Reland." In *Memoires de Trevoux.* Sept. 1705. 1643-1648. [603/ 2501].

1268. **Galbiati, Giovanni.** "Materiali per un corpus Iuris dei Samaritani nei Fontes Ambrosiani." In **P. Hennequin,** editor, *Mélanges Eugene Tisserant, Studii e Texti.* Rome, 1964. 1: 209-215. [103/ 1106].

1269. **Galton, Francis.** "Nabloos and the Samaritans (in 1861)." In **G. Grove,** *Narrative of an Explorer in Tropical South Africa, also Vacation Tours in 1860 and 1861.* Melbourne: Ward Lock, 1889. 241-258. [Other editions]. [813/ 903].

1270. **Garber, Z.** "The Samaritan Passover." *CCAR* 22 (1975): 41-44. [1404].

1271. **García Martínez, Florentino.** Reviewer. **A. D. Crown,** "The Samaritans." *JSJ* 21.1 (1990): 102-104. [107/ 200].

1272. **Garner, G. G.** "The Temples of Mt. Gerizim—Tel er Ras. The Probable Site of the Samaritan Temple." *Buried History* 11 (1975): 33-42. [406/ 415/ 600/ 1305].

1273. **Garratt, S.** "Date of the Samaritan Pentateuch." *Thinker* 1 (August, 1892): 112-114. [2300].

1274. —————. "The Samaritan Pentateuch." *JTVI* 36 (1904): 197-213.
      [2300].

1275. **Gaster, Moses.** *The Asatir, The Samaritan Book of the Secrets of Moses Together
      with the Pitron or Samaritan Commentary and the Samaritan Story of the Death
      of Moses.* London: Oriental Translation Fund, N. S. Vol. 26, 1927. [Printed in
      Leipzig].
      [1801].

1276. **Gaster, Moses.** "The Biblical Lessons: A Chapter on Biblical Archaeology." *The
      Jewish Review* (1913): 88f. [Reprinted in Studies and Texts 1: 503-599].
      [1304/ 1400/ 2308].

1277. —————. "The Chain of the Samaritan High Priests. A Synchronistic
      Synopsis." *JRAS* (1909): 393-420. [Reprinted, *Studies &Texts* 3:131-138].
      [700/1302].

1278. —————. "Das Buch Josua in hebräisch-samaritanischer Rezension. Entdeckt
      und zum ersten Male herausgegeben." *ZDMG* 62.209-279, 494-549 (1908).
      [Reprinted, Leipzig 1908: 127 pp].
      [1604].

1279. —————. "Das samaritanische Buch Josua." *AZJ* 72 (1908): 307-309.
      [1604].

1280. —————. "Die 613 Gebote und Verbote der Samaritaner (Ibrahim al Kabasi)."
      (German & Hebrew) in *Festschrift zum 75-jahrigen Bestehen des jüdisch
      theologischen Seminars Fraenkelscher Stiftung.* Breslau, 1929. 2: 393-404 & 35-
      67 (Hebrew section). [The Hebrew title is different : 'Taryag Mitzvot shel
      haShomronim'].
      [1102/ 1108].

1281. —————. "Die Ketubbah bei den Samaritanern." *MGWJ* 54 (1910): 174-188;
      289-304; 433-451; 571-587. [Reprinted in *Studies and Texts* 3:139-204].
      [1207].

1282. —————. Reviewer. J. Jeremias, "Die Passahfeier der Samaritaner." *MGWJ* 77
      (1933): 308-312. [Idem *JRAS* (1934) 805-807].
      [107/ 1303/ 1404].

1283. —————. "Eine samaritanische Buch Josua." *Die Welt* 24 (1908): 18-19.
      [1605].

1284. —————. "The Feasts of Jeroboam and the Samaritan Calendar." *ET* 24
      (1913): 198-201.
      [1001/ 1400].

1285. —————. "The Genuine Samaritan Book of Joshua." *The Times* (9 June 1908
      & 17 June 1908): 6, 18.
      [1605].

1286. —————. "Jewish Knowledge of the Samaritan Alphabet in the Middle Ages."
        JRAS .613-626 (1913): [Reprinted in *Studies and Texts* 1:600-613].
        [105].

1287. —————. "The Jewish Sects: The Samaritans." *The Jewish World* 51.19 (3
        February 1899): 295-296.
        [202].

1288. —————. *Les Samaritains (leur histoire, leurs doctrines, leurs littérature).*
        Translator. Bernard Duborg. Paris: QEIL, 1984. [= the Schweich lectures, *The
        Samaritans*].
        [200].

1289. —————. "Magic (Jewish)." *ERE* 8 (1917): 300-305.
        [1104].

1290. —————. "Massoretisches im Samaritanischen." In **C. Bezold**, editor,
        Orientalische Studien Theod. Nöldeke zum 70sten Geburstag (2 März 1906).
        Giessen, 1906. 513-536. [Reprinted in Studies and Texts 1: 614-637].
        [2306.1].

1291. —————. Reviewer. **A. Merx**, "Der Messias; oder Ta'eb der Samaritaner."
        ZDMG 64 (1910): 445-455.
        [107/ 1107].

1292. —————. "Molad Mosheh: The Samaritan Legends of the Birth of Moses."
        The Quest 21 (1930): 358-372.
        [1802].

1293. —————. "On the Newly Discovered Samaritan Book of Joshua." *JRAS*
        (1908): 759-809, 1143-1156.
        [1604/ 1605].

1294. —————. "Ordination, Jewish." *ERE* 9 (1917): 552-555.
        In.
        [1302].

1295. —————. "Parsiism in Judaism." *ERE* 9 (1917): 637-640.
        [1100].

1296. —————. "The Passing of a Nation." *Reflex* 1 (1927): 23-27.
        [202].

1297. —————. "Popular Judaism at the Time of the Second Temple in the Light of
        Samaritan Traditions." *Transactions for the Third International Congress for the
        History of Religions* 1 (1908): 298-302. [An abstract].
        [1001].

1298. —————. "Reply to the letter of E. N. Adler on the 'Samaritan Book of
        Joshua'." *JRAS* (October, 1908): 1148-1156.
        [1605].

1299. ——————. "The Samaritan Book of Joshua and the Septuagint." *PSBA* 31
      (1909): 115-127; 149-153.
      [1605/ 2400].

1300. ——————. "The Samaritan Calendar." *The Jewish Review* (Sept. 1913): 243-
      262.
      [1400].

1301. ——————. "The Samaritan Hebrew Sources of the Arabic Book of Joshua."
      JRAS (1930): 567-600, plate 6.
      [1604/ 1605].

1302. ——————. "The Samaritan Literature." (Supplement to the Author's Article
      "The Samaritans") in *Encyclopaedia of Islam*. Leiden: Brill, 1925. [Reprinted as
      "Die Samaritanische Litteratur" in Dexinger and Pummer, *Die Samaritaner*
      141-186].
      [1550].

1303. ——————. "A Samaritan Manuscript of the Second or Third Century: A
      Palaeographic Study." *JRAS* (1918): 68-83. [Reprinted in *Studies and Texts*
      1:462-482].
      [103/ 2501.1].

1304. ——————. *The Samaritan Oral Law and Ancient Traditions 1. Samaritan
      Eschatology*. London: Search Publishing Co., 1932. [Vol. 1. only was
      published].
      [1106/ 2306.1].

1305. ——————. "The Samaritan Passover." *JC* (27 March 1896): 19.
      [1404].

1306. ——————. Reviewer. **A.F.Von Gall**, "The Samaritan Pentateuch (=Der
      Hebräische Pentateuch der Samaritaner)." *JC* (16 Jan. 1920).
      [107/ 2300].

1307. ——————. "Samaritan Phylacteries and Amulets." *PSBA* 37-40 (1914-1917):
      38:96-107, 135-144, 163-174; 39:70-79, 96-104, 186-195, 202-237; 40:16-26,
      45-50. Plates 1-3. [Reprinted in *Studies and Texts* 1: 387-482].
      [601/ 1211].

1308. ——————. "The Samaritan Pilgrims (An Editorial Note)." *The Jewish World* (30
      November 1906).
      [309.2/ 1400].

1309. ——————. "Samaritan Scroll of the Law." *JC* (10 Feb.1899): 31.
      [2301].

1310. ——————. "A Samaritan Scroll of the Hebrew Pentateuch." *PSBA* 22 (1900):
      240-269.
      [2300/ 2309.1].

1311. ——————. "The Samaritan Scroll of the Law." *The Jewish World* (23 November 1906, pt.1) (30 November 1906, pt. 2): 611, 622-623.
[2301].

1312. ——————. "The Samaritans." *JC* (3 Feb. 1899): 21.
[200].

1313. ——————. "Samaritans." In *The Encyclopaedia of Islam*. Leyden: Brill, 1924. Vol.4: 132-138.
[201].

1314. ——————. "The Samaritans." *The Jewish Forum* no.151.5-6 (March 1929): 113-119, 251-257.
[200/ 202].

1315. ——————. "The Samaritans in London." *The Jewish World* (24 August 1906): 336.
[813.2/ 903].

1316. ——————. *The Samaritans, Their History, Doctrines and Literature*. London: Schweich Lectures for 1923, 1925. [Reprinted 1980, and by the Gordon Press, 1976].
[200/ 800/ 1550].

1317. ——————. "The Story of the Daughter of Amram: the Samaritan parallel to the Apocryphal Story of Susanna." *Studies and Texts* 1 199-210. [Reprinted from JA].
[1800].

1318. ——————. *Studies and Texts in Folklore, Magic, Medieval Romance, Hebrew Apocrypha and Samaritan Archaeology*. London: Maggs Bros. 1925-1928. 3 volumes. [Reprinted, Ktav, New York,1971].
[200/ 1000/ 1100/ 1200/ 1300/ 1400/ 1600].

1319. ——————. "Transmigration (Jewish)." *ERE* 12: 435-440.
[1100].

1320. ——————. "Water, Water Gods." In *ERE*. Vol. 12: 713-716.
[1110].

1321. **Gaster, Moses and Theodor H. Gaster.** "Rites and Beliefs of the Samaritans Relating to Death and Mourning." *JPOS* 19 (1939-1940): 180-212.
[1203/ 2103].

1322. **Gaster, M., B. Schindler, A. S. Yahuda and D. Yellin.** "The Samaritan Book of Joshua." (An exchange of letters) *The Times (9, 17 June, 3, 5 Oct.,3, 5 Nov. 1908) The Sunday Times (18 Oct.1908) The Jewish World (3 July 1908; 9 April 1909) The Jewish Chronicle (10 July, 30 Oct. 1908)*.
[1604/ 1605].

1323. **Gaster, Theodor H.** "Samaritan Proverbs." *Studies and Essays in Honour of Abraham A. Neuman*. Leiden: Brill, 1962. 228-242.
[1108].

1324. —————. "The Samaritans." In G. A. Buttrick, editor, *Interpreter's Dictionary of the Bible*. Nashville: Abingdon Press, 1962. Vol. 4: 190-197. [200/ 201].

1325. —————. "The Samaritan Book of Joshua." In *The Universal Jewish Encyclopaedia*. New York, 1948. [201/ 1604/ 1605].

1326. —————. Reviewer. E. Robertson, "Samaritan Manuscripts." (= Review of *Catalogue of the Samaritan Manuscripts vol. 1*) *Journal of Jewish Bibliography* 2.1 (October, 1940): 127-135. [101/ 103/ 107].

1327. —————. "A Samaritan Poem About Moses." In A. Berger, L. Marwick and I. S. Meyer, *Studies in Booklore and History: The Joshua Bloch Memorial Volume*. New York: New York Public Library, 1960. 115-139. [Includes a long comment on and corrections to S. Miller, *Molad Mosheh*.]. [107/ 3008].

1328. —————. "The Samaritans." In *The Universal Jewish Encyclopaedia*. New York, 1948. 9: 335-339. [200/ 201].

1329. Gatt, G. "Das Osteropfer der Samaritaner nach samaritanischen Quellen." *DHL* 2 (1897): 29-31. [1303/ 1404].

1330. —————. "Das Pfingstfest der Samaritaner nach samaritanischen Quellen." *DHL* 4 (1899): 51f. [1407].

1331. —————. "Die Kibla oder der auserwahlte ort nach d. Anschauungen der Samaritaner." *DHL* 2 (1897): 31-35. [1003.3/ 1100].

1332. —————. "Die Sabbathfeier der Samaritaner nach samaritanischen Quellen." *DHL* 1 (1896): 228-230. [1303/ 1405].

1333. —————. "Der grosse Buss und Verhsohnungstag der Samaritaner nach samaritanischen Quellen." *DHL* 1 (1896): 230f. [1111/ 1401].

1334. Geiger, Abraham. "Bibelkritische Miscellen" 7. "Samaritanische Lesarten in der Halachah." *JZWL* 4 (1866): 42-43. [1106/ 2300].

1335. —————. "Biblische und talmudische Miscellen, 10. Ketav Livonah und Milon." *JZWL* 5 (1867): 115-117. [2501.1].

1336. ——————. Reviewer. T. Nöldeke, "Die hebräische Grammatik bei der Samaritanern." (=Review of Über die aussprache) *ZDMG* 17 (1863): 718-725. [107/ 2602].

1337. ——————. "Einleitung in die biblischen Schriften" 11." Der samaritanische Pentateuch" 20. Uebersetzungen unter den Samaritanern." In *Nachgelessene Schriften*. Berlin, 1876. 4: 54-67, 121-132. [2300/ 2401].

1338. ——————. "Genesis 6, 3 bei den Samaritanern." *ZDMG* 28 (1874): 489-491. [2305].

1339. ——————. "Nachträgliche Bemerkung zu Bd.XX dieser Zeitschrift." *ZDMG* 21 (1867): 279-281. [1003.4/ 1100/ 2300].

1340. ——————. Reviewer. M. Heidenheim, "Neuere Mitteilungen über die Samaritaner." (=includes a review of Untersuchungen über die Samaritaner) *ZDMG* 16-22 (1862-1868): 1(1862) 714-728; 2-3 (1864): 590-597; 4 (1865): 601-615; 5 (1866): 143-170; 6 (1867): 169-182; 7 (1868) 528-538. [200].

1341. ——————. "Der samaritanische Pentateuch." In *Nachgelassene Schriften*. Berlin, 1876. Vol.4. [2300].

1342. ——————. "Über die gesetzlichen Differenzen zwischen Samaritanern und Juden." *ZDMG* 20 (1866): 527-575. [Reprinted in *Nachgelasse Schriften* 3: 283-321]. [1003.4/ 1100/ 2300].

1343. ——————. *Urschrift und übersetzungen der Bible.* Breslau, 1857. [2nd. edn. Frankfurt, 1928. 1st. Hebrew edn. *Hamiqra vetargumav*, trs. Y. L. Baruch, Jerusalem, 1949. 2nd. Hebrew edn. 1972]. [2300/ 2307].

1344. ——————. *Was Hat Mohammed aus dem Judenthum aufgenommen?* Baden, 1833. [Reprinted Leipzig, 1902 & Osnabrück, 1971: reprinted in F. M. Young's translation, 1896 and by Ktav, New York, 1970, with a prolegomenon by Moshe Pearlman. See especially the treatment of the Samiri, p.130f in the English version and p.162f in the original]. [200/ 307/ 1003.3].

1345. ——————. "Zur Theologie und Schrifterklärung der Samaritaner." *ZDMG* 12 (1858): 132-142. [Reprinted in *Nachgelessene Schriften*, 3: 255-266]. [1100/ 2300].

1346. Geiger, Ludwig, editor. *Abraham Geiger's Nachgelessene Schriften.* Berlin, 1875-1878. 5 vols. [200].

1347. Gelbhaus, Sigmund. *Eine absterbende Rebe am Weinstocke Israels.* Wien: 1894. [1003.3/ 1109].

1348. **Gelhaus, I.** "Contributions à l'histoire des Samaritains." *Sammelbuch für Wissenschaft und Literatur* 1.Krakau (1905).
[800].

1349. **Genna, Giuseppe E.** "Antropologia dei Samaritani." *16th International Congress of Anthropology and Prehistoric Archaeology.* 1935. Brussels, 1935. 128-135.
[2900/ 2901].

1350. —————. *I Samaritani. 1: Antropologia.* Roma: Comitato italiano per lo studio dei problemi della popolazione, ser. 5; Spedizioni scientifiche vol. 1, 1938.
[2900/ 2901].

1351. —————. "Una inchiesta sui Samaritani." *Revista di Antroplogia.* Roma (1933/4): 483-487.
[2900/ 2901].

1352. **Genuyt, F.** "Evangile de Jean. L'entretien avec la Samaritaine, 4,1-42. Analyse sémiotique." *Sémiotique et Bible* 36 (1984): 15-24.
[1502.1].

1353. **Gerhardsson, G.** "The Good Samaritan—The Good Shepherd." *CNT* 16 (1958).
[1502.3].

1354. —————. "Joh. 4: 5-26, Joh. 4: 27-42." *Kommentar till evangelienboken* 2 (1964): 204-209.
[1502.1].

1355. **Gerlemann, Gillis.** *Synoptic Studies in the O.T.:* Lunds Universitet Årsskrift n.f.54, 1948. vol. 5: 36pp.
[2300/ 2400].

1356. **Germer-Durand, J.** "Épigraphie palestinienne." *RB* 3 (1894): 153-154, 248-257.
[2502].

1357. —————. "Sceau de Balian, seigneur de Naplouse." *Echos d'orient* 8 (1905): 13f.
[306/ 810].

1358. **Gerson-Kiwi, Edith.** "Zur Musiktradition der Samaritaner." *Baessler Archiv (Beiträge zur völkerkunde)* 23 (1975): 139-144.
[3300].

1359. **Gese, H.** Reviewer. J. Macdonald, "Samaritan Chronicle II." *OLZ* 69 (1974): 151-157.
[107/ 1603].

1360. **Gesenius, F. H. W.** *Carmina Samaritana e codicibus Londinensibus et Gothanis editit et interpretatione Latina cum commentario illustravit.* Anecdota Orientalia. Leipzig: C. G. Vogel, 1824. Part 1. [Nothing further published].
[101/ 103].

1361. —————. *Geschichte der hebräischen Sprache und Schrift.* Leipzig, 1815. [Pp. 84-87. Reprinted, Hildesheim, 1973]. [2600/ 2501].

1362. —————. *De pentateuchi samaritani origine, indole et auctoritate: commentatio philologico-critica.* Halae, 1815. [2300].

1363. —————. *De Samaritanorum theologia ex fontibus ineditis commentatio.* Halae, 1822. [1100].

1364. —————. *Scripturae Linguaque Phoeniciae Monumenta Quotquot Supersunt.* Leipzig, 1837. §52 Scriptura Samaritanorum p. 79ff. [2300].

1365. —————. *Thesaurus Philologicus Criticus Linguae Hebraeae et Chaldaeae Veteris Testamenti.* Lipsae, 1829. [In this early edition of the Thesaurus many examples were presented from Samaritan lexicography and grammar]. [2602/ 2603].

1366. **Geshuri, M. S.** "Samaritan Music." (Hebrew) *Proceedings for the Israel Institute for Religious Music* 3 (1962): 87-89. [3300].

1367. **Gevaryahu, H. M. I.** "Lecture on Problems of Samaritan Hebrew." *BM* 1 (1956): 126-127. [1000].

1368. **Geysar, A. S.** "Israel in the Fourth Gospel." *Neotestamentica* 20 (1986): 13-20. [1502.1].

1369. **Giavini, G.** "Il 'prossimo' nella parabola del buon Samaritano." *Rivist. Bib.* 12.4 (1964): 419-421. [Reprinted *NTAb* 10 (1965) no. 153]. [1502.3].

1370. **Gichon, M.** "The Plan of a Roman Camp Depicted on a Lamp from Samaria." *PEQ* 104 (1972): 38-58. [605].

1371. **Gil, J.** "The Abisha Scroll." (Hebrew) *BM* 44.1 (1970/71): 74-84. [2301].

1372. —————. "The Abisha Scroll: The Old Samaritan Scroll at Shechem." (Hebrew) *Katif* 12/13 (1978): 249-258. [2301].

1373. **Gil, Moshe.** "The Samaritans." In *A History of Palestine, 634-1099.* Cambridge: CUP, 1992. 820-825. [809/ 810].

1374. **Gilboa, Gila.** "Aspects in Samaritan Music." *A–B* (1979): 242-243. [2300].

1375. **Gill, John.** *Notices of the Jews and Their Country by the Writers of Classical Antiquity.* London, 1870. [2nd edn. revised and enlarged, 1872. Reprinted, 1972].
[300/ 305].

1376. **Gillespie, Charles George Knox.** *The Burden of Babylon...The Hebrew Text of Isaiah XIII. 1—XIV.23 compared with the Targum of Jonathan ben Uzziel and the Samaritan Pentateuch.* Stockport: Gillespie, 1890. [8pp.].
[2300].

1377. **Ginat, S.** (Hebrew) *The Samaritan Community in Israel.* 28pp Sulam Tzor: Regional Council, 1963. [Klau Library FQ/G].
[200].

1378. **Gini, C.** "I Samaritani." *Genus* 1.1-2 (1934).
[2901].

1379. **Ginzberg, Louis.** *The Legends of the Jews.* Philadelphia: Jewish Publication Society, 1911-1938, 1956, 1978. [Lost tribe and Joshua legends].
[304/ 1800].

1380. —————. *An Unknown Jewish Sect.* New York, 1970. [Reprinted from *MGWJ* nos. 55-58. See especially chapter 4].
[1003.3/ 1005].

1381. **Girard, Marc.** "Jésus en Samarie (Jean 4:1-42)." *ET* 17 (1986): 275-310.
[1502.1].

1382. **Girón-Blanc, Luis F.** "Cryptograms in a Samaritan Pentateuch Manuscript (Istanbul, Topkapi Serai)." *Proceedings of the Ninth World Congress of Jewish Studies* 1.(1986) (1985): 37-43.
[2300/ 2306.1].

1383. —————. "Datos para una historia de los samaritanos y los orígenes de su Pentateuco." *El Olivo* 22 (1985): 149-174.
[801.1/ 2300].

1384. —————. Edición Científica del Pentateuco Samaritano sobre la Base de Manuscritos Inéditos. (Doctoral thesis) Madrid: University Complutense, 1975. [The published version of Genesis has 37 pp].
[2300].

1385. —————. "El hebreo samaritano. Estado de la cuestión." *Simposio Bíblico Español (Salamanca, 1982).* Madrid: Universidad Complutense, 1984. 143-148.
[2600].

1386. —————. "Estudios samaritanos, 1985-1988." *Sefarad* 49.1 (1989): 167-178.
[100].

1387. —————. "Los Samaritanos, Puente entre judaismo y cristianismo." *El Olivo* 11 (1980): 35-43.
[1003.1/ 1003.4].

1388. —————. *Pentateucos hebreo-Samaritano, Genesis; Edición crítica sobre la base de manuscritos inéditos.* Madrid: Textus y Estudios "Cardenal Cisneros" Consejo Superior de Investigaciones Científicas, 1976.
[2300].

1389. —————. "Problemas en torno a la tradición samaritana en la Pentateuco." In *Memoria de Licenciatura Inédita.* Madrid: Fac. de F. Y. L. Universidad Complutense, 1973.
[2300].

1390. —————. "Un signo controvertido en la vocalización del Pentateuco hebreo-samaritano." In **Rothschild and Sixdenier,** editors, *Etudes samaritaines.* Louvain-Paris, 1988. 95-106.
[1004].

1391. —————. "La Tradición Samaritana del Pentateuco. Estado de la cuestión, bibliografia y camparación estadica de dos manuscritos." *Sefarad* 34 (1974): 387-399.
[103/ 2300].

1392. **Glaser, Hermann.** "Die Samaritaner." *Menorah* 4 (1926): 5-8. [Illustrated].
[200].

1393. **Glaue, P. and A. Rahlfs.** "Fragmente einer griechischen Übersetzung des samaritanischen Pentateuchs." *NKGW, Philol.-hist. Klasse* (1911): 167-200, 263-266. 1 plate. [Reprinted, Berlin, 1911, as *Mitteilungen des Septuaginta unternehmens der Königlichen Gesellschaft der Wissenschaften zu Göttingen, Heft 2, Fragmente einer griechischen Übersetzung des samaritanischen Pentateuchs*].
[2300/ 2309].

1394. —————. "Fragmente einer Übersetzung des samaritanischen Pentateuchs." *RB* 8 (1911): 628f.
[2309].

1395. **Glombitza, Otto.** "Der Dankbare Samariter–Luke xvii, 11-19." *NT* 11.4 (1969): 241-246.
[1502.4].

1396. —————. "Zur Charakterisierung des Stephanus in Acts 6 und 7." *ZNW* 53 (1962): 238-244.
[1502.2].

1397. **Godbey, Allen H.** "Samaritans, Sadducees and Karaites (= chapter 14)." In *The Lost Tribes: A Myth. Suggestions Towards Rewriting Hebrew History.* Durham, N.C., 1930. [2 maps, 22 plates. Bibliography, pp. 711-754].
[100/ 801.2].

1398. **Goedendorp, P. R.** Reviewer. **A. D. Crown,** "Bibliography of the Samaritans." *JSJ* 16 (1985): 263-264.
[100/ 107].

1399. —————. "If you are the Standing One I will Worship You." In **A. Tal and M. Florentin,** editors, *Proceedings of the First International Congress of the Société*

d'Études Samaritaines. Tel Aviv: Chaim Rosenberg School for Jewish Studies, University of Tel Aviv, 1991. 61-78.
[1003.1].

1400. —————. Reviewer. "Josephus Flavius und die Samaritaner." *JSJ* 18.2 (1987): 232-233.
[107/ 303.5].

1401. **Goege, M. D. de**, editor. **Abu Djafar At-Tabari,** *Annales.* Leiden: Brill, 1964. First series: vol. II.
[307/ 307.2].

1402. **Goeje, M. J. de.** *Catalogus Codicum Orientalium bib. Acad. Lugduni Batavae.* Leiden: Brill, 1873. 5: 63.
[101].

1403. **Gold, Y. Roland.** "The Mosaic Map of Madeba." *BA* 21.3 (1958): 50-71. [A discussion of Neapolis: figs. 1-6].
[305.4/ 400].

1404. **Goldberg, Leah.** *Das samaritanische Pentateuchtargum: eine Untersuchung seiner handschriftlichen Quellen.* Stuttgart: Bonner orientalischen Studien, XI, 1935.
[103/ 2401].

1405. **Golding, Louis.** "The Samaritan Doom." In *Those Ancient Lands.* New York, 1928. Chapter 10, 126-136.
[200].

1406. **Goldziher, Ignaz.** "La Misasa." *Revue Africaine* 268 (1908): 23-28.
[1501].

1407. —————. "Muhammedanische Traditionen über den grabsort des Josua." *ZDPV* 2 (1879): 13-17. [Reprinted, *Gesammelte Schriften,* 1968:71-75].
[407.2].

1408. —————. "Pinchas-Mansûr." *ZDMG* 56 (1902): 411-412.
[3009.1].

1409. **Gollwitzer, Helmut.** "Das Gleichnis vom Barmherzigen Samariter." *BSt* 34 (1962).
[1502.3].

1410. —————. "Predigtmeditation über Luk 10, 23-37." *Göttinger Predigtmeditationen* (1954/5): 213-216.
[1502.3].

1411. **Goodwin, Thomas.** "Moses and Aaron cum Joh. Henrici notis." In **Ugolini,** *Thesaurus.* Venice, 1761. Vol. 3: 124-132.
[1502.4/ 3000.1/ 3008].

1412. **Goroncszik, M.** "With the Samaritans on Mt. Gerizim on the Day of the Passover Sacrifice." *A–B* 258-259 (28/4/80): 5-7.
[1404].

1413. **Gottheil, Richard.** "The Dating of Their Manuscripts by the Samaritans." *JBL* 25
       (1906): 29-48. [2 figs].
       [103/ 700].

1414. ——————. "An Eleventh Century Document Concerning a Cairo Synagogue."
       JQR 19 (1907): 467-539.
       [505].

1415. ——————. "Syriac and Assyrian." *Hebraica* 3 (1887): 187.
       [2600].

1416. **Goulder, Michael.** "The Samaritan Hypothesis." In *Incarnation and Myth: The
       Debate Continued.* London/Grand Rapids, Michigan: SCM/Eerdmans, 1979.
       247-250.
       [1003.1].

1417. ——————. "The Two Roots of the Christian Myth." In J. **Hicks,** ed., *The Myth
       of the God Incarnate.* Philadelphia: SCM, 1977. 64-86. [Discusses Samaritan
       Missionaries in Corinth and Ephesus and the influence of the Samaritans on
       Christology].
       [502/ 506/1003.1].

1418. **Gourgues, Michel.** "Esprit des commencements et esprits de prolongements dans
       les Actes: notes sur la 'Pentecôte des Samaritains' L'Acts 8, 5-25." *RB* 93.3
       (1986): 376-385.
       [1407/ 1502.2].

1419. **Gowan, Donald E.** *Bridge Between the Testaments—a Reappraisal of Judaism from
       the Exile to the Birth of Christianity.* Pittsburgh: Pittsburgh Theological
       Monographs 14, 1976. [Especially 163-178].
       [200/ 2300].

1420. **Grabbe, Lester.** "Chronography in Hellenistic Jewish Historiography." *Society of
       Biblical Literature* 2 (1979): 43-68.
       [804/ 805].

1421. **Graf, E.** "Theology at Jacob's Well. Chapters from the Gospel of St. John."
       Homiletic and Pastoral Review 59 (1959): 1099-1104.
       [1502.1].

1422. **Graf, Georg.** "Jesus und die Samariter." *Bi.Ki.* (1951): 99-144.
       [1003.1].

1423. ——————. "Zum Alter des samaritanischen Buches Josue." *Biblica* 23 (1912):
       62-67.
       [1604/ 1605].

1424. **Grajewsky, Pinhas ben Zvi.** "Two Samaritan Ketubbot." (Hebrew) *East and West
       (= Mizrah Uma'arav)* 2 (1915): 229-231.
       [2500].

1425. ——————. Hebrew *Two Samaritan Ketubbot and One Karaite Ketubbah.* 19pp
       Jerusalem: Y. Walker, Hebrew Press, 1927-1928. The last page of the booklet

contains a piece entitled "An interesting Samaritan Amulet".
[1207].

1426. **Granados, J. and C. Moliner.** "Jésus y los Samaritanos; análisis estructural de Juan 4: 4-44." *Cuadernos de Teologia* 6.3 (1973): 19-33.
[1502.1].

1427. **Grant, Robert M.** *Gnosticism: A Source Book of Heretical Writings from the Early Christian Period.* New York: Harper, 1917. [2nd edn., 1961].
[1506/ 1506.1/ 1506.2].

1428. **Gray, J. B.** "The Derivation of Ebal." *Academy* 49 (1896): 510.
[404].

1429. **Green, L. C.** A Critical Edition and Translation of the Samaritan Feast of Hag haSuccoth with Special Reference to the Historical Development Involved. (Doctoral thesis) Leeds: University of Leeds, 1958.
[1409].

1430. **Greenberg, Moshe.** "The Stabilization of the Text of the Hebrew Bible Reviewed in the Light of the Biblical Materials from the Judean Desert." *JAOS* 76 (1956): 157-167.
[2300/ 2307].

1431. **Greenfield, Jonas C.** Reviewer. **J.-P. Rothschild, G. D. Sixdenier,** "Études samaritaines." *IEJ* 42 (1992): 125-126.
[107/ 200].

1432. ————. Reviewer. **Z. Ben-Hayyim,** "Samaritan Hebrew and Aramaic in the Work of Prof. Zev Ben-Hayyim." *Biblica* 45.2 (1964): 261-268.
[107/ 1600/ 2600].

1433. ————. Reviewer. **A. D. Crown,** "The Samaritans." *IEJ* 42 (1992): 125-126.
[107/ 200].

1434. **Grégoire, Henri Baptiste.** *Histoire des sectes religieuses qui se sont nées depuis le commencement du siècle dernier jusqu'à l'époque actuelle.* Paris, 1814. [Other editions, 1828-1835].
[200/ 800].

1435. **Gregory the Great.** "Letter to Leo of Catena Regarding Samaritans who have bought Pagan Slaves" and "Letter to the Bishop of Syracuse Regarding Felix, Given in Slavery to a Samaritan." In *Works.* Book V, cap. 32 and VII: cap.22.
[811/ 1003.1].

1436. **Grimm, Joseph.** *Die Samariter und ihre Stellung in der Weltgeschichte. Mit besonderer Rücksicht auf Simon den Magier.* München, 1854.
[1002].

1437. **Grintz, J. M.** "Gerizim, Mount." In *EJ.* Jerusalem, 1971. 7: 436-438.
[406].

1438. —————. "The Samaritan Torah." (Hebrew) In *Introduction to the Bible*.
       Jerusalem, 1972. 83-96.
       [2300].

1439. **Grob, Francis.** "La femme samaritaine et l'eau du puits (Jean 4, 13-14)." *ETR* 55.1
       (1980): 86-89.
       [1502.1].

1440. **Groningen, G. van.** Reviewer. **J. Fossum,** "The Name of God and the Angel of
       the Lord." *Vox Reformata* 46 (May, 1986): 33b-35a.
       [107/ 1101].

1441. **Gropp, Douglas M. E. M. Cook,** "The Language of the Samaria Papyri: A
       Preliminary Study." *Maarav: Sopher Mahir: N.W.Semitic Studies presented to
       Stanislav Segert* 5-6 (1990): 169-187.
       [303.3/ 2600].

1442. —————. "The origin and development of the Aramaic 'sallit' clause." *JNES*
       52.1 (1993): 31-36.
       [303.3/ 2800].

1443. —————. The Samaria Papyri from the Wadi ed-Daliyeh: The Slave
       Sales.(Ph.D. dissertation) Harvard, 1986.
       [303.3/ 2600].

1444. **Grossberg, Asher.** "The Structure on Mt. Ebal and the Laws of the Altar."
       (Hebrew) in **Z. Ehrlich,** editor, *Samaria and Benjamin.* Jerusalem, 1987. 148-
       152.
       [404/ 1303].

1445. **Grossman, David.** "Northern Samaria; a Process-Pattern Analysis of Rural
       Settlement." *Canadian Geographer* 26.2 (1982): 110-127.
       [400.3].

1446. **Grossman, David and Z. Safrai.** "Satellite Settlements in Western Samaria."
       Geographical Review 70 (1980): 446-461.
       [400.3].

1447. **Grove, George.** "Sychar","Sychem", "Shechem." In **W. Smith,** *A Dictionary of the
       Bible.* London, 1863. 3: 1234-1240; 1395-1396.
       [412/ 413].

1448. **Grünbaum, M.** "Einige Bemerkungen in Bezug auf die in dieser Zeitschrift Bd. XI
       s. 730 und Bd.XII s. 132 mitgetheilten Aufsätze über die Samaritaner." *ZDMG*
       16 (1862): 389-416. [Refers to articles by Rappoport and Geiger].
       [107/ 200].

1449. —————. "Nachträge zu den 'Bemerkungen über die Samaritaner'." *ZDMG* 23
       (1869): 615-641.
       [200].

1450. —————. "Nachträgliche Bemerkung zu Bd XX dieser Zeitschrift." *ZDMG* 21 (1867): 279-281. [200/ 406/ 408].

1451. —————. "Nachträgliches zu Nabulus und Garizim." *ZDPV* 7 (1884): 131. [406/ 408].

1452. —————. "Zu Awarta." *ZDPV* 6 (1883): 195. [402].

1453. **Grunpier, J. C.** Reviewer. **Sylvia Powels,** "Der Kalender der Samaritaner." *JNES* 40 (1981): 148. [107/ 1400].

1454. **Guenzberg, Mordechai Aaron.** "The Samaritans." (Hebrew) In J. Edelstein, editor, *Ketavim Nivcharim.* Warsaw: Tushiyyah, 1911. 23-33. [200/ 202].

1455. **Guérin, V.** "Samarie." In *Description géographique, historique et archéologique de la Palestine.* Paris, 1875. Part 2. [410].

1456. —————. *La terre sainte.* Paris: 2 vols., 1886. 1. 254-268. [200/ 400].

1457. —————. "Le tombeau de Josué." *Revue Archéologique* 77 (1865): 100-108. [407.2].

1458. **Guidi, I.** Reviewer. **J. H. Petermann and K. Vollers,** "Pentateuchus Samaritanus." *GSAG* 5 (1891): 200f. [107/ 2300].

1459. **Guidi, I. et al.,** editor and translator. *Chronica Minora.* (Scriptores Syri, 3rd series). Louvain, 1903-1907. 4: 411f. [Samaritans at the time of the Moslem conquest]. [305.6/ 809].

1460. **Guignes, Joseph de.** *Essai historique sur la typographie orientale et grecque de l'Imprimerie Royale.* Paris, 1787. [An English translation, London, 1789]. [105].

1461. **Gulkowitsch, L.** "Der Kleine Talmudtraktat über die Samaritaner." *Angelos* 1.1-2 (1925): 48-59. [304.2].

1462. **Günther, Hans F. K.** *Rassenkunde des jüdischen Volkes.* Munchen, 1930. ["Samaritan Anthropology" 149-158]. [2901].

1463. **Gunzig, Israel.** "Samaritaner." In *Jüdisches Lexicon.* Berlin, 1930. Vol. 4: 2.(S-Z). [201/ 202].

1464. **Guthe, H.** "Die Pilgerfart des russischen Abtes Daniel ins heilige Land 1113-1115." *ZDPV* 7 (1884).
[306.2/ 400].

1465. **Gutman, Y.** (Hebrew) *The Beginnings of Jewish Hellenistic Literature.* Jerusalem, 1958-63. Vol.2.
[2000].

1466. **Guyldforde, Sir Richard. H. Ellis,** editor, *Pylgrimage to the Holy Land, A.D. 1506.* London: Camden Society Publication 51, 1851.
[306.3/ 400].

1467. **Gyllenberg, R.** "Le samaritain misericordieux." *Svensk Exegetisk Årsbok* 12 (1947): 163-174.
[2100].

H

1468. Haacker, Klaus. "Assumptio Mosis—eine samaritanische Schrift?" *TZ* 25.6 (1969): 385-405.
[2000/ 2007].

1469. —————. "Die Schriftzitate der samaritanische Chronik II." *Institutum Judaicum der Univ. Tübingen* 1968-1970 (1970): 38-47.
[1603].

1470. —————. *Die Stiftung des Heils. Untersuchungen zur Struktur der johanneischen Theologie.* Stuttgart: Arbeiten Zur Theologie I, Heft 47, 1972. [Originally a dissertation from the University of Mainz, 1970].
[1502.1].

1471. —————. Reviewer. **H. G. Kippenberg,** "Garizim und Synagoge." *TZ* 29 (1973): 435-436.
[107/ 806/ 807].

1472. —————. "Gottendienst ohne Gotteseinandersetzung. Joh 4, 22 von dem Hintergrund des Jüdisch-samaritanischen Auseinandersetzung." In **B. Benzing,** editor, *Wort und Wirklichkeit:Festschrift für Eugen Ludwig.* Meisenheim, 1976. 110-126.
[1502.1].

1473. —————. "Samaria", "Samaritan." In *New International Dictionary of New Testament Theology.* Exeter: Paternoster Press, 1978. 3: 449-467. [Translated from the German edition, Wuppertal, 1971].
[200/ 410].

1474. **Haacker, Klaus and P. Schaefer.** "Nachbiblische Traditionen vom Tod des Moses." In *Josephus Studien, Festschrift für O. Michel.* Göttingen, 1974. 147-174.
[1802/ 1803/ 3008].

1475. **Haag, H.** "Samaria." In *Lexicon für Theologie und Kirche.* Freiburg: Herder, 1964. 9: 292-295.
[410].

1476. **Haarbrucker, Th.** *Abu'l Fath' Muhammad ash-Schahrastani's Religionspartheien und philosophen-Schülen.* Halle, 1850/51. 2 vols. [Reprinted, Hildesheim, 1969. Description of the Samaritans, 257-259].
[307.2].

1477. **Haberman, A. M.** "Samaritans and Karaites—Bibliography." (Hebrew) in *Toldot Hapiyyut vehaShirah.* Jerusalem/Ramat Gan, 1970. 78-83.
[100/ 1004].

1478. —————. "Studies in the Dead Sea Scrolls." (Hebrew) *Sinai* 32 (1952): 101-107.
[1005].

1479. Hachicho, M. Ali. "English Travel Books About the Arab Near East in the Eighteenth Century." *World of Islam* (1964): 9.
[306.3].

1480. Hadassi, Judah b. Elijah. *Eshkol Hakofer.* Eupatoria, 1836. 96-97 (41a-41b).
[304.3/ 1004].

1481. Hadot, J. Reviewer. A. Isser, "The Dositheans." *Archives de Sciences Sociales des Religions* 22.44 (1977): 247.
[1503].

1482. Haefeli, Leo. *Geschichte der Lansdschaft Samaria von 722 vor Chr. bis 67 nach Chr.* Münster: Alttestamentliche Abhandlungen 8, bd. 1-2, 1922.
[800/ 801/ 804/ 806].

1483. —————. "Les Samaritains dans le Coran." *Revue Sémitique* 16 (1908): 419-429.
[307/ 1003.3].

1484. —————. *Samaria und Peräia bei Flavius Josephus.* Freiburg, 1913. [Also appears as a doctoral dissertation, Tübingen, 1913].
[303.5].

1485. Haenchen, E. "Gab es eine vorchristliche Gnosis." *ZTK* 49 (1959): 316-349.
[1506].

1486. —————. "Simon Magus in der Apostelgeschichte." In K. W. Tröger, editor, *Gnosis und Neues Testament.* Gütersloh, 1973. 267-279.
[1506.2].

1487. Hag, H. "Samaria","Samaritaner." In M. Buchberger, editor, *Lexicon für Theologie und Kirche.* Freiburg: Herder, 1964. 9: 292-295.
[201/ 202/ 410].

1488. Hahn, F. "Das Heil kommt von den Juden. Erwägungen zu Joh 4, 22b." In B. Benzing, *et al.*, editors, *Wort und Wirklichkeit: Festschrift für Eugen Ludwig.* Meissenheim, 1976. 67-84.
[1502.1].

1489. Hai ben Shrira Gaon. (Hebrew) *Sefer Hamekah vehaMimkar (The Book of Commercial Transactions).* Venice, 1602. [Reprinted, Vienna, 1800. Observations on the Dositheans which seem to be based on the author's personal acquaintance with Samaritan sects].
[1503/ 3004].

1490. Halévy, J. "Découverte d'une inscription bilingue en Palestine." *N. A. de Philos. Cath.* 3 (1881): 464f. [Greek and Samaritan in Amwas].
[2502].

1491. —————. "Découvertes épigraphiques en Arabie." *REJ* 9 (1884): 1-20. [See especially 8-16].
[802].

1492. ——————. *Mélanges de critique d'histoire relatifs aux peuples sémitiques.* Paris, 1883.
[200/ 1000].

1493. ——————. "Sens et origine de la parabole évangelique dite du bon samaritain." *REJ* 4 (1882): 249-255. [Reprinted in *Mélanges*: 234-240].
[1502/ 1502.3].

1494. Halkin, A. S. "The 613 Commandments Among the Samaritans." (Hebrew) In *The Ignace Goldziher Memorial Volume.* Jerusalem, 1958. 2.
[1004/ 1108].

1495. ——————. "Controversies in the Samaritan Masail al Khilaf." *PAAJR* 46/47.1 (1980): 281-306.
[2203.1/ 2205].

1496. ——————. "From Samaritan Exegesis—the Commentary of Abu'l Hasan al Suri on Deuteronomy 31." (Hebrew) *Leshonenu* 32.1-2 (1968): 208-246.
[2304/ 3002].

1497. ——————. "Introduction." In J. A. Montgomery, *The Samaritans.* New York: Ktav reprint, 1968.
[200].

1498. ——————. "The Relations of the Samaritans to Saadia Gaon." *PAAJR (Saadia Anniversary Volume)* 2 (1943): 271-325.
[1003.4/ 2205].

1499. ——————. "The Righteous and Their Experiences According to the Samaritan Abraham Qabassah." (Hebrew) in M. Bar-Asher, editor, *Hebrew Language Studies Presented to Ze'ev Ben-Hayyim.* Jerusalem: Magnes Press, 1983. 177-194.
[1105/ 3002.2].

1500. ——————. "Samaritan Polemics Against the Jews." *PAAJR* 7 (1935-36): 13-59.
[1003.4/ 1100/ 2205].

1501. ——————. "The Scholia to Numbers and Deuteronomy in the Samaritan-Arabic Pentateuch." *JQR* 34.(New series) (1943-1944): 41-59.
[103/ 2302].

1502. Hall, Bruce W. "The Samaritans in the Writings of Justin Martyr and Tertullian." In A. Tal & M. Florentin, editors, *Proceedings of the First International Congress of the Société d'Études Samaritaines.* Tel Aviv: Chaim Rosenberg School for Jewish Studies, University of Tel Aviv, 1991. 115-122.
[305].

1503. ——————. "From John Hyrcanus to Baba Rabba." In A. D. Crown, editor, *The Samaritans.* Tübingen: Mohr, 1989. 32-54. [First appeared as a doctoral dissertation, Sydney University, 1985].
[806/ 1003.1/ 1003.4].

1504. —————. *Samaritan Religion; Hyrcanus to Baba Rabbah.* Sydney: Mandelbaum Judaica Series 2, 1986.
[806/ 1003.1/ 1003.4].

1505. **Hall, D. R.** "The Meaning of sugcraomai in John 4: 9." *ET* 83 (1971/72): 56-57.
[1502.1].

1506. **Hall, G. M.** "Simon Magus." In *ERE.* Edinburgh, 1920. Vol. 9: 514-525.
[1506.2].

1507. **Hall, I. H.** Presented by C. H.Toy. "On a Manuscript of the Samaritan Pentateuch." *JAOS* 11.Proceedings (1881): lxix-lxx.
[2300].

1508. **Hamaker, H. A.** "Aanamerkingen over de Samaritanen en hunne Briefwisseling met eenige Europesche Geleerden: ter Gelgenheid van eenen nog onbekenden Samaritaanschen Brief." *Archief voor Kerkelijke Geschiedenis* 5 (1834): 3-56.
[Illustrated. Correspondence with Scaliger].
[1705].

1509. **Hamartolus, Georgius.** "Chronicon." *PG* 110 70-71, 867-870.
[305].

1510. **Hamburger, A.** "A Greco-Samaritan Amulet from Caesarea." *IEJ* 9 (1959): 43-45.
[601].

1511. **Hamburger, Jacob.** "Samaritaner." In *Real-Encyclopädie des Judenthums.* Leipzig, 1870. 1: 892-894 & 2: 1062-1071.
[201/ 202].

1512. —————. "Text der Bibel." In *Real-Encyclopädie für Bibel und Talmud.* Leipzig, 1883. 2: 1211-1220.
[2300].

1513. **Hamelsveld, Y. Van.** De weigering der Joden am den Samaritanen deelgenootschap te geven aan den hebrouw van Runnen Tempel verdedigo. (Ph.D. dissertation) Utrecht: University of Utrecht, 1784. [Only copy known, Utrecht University library].
[1300].

1514. **Hamilton, H.** *Schedule of Historical Monuments and Sites.* Supplement 2 to Palestine Gazette Extraordinary, no.1575. 24 November 1944.
[410/ 801].

1515. **Hamilton, R. W.** "The Domed Tomb at Sebastiya." *QDAP* 8 (1939): 64-71.
[Figs. 1-3, plates 38-40].
[410/ 602].

1516. **Hammer, Heinrich.** *Traktat vom Samaritanermessias.* Bonn: Studien zur Frage der Existenz und Abstammung Jesu, 1913. 2 plates, 101pp.
[1003.1/ 1107].

1517. **Hammerton, J. A.** "Samaritans." In *Harmsworth's Universal Encyclopaedia.* London, n.d. 8.
[201/ 202].

1518. **Hammond, Canon.** "The Samaritan Passover of the Year 1861." *JTVI* 36 (1904): 213-223.
[1404].

1519. **Hanhart, R.** "Zu den ältesten Traditionen über das samaritanische Schisma." *EI* 16 (1982): 106-115.
[801.1].

1520. **Hanover, Siegmund.** *Das Festgesetz der Samaritaner nach Ibrâhîm ibn Ja'kûb. Edition und Uebersetzung seines Kommentars zu Lev. 23: nebst Einleitung und Anmerkungen.* Berlin: H. Itzkowski, 1904. [Reprint of inaugural dissertation, University of Jena].
[2102/ 2304].

1521. **Haparhi, Ahstori.** "Excerpts from the Travels of Ashtori Haparhi." (Hebrew) in A.Ya'ari, editor, *Travellers to the Holy Land.* Ramat Gan, 1976. 98-104.
[304.4].

1522. **Happel, J. H.** *Brevis Institutio Linguae Arabicae...Hebraicae...Samaritanae... Harmonica.* Francofurti, 1707.
[2600].

1523. **Haran, Menachem.** "The Concept of "Taheb" in the Samaritan Religion." (Hebrew) *Tarbiz* 23 (1951/2): 96-111.
[1107].

1524. ———. "The Liturgical Commandments of Aaron ben Manir, a Samaritan Piyyut for Yom Kippur on the 613 Principles of Maimonides." (Hebrew) *IASH* 4:15 (1971): 229-280. English version, *IASH* 5: 7 (1974): 174-209. Reprinted 1974, 36pp.
[1003.4/ 1401/ 2102].

1525. ———. "Maimonides' Catalogue of Religious Precepts in a Samaritan Piyyut." (Hebrew) *EI* 4 (1956): 160-169.
[1003.4/ 1004/ 1108].

1526. ———. "Shechem Studies." (Hebrew) *Zion* 38 1-32.
[1001].

1527. **Hardouin, Jean.** "Explication de deux médailles samaritaines." *Mémoires de Trevoux* (Mai, 1712): 841-859. [Reprinted as "Expositio de duobus nummis Samaritanis", in Ugolini, *Thesaurus,* 28 (1765): 1065-1076].
[603].

1528. ———. "Lettre du R.P. Hardouin touchant quelques médailles samaritaines. De Nummis Samaritanis." *Bibliothèque universelle et historique* 21 (1692): 130-136. [Reprinted as "Epistola de nummis Samaritanis" in Ugolini, *Thesaurus,* 28 (1765): 1077-1078].
[603].

1529. **Harkavy, A.** *Catalog der Hebräischen und Samaritanischen Handschriften der Kaiserlichen öffentlichen Bibliothek in St. Petersburg.* St Petersburg, 1875. [Russian sub-title: Opisanie samaritjanskikh rukopisej khrajascikhsja v. Imperatorskoj Publicnoj biblioteke. Vol.2 only relates to the Samaritan manuscripts]. [101/ 103].

1530. —————. "The Collection of Samaritan Manuscripts at St. Petersburgh." In J. W. Nutt, *Fragments of a Samaritan Targum.* London, 1874. 153-167. [Printed also as "Die samaritanische Handschriftensammlung in St Petersburg," *Russische Rundschau* (1874) 4:74-80]. [101/ 103].

1531. **Harl, K. W.** "The Coinage of Neapolis in Samaria, A.D. 244-253." *American Numismatic Society Museum Notes* 29 (1984): 61-97. [603].

1532. **Harozen, I.** "Thoughts on the Samaritan Tribe." (Hebrew) *Bama'aracha* 11.122 (1971): 26-27. [200].

1533. **Harper, H. A.** "Ebal and Gerizim." *PEFQS* (1896): 85f. [404/ 406].

1534. **Harrington, Daniel J.** Reviewer. **A. D. Crown,** "The Samaritans." *Critical Review of Books in Religion* (1991): 355-357. [107/ 200].

1535. **Harris, B. F.** "Simon Magus." In **M. C. Tenny,** *et al.,* editors, *The Zondervan Pictorial Encyclopaedia.* Grand Rapids, 1975. 5: 442-444. [1506.2].

1536. **Hartman, L.** Reviewer. **S. Saller,** "The Memorial of Moses on Mt. Nebo." *CBQ* 5.1 (1943): 104-106. [107/ 409/ 600].

1537. **Hartmann, Johann Philipp.** *Hoc est grammatica Aethiopica Henr. Maji. Hebr. chaldaic. syr. atque samarit...harmonica.* Francofurti, 1707. [2600].

1538. **Hartum, M.** "S. D. Luzatto's Introduction to the Torah." (Hebrew) *BM 33* (1968): 123-128. [2300].

1539. **Hasse, Johann Gottfried.** *Lectiones syro-arabico-samaritano-aethiopica, Congessit ac tabulis...instruxit.* Lipsae: Hartung, 1788. [2600].

1540. —————. *Praktischer Unterricht über die gesammten orientalischen Sprachen. Part 3: Praktisches Handbuch der aramäischen oder syrisch-chaldaisch-samaritanischen Sprache.* Jena, 1786-1789. [2600].

1541. Hassencamp, Johann M. *Commentatio philologico critica de Pentateucho LXX interpretum graeco, non ex hebraeo sed samaritano textu converso.* Part 1 Marburg, 1765. [Second printing, Rinteln, 1783]. [2300/ 2400].

1542. ————. *Der entdekte wahre ursprung der alten Bibelübersetzung...und der gerettete samaritanische text...* Minden, 1775. [2nd edn. Frankfurt and Leipzig, 1790]. [2300/ 2307].

1543. Hauber, Eberhard David. *Nachtricht von den jüdischen insgemein genannten samaritanischen münzen und den davon herausgekommenen schriften.* Kopenhaven und Leipzig: 1778. [603].

1544. Hayes, J. H. and J. K. Kuan. "The Final Years of Samaria (730-720 BC)." *Biblica* (1991): 153-181. [801.1].

1545. Hayman, H. "Samaritan Acceptance of the Pentateuch." *Thinker* (Sept. 1892): 206-211. [2300].

1546. Hedin, Sven Anders. *Till Jerusalem.* Stockholm, 1917. 200-221. [308].

1547. Heichelheim, Friederich M. "Die auswärtige Bevölkerung im Ptolemäerreich." *Klio* 18.NF5 (1925): 70-71. [Reprinted, 1963]. [805].

1548. Heidenheim, Moritz. *Bibliotheca Samaritana, Texte aus Samaria und Studien zum Samaritanismus 1. Die Samaritanische Pentateuch-version II. Die samaritanische Liturgie. Eine Auswahl der wichtigsten Texte. III. Commentar zum Samaritanischen Pentateuch von Marqah der Samaritaner.* Leipzig and Weimar, 1884-1896. [Reprinted Georg Olms, Philo Press, Amsterdam, 1971]. [1803/ 2100/ 2300].

1549. ————. "Die litanei Markas." *DVJ* 2.4 (1865): 472-487. [1803].

1550. ————. "Die Literatur der Samaritaner." *DVJ* 1 (1861): 278-279, 408-420. [1550].

1551. ————. "Die neue Ausgabe der versio Samaritana zur Genesis (Bibliotheca Samaritana I)." *ZDMG* 40 (1866): 516-522. [2300].

1552. ————. "Die samaritanische Chronik des Hohenpriesters Elasar aus dem 11. Jahrhundert übersetzt und erklärt." *DVJ* 15.3 (1870): 347-389. [1600/ 1607].

1553. ————. "Gebet Ab Gelujah's." *DVJ* 2.2 (1865): 213-231. [2100,].

1554. —————. "Nachrichten über die Samaritaner aus einem handschriftlichen Reisejournale aus dem 15 Jahrhundert." *DVJ* 3 (1867): 354-356. [306.3].

1555. —————. "Über die Wichtigkeit der samaritanischen Literatur für die semitische Sprachwissenschaft." *Verhandlungen der 39 Versamm. deutscher Phil. und Schülmänner.* Zurich and Leipzig (1887-1888): 148-160. [1550/ 2600].

1556. —————. "Untersuchungen über die Samaritaner." *DVJ* 1 (1861): 2ff, 78ff, 374ff. [200].

1557. —————. (Hebrew) *The Wonders of Marqah.* 61 pp. Weimar & Berlin, 1895. [With comments by M. Hildesheimer]. [1803].

1558. —————. "Zur Logoslehre der Samaritaner." *DVJ* 4.1 (1868): 126-128. [2605].

1559. —————. "Zur samaritanischen Angelologie und Astrologie; ein samaritanisches Gebet." *DVJ* 44 (1871): 4f. [1101/ 2100].

1560. Heidet, L. "Samarie." In F. Vigouroux, *Dictionnaire de la Bible.* 2nd. Paris, 1928. 5: 1401-1421. [410].

1561. Heie, J. C. N. *Ten forskjellige Alphabeter.* Kjøbenhavn: Chr, Steen & Sons, 1869. [Especially p. 14 for a Danish version of the German type face.]. [105].

1562. Heinemann, Joseph. "Anti-Samaritan Polemics in the Aggadah." *Proceedings of the Sixth World Congress of Jewish Studies.* Jerusalem: Magnes Press, 1977. 3: 57-69. [304/ 1003.4].

1563. Heller, Bernhard. "Al-Samiri." In *Encyclopaedia of Islam.* Leiden: Brill, 1924. [See also the *Shorter Encyclopaedia of Islam*, 1961]. [200/ 307].

1564. —————. "Die Susannaherzählung: ein Märchen." *ZAW* 54 (1936): 281-287. [1800].

1565. —————. Reviewer. M. Gaster, "Samaritanisches." (= Review of *The Asatir*) *MGWJ* 77 (1933): 300-305. [107/ 1801].

1566. Heller, Chaim. (Hebrew) *The Samaritan Pentateuch Version and the Masoretic Version.* Berlin, 1923/4. [Reprinted, Jerusalem 1972, 108 pp. Includes a comparison of the variants from the Samaritan Pentateuch, Sa'adiah's version and the LXX]. [2300/ 2400].

1567. **Helton, R. Arlington.** The Samaritans and the Jews. (Ph.D.) Southern Baptist
Theological Seminary, 1941.
[200/ 1003.4].

1568. **Hempel, J.** "Innermasoretische Bestätigungen des Samaritanus." *ZAW* (1934): 254-
274.
[2300].

1569. ——————. "Samaria." In *Religion in Geschichte und Gegenwart.* 2nd. Tübingen,
1931. 5: 99-101.
[410].

1570. **Hengel, Martin.** *Judentum und Hellenismus.* Tübingen: J.C.B. Mohr, 1973. [An
English edition, *Judaism and Hellenism,* Studies in Their Encounter in Palestine
During the Early Hellenistic Period,Philadelphia, 1974].
[804/ 1002/ 1003.1].

1571. ——————. "Zwischen Jesus and Paulus: die 'Hellenisten', die 'Sieben' und
Stephanus (Apg. 6, 1-15:7, 54—8, 3)." *ZTK* 72 (1975): 151-206. [English
translation, in *Between Jesus and Paul* Fortress Press/SCM, 1983. 1-29; 129-
156. Includes a good bibliography].
[1002/ 1003.1].

1572. **Hengstenberg, Ernest Wilhem.** *Beiträge zur Einleitung ins alte Testament. 1. Die
Authentie des Pentateuchs.* Berlin, 1836. [An English translation by J.E.Ryland,
Dissertations on the Genuineness of the Pentateuch, Edinburgh, 1847, 2 vols.].
[2300].

1573. **Henkel, Linda.** "The Samaritans: History and Religion." *A–B* 456-457
(15/3/1988): 51-54. [A report of a project carried out with the aid of the
Samaritan Institute, Holon].
[200/ 800].

1574. **Hennessy, J. Basil.** "Excavations at Samaria—Sebaste, 1968." *Levant* 2 (1970): 1-
21. [15 figs., pls. I–XII].
[410/ 600].

1575. ——————. "Samaria." In *IDB* Supplementary volume. New York & Nashville:
Abingdon, 1976. 771-772.
[410].

1576. **Hennessy, J. Basil and D. Homès-Fredericq.** *Archaeology of Jordan I. Bibliography
II. i & ii Field Reports, Surveys & Sites A-K, L-Z.* Leuven: Peters, 1986-1989.
[See Siyagha and Shaubak].
[100/ 508/ 600].

1577. **Henrion, Nicolas.** "Sur les médailles samaritaines qui portent le nom de Simon."
Histoire de l'Académie Royale des Inscriptions et Belles-Lettres 2 (1724): 306-310.
[603].

1578. **Henry, H. T.** "The Good Samaritan." *Homiletic and Pastoral Review* 38 (1937):
1134-1142.
[1502.3].

1579. **Herbert, A. S.** Reviewer. J. Bowman, "The Importance of Samaritan Researches." *ZAW* 72 (1960): 272.
[106/ 107].

1580. **Hermann, I.** "Wem ich der Nächste bin Auslegung von Lk.10, 25-37." *BL 2* (1961): 17-24.
[1002/ 1003.1/ 1502.3].

1581. **Herr, J.** "Johannische Botschaft: die Mission in Samaria." *Sammlung und Sendung.* 1958. 33: 99-112.
[1002/ 1003.1].

1582. **Herrmann, Hugo.** "Das Pessach der Samaritaner aus einem gespräch mit ehrem Hohepriester." In *Chad Gadja, Das Pesachbuch.* Berlin: Jüdischer Verlag, 1914. 109-110.
[1404].

1583. **Herrmann, Karl H.** "Chaldaisch und Samaritanisch." In *Bibliotheca Orientalis et Linguistica...1858...1868 in Deutschland.* Halle, 1870. 83-89.
[100/ 101].

1584. **Herschell, Ridley H.** *A Visit to my Fatherland, Being Notes of a Journey to Syria and Palestine in 1843, with Additional Notes of a Journey in 1854.* London, 1896. 94-101.
[308].

1585. **Herskovits, Y.** "The Cutheans in Tannaitic Literature—A Second Collection." (Hebrew) in *The Asaph Festschrift on his Fiftieth Birthday.* Jerusalem, 1940.
[304].

1586. —————. "The Samaritans in Tannaitic Literature." (Hebrew) *Yavneh 2* (1940): 71-105.
[304].

1587. **Hertzberg, H. W.** "Die Botschaft von Anfang." *Beiträge zur Traditionsgeschichte und Theologie des alten Testaments.* Göttingen: Vandenhoeck & Ruprecht, 1962. 162-186.
[1002].

1588. —————. "Die Tradition in Palästina." *PJ* 22 (1926): 84-105.
[1404].

1589. —————. "Garizim." In *Die Religion in Geschichte und Gegenwart.* Tübingen, 1958. 2.
[406].

1590. —————. "Zum samaritanischen Passah." *Sammlung und Sendung (the Rendtorff Festschrift)* (1958): 120-136.
[1404].

1591. —————. "Zum samaritanischen Passah." *Beiträge zur Traditionsgeschichte und Theologie des alten Testaments.* Göttingen: Vandenhoeck & Ruprecht, 1962.

126-133.
[1404].

1592. **Herzog, Avigdor.** "Musical Forms in Samaritan Prayers." *A–B* 109 (1974): 8.
[2100/ 3300].

1593. ————. "The Singing of Exodus XIV by the Samaritans." *A–B* 194 (1977):
4-12.
[2300/ 3300].

1594. **Hessey, J. A. H.** "Samaria", "Samaritans." In W. **Smith,** editor, *A Dictionary of the
Bible.* London, 1863. Vol. III.
[200/ 410].

1595. **Heutger, Nicolaus.** "Die lukanischen Samaritanererzählungen in
religionspädagogischer Sicht." In **Wilfrid Haubeck and Michael Bachmann,**
eds., *Wort in der Zeit.* Leiden: Brill, 1980. 275-287.
[1502.3].

1596. **Heyd, Uriel.** "Jews and Samaritans." In *Ottomon Documents on Palestine, 1552-
1616.* Oxford: OUP, 1960. Chapter 10.
[813.1].

1597. **Hickman, Charles.** *A Sermon Preached before the Right Honorable George, Earl of
Berkely, Governor of the Company of Merchants of England Trading in the
Levant Seas at St. Peter's Church in Broadstreet Jan 25th 1680 by Charles
Hickman.* London, 1681. [Reprinted in microform in the series, *Early English
Books, 1641-1700*].
[200].

1598. **Hieronymi, E. G. von.** *Briefwechsel der Samaritaner zu Naplusa mit europäischen
Gelehrten nebst Nachtrichten über ihr Gebräuche...I Welches die literarische
Einleitung enthält.* Schönberg, 1836.
[1700/ 1701].

1599. **Higger, Michael.** "Cuthim." (Hebrew) in *Seven Minor Tractates.* New York, 1930.
[304.2].

1600. **Higgins, J. B. and John Macdonald.** "The Beginnings of Christianity." *NTS* 18.1
(1971): 54-80.
[1003.1/ 1603].

1601. **Hildesheimer, Meir.** *Des Samaritaners Marqah Buch der Wunder (Nach einer
Berliner Handschrift hrsg. übersetzt und mit noten und Anmerkungen versehen).*
Berlin, 1898. [Inaugural dissertation, 61 pp].
[1803].

1602. **Hilgenfeld, A.** *Die Ketzergeschichte des Urchristentums, Urkundlich Dargestellt.*
Leipzig, 1864. [Die Vorchristlichen Häresien in Israel: Essaer, Samariter, Simon
Magus].
[200/ 1500/ 1506.2].

1603. Hilgenfeld, A. "Nachtrag zu dem Taheb der Samariter." *ZWT* 38 (1895): 156.
[1107].

1604. ──────. Reviewer. A. Merx, "Der Taheb der Samaritaner, nach einer neu
aufgefundenen Urkunde." *ZWT* 37 (1894): 233-244.
[107/ 1107].

1605. Hill, Craig C. *Hellenists and Hebrew: Reappraising Division within the Earliest
Church.* Minneapolis: Fortress Press, 1992.
[1003.1/1502.2].

1606. Hill, G. F. "Some Palestinian Cults in the Graeco-Roman Age." *Proceedings of the
British Academy* 5 (1911-1912): 411-427.
[1002].

1607. Hillel, David de Beth. "The Travels of David de Beth Hillel." (Hebrew) in A.
Ya'ari, *Travellers to the Holy Land.* Ramat Gan, 1976.
[309].

1608. Hilliger, Johann Wilhelm. *Summarium Linguae Aramaeae i.e. Chaldaeo-Syro-
Samaritanae Olim in Academia Wittenbergensi.* Wittenbergae: University Press,
1679. [2nd edn. Leipzig, 1711].
[2600/ 2800].

1609. Hillprecht, H. V. *Explorations in Bible Lands During the Nineteenth Century.*
Edinburgh, 1903.
[308].

1610. Hippolytus and Origen? "Contra Haereses." In Migne, *PG.* 16: 3205-3212;3221-
3228; 3409-3412.
[200/ 305.4].

1611. Hirschberg, H. Z. (J. W.). "Judah and Ephraim—A Conflict of Generations."
(Hebrew) in *Eretz Shomron.* Jerusalem: IES, 1973. 99-105.
[1003.4].

1612. Hitti, P. K., editor. *Al-Baladhuri, The Origins of the Islamic State.* New York,
1916. 1.
[307.2/ 501/ 1003.3].

1613. Hoade, E. *Western Pilgrims—The Itineraries of..Fitsimons...Brygg and other pilgrims.*
Jerusalem: Franciscan Press, 1952. [2nd edition, 1970].
[306.3].

1614. Hody, Humphrey et al. *Aristeae Historia LXX interpretum. Accessere veterum
testimonia de eorum versione.* Oxford, 1692. [See E. Bernard].
[2300/ 2400].

1615. Hoenig, Johannes Caspar. *De Conversione Samaritanorum ad Christianismum...ex
historia colloquii Samaritani John iv.1-43.* Halle, 1696. 43 pp. 4°.
[1003.1 /1502.1].

1616. **Hoffman, Christian.** "Samaritanismi." *Umbra in Luce: Siva ConsensusJudaismi Samaritanismi cum Veritate Christiana.* Ienae, 1667. [2nd edn. 1680]. Both printed by John Jacob Bauhofer.
[1003.1].

1617. **Hoffman, Georg.** "Lexicalisches"=(Ketav Livona and Ketav Daatz)." *ZAW* 1 (1881): 334-338.
[2501].

1618. **Hofius, Otfried.** "Vergebungszuspruch und Vollmachtsfrage Mk 2, 1-12 und das Problem priestlicher Absolution im antiken Judentum." In *"Wenn nicht Jetzt".* editors. Hans-Georg Geyer and J. Schmidt. Neukirchen-Vluyn: Neukirchener, 1983. 115-127.
[1502/1803].

1619. **Hofman, S.** "The Four Differentiae in the Samaritan Reading of the Law." (Hebrew) in *Papers of the Fourth World Congress of Jewish Studies.* Jerusalem: Magnes, 1968. II: 208-209, 385-394. [Abstracted in the Fourth World Congress Abstracts, *Jewish Music,* 1965:11-13, 9-10 (Hebrew)].
[2308/ 3302].

1620. ⸺. "The Samaritan Reading of Marqah's Piyyutim." (Hebrew) *Yuval* 1 (1968): 36-51. [English summary: 251-252].
[2100/ 2604/ 3300].

1621. ⸺. "Samaritans (Supplementary section) Musical Tradition." *EJ.* Jerusalem, 1971. 16: 1555-1558.
[3300].

1622. **Hogan, M. P.** "The Woman at the Well (Jn. 4,1-42)." *Bible Today* 82 (1976): 633-669.
[1502.1].

1623. **Holloway, Benjamin.** *Remarks on Dr Sharps pieces...some account is given of the Chaldee, Syriac, Samaritan and Arabic dialects; showing them to have been all anciently one language.* Oxford, 1751.
[2600].

1624. **Hölscher, Gustav.** "Das neuentdeckte 'Josuabuch' der Samaritaner." *Allg.ev.Luth.K.Z* 41 (1908): 759-762.
[1604/ 1605].

1625. ⸺. "Palästina in der persischen und hellenistischen Zeit. Eine historischgeographische Untersuchung." In *Quellen und Forschungen zur alten Geschichte und Geographie.* Berlin, 1903.
[803/ 804].

1626. ⸺. "Samaritaner." In *Protestant Realencyklopädie.* 1913. 24.
[200/ 201].

1627. ⸺. Reviewer. **J. A. Montgomery**, "The Samaritans." *TLB* 29 (1908): 384.
[107/ 200].

1628. —————. "Sichem und Umgebung; Bemerkungen zur Topographie Palästinas."
ZDPV 33 (1910): 98-106.
[400/ 412].

1629. **Honig, Sarah.** "Samaritan Baby Boom." *Jerusalem Post.* 22/2/77.
[903/ 2904].

1630. **Hoonacker, Albin van.** *Une communauté judéo-araméene à Eléphantiné en Égypte au VIᵉ siècle av.J.C.* London, 1915.
[303.1/ 803].

1631. **Horbury, W.** Reviewer. **J. S. Isser,** "The Dositheans." *JTS* 29 (1978): 218-222.
[107/ 1503].

1632. **Horn, Georg.** *Defensio Dissertationis de vera aetate mundi contra Castigationes Isaaci Vossii: qua Hebraea Biblia... ex LXX interpr.* Lugduni Batavorum: Elsevier, 1659.
[Has a section on Samaritan language and letters].
[2501/ 2600].

1633. **Horn, S. H.** "Objects from Shechem, Excavated 1913 and 1914." *JEOL* 20
((1967-1968) 1968): 71-890. [5 figs. plates XV-XIX].
[606.1].

1634. —————. "Scarabs from Shechem." *JNES* 21 (1962): 1-14.
[412/ 607].

1635. **Horn, S. H. and L. G. Moulds.** "Pottery from Shechem, Excavated 1913 and
1914." *Andrews University Seminary Studies* 7.1 (1969): 17-46. [9 plates].
[606.1].

1636. **Horne, T. H.** *Introduction to the Critical Study and Knowledge of the Holy Scriptures.* London, 1818-1821. [Numerous printings].
[2300].

1637. **Horsley, G. R.** *New Documents Illustrating Early Christianity.* Sydney: Macquarie
University, 1981.
[2500/ 2513].

1638. **Horst, Pieter van der.** *Essays on the Early World of Christianity.* Novus
Testamentum et Orbis Antiquus 14. Göttingen: Vanderhoeck & Ruprecht,
1990. [The volume contains a reprint of the author's study of the Samaritan
Diaspora].
[500].

1639. —————. "De Samaritaanse diaspora in die oudheid." *NTT* 42 (1988): 134-
144.
[500].

1640. —————. Reviewer. **A. D. Crown,** "The Samaritans." *NTT* 45.4 (1991): 341-
342.
[107/ 200].

1641. **Hospers, J. H.** *A Basic Bibliography for the Study of the Semitic Languages.* Leiden: Brill, 1973. Vol. 1: 211-214.
[100/ 2600].

1642. **Hottinger, Johann Heinrich.** *Dissertationum theologico-philologicarum fasciculus III. De translationibus bibliorum in varias linguas vernaculas.* Heidelberg, 1660.
[2300].

1643. —————. *Enneas dissertationum philologico-theologicarum Heidelbergensium.* Tiguri, 1662.
[2300].

1644. —————. *Etymologicum orientale; sive Lexicon. sed et...samaritanae...brevis apologia contra Abrahamum Ecchellensem...* Francofurti, 1661. [Reprinted Hildesheim, 1977].
[2600/ 2603].

1645. —————. *Exercitationes anti-Morinianae de Pentateucho Samaritano, ejusque udentica authentia: oppositae canonicae ejusdem authentia à Johanne Morino...temerè assertae.* Tiguri: J. Bodmer, typis, 1644.
[2300].

1646. —————. *Historia Orientalis Quae ex variis Orientalium Monumentis Collecta agit...* Tiguri, 1660.
[200/ 801].

1647. —————. *Promtuarium, sive Bibliotheca Orientalis exhibens Catalogum.* Heidelberg, 1658.
[101/ 1550].

1648. —————. *Smegma Orientale Sordibus Barbarismi Contemtui Praesertim Linguarum Orientalium Oppositum.* Heidelberg: Academ. Bibliopolae & Typographi,[Typis. A. Wyngaerten].
[2300/ 2307/ 2600].

1649. —————. *Thesaurus philologicus seu Clavis Scripturae..samaritanismo.* Tiguri, 1649. [2nd edn. 1659, 1696. 3rd edn. 1698].
[2300].

1650. **Houbigant, Charles François.** *Biblia Hebraica cum notis criticis versionis Latina ad notas criticas facta.* Paris, 1753. [See especially vol.1: I-CXCI and the prolegomenon: LXI-XCIV. Notes are added both from Samaritan sources and from the Samaritan pentateuch].
[2300].

1651. **Hude, H. von der.** *Der Forma Pentateuchi Samaritani Externa.* Wittenberg, 1755.
[2300].

1652. **Hudry-Clergion, C.** "De Judée en Galilée. Étude de Jean 4, 1-45." *NRT* 103 (1981): 818-830.
[1003.1/1502.1].

1653. **Huetii, Pierre Daniel.** *De Interpretatione Libri Duo-Editio post Parisinian Primam altera et emendatio.* Paris and Stadae, 1680. [An earlier edition, Paris, 1661, not seen].
[2300].

1654. **Hug, J. L.** "Beiträge zur Geschichte des samaritanischen Pentateuchs." *Freyburger Zeitschrift* 7 (1834).
[2300].

1655. **Huntington, Robert.** *D. Rob. Huntingtoni, Episc.Ropotensis, Epistolae-Praemittuntur D. Huntingtoni et D. Bernardi Vitae.* London: Thomas Smith, 1704.
[1702].

1656. ——————. "Versio latina epistolae samaritanarum qui Sichem incolunt, ad fratres suos in Anglia." In **Ugolini,** *Thesaurus antiquitatum sacrorum.* Venice, 1759. 661-666.
[1702].

1657. **Hurst, L. D.** "The Case for a Samaritan Background." In *The Epistle to the Hebrews.* Cambridge: CUP, 1990. 67-74.
[1502/ 1502.1/ 1502.2].

1658. ——————. "The Samaritans." In *The Epistle to the Hebrews.* Cambridge: CUP, 1990. 75-82. [A very useful survey of the Samaritan background to the book of *Hebrews*].
[1502/ 1502.1/ 1502.2].

1659. **Huttenmeister, F. and G. Reeg.** *Die antiken Synagogen in Israel.* Wiesbaden, 1977. [Vol. 2, Samaritan Synagogues].
[602/ 1304].

1660. **Huxley, Henry Minor.** "Zur Anthropologie der Samaritaner." *Zeitschrift für Demographie und Statistik der Juden* 2 (1906): 137-139. [Translated from the *Jewish Encyclopaedia,* vol. 10 (1905): 674-676.].
[2901].

1661. **Hwiid, Andreas C.** *Specimen ineditae versionis Arabico-Samaritanae Pentateuchi e codice manuscripto Bibliothecae Barberinae.* Romae, 1780.
[2302].

1662. **Hyamson, A. M.** *The British Consulate in Jerusalem in Relation to the Jews in Palestine 1838-1914.* London: Jewish Historical Society of Great Britain, 1939.
[813/ 813.1].

1663. **Hyde, Thomas.** *Itinera Munda sic dicta nempe Cosmographia, autore Abrahamo Peritsol.* London: H. Bonwick, 1691. [The English edition contains quotations from the Samaritan Pentateuch that were not in the original Hebrew editions.].
[200].

1664. **Hyvernat, H.** "Arabes (Versions) des écritures." In *DB.* Paris, 1894. 1: 846-848.
[2302].

I

1665. **Ibn el Athir.** "Anecdotes et beaux traits de la vie du Sultan Youssof (Salâh Ed-Dîn)." *RHC (historiens orientaux)* 3 (1884). [307.1/ 809/ 810].

1666. **Ibn el Athir el Djezer.** "Extrait de la chronique titulée Kamel Altevarykh." *RHC (historiens orientaux)* 1 (1872). [307.1/ 809/ 810].

1667. **ibn Yahya, Gedalyah.** (Hebrew) *Sefer Shalshelet Haqabalah.* Warsaw, 1877. 30-33. [800].

1668. **Idelsohn, A. Z.** "Die gegenwärtige Aussprache des Hebräischen bei Juden und Samaritanern." *MGWJ* 57 (1913): 527-545, 697-721. [2604/ 2607].

1669. ————. "Die Vortragzeichen der Samaritaner." *MGWJ* 61 (1917): 117-126. [2607].

1670. ————. (Hebrew) *A History of Hebrew Music.* Tel Aviv: Dvir, 1923. [3300].

1671. ————. "The Samaritan Vowel System." (Hebrew) *JJ* 11 (1916): 343-344. [2607/ 3300].

1672. **Ilan, Zvi and U. Dinur.** "Giveit, An Ancient Settlement in the Desert of Shomron." (Hebrew) in Z. Ehrlich, editor, *Samaria and Benjamin.* Jerusalem, 1987. 114-130. [400/ 400.1].

1673. **Ilan, Zvi and E. Damati.** "Ancient Roads in the Wilderness of Samaria." (Hebrew) *Yearbook of the Museum Haaretz* 17/18 (1975): 43-52. [400.2].

1674. **Ilan, Zvi.** "Riddle of the Samaritan Desert." *Teva Va'arets* 19.4 (May, June, 1977). [Same as the following article of Ilan]. [400.3].

1675. ————. "Riddle of the Samaritan Desert." *Israel, Land and Nature* 2.4 (1977): 150-155. [On the site of Jib't in the *Kitab Tarikh of Abu'l Fath*]. [400.3].

1676. **Irmscher, Johannes.** "Zum diatagma Kaisaros von Nazareth." *ZNW* 42 (1949): 172-184. [1003.1].

1677. **Irwin, R. H.** "Les sanctuaires pré-monarchiques." *RB* 72 (1965): 170-171. [406].

1678. **Isaac, B. and A. Oppenheimer.** "The Revolt of Bar Kochba: Ideology and Modern Scholarship." *JJS* 36.1 (1985): 33-60.
[808/ 1601/ 1602].

1679. **Isaac ibn al-Fara.** "The Travels of Isaac ibn al-Fara of Malaga." (Hebrew) in **A. Ya'ari,** *Travellers to the Holy Land.* Givat Ram: Magnes Press, 1976. [Sacred places at Awerta and Shechem].
[306.3/ 402/ 412].

1680. **Ish-Shalom. M.** (Hebrew) *Christian Travellers to the Holy Land.* Tel Aviv, 1965.
[306.3/ 402/ 412].

1681. **Isidorus Pelusiota. Migne,** "Epistles." *PG* 78 1195-1198.
[305.4].

1682. **Israeli, A.** "Samaritans." In *The Jews in Our Times; Essays in the Sociology of the Jews.* 1967. 25-26.
[903].

1683. **Issa, A. O.** *Les minorités chrétiennes de Palestine à travers les siècles.* Jerusalem: Franciscan Press, 1978.
[900].

1684. **Isser, Jerome Stanley.** Reviewer. **A. D. Crown,** "The Samaritans." *Shofar* 8.3 (1990): 93-94.
[107/ 200].

1685. —————. *The Dositheans, A Samaritan Sect in Late Antiquity.* Leiden: Brill, 1976.
[1503].

1686. —————. "Dositheus, Jesus and a Moses Aretology." In **J. Neusner,** editor, *Christianity, Judaism and other Greco-Roman Cults. Studies for Morton Smith at Sixty.* Studies in Judaism in Late Antiquity XII. Leiden: Brill, 1975. 4: 167-189.
[1503].

1687. —————. Reviewer. **H. Kippenberg,** "Garizim und Synagoge." *BO* 29.5/6 (1972): 334-335.
[107/ 1001/ 1002].

1688. —————. "Jesus in the Samaritan Chronicles." *JJS* 32.2 (1981): 166-194.
[1003.1].

1689. —————. Reviewer. **S. Lowy,** "The Principles of Samaritan Exegesis." *JTS* (1978): 551f.
[107/ 2305].

1690. —————. Reviewer. **S. Lowy,** "The Principles of Samaritan Exegesis." *JBL* 98 (1979): 471-473.
[107/ 2305].

1691. —————. Reviewer. R. Coggins, "Samaritans and Jews." *JBL* 96 (1977): 131-
132.
[107/ 801/ 804].

1692. Iturriaga, A. Reviewer. Jarl Fossum, "The Name of God and the Angel of the
Lord." *Studia Monastica (Abadia de Montserrat, Barcelona)* 28.2 (1986): 413.
[107/ 2605].

I

1693. **Jacob, B.** "Das Hebräische Sprachgut im Christlich-Palästinischen." *ZAW* 22 (1902): 83-113.
[2600].

1694. **Jacob ben Aaron. W. E. Barton,** "The Book of Enlightenment—Translated from the Arabic by Abdullah ben Kori." *BS* 70 (1913): 313-346. [Reprinted as *The Book of Enlightenment for the Instruction of the Enquirer*, Sublette, Illinois, Puritan Press, 1913, 84 pp].
[200/ 800/ 1100].

1695. —————. **W. E. Barton,** "Circumcision Among the Samaritans—Translated from the Arabic by Abdullah b. Kori." *BS* 65 (1908): 694-710.
[1204].

1696. —————. "The History and Religion of the Samaritans, with an Introduction by W.S. Barton." *BS* 63 (1906): 385-426. [Reprinted, Oak Park, Ill.,1906, 46pp].
[200/ 800/ 1100].

1697. —————. "(La pâque) Chez les Samaritains." In *La pâque dans la conscience Juive*. Paris, 1959. 81-89.
[1404].

1698. —————. **W. E. Barton,** "The Messianic Hope of the Samaritans—Translated from the Arabic by Abdullah b. Kori." *Open Court* (1907): 272-296. [Reprinted 1907; 36 pp].
[1107].

1699. —————. **W. E. Barton,** "Mt.Gerizim, the One True Sanctuary—Translated from the Arabic by Abdullah b. Kori." *BS* 64 (1907): 498-518. [Reprinted, Puritan Press, Oak Park, Ill., 1907, 32pp].
[406].

1700. —————. **W. E. Barton,** "The Samaritan Sabbath—Translated from the Arabic by Abdullah b. Kori." *BS* 65 (1908): 430-444.
[1405].

1701. —————. *Samaritjansker rasskazyo Pervonacal noj istorii Samaritjan.* Kazan, 1911.
[200].

1702. **Jacob ben Ozzi, HaCohen.** *The Celebration of Passover by the Samaritans.* Jerusalem: Greek Convent Press, 1934. [2nd edition, 1935-115 pp. Translated from the Arabic by Abraham b. Zebulun. A Hebrew edition is known, 1934].
[1404].

1703. —————. *The Samaritans, Their History, Customs, Religion.* Nablus: Samaritan Community, SD.
[200/ 800].

1704. —————. *Who were the Samaritans?* Nablus: Samaritan Community, 1968.
      [800].

1705. **Jacob, E.** Reviewer. **J. Macdonald,** "Samaritan Chronicle II." *Revue d'histoire et philosophie religieuse* 53 (1973): 75.
      [107/ 1603].

1706. **Jacob, H. and J. D 'Allemand.** *Biblia Hebraica. Sepher Esrim ve'arba, Adjiciuntur Variae Lectiones Pentateuchi Hebraei et Hebraeo-Samaritani.* London, 1825.
      [2300].

1707. **Jacobé, F.** "L'hypogée d'el-Berith à Sichem. Note d'archéologie biblique." *RHLR* 2 (1897): 134-140.
      [412/ 606.1/ 1110].

1708. **Jacobs, J. and Lucien Wolf.** "The Crawford Collection & Manuscripts." In *Catalogue of the Anglo-Jewish Historical Exhibition, Royal Albert Hall, London, 1887.* London: F. Haes, 1888. 140-142, 193-194,.
      [101].

1709. **Jacobson, Howard.** *The Exagoge of Ezekiel.* Cambridge: CUP, 1983.
      [2002].

1710. **Jacoby, D. and Y. Tsafrir.** (Hebrew) *Jews, Samaritans and Christians in Byzantine Palestine.* Jerusalem: Yad Izhak Ben-Zvi, 1988.
      [808].

1711. **Jacoby, F.** *Die Fragmente der griechischen Historiker.* Leiden, 1957. 3 vols.
      [2000].

1712. **Jaffe, Chava Lazarus.** "Ezra Azir: A Pre-Islamic Polemic Motif: An Islamic Approach to the Origins of Biblical Criticism." *Tarbiz* 45.3 (Nisan-Sivan, 1987): 359-379. [Refers to the Karaite-Samaritan nexus].
      [1004].

1713. **Jaffe, O.** The Relationship Among Socio-Cultural, Socio-Economic and Personality Variables in Young Male Samaritans Living in Jewish Israeli Society. (Hebrew) Tel Aviv: Tel Aviv University, 1969. Unpublished M.A. thesis.
      [1500].

1714. **Jamgotchian, Haroutun S.** "Fragments inconnus de la traduction arabe du Pentateuque par Sa'adia al-Fayyoumi dans une adaptation samaritaine." In **A. Tal & M. Florentin,** editors, *Proceedings of the First International Congress of the Société d'Études Samaritaines.* Tel Aviv: Chaim Rosenberg School for Jewish Studies, University of Tel Aviv, 1991. 225-244.
      [2302].

1715. —————. "Le dictionnaire des manuscrits samaritains: sa préparation: objectif et méthode de travail." In **Rothschild and Sixdenier,** editors, *Etudes samaritaines.* Louvain-Paris, 1988. 193-201.
      [103].

1716. Jamieson, J. W. "The Samaritans." *Mankind Quarterly* 23.2 (1982): 141-148. [200].

1717. Jampel, S. "Die Wiederherstellung Israels unter den Achämeniden: vii Untersuchung von Esra iv, 1-5." *MGWJ* 46 (1901): 395-407. [803].

1718. Janssens, Yvonne. "L'épisode de la samarie chez Heracléon." *Sacra Pagina Bibl. Ephem. Theol. Lov.* 12-13 (1959): 77-85. [808].

1719. Japhet, H. A. "The Samaritans and Their Festivals." (Hebrew) Holon: Samaritan Community, 1968. [200/ 1100/ 1400].

1720. Japhet, Sarah. "The People of Israel." In *The Ideology of the Book of Chronicles and its Place in Biblical Thought.* Frankfurt, Bern and New York: Peter Lang, 1989. 267-351. [801.1].

1721. ——————. "The Temple in the Restoration Period: Reality and Ideology." *Union Seminary Quarterly Review* 44 (1991): 195-251. [802].

1722. Jaros, Karl. *Sichem, eine archaeologische und religionsgeschichtliche Studie mit besonderer Berucksichtung von Jos. 24.* Orbis Biblicus et Orientalis 11, Göttingen: Vandenhoeck & Ruprecht, 1976. [412/ 600].

1723. Jaros, Karl and B. Deckert. *Studien zur Sichem Area.* Orbis Biblicus et Orientalis-Freiburg 11a. Göttingen: Vandenhoeck & Ruprecht, 1976. [411/ 500].

1724. Jastrow, M. "On Assyrian and Samaritan." *JAOS* 13 (1889): 146-150. [2600].

1725. Jaubert, Annie. "La symbolique du puits de Jacob: Jean 4, 12." In *L'homme devant Dieu. Mélanges offerts au Père Henri de Lubac.* Aubrin, 1963. 1: 63-73. [407].

1726. Jaussen, J. A. *Coutumes Palestiniennes I. Naplouse et son district.* Paris, 1927. [903].

1727. ——————. "Inscription arabe du sanctuaire de sitt sulaymiyah au mont Ebal à Naplouse." *JPOS* 5 (1925): 75-81. [404/ 1110].

1728. Jeffrey, A. Translator. "Ghevond's Text of the Correspondence Between Umar II and Leo III." *HTR* 37 (1944): 269-332. [The Samaritans and early Islam]. [1003.3].

1729. Jellicoe, S. *The Septuagint and Modern Study*. Oxford, 1968. [Reprinted, New York, 1974].
[2400].

1730. Jens, Walter. *Der Barmherzige Samariter*. Stuttgart: Kreuz Verlag, 1973. [A Dutch translation, *Der Barmhartige Samariter*, Baarn, 1975].
[1502.3].

1731. Jepsen, A. Reviewer. E. Robertson, "Catalogue of the Samaritan Manuscripts in the John Rylands Library—The Gaster Manuscripts." *TLZ* 92 (1967): 507-508.
[103/ 107].

1732. Jeremias, Joachim. *Die Passahfeier der Samaritaner und ihre Bedeutung für das Verständnis der alttestamentlichen Passahüberlieferung*. 109 pp. Giessen: BZAW, 1932. 59.
[1404].

1733. ————. "Die Samaritaner." In *Jerusalem zur Zeit Jesu. Kultur Geschichtliche Untersuchung*. Göttingen, 1937. 224-231. [2nd edn. 1958, 3rd edn. 1962. French version, Paris, 1967, *Jerusalem au temps de Jésus*. An English edn., *Jerusalem in the Time of Jesus*, London, 1969, and 2nd English edn. 1973].
[200/ 800].

1734. ————. "Samareia", "Samarites", "Samiritis." In G. Friederich, editor, *Theological Dictionary of the New Testament*. Grand Rapids: Eerdmans, 1971. 88-94. [Reprinted, 1975. This is a reprint and translation of Kittel, *TWNT* 1960, 7. 88-94].
[410/ 804/ 806].

1735. ————. "The Samaritan Passover—a note." *ZAW* 13 (1936): 137.
[1404].

1736. Jervell, Jacob. "The Lost Sheep of the House of Israel, the Understanding of the Samaritans in Luke—Acts." In *Luke and the People of God. A New Look at Luke Acts*. Minneapolis: Augsburg Publishing, 1972. 113-132.
[1502.2/ 1502.4].

1737. Jervis, John Jervis-White. *Genesis Elucidated. A New Translation from the Hebrew, Compared with the Samaritan Text and the Septuagint and Syriac Versions, with Notes*. London: Samuel Bagster, 1852. [BL 3050.d.17].
[2300].

1738. Jewish Chronicle. "Untitled entries on the Samaritans." 17/10/1845 (History) (Shechem); 17/12/1858; 31/12/1858; 13/6/1862; 4/11/1864; 11/11/ 1864; 20/1/1865 (Cairo, Egypt); 5/5/1865 (Samaritan Pentateuch); 12/1/1866; 27/7/1866 (Palestine Exploration); 31/1/1868 (Oxford University MSS); 12/2/1869 (Library, France-Pentateuch); 3/1/1875; 17/12/1879 (Biblical Archaeology); 24/11/1884 (Visit of Es-Shellaby); 18/3/1887 (Visit of Es-Shellaby).
[200/ 103/ 106/ 600/ 2300/ 3006].

1739. **Jirku, Anton.** "Das Inschriftenmaterial der amerikanischen Ausgrabungen in Samarien." *OLZ* 28 (1925): 273-281.
[410/ 600].

1740. **John of Damascus.** "De Haeresibus Liber." Migne, *PG.* 94: 679-692, 694.
[305.4].

1741. **John of Nikiu. R. H. Charles,** editor, *The Chronicle of John, Coptic Bishop of Nikiu.* London, 1916. [Reprinted Amsterdam, Philo Press, n.d.].
[305.3].

1742. **Johnson, A. C., P. R. Coleman-Norton and F. C. Bourne.** *Ancient Roman Statutes.* Austin, 1961. [Edicts against violation of sepulchres].
[808].

1743. **Johnson, A. M.** "Philip the Evangelist and the Gospel of John." *AN* 16 (1976): 49-72.
[1502.1].

1744. **Jonas, Hans.** *The Gnostic Religion.* Boston, 1958. [2nd English edn.1963; 2 volume German edn., *Gnosis und Spätantiker Geist* 1934, 1954].
[1506].

1745. **Joshua, I.** *The Samaritan Book of Joshua.* Holon: Samaritan Community, 1965.
[1604/ 1605].

1746. **Joshua, S., I. Joshua and B. Marhiv.** *Pessah b'Bet-El.* Nablus, 1972. 44 pp.
[1404].

1747. **Joshua, S., A. Marhiv and B. Marhiv.** *Sepher Yehoshua Hashomronim.* Holon, 1976. [Limited edition of 100 copies].
[1604/ 1605].

1748. **Jost, Isaac M.** *Geschichte des Judentums und seiner Secten.* Leipzig, 1857. Vol. 1. 44-89.
[1500].

1749. **Justin Martyr.** "First Apology", "Second Apology", "Dialogue with Trypho." In Migne, *PG.* 6: 367-390, 403-410, 467-470, 755-758.
[305.4].

1750. **Justinian—Emperor.** "De Samaritanis (= Novella 144)." In Migne, *PL.* 72: 1050-1051.
[305.5].

1751. **Juynboll, T. G. J.** *Commentarii in historiam gentis Samaritanae.* Lugduni Batavorum: Luchtmans, 1846.
[800].

1752. —————. *Chronicon Samaritanum Arabice conscriptum, cui Titulus est Liber Josuae.* Lugduni Batavorum: Luchtmans, 1848.
[1604].

1753. ——————. "Commentatio de versione Arabico-Samaritana, et de scholiis, quae ccodicibus Parisiensibus n. 2 et 4 adscripta sunt." *Orientalia* 2 (1846): 115-157. [103/ 2302].

K

1754. **Kahen, Hasanein Wasef.** *Les Samaritains: histoire, coutumes, religion.* Nabluse—Jordania (!), 1965. 16 pp.
[200/ 800/ 1100].

1755. ―――. *The Samaritans, Their History, Religion, Customs.* Nablus, 1969. 24 pp. [Reprinted, 1974 as *The Samaritans, Their History, Religion, Custums(!)*].
[200/ 800/ 1100].

1756. ―――. *The Samaritans, Their History, Identity, Religion and Subdivisions, Literature and Social Status.* Jerusalem: Greek Convent Press, 1966.
[200].

1757. ―――. *Feastes (!) of the Samaritans: Passover (Sacrifice)—Pentecost (Shavuoth) Tabernacle (!).* Nablus, 1968. 10 pp.
[1100/ 1400].

1758. **Kahle, Ernest.** "The Problem of Saraat in the Viewpoint of Samaritan Exegesis." *Koroth* 8.5/5 (1982): 48-56. Proceedings of the First International Symposium on Medicine in the Bible.
[2305/ 3500].

1759. **Kahle, Paul.** "The Abisha' Scroll of the Samaritans." In *Studia Orientalia Ioanni Pedersen, Septuagenario a collegis discipulis amicis dicata.* Havniae, 1953. 188-192.
[2300/ 2301].

1760. ―――. "Aus der Geschichte der ältesten hebräischen Bibelhandschrift." *Abh. zur Semit. Religionskunde...Baudissin.* BZAW 33, 1918. 247-260.
[103/ 2300/ 2301].

1761. ―――. *The Cairo Geniza.* Oxford: Blackwell, 1959, 2nd edn. Reprinted: Berlin, 1962].
[103/ 2102.1/ 2300/ 2302/ 2306.1].

1762. ―――. Reviewer. **E. Robertson,** "Catalogue of the Samaritan Manuscripts in the John Rylands Library." *ZDMG* 92 (1938): 682-687.
[101/ 107].

1763. ―――. "Das Problem der Grammatik des Hebräischen." *Indogermanische Forschungen (Thurneysen Festschrift)* 45 (1928): 395-410. [Reprinted, *Opera Minora*: 54-67].
[2600].

1764. ―――. "Die Punktation der Masoreten in Alten Testament." *BZAW (Marti Festschrift).* Giessen, 1925. 167-172.
[2306.1].

1765. ―――. *Die arabischen Bibelübersetzungen. Texte mit Glossar und Literaturübersicht.* Leipzig: 1904,60 pp.
[2302].

1766. —————. "Die Aussprache des Hebräischen in Palästina vor den zeit der tiberischen Masoreten." *VT* 10 (1960): 375-385. [2600/ 2604].

1767. —————. *Die hebräischen Handschriften aus de Höhle.* Stuttgart, 1951. [101/ 103].

1768. —————. "Die Lesezeichen bei den Samaritanern." In **C. Adler & A. Ember**, editors, *Oriental Studies Published in Commemoration of the Fortieth Anniversary (1883-1923) of Paul Haupt.* Baltimore & Leipzig, 1924. 425-436. [Reprinted, *Opera Minora*, Brill, Leiden, 1956: 167-179]. [2607].

1769. —————. "Die Samaritaner im Jahre 1909 (AH 1327)." *PJ* 24 (1930): 89-103. [=*Dalman (Textschrift) Festschrift*]. [813/ 903].

1770. —————. "Die überlieferte Aussprache des Hebräischen und die Punktation der Masoreten." *ZAW* 39 (1921): 230-239. [2604].

1771. —————. "Die zwölf Marka-Hymnen aus dem 'Defter' der samaritanischen Liturgie." *Oriens Christianus,*3rd series, 7 (1932): 77-106. [= *Festschrift Anton Baumstark.* Reprinted, *Opera Minora*: 186-212]. [2102.1].

1772. —————. "Fragmente des samaritanischen Pentateuchtargums herausgegeben und erläutert." *ZA* 16/17 (1902/1903): 79-101; 1-22. [2401].

1773. —————. *Masoreten des Westens I.* Stuttgart, 1927. [2300/ 2306.1].

1774. —————. Reviewer. **A. Murtonen**, "Materials for a non-Masoretic Hebrew Grammar." *JSS* 3 (1958): 388-389. [107/ 2600].

1775. —————. Reviewer. **A. Merx**, "Der Messias oder Ta'eb." *TLZ* 36 (1911): 198-200. [107/ 1107].

1776. —————. *Opera Minora.* Leiden: Brill, 1956. [200].

1777. —————. Reviewer. **M. Gaster**, "Samaritan Joshua." *RB* 6 (1909): 154. [107/ 1605].

1778. —————. Reviewer. **M. Gaster**, "Samaritan Joshua." *DL* 30 (1909): 333-336. [1605].

1779. —————. Textkritische und lexicalische Bemerkungen zum samaritanischen Pentateuchtargum. (Ph.D.) Leipzig: Halle, 1898. [2300/ 2603].

1780. —————. "Untersuchungen zur Geschichte des Pentateuchtexres." *Theologische Studien und Kritiken* 88 (1915): 399-439. [Reprinted in *Opera Minora*: 3-37]. [2300].

1781. —————. "Zu den in Nablus befindlichen Handschriften des samaritanischen Pentateuchtargums." *ZDMG* 61 (1907): 909-912. [103/ 2401].

1782. —————. Reviewer. A. S. Yahuda, "Zum hebräische Buch Josua der Samaritaner." *ZDMG* 62 (1908): 550-551. [107/ 1604/ 1605].

1783. —————. Reviewer. A. S. Yahuda, "Zum samaritanischen Josua—Eine Erklärung." *Die Jüdische Rundschau* 4.71 (1908): 90-98. [107/ 1604/ 1605].

1784. —————. Reviewer. A. S. Yahuda, "Zum samaritanischen Josua—Eine Erklärung." *Die Welt* 12 (1908): 35. [107/ 1604/ 1605].

1785. —————. Reviewer. A. S. Yahuda, "Zum samaritanischen Josua—Eine Erklärung." *DL* 30 (1909): 336-360. [107/ 1604/ 1605].

1786. —————. "Zur Aussprache des Hebräischen bei den Samaritanern." In *Bertholet Festschrift*. Tübingen, 1950. 281-286. [Reprinted, *Opera Minora*: 180-185]. [2600/ 2604].

1787. **Kahlefeld, H.** "Wer ist mein Nächster? Das Lehrstück vom barmherzigen Samariter und die heutige Situation." *Bi.Ki* 24 (1969): 74-77. [1502.3].

1788. **Kamsler, H. M.** "The Samaritans." *Jewish Heritage* 12 (1970): 39-42. [200/ 903/ 2900].

1789. **Kaplan, Chaya.** "Remarks on the Suggested Reading of Yoram Tsafrir." (Hebrew) *Qadmoniot* 12.1[45] (1979): 30. [1003.1/ 1301/ 1304].

1790. —————. "On the Samaritan Church at Tel Qasile—Reply to Zev Safrai." (Hebrew) *Qadmoniot* 12.1 (1979): 30-31. [1003.1/ 1301/ 1304].

1791. —————. "A Samaritan Church in the Precincts of the Museum Ha'aretz." (Hebrew) *Qadmoniot* 11.2-3 (1978): 78-80. [Reprinted in *A–B* 1978:25-27]. [1003.1/ 1301/ 1304].

1792. **Kaplan, Jacob.** "Chronique Archéologique: Tel Aviv (a) Ramat Hahayal." *RB* 74 (1967): 86-88. Plate XIVb. [600].

1793. —————. "Chronique archéologique; Ramat Aviv." *RB* 84 (1977): 284f.
[414/ 1304].

1794. —————. "An Inscription from the Samaritan Synagogue at Yabneh."
(Hebrew) *Yediot* 13 (1946): 156-166. [Illustrated. Reprinted: *Yediot Reader,* 1
no. 1: 232-233].
[1304/ 2515].

1795. —————. "A New Interpretation for a Samaritan Inscription from Beth Shean."
Bulletin of the Museum Ha'aretz 17.8 (1975): 22-25.
[2503.1].

1796. —————. "A Samaritan Amulet from Corinth." *IEJ* 30.3-4 (1980): 196-198.
Plate 21.
[601].

1797. —————. "Samaritan Settlements of Byzantine Date in the Yarkon Basin."
Bulletin of the Museum Haaretz 8 (1966): 65-66 (English version): 55-56
(Hebrew Version).
[400.3/ 808].

1798. —————. "A Second Samaritan Amulet from Tel Aviv." *EI (Shazar Volume)* 10
(1971): 255-257. [English summary p. ix; plate 67].
[601].

1799. —————. "Two Samaritan Amulets." (Hebrew) *Yediot* 30 (1966): 239-244.
[601].

1800. —————. "Two Samaritan Amulets." *IEJ* 17 (1967): 158-162.
[601].

1801. Karasszon, I. Reviewer. J. Chappuis, "Jésus et la samaritaine." *Theologiai Szemle*
29 (1986): 119-121.
[1502.1].

1802. Karmon, Y. "The Samaria Mountains—Physiographic Structure and Road
Network." (Hebrew) *Eretz Shomron.* IES: Jerusalem, 1973. 114-120.
[400.2/ 400.4].

1803. Karst, Josef. *Eusebius Werke—Die Chronik aus dem Armenischen, übersetzt.*
Leipzig, 1911.
[305.4/ 500.1].

1804. Kartveit, Magnar. "Samaritanane i nyare forsking- ei gammel sekt som vert yngre
me ara?" *Tidsskrift for Teologi og Kirke* 52 (1982): 1-18.
[200].

1805. Kashani, R. "Samaritans; Origins, Traditions and Customs." (Hebrew) *Bitefutsot
Hagolah* 13 (1971): 202-219.
[200/ 801.1/ 1100/ 1200].

1806. Kasher, Aryeh. "Some Suggestions and Comments Concerning Alexander of
Macedon's Campaign in Palestine." (Hebrew) *BM* 62.1[20] (1975): 187-208

(Hebrew): 311-312 (English).
[804].

1807. **Katz, Ruth.** "The Reliability of Oral Transmission: The Case of Samaritan Music."
Yuval 3 (1974): 109-135. [Reprinted, Jerusalem, 1974].
[3300].

1808. —————. "Samaritan Music." In **A. D. Crown,** editor, *The Samaritans.*
Tübingen: Mohr, 1989. 743-770.
[3300].

1809. **Kaufman, Alfred.** "Auf Dem Garizim (Samaritaner—Passah)." *Orient-Rundschau*
(1932): 28-30. Illustrated.
[1404].

1810. **Kaufman, M.** "Christianity in Samaria." *A–B* 175 (1976): 12-13.
[1003.1].

1811. **Kaufman, Yehezkel.** (Hebrew) *Golah Venekhqar (=Exile and Estrangement).* Tel
Aviv, 1928. 1: 239-248.
[1100].

1812. —————. *History of the Religion of Israel.* New York, 1977. Vol. 4. 619-628.
[801.1/ 802].

1813. **Kautzsch, E.** "Ein Brief des Hohenpriesters der samaritaner Jakub ibn Harun."
ZDPV 8 (1885): 149-154.
[1300/ 1302].

1814. —————. "Samaria", "The Samaritans." In *The New Schaff-Herzog*
Encyclopaedia of Religious Knowledge. 1908-1914. 10: 185-191. [Includes a
substantial bibliography].
[100/ 201/ 410].

1815. —————. "Samaritaner", "Samariter." In *PRE.* 1884. 13: 340-355. [See also vol.
18: 1888 edn. 704, vol. 17 1906 edn. 428-445].
[201/ 410].

1816. **Kearney, P. J.** "Samaria." In *The New Catholic Encyclopaedia.* New York: McGraw
Hill, 1967. 12: 1007-1008.
[201/ 410].

1817. **Kedar, Benjamin Z.** "A Dangerous Baptism at Khisfin in the Late Sixth Century."
(Hebrew) in **Jacoby and Tsafrir,** editors, *Jews, Samaritans and Christians in*
Byzantine Palestine. Jerusalem: Yad Izhak Ben-Zvi, 1988. 238-241.
[808/ 1201].

1818. —————. "The Frankish Period." In **A. D. Crown,** editor, *The Samaritans.*
Tübingen: Mohr, 1989. 82-94.
[810/ 811].

1819. ——————. "Jews and Samaritans in the Crusader Kingdom of Jerusalem." (Hebrew) *Tarbiz* 53.3 (1984): 387-408.
[810].

1820. **Kee, H. C.** "Tell er-Ras and the Samaritan Temple." *NTS* 13 (1966-1967): 401-402.
[415/ 1305].

1821. **Keilholz, F.** *De Antiquissima Pentateuchi Versione Samaritana.* Wittenberg, 1756. [=Exercitatio V pp.140-185 in Imm. Schwarz].
[2300].

1822. **Keith, M. et al.** *Les juifs d'Europe et de palestine, voyage de M. M. Keith, Black, Bonar et MacCheyne envoyés par l'église d'Écosse.* Paris, 1844. 195-214.
[308/ 903].

1823. **Kelso, James L.** "Samaria", "Samaritans." In *Zondervan Pictorial Encyclopaedia of the Bible.* Grand Rapids, 1975. 5: 244-246.
[201].

1824. **Kennedy, A. R. S.** Reviewer. J. E. H. Thomson, "The Samaritans." *ET* 31 (1919-1920): 374-375.
[107/ 200].

1825. **Kennett, R. H.** "Israel." *ERE.* 1914. 7: 439-456.
[801].

1826. **Kennicott, Benjamin.** *An Answer to a Letter from...T. Rutherforth, by B. Kennicott D.D. in Defence of his Second Dissertation.* London, 1762.
[200/ 2300].

1827. ——————. *The State of the Printed Text of the Old Testament Considered. Dissertation the Second Wherein the Samaritan Copy of the Pentateuch is Vindicated.* Oxford, 1759.
[2300].

1828. ——————. *Vetus Testamentum Hebraicum cum variis lectionibus.* Oxford, 1776-1780. [Reprinted by Benjamin Blayney, 1790].
[2300].

1829. **Kenyon, Sir Frederick.** *Our Bible and the Ancient Manuscripts.* Revised edn. New York, 1958.
[2300].

1830. **Kerkhof, V. I.** "Catalogue of the Shechem Collection in the Rijksmuseum van Oudheden in Leiden =('Oudheidkundige Medadelingen uit het Rijksmuseum van Oudheden te Leiden')." *Nuntii ex Museo antiquario Leidensi* 50 (1969): 28-109. [34 figs.].
[101/ 600/ 606.1].

1831. ——————. "An Inscribed Stone Weight from Shechem." *BASOR* 184 (1966): 20-21. [1 fig.].
[606.1].

1832. **Keronyant de Tresel, P. B.** *Thesis Theologico Hebraicae Samaritanae et Graecae.*
Paris, 1774. [Held in Bibliothèque Nationale; D 8295].
[1100].

1833. **Kiesling, Emil.** *Sammelbich greichischer Urkunden aus Ägypten.* Wiesbaden, 1960.
Vol. 6, part 2.
[305.4/ 506].

1834. **Kilgallen, J.** "The Function of Stephen's Speech (Acts 7, 2-53)." *Biblica* 70.2
(1989): 173-193.
[1003.1/ 1502.2].

1835. ——————. A Literary and Redactional Study of Acts 7, 2-53. (Dissertation)
Rome: Pontifical Biblical Institute, 1973.
[1003.1/ 1502.2].

1836. ——————. *The Stephen Speech. A Literary and Redactional Study of Acts 7, 2-53.*
Analecta Biblica 67. Rome: Pontifical Institute, 1976.
[1003.1/ 1502.2].

1837. **Kilpatrick, G. D.** "John 4: 9." *JBL* 87.3 (1968): 327-328. [Samaritana and
Samaritanis/Samaritis is a Homoieteleuton].
[800/ 1502.1].

1838. **King, J. S.** "Sychar and Calvary. A Neglected Theory in the Interpretation of the
Fourth Gospel." *Theology* 77 (1974): 417-422.
[413/ 1003.1/ 1502.1].

1839. **King, P. J.** "Shechem." In *American Archaeology in the Mid East.* New York:
AASOR Monograph series, 1983. 141-146, 185-186.
[412].

1840. **Kippenberg, Hans G.** Reviewer. J. S. Isser, "The Dositheans." *JSJ* 8 (1977): 89-90.
[107/ 1503].

1841. ——————. "Ein Gebetbuch für den samaritanischen Synagogengottesdienst aus
dem 2. Jh. n. Chr." *ZDPV* 85.1 (1969): 76-103.
[2100/ 2102.1].

1842. ——————. *Garizim und Synagoge. Traditionsgeschichtliche Untersuchungen zur
samaritanischen Religion der aramäischen Periode.* Berlin, 1971.
[804/ 805/ 806/ 1002].

1843. **Kippenberg, Hans G. and G. A. Wewers.** *Textbuch zur neutestamentischen
Zeitgeschichte (Grundrisse zum neuen Testament. Das neue Testament Deutsch).*
Gottingen, 1979. [Pp.145-171 reprinted in Dexinger and Pummer, *Die
Samaritaner,* as "Die Synagogue", 331-360].
[806/ 1002].

1844. **Kircher, Athanasius.** *Prodromus Coptus sive Aegyptiacus.* Rome, 1636.
[505/ 1100].

1845. **Kirchheim, Raphael.** Reviewer. J. W. Nutt, "Fragments of a Samaritan Targum."
       JZWL (1875): 220-273.
       [107/ 800/ 2401].

1846. —————. (Hebrew) *Karme Shomron= Introductio in librum Talmudicum 'de
       Samaritanis'.* Francofurti ad Moenum: Kaufman, 1851. [Reprinted, Kedem,
       Jeusalem 1970 and Reuben Mass, Jerusalem 1976; see also S. D. Luzzatto].
       [200/ 304.2/ 800].

1847. —————. "Massekhet Kuthim." In *Septem libri Talmudici parvi Hierosolymitana
       editit in eosque commentarium composuit.* Frankfurt, 1851. 31-37. [Reprinted,
       with a Hebrew title page, Frankfurt, 1860 and Jerusalem, 1960].
       [304.2].

1848. **Kirkland, J. R.** "The Incident of Salem: A Re-examination of Genesis 14:18-20."
       Studia Biblica et Theologica 7 (1977): 3-23.
       [410.1].

1849. **Kirsch, J. S.** "The Samaritans and the Passover." *Sunday Magazine* 33 : 256f.
       [1404].

1850. **Kirschner, B.** "A Page from an Old Samaritan Bible." (Hebrew) *Yeda 'am* 8
       (1962): 34-36.
       [2300].

1851. **Kirshner, S.** "The Samaritans: A People Apart." *Jewish Digest* 28 (November,
       1982): 39-40.
       [200].

1852. **Klein, R. W.** "Samaria Papyrii." In *IDB.* Nashville: Abingdon, 1976.
       Supplementary volume: 722.
       [303.3].

1853. —————. Reviewer. R. **Coggins,** "Samaritans and Jews." *Currents in Theology
       and Mission* 3 (1976): 368.
       [107/ 801.1].

1854. **Klein, S.** "The Land of the Samaritans in the Time of the Talmud." (Hebrew) *JJ*
       10 (1913): 133-160.
       [400/ 807/ 808].

1855. **Klemm, H. G.** *Das Gleichnis vom barmherzigen Samariter.* Stuttgart, 1973.
       [1003.1/ 1502.3].

1856. —————. "Schillers ethisch-ästhetische Variationen zum Thema Lk.10, 30ff."
       KD 17 (1971): 127-140.
       [1003.1/ 1502.4].

1857. **Klijn, A. F. J.** "Stephen's Speech—Acts 7, 2-53." *NTS* 4 (1957): 25-31.
       [1502.2].

1858. **Klumel, M.** *Mischpâtim, ein samaritanisch-arabischer Commentar zu Ex.21-22, 15 von Ibrahim ibn Jakub.* Berlin, 1902.
[2200/ 2304].

1859. **Knaani, H.** "Shomronim." In *Encyclopaedia of Social Sciences.* 1970. 5: 663-666.
[201].

1860. **Knibb, Michael A.** "A Note on 4Q372 and 4Q390." In F. **García Martinez, A. Hilhorst and C. J. Labuschagne,** editors, *The Scriptures and the Scrolls.* Leiden, New York & Köln: Brill, 1992. 164-177.
[1005].

1861. **Knobel, A.** *Zur Geschichte der Samaritaner.* Giessen: Denkschriften der Gesellschaft für Wissenschaft und Kunst in Giessen, 1847. 1: 129-172.
[800].

1862. **Knox, E. A.** "The Samaritans and the Epistle to the Hebrews." *Churchman* (1927): 184-193. [Written to Christian Samaritans].
[1003.1/ 1502].

1863. **Kobert, R.** Reviewer. **H.Pohl,** "Kitab al Mirath." *Orientalia* 44 (1975): 139.
[107/ 2204].

1864. **Koch, Cornelius Dietrich.** "Dissertatio de nummorum hebraicorum inscriptionibus Samaritanis." In **Ugolini,** *Thesaurus.* Venice, 1765. 28: 1293-1308.
[603].

1865. —————. *De nummorum hebraicorum inscriptionibus Samaritanis.* Helmstadii, 1712.
[603].

1866. **Koch, K.** "Ezra and the Origins of Judaism." *JSS* 19 (1974): 173-197.
[801/ 802].

1867. —————. "Haggais unreines Volk [Hag. 2:4]." *ZAW* 79.1 (1967): 52-66.
[801].

1868. **Koeppel, P. Robert.** *Palästina die Landschaft in Kartern und Bildern.* Tübingen: Mohr, 1930.
[102/ 400.4].

1869. **Koester, Craig R.** "'The Savior of the world' (John 4:42)." *JBL* 109.4 (1990): 665-680.
[1100/ 1502.1].

1870. **Kohl, Heinrich and Carl Watzinger.** *Antike Synagogen in Galilaea.* Leipzig, 1916.
[1304].

1871. **Kohler, C.** "Description de la terre sainte par un franciscain anonyme." *ROL* 12 (1911): 1-67.
[306.2/ 400].

1872. **Kohler, Kaufman.** "Dositheus, the Samaritan Heresiarch, and His Relations to Jewish and Christian Doctrines and Sects." *AJT* 15.3 (1911): 405-435. [Reprinted, 1911]. [1503/ 1504].

1873. —————. "Dositheus, the Samaritan Heresiarch." In *Studies and Addresses and Personal Papers.* New York, 1931. [1503/ 1504].

1874. **Kohn, Samuel.** Reviewer. H. **Petermann and K. Vollers,** "Die samaritanische Pentateuchübersetzung nach der Ausgabe von Petermann und Vollers." *ZDMG* 47 (1893): 626-697. [107/ 2300].

1875. —————. "Ibn-Ezra Polemisirt gegen die Samaritanen." *MGWJ* 22 (1873): 478-480. [1004/ 2205].

1876. —————. De Pentateucho Samaritano ejusque cum versionibus antiquis nexu. (D. Phil) Lipsiae: University of Leipzig, 1865. [2300].

1877. —————. "Samareitikon und Septuaginta." *MGWJ* 37 (1874): 1-7, 49-67. [2309/ 2400].

1878. —————. "Samaritanische Studien. Beiträge zur samaritanischen Pentateuchübersetzung und Lexicographie." *MGWJ* (1866, 1867): (1866) 15-32, 56-68, 109-119, 217-231, 268-272; (1867) 174-189, 216-222, 252-269. [Reprinted; Breslau (1868) 114 pp. + vi]. [2300/ 2603].

1879. —————. "Zur neueste literatur über die Samaritaner." *ZDMG* 39 (1885): 165-226. [100/ 107/ 200].

1880. —————. "Zur Sprache, Literatur und Dogmatik der Samaritaner. I. Aus einer Pessach Haggadah der Samaritaner. II. Das samaritanische Targum. III. Die Petersburger Fragmente des samaritanische Targum. IV. Nachträge." *AKM* 5.4 (1876): 1-238. [Reprinted, Lichtenstein, Kraus 1966]. [1100/ 1550/ 2600].

1881. **König, E.** "Samaritan Pentateuch." In J. D. **Hastings,** editor, *Dictionary of the Bible.* Edinburgh & New York, 1904. Additional volume: 68-72. [2300].

1882. —————. "Der samaritanische Pentateuch und die Pentateuchkritik." *JBL* 34 (1915): 10-16. [2300].

1883. **Königsberger, B.** "Von den Samaritanern." *AZJ* 60.2 (1896): 20-22. [200].

1884. **Körner, J.** Reviewer. **R. Macuch,** "Grammatik des samaritanischen Hebräisch." *TLZ* 98 (1973): 21-25. [107/ 2601].

1885. **Kortholt, Christian.** "De Pentateucho Samaritani." In *De Variis scripturae editionibus Tractatum Theologico Historico-Philologicum.* Cologne, 1686. [2300].

1886. **Kotsuji, Abram Setsuzau.** *The Origin and Evolution of the Semitic Alphabets.* Tokyo, 1937. 202-207. [2501].

1887. **Kovacic, E. S.** Reviewer. **A. D. Crown,** "Bibliography of the Samaritans." *Choice* (February, 1985): 792. [100/ 107].

1888. **Kraabel, A. T.** "New Evidence of the Samaritan Diaspora Has Been Found on Delos." *BA* 47.1 (1984): 44-46. [504].

1889. **Kraemer, J. C.** *Excavations at Nessana: 3 The Non-Literary Papyri.* Princeton, 1958. [303.2].

1890. **Kramers, J. H. and G. Wiet,** editors. (Arabic) **Ibn Hauqal,** *The Configuration of the Land.* Paris, 1964. Vol. 1. [307.1/ 400].

1891. **Kraus, J.** "The Good Samaritans, Somehow They Have Survived." *Pr. T.* 6.4 (1979): 53-57. [200].

1892. —————. "Os Bons Samaritanos." *Shalom Sao Paulo* 180 (1980): 54-58. [Translated from the English version in *Present Tense*]. [200].

1893. **Kraus, R.** "Samaritan Cooking." *A–B Samaritan News* 228 (1/2/1979). [3600].

1894. **Krauss, Samuel.** "Antioche." *REJ* 45 (1902): 27-49. [1503/ 1504].

1895. —————. "Dosithée et les Dosithéens." *REJ* 42 (1901): 27-42. [1503/ 1504].

1896. —————. Reviewer. **J. A. Montgomery,** "The Samaritans." *LZ* 58 (1907): 1532-1534. [107/ 200].

1897. **Kressel, G.** "Samaritan Newspapers." *Hadoar* 51 (1972): 32-37. (Hebrew). [100/ 106].

1898. —————. "The Torah in Samaritan Tradition." (Hebrew) in *The Tanach Among the Jewish Tribes*. Tel Aviv, 1962. [2300].

1899. **Krumbacker, K.** Reviewer. A. **Wirth,** "Aus orientalischen Chroniken." *BZ* 3 (1894): 607-675. [See also *LZ* 46 (1895): 5ff.]. [1600].

1900. **Kuenen, Abraham.** *Libri Exodi et Levitici Secundum Arabicam Pentateuchi Samaritani Versionem ab Abu Saido Conscriptam.* Leiden: Brill, 1854. [2302].

1901. —————. A. H. **May,** translator, *The Religion of Israel.* London and Edinburgh, 1875. Vol. 3. [1100].

1902. —————. *Specimen Theologicum continens Geneseos libri capita xxxiv priora ex Arabici Pentateuchi Samaritani versione nunc primum edita cum prolegomenis.* Leiden, 1851. [An alternative title page—Liber Geneseos Secundum]. [2302].

1903. **Kugel, James.** "The Story of Dinah in the Testament of Levi." *HTR* 85.1 (1992): 1-34. [801].

1904. **Kuiper, K.** "Le poète juif Ezechiel." *REJ* 46 (1903): 48-73, 161-177. [2002].

1905. **Kunert, Christian Samuel.** "Exercitatio IV." In I. **Schwarz,** *Exercitationes historic-criticae.* Wittenberg, 1756. 188-216. [2300].

1906. **Kunitzsch, P.** Reviewer. S. **Powels,** "Der Kalender der Samaritaner." *ZDMG* 198 (1978): 416. [107/ 1400].

1907. **Kunstlinger, I.** "De la prétendue influence des Samaritains sur Muhammed et sur l'Islam." *Rocznik Orientalistyczny* 4 (1925): 269-275. [1003.3].

1908. **Kupliuk, M.** "Gerizim." *Keshet* 12 (1970): 150-166. [406/ 1404].

1909. —————. "Night Watch on Mt. Gerizim." (Hebrew) in Y. L. **Baruch** and **Yom-Tov Levinski,** *Sepher Hamoadim (Pessach).* 2nd edn. Tel Aviv, 1952. 3: 407-410. [1404].

1910. **Kutscher, E. Y.** Reviewer. Z. **Ben-Hayyim,** "The Aramaic of the Samaritans (= The Literary and Oral Traditions of the Samaritans)." *Tarbiz* 37 (1968): 397-419. [Reprinted in *Hebrew and Aramaic Studies*, Jerusalem, 1977]. [107/ 2600].

1911. —————. *The Language and Linguistic Background of the Dead Sea Isaiah Scroll.*
Tel Aviv, 1959. (Hebrew).
[2600].

1912. **Kysar, Robert.** *The Fourth Evangelist and His Gospel. An Examination of Contemporary Scholarship.* Minneapolis: Augsburg Publishing, 1975. [The Samaritan mission].
[100/ 106/ 1502.1].

1913. —————. "The Fourth Gospel: A Report on Recent Research." In **Wolfgang Haase,** editor, *Aufstieg und Niedergang de römischen Welt.* Berlin: Walter de Gruyter, 1985. II: 2389-2480.
[100/ 1502.1].

L

1914. **La Haye, A.** *Lettres juives ou correspondance philosophique-historique et critique.* Paris, 1764. Vol. 5 letter 145:223-243.
[800].

1915. **Lacheman, E. N.** "A Matter of Method in Hebrew Paleography." *JQR* 40 (1949): 15-39. With plates.
[2501.1].

1916. **Lagrange, Marie Joseph.** "Découverte d'une inscription en caractères samaritains à Amouas." *Rev. ill. de la Terre Sainte* 7 (1890): 339.
[2502].

1917. ————. "Épigraphie sémitique." *RB* 6 (1897): 106.
[2501].

1918. ————. "Inscription samaritaine d'Amwas." *RB* 2 (1893): 114-116. [Reprinted in Chabot, *Répertoire d'épigraphie sémitique I* no. 366:229-230; see de Vogüé].
[2502].

1919. ————. "L'inscription samaritaine d'Amwas." *Rev. ill. de la Terre Sainte* 8 (1891): 83-84.
[2502].

1920. ————. "La secte juive de la nouvelle alliance en pays de Damas." *RB* 9 (1912): 213-240, 321-360.
[503/ 1003.4/ 1503].

1921. **Laibl, D.** "The Influence of the Five Final Letters on the Bible Version." (Hebrew) *BM* 28.4 (1966): 77-86.
[2300].

1922. **Laine, Genevieve.** "Itinéraire du pèlerin: la Samarie." *Terre Sainte* 2 (1971): 34-42.
[400/ 407].

1923. **Lambdin, T. O.** "The Gospel of Thomas (II:2)." In **J. M. Robinson,** editor, *The Nag Hammadi Library in English.* London, 1977. 118-130.
[1003.1/ 1506].

1924. **Lambert, M.** "Note exégétique." *REJ* 49 (1904): 147-148.
[2602].

1925. **Lambrecht, J.** "De Barmhartige Samaritaan (Lk.10:25-37)." *OGL* 51 (1974): 91-105.
[1502.3].

1926. ————. "The Message of the Good Samaritan: Luke 10: 25-37." *Louv. Stud.* 5.2 (1974): 121-125. [*NtAb* 19 (1975) 980].
[1502.3].

1927. **Landau, J. M.** *Abdul Hamid's Palestine.* London, 1979. [Illustrations, pp. 87-95]. [102].

1928. **Landers, G. M.** Reviewer. **A. Murtonen,** "Materials for a Non-Masoretic Hebrew Grammar II." *JBL* 80 (1961): 96-97. [107/ 2600].

1929. **Landersdorfer, S.** "Ein samaritanischer Psalterium." *T und G* (1924): 39-46. [2100].

1930. **Langen, A.** "Ein samaritanischer Psalter." *Beilage zur Wochenschrift für homiletische Wissenschaft* 1.2 (1923/1924): 65-66. [2100].

1931. **Lapp, Nancy L.,** editor. "The Cave Clearances in the Wadi ed-Daliyeh." In *The Tale of the Tell.* Pittsburgh: Pittsburgh Theological Monograph Series, 5, 1975. 66-76. [303.3].

1932. ——————. "Pottery from Some Hellenistic Loci at Balâtah (Shechem)." *BASOR* 175 (1964): 14-26. [Figs. 1-4]. [412/ 606.1].

1933. ——————. "The Stratum V Pottery from Balâtah (Shechem)." *BASOR* 257 (Winter/February 1985): 19-44. [606.1].

1934. **Lapp, Paul W.** "Bedouin Find of Papyri. Three Centuries Older Than the Dead Sea Scrolls." *BAR* 4.1 (1978): 16-24. [303.3].

1935. ——————. "The Samaria Papyri." *Archaeology* 16.3 (1963): 204-206. Two figs. [303.3].

1936. ——————. "Wadi ed-Dâliyeh, chronique archéologique." *RB* 72 (1965): 405-411. [303.3].

1937. **Lapp, Paul W. and N. Lapp.** "Discoveries in the Wadi ed-Dâliyeh; An Account of the Discovery." *AASOR* 41 (1974): 1-6. [Pp. 1-106 of this issue are concerned with the archaeological implications of this find]. [303.3].

1938. **Larned, J. N.** "Samaria—Samaritans." In *History for Ready Reference.* Springfield, 1901. 4. [200/ 201].

1939. **Larousse, P.** "Samaritaine." In *Grand Dictionnaire Universel du XIXe Siècle.* Paris, 1875. 14. [200/ 201].

1940. **Larsson, G.** *The Secret System. A Study in the Chronology of the Old Testament.*
Leiden: Brill, 1973.
[700].

1941. **Le Comte Beugnot, M.** "Assises de Jérusalem." *RHC* 1 & 2 (1841-1843): 1: 396-
399, 612-633; 2:55-57, 171-173, 452-453.
[809/ 810].

1942. **Le Jay, Guy Michel.** *Pentateuchus Syriacus, Arabicus et Samaritanus.* Paris, 1632.
[2300].

1943. **Le Jay, Guy Michel and Morin et al.** *Biblia Polyglotta... 2. Samarita...Quibus
textus originales totius Scripturae Sacrae.* Paris: 9 vols., 1645. [The Samaritan
text is in vol. 6 of the Paris polyglot].
[105/ 2300].

1944. **Le Long, Jacob.** *Bibliotheca Sacra seu syllabus omnium ferme Sacrae Scripturae
editionum ac versionum. Pars prima.* Paris, 1709. [Notes by Chr. Fried. Boerner,
Lipsae, 1709; a new edition Halle, 1781 ed. A. G. Masch].
[105/ 2300].

1945. **Lebedev, V. V.** "The Samaritan Method of Speaking Hebrew." (Yiddish) *Sovietish
Heimland* 7 (1974): 157-159.
[2606].

1946. **Lebram, J. C. H.** "Ein Streit um die hebräische Bibel und die Septuaginta." In T.
H. L. Scheurleer and G. H. M. P. Meyjes, *Leiden University in the
Seventeenth Century.* Leiden: Brill, 1975. 21-64.
[1700/ 2300].

1947. ——————. "Jakob segnet Josephs Söhne, Darstellungen von Gen. XLVIII in der
Überlieferung und bei Remrandt." *OTS* 15 (1969): 145-169.
[102/ 800].

1948. ——————. Reviewer. **J. Macdonald,** "Memar Marqah." *VT* 15 (1965): 176f.
[107/ 1803].

1949. ——————. "Nachbiblische Weisheitstraditionen." *VT* 15.1 (1965): 167-237.
[1803].

1950. ——————. Reviewer. **J. Macdonald,** "Samaritan Chronicle II." *NTT* 25 (1971):
204-205.
[107/ 1603].

1951. ——————. Reviewer. **James Purvis,** "The Samaritan Pentateuch." *BO* 26
(1969): 382-383.
[107/ 2300].

1952. **Leclercq, Henri M.** "Samaritaine." In *Dictionnaire d'archéologie chrétienne et de
liturgie.* Paris, 1903, 1950. 15a: 726-734. [Other editions].
[200/ 201].

1953. **Leconte, R.** "Chez les samaritains." In *Terre biblique. La Palestine aux trois dimensions.* Paris and Brussels, 1960. chapter 3: 37-54.
[308/ 903].

1954. **Lee, Samuel.** *Biblia Sacra Polyglotta.* Paris, 1831. [Reprinted, 1869, by Samuel; Bagster; only the quarto edition contains a Samaritan text of the Pentateuch].
[2300].

1955. **Leenhardt, Franz J.** "Das Gleichnis vom barmherzigen Samariter." In H. Gollwitzer, editor, *Das Gleichnis vom barmherzigen Samariter.* Neukirchen: BSt 34, 1962.
[1502.3].

1956. ——————. "La parabole du Samaritain. (Schema d'une exégèse existentialiste)." In *Aux sources de la tradition chrétienne: Mélanges offerts à Maurice Goguel.* Neuchâtel-Paris, 1950. 132-138.
[1502.3].

1957. **Legendre, A.** "Garizim." *DB* 3 (1899): 106-113.
[406].

1958. ——————. "Sur les ruines de samarie (Sebastiyeh)." *Revue des facultés catholiques de l'ouest* 8.5 (1898): 645-662.
[410].

1959. **Leidig, Edeltraud.** *Jesu Gespräch mit der Samaritanerin und weitere GesprächeJesus im Johannesevangelium.* Basel: Reinhardt Kommissionsverlag, 1979. [Revision of a doctoral thesis for Basel University, 1978].
[1003.1/ 1502.1].

1960. **Leipoldt, Johannes.** Reviewer. J. Jeremias, "Die Passahfeier der Samaritaner." *ZDMG* 86 (1933): 232-233. [See also, Vollers; Leipoldt was a contributor to Vollers' catalogue of Samaritan manuscripts].
[107/ 1404].

1961. **Leisegang, Hans.** *Die Gnosis.* Leipzig, 1924. [Reprinted as *La Gnose*, Paris, 1951. See especially pp. 47-79. Another edn. 1971].
[1506/ 1506.2].

1962. **Leith, Mary Joan Wynn.** Greek and Persian Images in Pre-Alexandrine Samaria: The Wadi ed-Daliyeh Seal Impressions. (Ph. D. dissertation) Harvard University: 1990.
[303.3].

1963. **Leitner, Martin.** "Die samaritanischen Legenden Mosis. Aus der arabischen Handschrift des britischer Museums übersetzt." *DVJ* 4 (1868): 185f.
[1802/ 1803].

1964. **Leivestad, Ragnar.** Reviewer. Jarl Fossum, "The Angel of the Lord." *Norsk Teologisk Tidsskrift* 87 (1986): 125-126.
[107/ 1500].

1965. **Lemaire, A.** "Samarie." In *Encyclopaedia Universalis.* Paris, 1975. 20: 1719.
[200/ 410].

1966. **Lenglet, Adrien.** "Jésus de passage parmi les samaritains Jn 4,4-42." *Biblica* 66.4
(1985): 493-503.
[1502.1].

1967. **Lerner, I.** A Critical Investigation and Translation of the Special Liturgies of the
Samaritans for Their Passover and their Feast of Unleavened Bread. (Ph.D.)
Leeds: University of Leeds, 1956.
[1404/ 2102].

1968. **Lesètre, H.** "Samaritain." *DB* 5.2 (1928): 1421-1428.
[201].

1969. **Leusden, Jan.** "Dissertation Octava 'De Pentateucho Samaritano'." In *Philologus
Hebraeo-Mixtus: una cum Spicilegio Philologico.* Ultrajecti: F.Halma, 1682.
[2nd edn. 1682; 3rd edn. Leydae & Ultrajecti, 1699; 4th edn. Basilae, 1739].
[2300].

1970. —————. *Philologus Hebraeus Continens Quaestiones Hebraicas.* Utrecht, 1657.
[5th edn. Basilae, 1739].
[2300/ 2600].

1971. —————. *Scholae syriacae libri tres. Una cum dissertatione de literis et lingua
samaritanorum.* Ultrajecti: Meinardi à Dreuen, 1658. [Second edn, Ultrajecti,
1672. The title page of the second edn. varies].
[1550/ 2501/ 2600].

1972. **Levey, Robson and Franklyn.** *Specimens of Printing Types in the Offices of Levey,
Robson and Franklyn...Samaritan...and Arabic.* London, 1850. [BL 11899 e.8
(1)].
[105].

1973. **Levin, M.** "Samaritan Passover." *Conservative Judaism* (11 April 1966): 35-40.
[1404].

1974. —————. "The Samaritan Passover: Sacrifice on the Mountain." *Hadassah
Magazine* 46 (May, 1965): 4-5.
[1404].

1975. **Levine, Lee I.** *Ancient Synagogues Revealed.* Jerusalem: IES, 1981.
[1304].

1976. —————. "R. Simeon b. Yohai and the Purification of Tiberias." *HUCA* 49
(1978): 143-186.
[1003.4/ 2205].

1977. —————. "The Samaritan Community." In *Caesarea under Roman Rule.*
Leiden: Brill, 1975. Chapter 6. 107-112; 227-230.
[806/ 807/ 808].

1978. **Levinson, Joshua.** *The Hill of Samaria.* Tel Aviv, 1963. 48 pp. [In the series *Israel from Dan to Eilat*].
[410].

1979. **Levy, Isaac.** "Les samaritains." *Mémoires de Societé Philomathique de Verdun* 6 (1863): 175-202.
[200].

1980. **Lewin, L.** Reviewer. D. Rettig, "Memar Marqah." *MGWJ* 79 (1935): 267-270.
[107/ 1803].

1981. **Lidzbarski, Mark.** *Handbuch der nordsemitischen Epigraphik ausgewahlten Inschriften.* Weimar, 1898. Vol. 1:117, 440. Vol. 2: pl. 21.
[2501].

1982. **Lieberman, Saul.** "The Martyrs of Caesarea." *Annuaire de l'Institut de philologie et d'histoire orientales et slaves* 7 (1939-1944—New York, 1944): 395-446. [See the response by Sonne in *JQR* and Lieberman's response and rejoinder for a discussion of the Samaritans in the Jerusalem Talmud].
[304.2/ 808].

1983. ——————. "The Martyrs of Caesarea." *JQR* 36 (1946): 239-253.
[304.2/ 808].

1984. ——————. "The Martyrs of Caesarea—Rejoinder." *JQR* 37 (1946-1947): 329-336.
[304.2/ 808].

1985. **Lietzmann, H.** "Simon Magus." In *PRE.* new edition. second series. , 1927. III: 180f.
[1506.2].

1986. **Lifshitz, B. and J. Schiby.** "Une synagogue samaritaine à Thessalonique." *RB* 75.3 (1968): 368-378.
[512/ 600/ 1304].

1987. **Lightfoot, John.** Ugolini, "Disquisitio Chorographica in S. Johannem." *Thesaurus* 5 1118f.
[1002/ 1502.1/ 3004].

1988. ——————. R. Gandell, editor, *Horae Hebraicae et Talmudicae.* Oxford, 1859. 1: 115-125, 352-361. [For a list of the editions of Lightfoot see the preface to this edition].
[2300].

1989. **Lightly, J. W.** *Jewish Sects and Parties in the Time of Christ.* London, 1923.
[1002/ 1500/ 1503].

1990. ——————. Reviewer. J. E. H. Thomson, "The Samaritans." *TLS* (27 May 1920): 334. [Correspondence—10 June 1920: 368].
[107/ 200/ 2300].

1991. —————. Reviewer. J. E. H. Thomson, "The Samaritans and their Pentateuch." *London Quarterly Review* (April, 1920): 250-253.
[107/ 200/ 2300].

1992. **Linder, Sven.** "Die Passahfeier der Samaritaner auf dem Berg Garizim." *PJB* 8th year (1912): 104-120. Plate 5.
[1303/ 1404].

1993. —————. "Några anteckningar från samaritanernas påskhögtid på Garizim år 1912." *Bibelforskaren* 30 (1913): 169-193. Illustrated.
[102/ 1303/ 1404].

1994. **Lindijer, C. H.** "Oude en nieuwe visies op de gelijkenis van de barmhartige Samaritaan." *NTT* 15 (1960): 11-23. [*NTAb* 5 (1961) no. 734].
[1002/ 1502.3].

1995. **Linneman, E.** "The Story of the Good Samaritan." In J. Sturdy, translator, *Parables of the Good Samaritan.* London, 1966. 51-59. [Translated from the 3rd edn. of *Gleichnisse Jesu. Einführung und Auslegung,* Göttingen, 1964].
[1002/ 1502.3].

1996. **Lipinski, Eduard.** Reviewer. K. A. Mathews, "The Palaeo-Leviticus Hebrew Scroll (11QPaleo Lev.)." *BO* 44.3-4 (1987): 516-517.
[107/ 2309.1].

1997. **Liver, Jacob.** "Sanballat." (Hebrew) *EM* 5 (1968): 1057-1061.
[802.1].

1998. **Lobstein, Ioanne Michaele.** *Anhang zu dem von Johann Michael Lobstein.* Francofurti ad Moenum, 1781.
[103/ 2300].

1999. —————. *Codex Samaritanus Parisinus Sanctae Genovefae. Praemissa commentatio de Samaritanae gentis religione aevi recentioris.* Francofurti ad Moenum, 1781.
[103/ 2300].

2000. —————. *Commentatio historic-philologica de montibus Ebal et Garizim Deuteronomii xxvii.* Strasbourg, Argentorati, 1772/1773.
[404/ 406/ 2304].

2001. **Lockwood, Wilfred and Chiesa, Bruno.** *Ya'qub al-Qirqisani on Jewish Sects and Christianity.* Frankfurt and New York: Peter Lang, 1984. Judentum and Umwelt 10.
[307.2].

2002. **Loescher, Valentin August.** *De Causis Linguae Ebraeae.* Francofurti and Lipsae, 1706.
[2600].

2003. **Loewe, Herbert.** *Catalogue of the Printed Books and of the Semitic and Jewish Manuscripts in the Mary Frere Hebrew Library at Girton College, Cambridge.*

Cambridge: Girton College, 1916. 37 pp.
[101/ 103].

2004. ——————. "Judaism." In *ERE*. 1914. 7: 581-609.
[1003.4].

2005. ——————. *Unpublished Catalogue Notes of the Samaritan Manuscripts in the Library of the University of Cambridge.* [Available on request from the library].
[101].

2006. **Loewe, L.** "Briefe...aus dem Oriente." *AZJ* 3.36 (1839): 143-4, 186, 190, 202, 226.
[200/ 1700].

2007. **Loewe, R.** "'Salvation' is not of the Jews." *JTS* 32 (1981): 341-368.
[1003.1].

2008. **Loewenstamm, Ayalah.** "Dustan (el Dustan)." In *EJ*. Jerusalem. 6: 313-316.
[1504].

2009. ——————. Reviewer. **H. G. Kippenberg,** "Garizim und Synagoge." *IEJ* 22 (1972): 188-190.
[107/ 805/ 1002].

2010. ——————. Reviewer. **Sylvia Powels,** "Der Kalender der Samaritaner." *BSOAS* 42 (1979): 555-561.
[107/ 1400].

2011. ——————. "A Karaite Commentary on Genesis in a Samaritan Pseudo-morphosis." (Hebrew) *Sefunot* 8 (1963): 18-20, 167-204.
[1003.4/ 1004/ 2304].

2012. ——————. "The Karaite Jeshuah ben Jehudah, Author of a Pseudo-Samaritan Commentary on Genesis." (Hebrew) *Tarbiz* 41.2 (1972): 183-187. [English summary].
[1003.4/ 1004/ 2304].

2013. ——————. A Karaite Manuscript in a Samaritan Guise (= Bodley Opp.Add.4⁰ 99p 3086). (Doctoral thesis, Hebrew) Jerusalem: Hebrew University, 1962.[See *Sefunot* 8 (1963)].
[1003.4/ 1004/ 2304].

2014. ——————. "Remarks on the 613 Precepts in Samaritan Exegesis." (Hebrew) *Tarbiz* 41 (1972): 306-312. [English summary p.IV].
[1003.4/ 1004].

2015. ——————. "Samaritan Language and Literature." In *EJ*. Jerusalem. 14: 752-758.
[Abstracted *A-B* (1979):247-248].
[1550/ 2600/ 2700/ 2800].

2016. ——————. "A Samaritan Ring and the Identification of 'Ain Kushi'." (Hebrew) *Qadmoniot* 11.1 (41) (1978): 35.
[400/ 606.1].

2017. ————. Towards a History of Samaritan Exegesis. (Dissertation, Hebrew) Jerusalem: Hebrew University, [2305].

2018. **Loisy, Alfred.** Reviewer. "Der Messias." *Revue Critique* 69 (1910): 486f. [107/ 1107].

2019. **Lombardi, Guido.** "La Elfosajoj sur Monto Gerizim." *Biblio Revuo* 3 (1968): 33-43. [1305].

2020. **Lorenzini, E.** "L'interpretazione del dialogo con la Samaritana." *Orpheus* 7 (1986): 134-136. [1502.1].

2021. **Lortet, M.** "Das heutige Syrien." *Globus—Illustrierte Zeitschrift für Länder und Völkerkunde* 40.13 (1881): 180-184; 192-197. [102/ 200/ 903].

2022. **Lourenço, J.** "Os Samaritanos: um enigma na história bíblia." *Didaskalia* 15.1 (1985): 49-72. [200/ 801.1/ 1105].

2023. **Lowy, A.** "An Account given by a Samaritan in A.D. 1713 on the Ancient Copy of the Samaritan Pentateuch at Nablus." *PSBA* (Dec.1879): 13-15. [103].

2024. ————. "On the Samaritans in Talmudic Writings." *PSBA* (Dec. 1879): 11-13. [304.2].

2025. **Lowy, S.** "A Note on the Samaritan Amulets, Yat." *IEJ* 25 (1975): 250-253. [601].

2026. ————. The Principles of Samaritan Bible Exegesis. (Ph.D. thesis) Leeds: University of Leeds, 1975. [2305].

2027. ————. *The Principles of Samaritan Bible Exegesis.* Leiden: Brill, 1977. Studia Post Biblica 28. [2305].

2028. ————. "Some Aspects of Normative and Sectarian Interpretation of the Scriptures." *ALUOS* 6 (1966-68): 89-163. [2305].

2029. **Lozachmeur, Helene and Jean Margain.** "Une amulette samaritaine provenant de Tyr." *Semitica.* 32 (1982): 117-121. With plates. [507/ 601].

2030. **Lubegk, J. F.** *Exercitatio Philologica de Proseuchis Samaritanorum.* Wittenberg, 1682. [2600].

2031. **Ludemann, G.** *Untersuchungen zur simonianischen Gnosis.* Göttingen: Göttinger Theologische Arb., 1975.
[1506/ 1506.2].

2032. **Lüdemann, Gerd.** "The Acts of the Apostles and the Beginnings of Simonian Gnosis." *NTS* 33 (1987): 420-426.
[1506.2].

2033. **Ludewig, Jo Pet von.** "Altertum der abrahamischen Traumuntze und der samaritanischen Buchstaben." *Anmerkungen über allerhandwichtige Materien und Schriften* 2 (1744): 56-57.
[603/ 2501].

2034. **Ludolf, Job.** *Epistolae Samaritanae Sichemitarum ad Jobum Ludolfum...cum ejusdem Latina versione et annotationibus.* Cizae, 1688. [Reprinted under the title "Epistolae duae Sichemitarum ad Jobum Ludolfum" in Ugolini, *Thesaurus* (1759) 22:649-656 with "Notae Jobi Ludolfi" cols. 657-660; see above, Bruns].
[1700/ 1703].

2035. **Ludovici, C. H.** *Targum Shomroni de Sepher Bereshit.* Halle, 1750.
[2300/ 2401].

2036. **Ludovicus, Thomasib.** *La méthode d'étudier et d'enseigner christiennement et utilement la grammaire ou les langues par rapport à l'écriture sainte en les réduisant toutes à l'hébreu.* Paris, 1690.
[2300/ 2600].

2037. **Ludwich, Arthur.** *De Theodoti Carmine Graeco-Judaico. Commentatio.* Hartungiana: Acad Alb Regim., 1899. 7: 8f. [Includes the Greek text].
[2000/ 2005].

2038. **Luke, H. C.** *Ceremonies at the Holy Places...with Illustrations from Paintings by Philippa A. F. Stephenson.* London, 1932.
[102/400/ 1300].

2039. —————. *Prophets, Priests and Patriarchs. Sketches of the Sects of Palestine and Syria.* London, 1927.
[1500].

2040. **Luncz, A. M.** "Conversations with the Samaritan High Priest." *Luah Eretz Israel* 8 (1902): 51-68. [Reprinted, Jerusalem (1980) including abstracts from vols. 8-14: 245-262].
[903/ 1302].

2041. —————. "Verzeichnis der Ortschaften in Paschalik Nablus." (Hebrew, with German summary) *Luah Eretz Israel* 8 (1902): 27-34.
[1404].

2042. **Luncz, A. M. and David Yellin.** "The Samaritan Book of Joshua." (Hebrew) *JJ* 6.2 (1902): 138-155.
[1605].

2043. **Luria, Ben-Zion.** "The Beginning of the Samaritan Diaspora." (Hebrew) *Sefer Congreen.* Jerusalem: Society for Biblical Studies, Israel, 1963. 159-168. [500/ 801.1].

2044. —————. "The Beginnings of the Division Between the Judaean Captives and the Samaritans (Haggai, II:10-14)." (Hebrew) *BM* 23.1 (no. 62) (1977/78): 43-56. [801.1].

2045. —————. "In the Mountains of Judaea and Samaria in the Days of the Hasmonaeans." (Hebrew) *Ha'umah* 12 (1976): 376-377. [805].

2046. **Luzzatto, S. D.** "Letter About the Samaritans." (Hebrew) In **R. Kirchheim**, *Karmei Shomron.* Frankfurt, 1851. [200/ 304.2].

M

2047. Macalister, R. A. "A Bronze Object from Nablus." *PEFQS* (1908): 340-343. [606.1].

2048. —————. "Diary of a Visit to Safed with Travel Notes of the Journey from Nablus to Safed." *PEFQS* 39 (1907): 91-103. [308/ 408/ 903].

2049. —————. "Gleanings from the Minute Books of the Jerusalem Literary Society, XXV." *PEFQS* (1911): 28-33. [Samaritans in 1850]. [813/ 903].

2050. —————. "A Greek Inscription from Nablus." *PEFQS* (1902): 240-242. [2510.1].

2051. Macdonald, John. "Arab Musical and Liturgical Terms Employed by the Samaritans." *The Islamic Quarterly* 6 (1961): 47-54. [1003.3/ 1550/ 2100/ 3300].

2052. —————. "Comprehensive and Thematic Reading of the Law by the Samaritans." *JJS* 10.2-3 (1959): 67-74. [2308].

2053. —————. A Critical Edition of the Text of the Samaritan Yom-haKippur Liturgy with a Translation thereof and Comparison with the Corresponding Jewish Liturgies. (Ph.D. thesis) Leeds: University of Leeds, 1958. [2102].

2054. —————. "The Day of Judgment in Near Eastern Religions." *Indo-Iranica (Mulla Sadra Number)* (1961): 35-53. [1105].

2055. —————. "The Discovery of Samaritan Religion." *Religion* 2 (1972): 141-153. [Reprinted in Dexinger and Pummer, *Die Samaritaner*, 361-378]. [1100].

2056. —————. "Islamic Doctrines in Samaritan Theology." *The Muslim World* 50 (1960): 279-290. [1003.3/ 1100].

2057. —————. "The Leeds School of Samaritan Studies." *ALUOS* 3 (1961): 115-118. [106].

2058. —————. Reviewer. Z. Ben-Hayyim, "Literary and Oral Tradition III." *JSS* 13 (1968): 275-276. [107/ 1900/ 2600/ 2800].

2059. —————. *Memar Marqah (The Teaching of Marqah)*. Berlin: BZAW, 83, 1963. 2 vols. [1803].

2060. —————. Reviewer. **James Purvis**, "The Origin of the Samaritan Sect." *JJS* 21 (1970): 69-72.
[107/ 801.1].

2061. —————. "The Particle רֵאשׁ in Classical Hebrew: Some New Data on its Use with the Nominative." *VT* 14 (1964): 264-275.
[2602].

2062. —————. *The Samaritan Chronicle no. II (or: Sepher Ha-yamim)*. Berlin: BZAW, 107, 1969.
[1603].

2063. —————. *The Samaritan Day of Atonement Liturgy with Selected Translations.* Leeds: ALUOS Monograph Series, 3, 1963.
[2102].

2064. —————. "The Samaritan Doctrine of Moses." *SJT* 13 (1960): 149-162.
[3008].

2065. —————. "Samaritan History till 1300." *EJ* 14. 725-732.
[800].

2066. —————. "Samaritan Religion and Customs." *EJ* 14. 738-741.
[1100/ 1200].

2067. —————. Reviewer. **R. Coggins**, "Samaritans and Jews." *SJT* 29 (1976): 286-288.
[107/ 801/ 801.1].

2068. —————. "The Samaritans Under the Patronage of Islam." *Islamic Studies* (1962): 91-110.
[1003.3].

2069. —————. "The Structure of II Kings XVII." *TGUOS* 23 (1972): 29-41.
[801.1].

2070. —————. "The Tetragrammaton in Samaritan Liturgical Compositions." *TGUOS* 17 (1958-1959): 37-47.
[2100/ 2605].

2071. —————. "The Theological Hymns of Amram Darrah." *ALUOS* 2 (1959-1961): 54-73.
[1100/ 2102.2].

2072. —————. *The Theology of the Samaritans*. London: SCM Press, 1964.
[1100].

2073. —————. "An Unpublished Palestinian Tradition About Muhammad." *AJBA* 1.3 (1969): 3-12.
[1003.3].

2074. MacEwen, Rev A. R. "A Visit to the Samaritan Passover." *Good Words* (1894): 50-54.
[1404].

2075. Macler, Frédéric. *Histoire d'Heraclius par l'évêque Sebeos.* Paris, 1904.
[808].

2076. —————. "Note sur un nouveau manuscrit d'une chronique samaritaine." *REJ* 50 (1905): 76-83.
[103/ 1600].

2077. Macpherson, J. R., editor. *Fetellus.* London: Palestine Pilgrim's Text Society, 1896.
[306.2/ 400].

2078. Macrae, G. W. Reviewer. R. Coggins, "Samaritans and Jews." *American Ecclesiastical Review* 130 (1975): 362.
[107/ 800/ 801.1].

2079. —————. Reviewer. J. Macdonald, "The Theology of the Samaritans." *HJ* 6 (1965): 209-210.
[107/ 1100].

2080. Macuch, M., C. Müller-Kessler and B. G. Fragner. *Studia Semitica Necnon Iranica Rudolpho Macuch Septuagenario ab Amicis et Discipulis Dedicata.* Wiesbaden: Harrassowitz, 1989.
[200].

2081. Macuch, Rudolf. "Der gegenwärtige Stand der Samaritanerforschung und ihre Aufgaben." *ZDMG* 138.1 (1988): 17-25. [The offprint pagination may differ from the original pagination].
[107].

2082. —————. *Grammatik des samaritanischen Hebräisch.* Studia Samaritana 1. Berlin: de Gruyter, 1969.
[2800].

2083. —————. *Grammatik des samaritanischen Aramäisch.* Studia Samaritana 4. Berlin: de Gruyter, 1982.
[2600].

2084. —————. "Hermeneutische Akrobatik aufgrund phonetischen Lautwandels in aramâischen Dialekten." *Orientalia Suecana* 33-35 (1984-86): 269-283.
[2305/ 2401/ 2800].

2085. —————. "The Importance of Samaritan Tradition for the Hermeneutics of the Pentateuch." In A. Tal and M. Florentin, editors, *Proceedings of the First International Congress of the Société d'Études Samaritaines.* Tel Aviv: Chaim Rosenberg School for Jewish Studies, University of Tel Aviv, 1991. 13-32.
[2305].

2086. —————. Reviewer. Z. Shunnar, "Katalog samaritanischer Handschriften."
      OLZ 71 (1976): 570-576.
      [101/ 103/107].

2087. —————. Reviewer. S. Noja, "Kitab al Kafi." *OLZ* 69 (1974): 159-163.
      [107/ 1106].

2088. —————. "Les bases philologiques de l'herméneutique et les bases
      herméneutiques de la philologie chez les Samaritains." In Rothschild and
      Sixdenier, editors, *Etudes Samaritaines.* Louvain-Paris, 1988. 149-158.
      [2305/ 2600].

2089. —————. R. Stiehl & H. E. Stier, "Der liquid Apikal und die apikale Liquide
      des samaritanischen Hebräisch." *Beiträge zur Alten Geschichte Unteren
      Nachleben* 2 (1970): 169-175.
      [2602].

2090. —————. "A New Interpretation of the Samaritan Inscription from Tel
      Qasile." *IEJ* 35 (1985): 183-185.
      [2512].

2091. —————. Reviewer. I. R. M. Bóid, "Principles of Samaritan Halachah."
      ZDMG 141.1 (1991): 172-175.
      [1106].

2092. —————. "On the Problems of Arabic Translations of the Samaritan
      Pentateuch." *IOS* 9 (1979): 147-173.
      [2302].

2093. —————. "Samaritan Languages: Samaritan Hebrew, Samaritan Aramaic." In
      A. D. Crown, editor, *The Samaritans.* Tübingen: Mohr, 1989. 531-584.
      [2600/ 2800].

2094. —————. Reviewer. A. Broadie, "A Samaritan Philosophy." *BO* 39.5/6 (1982):
      661-670.
      [107/ 1550/ 1803].

2095. —————. Reviewer. A. Tal, "Samaritan Targum." *BSOAS* 44.3 (1981): 569-
      572.
      [107/ 2401].

2096. —————. Reviewer. J. A. Montgomery, "The Samaritans." (Reprint edn.)
      Orientalia 38 (1969): 586-591.
      [107/ 200].

2097. —————. Reviewer. R. Pummer, "The Samaritans." *OLZ* 85.4 (1990): 433-
      436.
      [107/ 200].

2098. —————. "Zur Grammatik des samaritanischen Hebräisch." *AO* 41.3 (1973):
      193-211.
      [2602].

2099. —————. "Zur Vorgeschichte der Bekenntnisformel lā ilāha illā llāhu." *ZDMG* 128 (1977): 20-28.
[1003.3/ 1210].

2100. **Madden, F. W.** *Coins of the Jews.* London: Trübner and Co., 1903. [Includes a reproduction of an inscription fromNablus and a discussion of its script].
[603 / 2510.1].

2101. —————. *A History of Jewish Coinage.* London, 1864. [Reprinted].
[603].

2102. **Magen, Y.** "The Ancient City and the Sacred Precinct on Mt. Gerizim." (Hebrew) *A–B Samaritan News.* 515-5116 (1/8/1990): 17-22.
[409.2/ 600/ 804].

2103. —————. "The Church of Mary Theotokos on Mount Gerizim." In *Christian Archaeology in the Holy Land, New Discoveries— Archaeological Essays in Honour of Virgilio C. Corbo.* Jerusalem, 1990. Collectio Maior XXXVI: 333-342.
[1301].

2104. —————. "A Fortified Town of the Hellenistic Period on Mt. Gerizim." *Qadmoniot* 19.3-4 (1986): 91-101.
[409.2/ 600/ 804].

2105. —————. The History and Archaeology of Shechem (Neapolis) in the 1st-4th Centuries AD. (Hebrew) Jerusalem: Hebrew University, 1988.
[408/ 600/ 808].

2106. —————. "Mt. Gerizim, A Temple City." (Hebrew) *Qadmoniot* 23.3-4 (91-92) (1990): 69-96.
[409.2/ 600/ 804].

2107. —————. (Hebrew) *The Qedem Museum and the Archaeological Finds at Qedumim.* Jerusalem, 1982.
[409.2/ 600].

2108. —————. "The Qedumim Miqvaot and the Observation of Purity Among the Samaritans." *Cathedra* 34 (1985): 15-26.
[409.2/ 606].

2109. —————. "Qedumim—A Samaritan Site of the Roman-Byzantine Period." *Qadmoniot* 16.2-3 (1983): 76-83.
[409.2/ 808].

2110. —————. "Samaritan Synagogues." *Qadmoniot* 25.3-4 (99-100) (1992): 66-90.
[1304].

2111. —————. "The Samaritans in Shechem and the Blessed Mountain of Gerizim." (Hebrew) in **Z. Ehrlich**, editor, *Samaria and Benjamin.* Jerusalem, 1987. 177-210.
[408/ 412].

2112. ——————. "The Temple of Zeus on Mt.Gerizim." (Hebrew) *Proceedings of the Twelfth Archaeological Congress.* Jerusalem: Israel Exploration Society, 1986. 14-15.
[406/ 602/ 1305].

2113. ——————. "The Western Mausoleum at Neapolis." (Hebrew) *EI* (1987): 72-91.
[415].

2114. **Mai, Angelo.** *Catalogus codicum Bibliothecae Vaticanae arabicorum...item eius partis hebraicorum et syriacorum quam Assemani in editioni praeterniserant.* Rome, 1831.
[101/ 103].

2115. **Maier, J.** Reviewer. **H. Kippenberg,** "Garizim und Synagoge." *ZDPV* 88 (1972): 98-99.
[107/ 805/ 808].

2116. ——————. Reviewer. **Sylvia Powels,** "Der Kalender der Samaritaner." *ZDPV* 91 (1975): 91-92.
[107/ 1400].

2117. **Majus, Joannes Henricus.** *Brevis Institutio Linguae Arabicae...Samaritanae...Opera J. H. Happelii.* Francofurti ad Moenum, 1707.
[2600].

2118. ——————. *Brevis institutio linguae Samaritanae...contexta a G. C. Borckeim.* Francofurti, 1697.
[2600].

2119. **Makrizi.** "The Samaritans." In **S. de Sacy,** editor, *Chrestomathie Arabe.* Paris, 1806. 1: 177-223.
[200/ 307.2/ 800/ 809].

2120. **Malalas, John.** "Chronographia." *PG* 97 147-150, 557-570, 667-670, 703-706.
[For a convenient English translation see M. Jeffreys].
[305.4/ 808/ 808.1].

2121. **Mandel, Seth Benjamin Joseph.** The Development of Samaritan Hebrew: A Historical Linguistic View. (Ph.D.) Boston: Harvard, 1978.Not available in University Microfilms publications.
[2600].

2122. **Mann, J.** "An Early Theologico-Polemical Work." *HUCA* 12-13 (1937-1938): 411-459.
[1004/ 2205].

2123. ——————. *The Jews in Egypt and Palestine Under the Fatimid Caliphs.* London, 1920. 2 vols.
[505].

2124. ——————. *Texts and Studies in Jewish History and Literature.* Cincinnati, 1931.
[Reprinted, Ktav, New York, 1972. See vol. 1].
[1004].

2125. **Manning, S.** "Samaritans, Guardians of the Faith." *CNI* 26.7 (1976): 6-11. [200].

2126. **Manning, Samuel.** *Those Holy Fields: Palestine Illustrated by Pen and Pencil.* London, 1874. [Reprinted, Jerusalem. On Nablus and its inhabitants]. [102/ 200].

2127. **Mansur, A.** "Jacob's Well." *PEFQS* (1910): 131-137. [407].

2128. **Mantel, H. D.** "The Secession of the Samaritans." (Hebrew) *Bar Ilan* 7-8 (1969/1970): 162-177. xxvi f. [801.1].

2129. **Marcel, J. J.** *Leçons de langue samaritaine données au Collège Royal de France.* Paris, 1819. [2600/ 2800].

2130. **Marcus, Ralph.** "Dositheus, Priest and Levite." *JBL* 64 (1945): 269-271. [1302/ 1503/ 3004].

2131. —————, editor. **Josephus,** *Jewish Wars. Antiquities of the Jews.* London: Loeb Classical Library, 1951-1963. 6-8. [303.5].

2132. —————. "Josephus on the Samaritan Schism (Ant. xi 297-347)." In *Josephus, Jewish Antiquities, Books IX-XI.* Cambridge, Mass., 1937. Loeb Classical Library vol. 6: 498-511. Appendix B. [303.5/ 804/ 805].

2133. **Mare, W. H.** "Acts 7: Jewish or Samaritan in Character?" *WTJ* 34.1 (1971): 1-21. [*NTAb* 16 (1972) no. 925]. [1502.2].

2134. **Margain, Jean.** "11Qtg Job et la langue targumique." *RQ (Mémorial Jean Carmignac)* 15.49-52 (1988): 525-528. [2309.1/ 2800].

2135. —————. "À propos des voyelles de transition en samaritain." *Comptes rendus du GLECS* 24-28 (1979-1984/ 1985): 85-89. [2607].

2136. —————. "À propos d'un phénomène de nunation en hébreu et en araméen. De 'Maryam' à 'Maria'." *Comptes rendus du GLECS* 24-28 (1979-1984/ 1985): 81-84. [2603.1/ 2607].

2137. —————. "Un anneau samaritain provenant de Naplouse." *Syria* 61 (1984): 45-47. [601].

2138. —————. Reviewer. H. Shehadeh, "The Arabic Translation of the Samaritan Pentateuch." *REJ* 140 (1981): 263-264. [2302].

2139. —————. "Bibliographie samaritaine." *JA* 268 (1980): 441-449. [100].

2140. —————. "Bibliographie samaritaine II." *JA* 271 (1983): 179-186. [Reprinted, *A–B* (1983) 65-67]. [100].

2141. —————. Reviewer. A. D. Crown, "A Bibliography of the Samaritans." *REJ* 145 (1986): 186. [100/ 107].

2142. —————. Reviewer. J.-P. Rothschild, "Catalogue des manuscrits samaritains." *REJ* 145 (1986): 404-406. [101/ 107].

2143. —————. "Deux hymnes samaritaines. I: l'hymne en araméen II: l'hymne en hébreu." *Henoch* 4.3 (1982): 331-342. [2100].

2144. —————. "Éléments de bibliographie samaritaine." *Semitica* 27 (1977): 152-157. [100].

2145. —————. Reviewer. R. Macuch, "Grammatik des samaritanischen Aramäisch." *REJ* 143.1/2 (1984): 162-164. [107/ 2800].

2146. —————. "Hébreu." In *Supplément au Dictionnaire de la Bible.* 1978. IX: 798-800. [2600].

2147. —————. "L'araméen du Targum samaritain en Exode 20 (Triglotte Barberini)." *Semitica* 35 (1985): 67-88. [2401/ 2800].

2148. —————. "Les particules a sens final dans le Targum samaritain." *Semitica* 27 (1977): 145-152. [2602].

2149. —————. "Les particules causales dans le Targum samaritain." *Semitica* 30 (1980): 69-87. [2401/ 2602].

2150. —————. "Les particules dans le targum samaritain de Genèse—Exode. Jalons pour une histoire de l'araméen samaritain." *REJ* 148.1-2 (1989): 193-195. [2401/ 2602].

2151. —————. Reviewer. Z. Ben-Hayyim, "The Literary and Oral Tradition of Hebrew and Aramaic Amongst the Samaritans, IV-V." *REJ* 140 (1981): 208-

210.
[107/ 2200/ 2600].

2152. —————. Reviewer. D. Talshir, "The Nomenclatura of the Fauna in the Samaritan Targum." *REJ* 143 (1984): 164-165.
[107/ 2401/ 2603].

2153. —————. "Note sur le particule *'yt* dans le Targum samaritain." *Semitica 36* (1986): 101-104.
[2603].

2154. —————. "Note sur l'économie des voyelles *o* et *u* en samaritain." *Comptes rendus du GLECS* 24-28 (1979-1984/ 1985): 81-84.
[2607].

2155. —————. "Note sur *lwt* et *lyd* dans la Targum samaritain." In **Maria Macuth et al,** *Studi Semitica Necnon Iranica: Rudolpho Macuch Septuagenario ab Amicis et Discipulis Dedicata.* Wiesbaden: Harrassowitz, 1989. 161-166.
[2603/ 2800].

2156. —————. "Note sur *qbl* et ses composés dans le Targum samaritain." *La vie de la Parole (Mélanges P. Grelot).* Paris, 1987. 95-99.
[2603/ 2800].

2157. —————. "Notes de lexicographie araméenne. Targum samaritain en Gn 1." *Sefarad* 44 (1984): 211-216.
[2401/ 2800].

2158. —————. "Une nouvelle amulette samaritaine portant le texte d'Exode 38, 8." *Syria* 59.1-2 (1982): 117-120.
[601].

2159. —————. "La Pâque samaritaine, bibliographie." *A–B* 307-308 (7/4/82): 58-63.
[100/ 1404].

2160. —————. "Le Pentateuque samaritain." In **Pierre Haudebert,** editor, *Le Pentateuque; débats et recherches. XIVe Congrès de l'ACFEB, 1991.* Paris: Cerf, 1992. 231-240.
[2300].

2161. —————. "Le prologue de Memar Marqa, translitération, transcription, traduction et commentaire philologique." *AEPHE* IVe section (1977-1978/1980): 155-164.
[1803].

2162. —————. "La racine *swy* en araméen samaritain." *Semitica* 29 (1979): 119-130.
[2800].

2163. —————. "Rapport sur les conférences (schèmes nominaux samaritains)." *AEPHE* (1981-1983) IVe section.livret 2 (1985): 48.
[200].

2164. ─────. "Remarques sur le consonantisme samaritain." *Comptes rendus du GLECS* xviii-xxiii (1973-1979): 235-239. [2600/ 2603.1].

2165. ─────. "Remarques sur le vocalisme samaritain." *Comptes rendus du GLECS* xviii-xxiii (1973-1979 (1981)): 257-278. [2600/ 2607].

2166. ─────. "Samaritaine (littérature)." In *Dictionnaire historique, thématique et technique des littératures.* Paris: Larousse, 1968. II: 1455-1456. [2200].

2167. ─────. Reviewer. A. Tal, "The Samaritan Targum to the Pentateuch, III-V." *REJ* 144 (1985): 259-260. [107/ 2401].

2168. ─────. Reviewer. A. Tal, "The Samaritan Targum to the Pentateuch, I-II." *REJ* 142 (1983): 173-175. [107/ 2401].

2169. ─────. "The Samaritan Version of the Torah." *A–B* 175 (1976): 10-11. [2300].

2170. ─────. Reviewer. R. Pummer, "The Samaritans." *JSJ* 19.2 (1988): 254. [107/ 200].

2171. ─────. Reviewer. L. Vilsker, "Samaritjanskie jazyk (la langue samaritaine)." *JA* 264 (1976): 175-178. [2600].

2172. ─────. "Select Bibliography." In A. D. Crown, editor, *The Samaritans.* Tübingen: Mohr, 1989. 795-801. [100].

2173. ─────. Reviewer. M. Haran, "The Song of the Precepts of Aaron ben Manir." *RHR* 496 (1976): 203-204. [107/ 1004].

2174. ─────. "Targum samaritain. Aspects de la langue du ms J." In Rothschild and Sixdenier, editors, *Études samaritaines.* Louvain-Paris, 1988. 123-129. [2401/ 2800].

2175. ─────. Reviewer. Z. Ben-Hayyim, "Tibåt Marqe-A Collection of Samaritan Midrashim." *RB* 98 (1991): 605-607. [1803].

2176. ─────. "Le traitement de la particule hébraïque 'pen' dans le targum samaritain." *Semitica* 28 (1978): 85-96. [2401/ 2602].

2177. ─────. "The Unity of Samaritan Aramaic." *A–B* 249-250 (16/12/1979): 35 & 52. [2800].

2178. —————. "Vision d'Abisha, poème en Samaritaine tardif." *Semitica* 33 (1983): 109-123.
[2100].

2179. **Margain, Jean and Ph de Robert.** "Les samaritains." *Le monde de la Bible* 14 (1980): 57-58.
[200].

2180. **Margain, Jean and J. Longton.** "Text de la Bible", "Version samaritaine." In *Dictionnaire encyclopédique de la Bible.* Paris: Brépols, 1987. 1256-1258, 1304.
[2300].

2181. **Margain, Jean and B.Outtier.** "Une feuille de garde en samaritain au patriarcat arménien de Jérusalem." *JA* 275 (1987): 35-44.
[103].

2182. **Margalith, Othniel.** "The political background of Zerubbabel's mission and the Samaritan schism." *VT* 41.3 (1991): 312-323.
[801].

2183. **Margoliouth, G.** "An Ancient Manuscript of the Samaritan Liturgy." *ZDMG* 51 (1897): 499-507.
[103/ 2102.1].

2184. —————. *Descriptive List of the Hebrew and Samaritan Manuscripts in the British Museum.* London, 1893.
[101].

2185. —————. "An Early Copy of the Samaritan Hebrew Pentateuch." *JQR* 15 (1903): 632-639.
[103/ 2300].

2186. —————. "Hymns." *ERE* 7 (1914): 48-49.
[2102.1].

2187. **Marhib, R., S. Yehoshua and I. Yehoshua,** editors.(Hebrew) Bezalel (Bezel-El) Newspaper. 1971-1973,
[104].

2188. **Marhiv, A. ben Yisakhar,** editor. (Hebrew) *Liturgy for Zimmuth Passover and the First New Moon (Nisan).* Holon, 1967. 217pp.
[1210/ 1404/ 2102].

2189. —————, editor. (Hebrew) *Prayer Book for Shemini Atzeret and Simhat Torah.* Holon, n.d. [186 pp. 25 x 17 cm].
[1210/ 2102/ 1408].

2190. —————, editor. (Hebrew) *Prayer Book for the Sabbath of the Zimmuth of Passover.* Holon, n.d. [241 pp. 25 x 17 cm].
[1210/ 1404/ 2102,].

2191. —————, editor. (Hebrew) *Sefer Eleh Devarim, Katav ufarash.* Holon? 1985.
[2300/ 2304].

2192. **Marín, José A.** "Les groupes politico-religieux en Israel du temps de Christ." *TS* 7/8 (1982): 170-178.
[806/ 807].

2193. **Marino, Sanuto.** *Secrets for True Crusaders to Help Them Recover the Holy Land, Written in A.D. 1321.* London, 1896. Trans. Aubrey Stewart.
[306.2/ 400].

2194. **Markham, Robert J.** "The Samaritan Pentateuch." *The Guardian* (12 July 1892): 1055.
[2300].

2195. **Marmardji, R. P. A.–S. le.** *Textes géographiques arabes sur la Palestine.* Paris, 1951.
[307.1/ 307.2/ 307.3/ 400].

2196. **Marrou, H.** *Dictionnaire d'archéologie chrétienne et de liturgie.* Paris, 1950. Vol. 15: 725-732.
[201/ 202].

2197. **Marsh, Rev. W.** *A Survey of the Holy Land.* Bath/London, n.d.
[306.3/ 400].

2198. **Marshall, T. H.** "The Problem of New Testament Exegesis." *JETS* 17 (1974): 67-73.
[1003.1].

2199. **Marti, K.** Reviewer. A. F. von Gall, "Der hebräische Pentateuch der Samaritaner." *TLZ* 40 (1915): 533-536.
[107/ 2300].

2200. **Martin, C. H. R.** "Alexander and the High Priest." *TGUOS* 23 (1972): 105-115.
[804].

2201. **Martin, M.** "Pentateuco Samaritano." *Enciclopedia de la Biblia.* Barcelona: Garriga, 1965. 1004-1008.
[201/ 2300].

2202. —————. "Samaritan Inscriptions." *Encyclopaedia Biblica.* London, 1965. 6.
[201/ 2500].

2203. **Marty, William Henry.** The New Moses. (Th.D.) Dallas Theological Seminary: 1984. AAC8500038 (publication nᵒ). [A long section on the Samaritans, the New Testament, and Qumran literature].
[1003.1/ 1005/ 1502].

2204. **Masch, Andreas Gottlieb, J. le Long and C. F. Boerneri,** editors. *Bibliotheca Sacra, Pt. II. de Versionibus Librorum Sacrorum Volumen primum de Versionibus Orientalibus (Section III. de Versionibus ex Samaritana lingua).* Halae, 1781.
[New edn. 1783].
[2300].

2205. **Masclef, François.** *Grammatica Hebraica, a punctis aliisque inventis Massorethicis liber. Accesserunt in hac secunde editione tres grammaticae, Chaldaica, Syriaca et*

Samaritana eiusdem instituti. 2nd edn. Paris: Vidua P. du Mesnil, 1731. 2 vols. [3rd edn. Paris, 1743]. [105/ 2600].

2206. **Mason, W. J.** "Parable of the Good Samaritan." *ET* 48 (1937): 179-181. [1502.3].

2207. **Matagne, C.** Reviewer. J. **Macdonald,** "Memar Marqah." *Nouvelle Revue Théologique* 89 (1967): 707-708. [107/ 1803].

2208. **Mathews, Kenneth Alan.** "11Q paleo Leviticus." *CBQ* 48.2 (1986): 171-207. [103/ 2307/ 2309.1].

2209. —————. Reviewer. J. **Sanderson,** "4QPaleo Ex^m and the Samaritan Tradition." *JBL* 107 (1988): 303-307. [107/ 2300/ 2309.1].

2210. —————. "The Background of the Paleo-Hebrew Texts at Qumran." In **Carole. L. Meyers** and J. **Murphy O'Connor,** *The Word of the Lord Shall Go Forth. Essays in Honor of David Noel Freedman on his 60 Birthday.* Winona Lake, 1983. 549-568. [103/ 2307/ 2309.1].

2211. —————. The Paleo-Hebrew Leviticus Scroll from Qumran. (Microfilm) Ann Arbor: University of Michigan, 1980. University Microfilms. [103/ 2307/ 2309.1].

2212. —————. "Paleo-Hebrew Leviticus Scroll from Qumran." *BA* 50.1 (1987): 45-54. [The *waw* used to mark section in the Palaeo-Hebrew scroll may be the precursor of the *waw* in the columnar form. Original height of the scroll 25-26cm]. [103/ 2307/ 2309.1].

2213. **Mattill, Andrew Jacob Jr.** "The Good Samaritan and the Purpose of Luke–Acts. Halévy reconsidered." *Encounter* 33 (1972): 359-376. [Cf. J. Halévy, *REJ* (1882).4]. [1502.3].

2214. **Matzo, B.** "Una fonte Sacerdotale anti-Samaritana di Giuseppe." In *Saggi do Storia e letterature giudeo-ellenistica.* Florence, 1924. [303.5].

2215. **Maundrell, Henry.** "A Journey from Aleppo to Jerusalem." In J. **Pinkerton,** editor, *A General Collection of Voyages and Travels.* London, 1811. 10. [See also Maundrell, Oxford, 1703 and other edns.]. [306.3].

2216. **Maximus, Abbas.** "Quaestiones ad Thalassium de Scriptura Sacra." *PG* 90 403-406. [305.4].

2217. **Mayer, L. A.** "Outline of a Bibliography of the Samaritans." (Hebrew) *EI* 4 (1956): 252-268. [Reprinted, Jerusalem 1956: Re-edited, D. Broadribb, *Bibliography of the Samaritans, Supplements to AN,* Leiden, 1964]. [100].

2218. ──────. "A Sixteenth Century Samaritan Hanging." (Hebrew) *Yediot* 13.3-4 (1947): 169-170. [Reprinted, *Yediot Reader A* (1965): 112-113]. [606.1].

2219. **Mayer, L. A. with A. Reifenberg.** "A Samaritan Lamp." *JPOS* 16 (1936): 44-45, plate 3. [605].

2220. **Mayer, R.** "Geschichtefahrung und Schriftauslegung zur Hermeneutik des frühen Judentums." In O. Loretz and W. Strolz, editors, *Die hermeneutische Frage in der Theologie.* 1968. 290-355. [2300].

2221. **Mayerson, Philip.** "Justinian's Novel 103 and the Reorganization of Palestine." *BASOR* 269 (1988): 65-71. [808.1].

2222. **Mayr, Joachim.** "Ein samaritanisches Psalterium." *Katholisch Kirchzeitung* (1924): 34-35. [2102].

2223. **Mazade, C.** Dissertation sur l'origine, l'âge et l'état critique du pentateuque samaritain. Geneva: University of Geneva, 1830. [2300].

2224. **Mazliah ben Pinhas.** (Hebrew) *Order of the Samaritan Passover on the Gerizim Mountain at Nablus.* Tel Aviv: 1932. [Reprinted with an English translation, Jerusalem]. [1404/ 2102].

2225. **McClymont, J. D.** The Samaritan Text of the Pentateuch. A Comparison of the Samaritan Text with the Massoretic Text. (Ph.D.) Glasgow: University of Glasgow, 1966-1967. [2300].

2226. **McElleny, N. J.** "Orthodoxy in Judaism After the First Christian Century." *JSJ* 4 (1973): 19-42. [Especially pp. 31-33]. [807].

2227. **McHardy, W. D.** Reviewer. J. Macdonald, "Theology of the Samaritans." *SOTS* (1965): 48-49. [107/ 1100].

2228. **McLaren, James S.** *Power and Politics in Palestine: The Jews and the Governing of Their Land 100BC–70AD.* Sheffield: Sheffield Academic Press, 1991. JSNT, Supplement Series 63. [806].

2229. Mead, G. R. S. *Simon Magus.* Cambridge: CUP, 1872. Reprinted, 1978.
       [1506.2].

2230. Mediolanensi, D. "Adventus Messiae." In G. Bartolocci, *Secundum Codicera
       Samaritanum.* Roma, 1675-1694. 5: 7ff. [Gregg Reprint, 1965].
       [1107].

2231. Meeham, Denis. *Adamnan's De Locis Sanctis.* Dublin: Scriptores Latini Hiberniae
       III, 1958.
       [306.2/ 401].

2232. Meeks, Wayne A. "Am I a Jew? Johannine Christianity and Judaism." In *Studies in
       Judaism in Late Antiquity, Christianity, Judaism and Other Greco-Roman Cults
       (Studies for Morton Smith at Sixty).* Leiden: Brill, 1975. 12: 163-186.
       [1105/ 1502.1].

2233. —————. Reviewer. J. Bowman, "The Fourth Gospel and the Jews."
       Interpretation 31 (1977): 442-444.
       [107/ 1502.1].

2234. —————. "Galilee and Judaea in the Fourth Gospel." *JBL* 85 (1966): 159-169.
       [400/ 1502.1].

2235. —————. "Moses as a King and Prophet in Samaritan Tradition." In *The
       Prophet King. Moses' Traditions and the Johannine Christology.* Supplements to
       NT 14. Leiden: Brill, 1967. 216-259, 286-319.
       [1105/ 1107/ 1502.1/ 3008].

2236. —————. "Moses as God and King." In J. Neusner, editor, *Religions in
       Antiquity—Essays in Memory of E. R. Goodenough.* Leiden: Brill, 1968. 354-
       371.
       [3008].

2237. —————. Reviewer. J. Macdonald, "The Samaritan Chronicle II." *JBL* 98
       (1970): 481-483.
       [107/ 1603].

2238. —————. Reviewer. J. Bowman, "Samaritan Problem." *JBL* 87 (1968): 448-
       450.
       [107/ 1503].

2239. —————. Reviewer. J. A. Montgomery, "The Samaritans." (Reprint edition)
       JAOS 91 (1971): 529-530.
       [107/ 200].

2240. —————. "Simon Magus in Recent Research." *Religious Studies Review* 3
       (1977): 137-142.
       [1506.2].

2241. Mehren, August Ferdinand. *Codices Persici, Turcici, Hindustanici variique alii
       Bibliothecae Regiae Hafniensis.* Hafniae, 1857.
       [101/ 103].

2242. **Menard, J.** Reviewer. **H. Kippenberg**, "Garizim und Synagoge." *RSR* 48 (1974): 166-167.
[107/ 805/ 806/ 1002].

2243. **Menchini, Charles.** Il discorso di S. Stefano protomartire nella letteratura e predicazione cristiana primitiva. (Doctoral dissertation) Roma: Pontifical Institute "Angelicum", 1951.
[1502.2].

2244. **Mendelsohn, I. and S. W. Baron.** *Descriptive Catalogue of Semitic Manuscripts (mostly Hebrew) in the Libraries of Columbia University.* Unpublished. [See pp. 380-393 for Samaritan MSS].
[101/ 103].

2245. **Mendelssohn, O.** "1800-1899: One Hundred Years of Isolation in Shechem." *A–B* 258-259 (28/4/80): 34-41.
[200/ 813/ 903].

2246. **Mendes, M.** "I Samaritani durante gli ultimi secli ed i loro contatti con l'Europa." *AION* 32 (1972): 388-393.
[813/ 903/ 1700].

2247. **Merx, Adalbert.** "Carmina Samaritana e cod. Gothano." *Atti della Reale Accademia dei Lincei* 3.1st sem. (1877): 261, 550-563. [See also 2nd sem. 160-172].
[103/ 2100].

2248. —————. "Ein samaritanisches Fragment über den Ta'eb oder Messias. Aus der Gothaer handschrift nr. 963." *Actes VIII Congrès Oriental.* (Section Sém. B) (1893): 117-139.
[103/ 1107].

2249. —————. "Exkurs über die samaritanische Gnosis." *Die vier kanonischen Evangelien* 11.2 (1911): 342-345.
[1502.1/ 1506].

2250. —————. *Der Messias oder Ta'eb der Samaritaner. Nach bisher unbekannten Quellen. Mit einer Gedachtniswort von Karl Marti.* Giessen: BZAW 17, 1909.
[103/ 1107].

2251. —————. "Samaritanisch." In **W. Pertsch**, editor, *Die orientalischen Handschriften der Herzoglichen Bibliothek.* Gotha, 1893.
[101/ 103].

2252. —————. "Samaritanisch." In *Marksteine aus der Weltliteratur in original Schriften.* Leipzig: Johannes Baensch-Drugulin, 1902. 77-88. [A limited edition].
[105].

2253. **Meshorer, Ya akov.** "The Mint of King Herod the Great (On two tablets uncovered in Samaria)." *The Shekel* 1 (1968): 29-31.
[603].

2254. —————. "Samaria (Shomron-Sebaste); Neapolis (Shechem)." *City Coins of Eretz Israel and the Decapolis.* Jerusalem: The Israel Museum, 1985. 43-52. [603].

2255. —————. "On Three Interesting Cults at Neapolis in Samaria." (Hebrew) *EI* 19 (1987): 92-96. [Includes comments on the Samaritan Dove cult]. [408/ 1002/ 1110].

2256. **Meshorer, Ya'akov and Shraga Qedar.** *The Coinage of Samaria in the Fourth Century BCE.* Jerusalem: Numismatic Fine Arts International, 1991. [Reviewed in *Qadmoniot* 24 1-2 (97-98) 1992: 58]. [603].

2257. **Meshullam of Volterra.** "Travels." (Hebrew) in **A. Ya'ari,** editor, *Travellers in the Holy Land.* Ramat Gan, 1976. 114-124. [309/ 401].

2258. **Metal, Z.** "The Samaritan Version in Targum Jonathan." *A–B* .200 (1977): 33-37. [2300].

2259. —————. "The Samaritan Version of the Torah in the Babylonian Talmud." *A–B* .147 (1975): 6-9. [304.2/ 2300].

2260. —————. "The Samaritan Version of the Torah in Targum Onkelos." *A–B.* 133/134 (1975): 8-12. [304/ 2300].

2261. —————. "The Samaritan Version of the Torah in the Jerusalem Talmud." *A–B.* 154 (1976): 6-7. [304.2/ 2300].

2262. —————. "The Samaritan Version of the Torah in Midrash Mechiltah." *A–B.* 162 (1976): 4-5. [304/ 2300].

2263. —————. "The Samaritan Version of the Torah in Sifre Deuteronomy Rabba." *A–B* .158/159, 170/171 (1976): 10-12, 16-17. [304/ 2300].

2264. —————. *The Samaritan Version of the Pentateuch in Jewish Sources.* Tel Aviv, 1979. [304/ 2300].

2265. —————. "Similarities Between the Samaritan Version of the Book of Genesis and the Septuagint." *A–B* .96 (1973): 2-4. [2300/ 2400].

2266. —————. "Similarities Between Exodus in the Samaritan and Septuagint Version." *A–B* .120/121 (1974): 7-10. [2300/ 2400].

2267. ——————. "Similarities Between Leviticus in the Samaritan and Septuagint Version." *A–B* .122 & 125 (1974): 13-16; 10. [2300/ 2400].

2268. **Meyer, R.** "Bemerkungen zur syntaktischen Funktion der Sorgenannten nota accusativi." *AOAT* 18 (1973): 137-142. [2600/ 2602].

2269. ——————. *Hebräisches Textbuch.* Berlin, 1960. 76-79. [2600].

2270. ——————. Reviewer. A. **Murtonen,** "Materials for a Non-Masoretic Grammar." *OLZ* 56 (1961): 606-608. [107/ 2300/ 2600].

2271. ——————. Reviewer. J. **Macdonald,** "Memar Marqah." *TZ* 20 (1964): 227-228. [107/ 1803].

2272. ——————. Reviewer. J. **Macdonald,** "Memar Marqah." *TLZ* 91 (1966): 659-661. [107/ 1803].

2273. ——————. Reviewer. R. **Coggins,** "Samaritans and Jews." *CBQ* 38 (1976): 90-91. [107/ 801.1].

2274. ——————. Reviewer. J. **Macdonald,** "Theology of the Samaritans." *TLZ* 91 (1966): 659-661. [107/ 1100].

2275. **Michael Glyca.** "Annals." *PG.*158. 375-378. [See J. B. Chabot's edn., Paris, 1900]. [200/ 305].

2276. **Michelant, H. and G. Reynaud.** *Itinéraires à Jerusalem et descriptions de la Terre Sainte.* Paris: Société de l'orient latin—série géographique III—itinéraires françaises, reprint, 1966. [305/ 306.2/ 401].

2277. **Michlin, H. B.** "Samaritan Stone on Mt. Gerizim." (Hebrew) *Jerusalem* 11-12 (1916): [406].

2278. **Migne, J. P.** "Samaritains","Hymnes des samaritains." In *Dictionnaire des apocryphes ou collection de tous livres apocryphes, relatifs à l'Ancien et au Nouveau Testament.* Paris, 1856-1858. 1-2: 885-920. [200/ 2100].

2279. **Mihoc, Vasile.** "Samaritenii." *Mitropolia Ardenlului* 25.7-9 (1980): 625-632. [200].

2280. **Miklin, H. M.** "Samaritan Places on Mt. Gerizim." *JJ* XI-XII (1916): 176-177. [406].

2281. **Mikolasek, Adrian.** "Le numérotation du Décalogue à la lumière de la tradition de l'Israêl de la loi." In **Rothschild and Sixdenier**, editors, *Etudes samaritaines.* Louvain-Paris, 1988. 85-93.
[1103].

2282. —————. "La samarianoj; gardetoj de la lego kontrau la profetoj." *Biblia Revuo* 6.3 (1970): 151-161. [A French version "Les samaritains, Gardiens de la Loi contre les prophètes" appeared in *Communio Viatorum* 12. 3 (1969) 139-148. An English translation, 15 pp., a summary of a thesis in preparation for the University of Strasbourg, is also available].
[200/ 801].

2283. —————. "Samaritani strazci zakona proti prorokum." *Krestanska Revue* 38. 2 (1971): 35-40.
[800].

2284. —————. "Silo et Salem à Sichem." In **A. Tal & M. Florentin,** editors, *Proceedings of the First International Congress of the Société d'Études Samaritaines.* Tel Aviv: Chaim Rosenberg School for Jewish Studies, University of Tel Aviv, 1991. 79-98.
[1002].

2285. **Milik, J. T.** Reviewer. **Z. Ben-Hayyim,** "Literary and Oral Tradition vols. I & II." *RB* 67 (1960): 103-107.
[107/ 1550/ 2300/ 2401/ 2600/ 2603].

2286. —————. "Note sui Manoscritti di 'Ain Feshka'." *Biblica* 31 (1950): 204-225.
[1005].

2287. —————. "La patrie de Tobie." *RB* 73 (1966): 522-530. [Suggests that Tobit was a Samaritan].
[303.1/ 1003.4].

2288. **Miller, Selig J.** The Samaritan Molad Mosheh. Samaritan and Arabic Texts Edited and Translated with Introduction andNotes. (Ph.D.) New York: Columbia University, 1949. [Reprinted, Philosophical Library, New York, 1949].
[1802].

2289. **Mills, D.** "Dissertatio de causis odii Judaeos inter atque Samaritanos." In *Dissertationes Selectae.* Lugduni Batavorum, 1743. xiv: 425ff.
[1003.4].

2290. **Mills, E.** "Report and Tables." *Census of Palestine.* Alexandria, 1933. I & II:
[813/ 903].

2291. **Mills, John.** "The Samaritan Pentateuch." *Journal of Sacred Literature* 3 (1863): 131-139. [Reprinted for private circulation, Mitchell and Sons, printers, 11 pp.].
[2300].

2292. ——————. *Three Months' Residence at Nablus and an Account of the Modern Samaritans.* London, 1864. [Reprinted, New York, 1982]. [200/ 813/ 903].

2293. **Milson, David.** "The Design of the Temple and Gates at Shechem." *PEQ* (July-December 1987): 97-105. [412/ 600/ 800].

2294. **Mittwoch, Eugen.** "Muslimische Fetwas über die Samaritaner." *OLZ* (1926): 845-849. [1003.3].

2295. ——————. "Der Wiederaufbau des jüdischen Tempels in Elephantine—ein Kompromiss Zwischen Juden und Samaritanern." In *Judaica Festschrift 70 Geburtstag Herman Cohen.* Berlin, 1912. 227-233. [802/ 803].

2296. **Moffat, James.** "The Samaritan Woman." *Expositor* 1.226 7th series. [1502.1].

2297. **Molinier, Auguste.** *Catalogue des manuscrits de la bibliothèque mazarine.* Paris, 1885. Vol. 1. [101/ 103].

2298. **Mollat, Donatien.** "Chez les samaritains le culte nouveau." *BTS* 4 (July, 1957): 3. [903].

2299. ——————. "Le puits de Jacob (Jn. 4,1-42)." *BVC* 6 (1954): 83-91. [407/ 1502.1].

2300. **Möller, W.** "Simon Magus." In *PRE.* 1884. 14: 246-256. [201/ 1506.2].

2301. **Monro, V.** *A Summer Ramble in Syria with a Tartar. A Trip from Aleppo to Stamboul.* London, 1835. Vol.2. [308].

2302. **Monselewski, W.** *Der barmherzige Samariter. Eine auslegungsgeschichtliche Untersuchung zu Lukas 10, 25-37.* Tübingen: Mohr, 1967. [1502.3/ 1502.4].

2303. **Montagu, Richard.** *Analecta ecclesiasticarum exercitationum.* London, 1622. [Section on the Dositheans in Exercitatione III]. [1503].

2304. ——————. *Apparatus ad origines ecclesiasticas.* Oxford, 1635. [1507].

2305. **Monte, J. L. la.** "The Viscounts of Naplouse in the Twelfth Century." *Syria* 19 (1938): 272-278. [408/ 810].

2306. **Montet, M. E.** "Le premier conflit entre Pharisiens et Sadducéens d'après trois documents orientaux." *JA* 9.8e série (1887): 415-423.
[1003.4/ 1601].

2307. **Montfauçon, Bernard de.** *Palaeographica Graeca.* Paris, 1708. 115-126.
[603].

2308. **Montgomery, James Alan.** Reviewer. M. Gaster, "The Asatir." *JQR* 19 (1929): 139-141.
[107/ 1801].

2309. —————. Reviewer. J. Jeremias, "Die Passahfeier der Samaritaner." *JQR* 24 (1933): 152f.
[107/ 1404].

2310. —————. "Notes from the Samaritan." *JBL* 25 (1906): 49-54.
[200/ 1101/ 2401].

2311. —————. Reviewer. A. E. Cowley, "The Samaritan Liturgy." *AJT* (1910): 277-280.
[107/ 2100].

2312. —————. Reviewer. Moses Gaster, "The Samaritans." *JQR* 17 (1927): 315-316.
[107/ 200].

2313. —————. The Samaritans, the Earliest Jewish Sect. (Ph.D.) Philadelphia: University of Pennsylvania, 1904.
[200].

2314. —————. *The Samaritans, the Earliest Jewish Sect. Their History, Theology and Literature.* Philadelphia, 1907. [Reprinted, Ktav, New York 1968, with an introduction by A. S. Halkin].
[200].

2315. —————. "Some Early Amulets from Palestine." *JAOS* 31 (1911): 272-281.
[601].

2316. —————. "Were the Samaritans Worthy or Unworthy." *Sunday School Times* (1906): 383f.
[1502].

2317. **Montmolin, Eduard de.** *Des samaritains et de l'origine de leur secte.* Geneva, 1951.
[200/ 801.1].

2318. **Moody, Robert E.** "Samaritan Material at Boston University: The Boston Collection and the 'Abisha Scroll'." *The Boston University Graduate Journal* 10 (1957): 158-160.
[101/ 2301].

2319. **Moore, George Foote.** "On a Fragment of the Samaritan Pentateuch in the Library of the Andover Theological Seminary." *JAOS* 14.Proceedings (1888): 35.
[103/ 2300].

2320. **Mor, Menahem.** "The High Priests in Judaea in the Persian Period." (Hebrew) *BM* 23. 1(no. 72) (1976-1977): 57-68. English summary 126-127. [803].

2321. ——. "More Bibliography on the Samaritans (with emphasis on Samaritanism and Christianity." *Henoch* 1. 1 (March, 1979): 99-123. [100/ 1003.1].

2322. ——. "The Persian, Hellenistic and Hasmonaean Period." In **A. D. Crown,** editor, *The Samaritans.* Tübingen: Mohr, 1989. 1-18. [802/ 803/ 804/ 805].

2323. ——. Samaritans and Jews in Persian, Hellenistic and Hasmonaean Periods. (Ph.D.) Haifa: University of Haifa, 1975. [802/ 803/ 804/ 805].

2324. ——. "Samaritans and Jews in the Ptolemaic and the Beginning of the Seleucid Periods." (Hebrew) In *Studies in the History of the Jewish People and the Land of Israel.* Haifa, 1980. 5: 71-81. [804/ 805].

2325. ——. "The Samaritans and the Bar-Kokhbah Revolt." In **A. D. Crown,** *The Samaritans.* Tübingen: Mohr, 1989. 19-31. [805].

2326. **Mor, M. and U. Rappaport.** *Bibliography of Works on Jewish History in the Hellenistic and Roman Periods, 1976-1980.* Jerusalem, 1982. [100].

2327. **Morag, Shlomo.** "Eppaya (Mark 7,34). Certainly Hebrew, not Aramaic." *JJS* 17 (1972): 198-202. [1003.1].

2328. **Morgernstern, J.** *Die Verleumdungen gegen die Juden und die der Juden gegen die Samaritaner. Ein Beitrag zur Kulturgeschichte derselben.* Berlin, 1878. [1003.4/ 2205].

2329. **Morin, Joanne.** *Biblia Hebraica, Samaritan, Chaldaica etc...quibus textus originales totius Scriptorae Sacrae.* Paris: Printed by Gaspard Meturas, 1629-1645. [The Paris polyglot: volume 6 was the work of Morin]. [105/ 2300].

2330. ——. *Diatribe...et animadversione in censurum exercitationum ad Samaritanorum Pentateuchum.* Paris, 1639. [105/ 2300].

2331. ——. *Ecclesiae Orientalis Antiquitates, clarissimor.* London: G.Wells, 1682. [Second edn. Leipzig and Frankfurt, 1683]. [105/ 1700/ 1705].

2332. ——. *Excercitationes Ecclesiasticae in utrumque Samaritanorum Pentateuchum. De illorum Religione et Moribus.* Paris: Anton Vitray, 1631. [394

pp + indices. Second edn. 1669].
[105/ 2300].

2333. —————. *Opuscula Hebraeo-Samaritica 1. Grammatica 2. Pentateuchi 3. Legis. 4. Grammaticorum 5. Varia lectiones 6. Lexicon Samaritanum.* Paris, 1657.
[105/ 2300/ 2600].

2334. —————. "Versio Epistolarum a Samaritanis Aegypti ad Scaligerum Scriptorum." In **Gassendius,** *Vita Peireskij.* 8.
[1705].

2335. **Moschus, Joannes.** "Pratum Spirituale." *PG* 87 (1860): 3032f.
[305].

2336. **Moses b. Eliyahu Halevi.** "Travels." (Hebrew) In **A. Ya'ari,** *Travellers to the Holy Land.* Ramat Gan, 1976. 305-322.
[401/ 408].

2337. **Moses, Marcus.** *Disputatio historico-philologico critica de Pentateucho ebraeo-Samaritano ab Ebraeo, eoqu masorethico, descripto exemplari, quam praeside Ol. Ger. Tychsen eruditorm examini subjicit.* Bützow, 1765.
[2300/ 2600].

2338. **Mosheim, Johann Lorenz von.** *Institutiones Historiae Christianae Majores.* Helmstadt, 1739.
[808/ 1002].

2339. **Motta Filho, J.** "Samaria Terra dos Paradoxos." *Revista de Univ. Cat. de São Paulo* 21.37 (1961): 89-104.
[200/ 410].

2340. **Motulsky, A. G.** Reviewer. **A. E. Mourant,** "The Genetics of the Jews." *Science* 203 (1979): 1102.
[107/ 903/ 2901].

2341. **Moulton, W. J.** "Das samaritanische Passahfest." *ZDPV* (1904): 194-201.
[1404].

2342. —————. "The Samaritan Passover." *JBL* 22 (1903): 187-194.
[1404].

2343. —————. "Samaritans." *ERE.* 1920/21. 11: 161-167.
[200/ 201].

2344. **Mourant, A. E., A. C. Kopec and Kazimiera Domaniewska-Sobczak.** *The Genetics of the Jews.* Oxford: Clarendon Press, 1978.
[2900/ 3500].

2345. **Mowbray, D. D.** A Critical Edition and Translation of the Samaritan Liturgies for the Zimmut Pesach and Zimmut Sukkot and Associated semi-Festival Liturgies.(Ph.D.) Leeds: University of Leeds, 1959.
[1404/ 2102].

2346. **Moyal, M. A.** "Samaritan Passover." *Asia and the Americas* 44 (1944): 549-554.
[1404].

2347. ——————. "Samaritan Passover." *History* (April, 1957): 1-5.
[1404].

2348. **Mulder, M. J.** Reviewer. **J. Macdonald**, "Samaritan Chronicle II." *Gereformeerd Theologisch Tijdschrift* 70 (1970): 179-183.
[107/ 1603].

2349. **Mülinen, Graf Eberhard von.** "Reise vom Karmelheim nach Nabulus und Zürück." *MNDPV* (1908): 36-40.
[308].

2350. **Müller, August.** *Katalog der Bibliothek der Deutschen Morgenlandischen Gesellschaft.* Leipzig, 1881.
[101/ 103].

2351. **Müller, D. H. and D. Kaufman.** "A Hymn Attributed to Samaritans." In *Sammlung Papyrus Erherzog Rainer.* Wien, 1886. 1: 38-44. [Republished with variants in *Beiträge zur jud. Altertumskunde,* Wien (1887) p. 116ff.].
[2102].

2352. **Müller, E.** "Ein Tag im alten Shechem." *Jüdische Zeitung* 3.42 (1909).
[200].

2353. **Müller, F. G.** *Jesus und die Samariterin. Zwei Predigten.* Stuttgart, 1865.
[1502.1].

2354. **Müller, H.** Reviewer. **H. Pohl,** "Kitab al Mirath." *Mundus* 11 (1975): 327-328.
[107/ 1100/ 2204].

2355. **Müller, Johann Gottfried.** *Disputatio philologico-critica de utilitate novae Pentateuchi Samaritani editionis.* Wittenbergae, 1728.
[2300/ 2600].

2356. **Müller, K.** Reviewer. **J. Bowman,** "Samaritan Problem." *BZ* 15 (1971): 150-151.
[107/ 1503].

2357. **Munk, Esriel.** Des Samaritaners Marqah Erzählung über den Tod Moses.(Hebrew and German) Berlin: Albertus-Universität zu Königsberg, 1890. Inaugural dissertation. [Reprinted, Berlin, 1890].
[1803].

2358. **Muñoz, A. S.** Reviewer. **J. Fossum,** "The Name of God and the Angel of the Lord." *Archivo Teologico Granadino* 49 (1986): 460.
[107/ 1101/ 1110].

2359. ——————. Reviewer. **A. D. Crown,** "The Samaritans." *Archivo Teologico Granadino* 52 (1989): 347-349.
[107/ 200].

2360. **Munro, J. Iverach.** *The Samaritan Pentateuch and Modern Criticism.* London: James Nisbet & Co., 1911. With an introduction by James Orr. [2300].

2361. ——————. "The Samaritan Pentateuch and Philological Questions." *JTVI* 44 (1912): 183-209. [2300/ 2600].

2362. **Murtonen, A. E.** *Hebrew in its West Semitic Setting: A Comparative Survey of Non-Masoretic Hebrew Dialects and Traditions.* Leiden: E. J. Brill, 1986, 1988. Pt. 1, A Comparative Lexicon & Pt. Ba: Root System: Hebrew Material. [2600].

2363. ——————. *I. Materials for a Non-Masoretic Hebrew Grammar II. An Etymological Vocabulary to the Samaritan Pentateuch III. A Grammar of the Samaritan Dialect of Hebrew.* Helsinki: Studia Orientalia, 1958-1964. [2300/ 2600].

2364. ——————. "On the Influence of the Development of Vocalization Upon the Form System in Samaritan Hebrew." *Akten des Vierundzwanzigsten Internationalen Orientalisten Kongress.* Wiesbaden, 1959. 257-259. [2602/ 2607].

2365. ——————. Reviewer. **Z. Ben-Hayyim,** "The Literary and Oral Tradition." *QS* 33 (1957-1958): 294-298. [107].

2366. ——————. "The Matres Lectionis in Biblical Hebrew." *AN* 16 (1976): 66-121. [2603.1].

2367. ——————, editor. "The Pronunciation of Hebrew by the Samaritans." In **P. Kahle,** *The Cairo Geniza.* 2nd edn. Oxford: Blackwell, 1959. 318-335. [2300/ 2604/ 2607].

2368. **Musil, Alois.** "Sieben samaritanische Inschriften." *Anz.Akad.Wiss. Wien* Phil-hist. Kl.39 (1902): 127f. [2500].

2369. ——————. "Sieben samaritanische Inschriften aus Damaskus." *Sitzungsberichte de K. K. Akad. d.Wiss., Munchen, Wien* (1903): 1-11. [2500/ 2506].

2370. **Mussner, Franz.** "Der Begriff des 'Nachsten' in der Verkundigung Jesu." In *Gesammelte Studien zu fragen und Themen des neuen Testamentes.* Dusseldorf, 1967. 123-132. [Reprinted, *TTZ* 64 (1975):91-99]. [1003.1/ 1502].

2371. **Myers, J. M.** Reviewer. **J. Bowman,** "Samaritan Problem." *CBQ* 39 (1977): 108-109. [107/ 1503].

N

2372. **Nagel, M.** "Un samaritain dans l'arsinoite au IIe siècle après J-C (à propos du nom Sambas)." *Chronique d'Égypte* 49.97 (January 1974): 356-365. [505].

2373. **Nagy, István Szerencsi.** "Exercitatio de Samaria et Samaritanis." In **Fr. Imm. Schwarz,** *Exercitationes historico-criticae in utrumque Samaritanum Pentateuchum.* Wittenberg, 1756. [200].

2374. **Nahon, G.** "Samaritains." In *Encyclopedia Universalis.* Paris, 1975. 20: 1719. [201].

2375. **Nallino, C. A.** "Abu'l Fath ibn Abu'l Hasan as Samiri." In *Enciclopedia Italiana.* ,1929. 1: 155. [201/ 1601/ 3001].

2376. **Narkiss, M.** "Une culte de Dioscures à Sebastiyeh." *RB* 42 (1933): 636. [1110].

2377. **Nau, F.** "Le canon biblique samaritano-chrétien des hérodiens." *RB* 39 (Juillet,1930): 396-400. [2300].

2378. —————. "Deux épisodes de l'histoire juive sous Théodore II (423 et 438) à après la vie de Barsauma le Syrien." *REJ* 83 (1927): [305.6/ 808].

2379. —————. "Juifs et samaritains à Eléphantine." *JA* 18.10th series (1911): 660-662. [803].

2380. —————. "Résumés de monographies syriaques." *Revue de l'orient chrétien* 8 (1913): 2nd series. [305.6].

2381. **Nauerth, C.** "Pilgersatten am Gerizim in Fruhchristlichen Zeit." *Dielheimer Blätter zum Alten Testament und Zeiner Rezeption in der Alten Kirche* 18 (1984): 17-45. [305/ 306/ 401].

2382. **Naveh, Joseph.** "Did Ancient Samaritan Inscriptions Belong to Synagogues?" In **Rachel Hachlili,** editor, *Ancient Synagogues in Israel, 3rd-7th Century CE.* Oxford: BAR International, 1989. 61-63. [2500].

2383. —————. *The Early History of the Alphabet.* Jerusalem, 1982. [2500/ 2600].

2384. ———————. "A Greek Dedication in Samaritan Letters." *IEJ* 31.3-4 (1981): 220-222.
[305.4/ 411/ 2500/ 2600].

2385. ———————. "Inscriptions on Pottery Lamps." (Hebrew) *EI* 19 (1987): 266-269.
[605].

2386. ———————. "Lamp Inscriptions and Inverted Writing." *IEJ* 38.1-2 (1988): 36-43 and plates 8 & 9. [Some Samaritan lamps discussed. See also *Eretz Israel* 19(1987): 266-269].
[605].

2387. ———————. "Some Considerations on the Ancient Samaritan Inscriptions." In **Maria Macuth, Christa Müller-Kessler and Bert G.Fragner,** editors, *Hokmot Baneta Beyta: Studia Semitica Necnon Iranica: The Macuch Festschrift.* Wiesbaden: Harrassowitz, 1989.
[2500].

2388. ———————. "Some Recently Forged Inscriptions." *BASOR* 247 (1982): 53-58.
[2500].

2389. **Nazianzus, Gregory.** "Orationes." *PG* 36 99-102, 407-410.
[200/ 305.4].

2390. **Negev, Abraham.** "Samaria." In **R. Stillwell,** editor, *The Princeton Encyclopedia of Classical Sites.* Princeton: Princeton University Press, 1976.
[201/ 410].

2391. **Nelson, Russell David.** Studies in the Development of the Text of the Tabernacle Account (Qumran, Old Greek, Samaritan). (Ph.D.) Boston: Harvard University, 1986.
[2300].

2392. **Nemoy, Leon.** "Abu Ishaq Ibrahim's Kitab al- Mirath." *JQR* 66 (1975): 62-65.
[2200/ 2204].

2393. ———————. "Al-Qirqisani's Account of the Jewish Sects." *HUCA* 7 (1930): 317-398.
[200/ 307.2/ 1500].

2394. ———————. *A Catalogue of Hebrew and Yiddish Manuscripts and Books from the Library of Scholem Asch Presented to Yale University Library by Louis M. Rabinowitz.* New Haven, 1945. Items 1663, 1664.
[101/ 103].

2395. ———————. Reviewer. **E. Robertson,** "Catalogue of the Samaritan Manuscripts II. The Gaster Manuscripts." *JBL* 81 (1962): 430-431.
[101/ 103/ 107].

2396. **Nestlé, E.** "Pinchas—Mansur." *ZDMG* 55 (1901): 701.
[1100/ 1302].

2397. —————. "Zu den samaritanischen Typen." *ZDMG* 57 (1903): 568-569.
      [105].

2398. **Netzer, E.** "The Augusteum at Samaria-Sebaste." (Hebrew) *EI* 19 (1987): 97-105.
      [410/ 600].

2399. **Neubauer, Adolf.** *Catalogue of the Hebrew Manuscripts in the Bodleian Library and in the College Libraries of Oxford, including Manuscripts in Other Languages which are Written with Hebrew Characters and a few Samaritan Manuscripts.* Oxford: Clarendon Press, 1886-1906. I & II: [Volume II was written with A. Cowley].
      [101/ 103].

2400. —————. "Chronique samaritaine suivie d'un appendice contenant de courtes notices sur quelques autres ouvrages samaritains." *JA* 14.6ᵉ series (1869): 385-470. [Republished separatum, Paris 1873].
      [1607].

2401. —————. "Un commentaire samaritain inconnu: deuxième appendice à la chronique samaritaine." *JA* 1.7th series (1873): 341-368.
      [1607/ 2304].

2402. —————. Reviewer. **E. Munk,** "Des samaritaners Marqah." *JQR* 4 (1892): 324-325.
      [107/ 1803].

2403. —————. *Facsimiles of Hebrew Manuscripts in the Bodleian Library Illustrting the Various Forms of Rabbinical Characters with Transcriptions.* Oxford: Clarendon Press, 1886. Plate 40.
      [103].

2404. —————. *La géographie du Talmud.* Paris, 1868. 165-175. [Reprinted, 1967].
      [304.2/ 400].

2405. —————. "Samaritan." *JQR* 2 (1890): 204. [Reprinted, Ktav, 1966. A review of Baneth and Wreschner].
      [107/ 200/ 1803].

2406. —————. "Sects Among the Jews." *JC* (12 November 1886): 12-13.
      [200].

2407. —————. "Where are the Ten Tribes?" *JQR* 1 (1889): 14-28, 95-114, 185-201, 408-423.
      [801.2].

2408. **Neumann, G. A.** Editor. "Ludolphus de sudheim; de itinéraire Terre Sainte." *AOL* 2 (1884): 304-377.
      [306.2].

2409. **Neumann, W.** "Studien über zwei Blätter aus einer alten samaritanischen Pentateuchhandschrift." *Abhandlungen aus dem Jahrbuch der Leo-Gesellschaft* (1896).
      [103/ 2300].

2410. **Neyrey, J. H.** "Jacob Traditions and the Interpretation of John 4:10-26." *CBQ* 41.4 (1979): 419-437.
[1502.1].

2411. **Niccolo of Poggibonsi.** **Theophilus Bellorini,** translator, *A Voyage Beyond the Seas (1346-1350).* Jerusalem: Franciscan Press, 1945.
[306.2/ 400].

2412. **Nicephorus Callistus.** "Ecclesiastical History." *PG* 145 cols. 847-850.
[200/ 305.4].

2413. **Nicholls, George F.** *A Grammar of the Samaritan Language with Extracts and Vocabulary.* London: Samuel Bagster, 1858.
[2600].

2414. **Nicolai, Johanne.** *Petri Cunaei de Republica Hebraeorum Liber Tres.* Lugdunum Batavorum, 1703. :301-318.
[200/ 406].

2415. **Nicoll, A.** *Notitia codicis Samaritano-Arabici in Bibliotheca Bodleiana adservati Pentateuchum complectentis.* Oxford, 1817. [Only sixty copies were printed of which only ten were on large paper. 11pp].
[101/ 103].

2416. **Nicoll, A. and W. Pusey.** *Bibliothecae Bodleianae codicum manuscriptorum orientalium catalogus.* Oxford, 1821-1835. [Nicoll edited the first volume on his own.].
[101/ 103].

2417. **Niebuhr, Berthold G.** *Corpus Scriptorum historiae Byzantiae.* Bonn, 1828-1894.
[305.4/ 808].

2418. **Nielsen, Eduard.** *Shechem: Traditio-Historical Investigations.* Copenhagen: G. E. C. Gad, 1959. [1st edn. 1955].
[412/ 801/ 801.1/ 2300].

2419. **Nilus.** "Epistles." *PG* 79 83-86.
[305.4].

2420. **Nobler, M.** "Samaritano-Pentateuco." In *Enciclopaedia Cattolica.* Rome, 1953. 10: 1736-1739.
[201/ 2300].

2421. **Nodet, Etienne.** *Essai sur les origines du judaisme: de Josue aux Pharisiens.* Paris: Cerf, 1992.
[801/ 804].

2422. —————. Reviewer. **Rita Egger,** "Josephus Flavius und die Samaritaner." *RB* 95.2 (1988): 288-294.
[107/ 303.5/ 805].

2423. **Noja, Sergio.** "Abu al-Hasan al Suri's Discourses on the Forbidden Degrees of
Consanguinity in Marriage in the Kitab al-Tabbah." *AN* 77 (1971): 110-115.
[1109/ 1208/ 2202/ 3002].

2424. —————. Reviewer. **Reinhard Pummer,** "The Book of Jubilees and the
Samaritans." *Henoch* 3 (1981): 97.
[1003/ 1003.4].

2425. —————. "Contribution à la bibliographie des samaritains." *AION* 33.n.s. 23
(1973): 98-113.
[100].

2426. —————. "Erklärung der 72 Lehren der Samaritaner." *ZDMG* 118 (1968):
270-273.
[1803].

2427. —————. "Gli Ultimi Dieci Anni di Studi Sui Samaritani." *Associazione Italiana
per lo Studio del Giudaismo Testi e Studi— Atti del congresso tenuto a S. Miniato
dal 12 al 15 Novembre 1984* (1987): 139-149.
[106].

2428. —————. "I Samaritani, le loro credenze, i loro riti." *Il Milione* 5 (1968):
[200].

2429. —————. *Il Kitab al-Kafi dei Samaritani.* Napoli, 1970. [Reprinted from *AION,*
n.s. 18:253-288; 19:17-44, 333-360; 20:167-207, 447-481].
[1106/ 2203].

2430. —————. "Il Samaritano, un Sopravvissuto di 2, 000 anni fa." *Bibbia et Oriente*
29.1 (1987): 39-41.
[200].

2431. —————. "The Last Decade in Samaritan Studies." In **A. D. Crown,** editor,
The Samaritans. Tübingen: Mohr, 1989. 802-814.
[106].

2432. —————. "Les préceptes des samaritains dans le manuscrit Sam. 10 de la
Bibliothèque Nationale." *RB* 74 (1967): 255-259.
[103/ 1108].

2433. —————. Reviewer. **Reinhard Pummer,** "New Evidence for Samaritan
Christianity." *Henoch* 3 (1981): 97.
[1003.1/ 1502].

2434. —————. Reviewer. **S. Lowy,** "Principles of Samaritan Bible Exegesis." *Henoch*
1.3 (1979): 410-411.
[107/ 2305].

2435. —————. "The Samareitikon." In **A. D. Crown,** editor, *The Samaritans.*
Tübingen: Mohr, 1989. 408-412.
[2309].

2436. ——————. Reviewer. J. Macdonald, "Samaritan Chronicle II." *ZDMG* 123 (1973): 148-149. [107/ 1600/ 1603].

2437. ——————. Reviewer. **A. D. Crown**, "Samaritan Majuscule Palaeography." *Henoch* 3 (1981): 98-100. [107/ 2501].

2438. ——————. Reviewer. **A. Broadie**, "A Samaritan Philosophy. A Study of the Hellenistic Cultural Ethos of the Memar Marqah." *Henoch* 8 (1986): 109-110. [107/ 1803].

2439. ——————. Reviewer. **A. Tal**, "The Samaritan Targum of the Pentateuch: A Critical Edition." *Henoch* 8 (1986): 249-250. [107/ 2401].

2440. ——————. "Studi Samaritani—Introduzione." *Revista di Storia e Letteratura Religiosa* 5.2 (1969): 413-414. [106].

2441. ——————. "Sulle fonti giuridiche Samaritane manuscritte in lingua araba." *Rendiconti del-l'Istituto Lombardo Class di Lettere* 100 (1968): 135-148. [1106].

2442. **Nöldeke, Theodor.** *Beitrage zur Geschichte des Alexanderromans.* Vienna, 1890. [804].

2443. ——————. "Über die Aussprache des Hebräischen bei den Samaritanern." *GGN* (1868): 485-504. [2600].

2444. ——————. "Über einige samaritanisch-arabische Schriften, die hebräische Sprache Betreffend." *GGN* 17 & 18 (23 July & 27 August 1862): 337-352; 385-416. [103/ 2600].

2445. **Nonnus of Panopolis.** "Paraphrase of John." *PG* 43 771-778. [305.4/ 1502.1].

2446. **North, Robert.** "Report from Palestine; Garizim Passover." *CBQ* 22 (1970): 424. [406/ 1404].

2447. ——————. "Samaritans and Pentateuch." *Israel's Chronicle.* St. Marys, Kansas: St. Louis University, School of Divinity, 1963. First preliminary edition: 315-322. [200/ 2300].

2448. **Noy, Dov.** "The Flaming Sword Which Turns." *A–B* 249-250 (16 December 1979): 33-35. [2305].

2449. ——————, editor. (Hebrew) *Samaritan Legends. Twelve Legends from Oral Tradition.* Haifa: Israel Folktale Archives Publication, 1965. Series 8. [Edited,

annotated and accompanied by an appendix; Samaritan folk traditions, selective bibliography. An English summary].
[1800].

2450. **Nutt, John W.** *A Sketch of Samaritan History, Dogma and Literature Published as an Introduction to "Fragments of a Samaritan Targum".* London: Trubner and Co., 1874. [Published as an introduction to *Fragments of a Samaritan Targum.* See next entry].
[200/ 800].

2451. —————. *Some Fragments of a Samaritan Targum. Edited from a Bodleian Manuscript with an Introduction, Containing a Sketch of Samaritan History, Dogma and Literature.* London: Trubner & Co., 1874. Appendix 1. A. Harkavy, The Collection of Samaritan Manuscripts at St. Petersburg: 153-167. Appendix 2. The Massekhet Kuthim or Tractate on the Samaritans.
[103/ 800/ 2401].

O

2452. **Oakman, Douglas E.** "Was Jesus a Peasant? Implications for Reading the Samaritan Story (Luke 10:30-35)." *Biblical Theology Bulletin* 22.3 (1992): 117-125.
[1003.1/1502.4].

2453. **Ockley, S.** *The Present History of the Jews.* London, 1707. [A translation of Leon di Modena's work].
[200/ 309].

2454. **O'Day, Gail R.** *Revelation in the Fourth Gospel.* Philadelphia: Fortress Press, 1954.
[1003.1/ 1502.1].

2455. **Odeberg, Hugo.** *The Fourth Gospel Interpreted in its Relation to Contemporaneous Religious Currents in Palestine and the Hellenistic-Oriental World.* Uppsala, 1929. [Reprinted, Amsterdam 1968].
[1502.1].

2456. **O'Ferrall, R.** "The Samaritan Passover: Extracts from the Letter of a Pilgrim." *Treasury* (April, 1920): 4-7. [Visit to Mt. Gerizim for Passover; 6 figs.].
[1404].

2457. **Ogawa, H.** "Chronology of the Cult of Kore at Samaria." (Japanese) *Palaeologia* (Kyoto, 1971): 233-243. [English summary, p. 250].
[1110].

2458. **Okure, Teresa.** *The Johannine Approach to Mission.* Wissenschaftliche Untersuchungen zum Neuen Testament 31. Tübingen: Mohr, 1988.
[1502.1].

2459. **Oliphant, L.** "Notes on a Tomb Opened at Jebata and on a monument found at Nablous." *PEFQS* (1885): 94-97.
[600].

2460. **Olsson, B.** *Structure and Meaning in the Fourth Gospel. A Text-Linguistic Analysis of John 2, 1-11 and 4, 1-42.* Lund: Lund University, 1974.
[1502.1].

2461. **Oplatka, (Prager) Rahamin Joseph Chaim.** *Travels of Rahamin Joseph Chaim Oplatka from Jerusalem to Meron.* Jerusalem, 1876. [Reprinted in A.Ya'ari, *Travels to the Holy Land*: 623-638. The original printing has a long polemic against Kirchheim over his views on the Samaritans expressed in *Karme Shomron*].
[309/ 800].

2462. **Oppenheim, D.** "Die Sekten der Samaritaner." *MGWJ* 9 (1860): 120-124.
[1500].

2463. **Oppenheimer, Aharon.** "The *'Ammei Ha-'aretz* and the Samaritans." In *The 'Am Ha-'aretz . A Study in the Social History of the Jewish People in the Hellenistic-*

Roman Period. Leiden: Brill, 1977. 229-238.
[808/ 1109].

2464. **Oppergelt, Friederich.** "Epistolae Samaritanorum ad Scaligerum duae." In *Jüdischen Lehren und ihren Exegesis.* Halle: Klemmen, 1730.
[1705].

2465. **Orbe, A.** *Aqua de Vida. Divagaciones sobre el Diálogo del Señor con la Samaritana (Joh. 4, 3-43).* Bilbao, 1962.
[1502.1].

2466. **O'Reilly, Bernal de.** *En Tierra Santa, La Judea, La Samaria y la Galilea.* Wiesbaden, 1896.
[306.2/ 400].

2467. **Origen.** "Against Celsus." *PG* 11 751-754.
[305.4].

2468. ————. "Commentary on John." *PG* 14 399-454, 651-658.
[305.4/ 1502.1].

2469. ————. "Commentary on Matthew." *PG* 13 1563-1566.
[305.4/ 1003.1].

2470. ————. "Commentary on the Epistle to the Romans." *PG* 14 912, 916-918.
[305.4/ 1502].

2471. ————. "On Exodus." *PG* 12 287-290.
[305.4/ 1003.3].

2472. ————. "Homilies on Luke." *PG* 13 1883-1890.
[305.4/ 1502.4].

2473. ————. "Homilies on Numbers." *PG* 12 763-766.
[305.4/ 1003.3].

2474. **Ormann, G.** Reviewer. J. Macdonald, "Memar Marqah." *QS* 39 (1964): 376-377.
[107/ 1803].

2475. **Ory, G.** "La 'conversion' de Simon le magicien." *CCER* 9 (1950): 20.
[1506.2].

2476. ————. "Jean le Baptiseur." *CCER* 10 (1956): 24.
[1502].

2477. ————. "Un rite magique de Simon le samaritain." *CCER* (1956): 37.
[1506.2].

2478. ————. "La Samarie, patrie d'un Messie." *CCER* 11 (1956): 16f.
[410].

2479. ————. "Simon (dit le magicien)." *CCER* 5 (1955): 16.
[1506.2].

2480. **Otho, Georgius.** *Palaestra, Linguarum Orientalium hoc est: Quator primorum capitum Geneseos 1) Textus Originalis tam ex Judaeorum Quam Samaritanorum Traditionibus 2) Targumim, Samaritana etc.* Francofurti ad Moenum, 1702. Second edn. 1704.
[2300/ 2401].

2481. —————. *Synopsis institutionum Samaritanarum, Rabbinicarum, Arabicarum, Aethiopicarum et Persicarum.* Francofurti ad Moenum, 1701. [Second edn. published as an appendix to Alting, *Fundamenta,* 1717. Third edn. 1735, Francofurti ad Moenum].
[200/ 2300].

2482. **Otho/Ottho, Johannes Henricus.** *Historia Doctorum Misnicorum.* Oxford, 1672. [Second edn. published anon. by Hadrian Reland, Amstelodami, 1699. The second edition is more important than the first for the study of the Samaritan Chronicles from a manuscript owned by Reland].
[1600/ 1601].

2483. **Ott, John Henry.** "Catalogues of Coins by J. H. Ott; containing coins of the Samaritans. 3 volumes." N.D. 18th century.
[103].

2484. **Otti, Johann B.** *Epistola de Numis Quibusdam Samaritanis as Adrianum Relandum.* Trajecti Ad Rhenum, 1704. [Reprinted in Ugolini, *Thesaurus* 28: 1216f. Venice (1765)].
[603].

2485. **Ouseley, Sir William,** editor. *The Oriental Geography of Ibn Haukhal: an Arabian Traveller of the Tenth Century.* London, 1800.
[307.1].

2486. **Ovadiah, A.** "The Greek Inscription from Tell Qasile Reexamined." *IEJ* 37 (1987): 36-39.
[2512].

2487. **Owen, H. P.** "Stephen's Vision in Acts 7:55-56." *NTS* 2 (1955): 224-226.
[1502.2].

2488. **Owen, Henry.** *A Brief Account, Historical and Critical of the Septuagint Version to which is added a Dissertation on the Comparative Excellence of the Hebrew and Samaritan Pentateuch.* London, 1787.
[2300].

2489. **Owen, John Ionnes.** *Orbis eruditi literaturam a charactae Samaritico hunc in modum favente Deo aedexit Eduardus Bernardus A.D. 1687.* Oxford, 1700.
[105/ 2501].

P

2490. **Paine, Timothy Otis.** *Solomon's Temple and Capital. Ark of the Flood and Tabernacle or the Holy Houses of the Hebrew, Chaldee, Syriac, Samaritan, Septuagint, Coptic and Itala Scriptures. Josephus, Talmud and Rabbis...with Plates.* London, 1886. New York, 1887.
[1305/ 2300].

2491. **Palacios, L.** *Grammatice Aramaico-biblica ad usum scholarum.* Rome, 1959. Appendix 5, p.1378 "Ex Targum Samaritano Gen. 37:12-22".
[2800].

2492. **Palfrey, John Gorham.** *Elements of Chaldee, Syriac, Samaritan and Rabbinic Grammar.* Boston, 1835. 2 plates.
[2600].

2493. **E. H. Palmer,** *A Descriptive Catalogue of the Arabic, Persian and Turkish Manuscripts in the Library of Trinity College, Cambridge, with an appendix containing a Catalogue of the Hebrew and Samaritan Manuscripts.* Cambridge, 1870. 232-235.
[101/ 103].

2494. **Pamment, Margaret.** "Is There Convincing Evidence of Samaritan Influence on the Fourth Gospel?" *ZNW* 73.3-4 (1982): 221-230.
[1502.1].

2495. **Panimole, Salvatore A.** "Il battesimo e la Pentacoste dei Samaritani." In **Giustino Fardini,** editor, *Traditio et Progressio: Studi liturgici in Honore del Adrien Nocent.* Rome. 413-436.
[1201/1407].

2496. **Pardee, Dennis.** Reviewer. Freedman, D. N., K.A. Mathews, "The Paleo-Hebrew Leviticus Scroll (11QpaleoLev)." *JNES* 49.2 (1990): 196-197.
[107/2307/2309].

2497. **Parker, M., K. Melis and H. D. L. Vervliet.** "Typographia Plantiniana, II." *De Gulden Passer* 38 (1960):
[105].

2498. **Parkes, Malcolm.** *The Medieval Manuscripts of Keble College, Oxford.* London: Scolar Press, 1979. [Section on the Samaritan manuscripts by A. D. Crown].
[101/ 103].

2499. **Parrot, André.** "Samarie, capitale du royaume d'Israël." In *Cahiers d'archéologie biblique, 7.* Neuchatel, Paris, 1956. [An English trans. by S. H. Hooke, London, SCM Press 1958].
[410/ 801].

2500. **Pastritius, Ioannes.** *Alphabetum plurima Linguarum et Dialectorum nempe Samaritanum etc.* N.D.
[105/ 2501/2600].

2501. **Patrick, D. and W. Geddie.** "Samaria", "Samaritan Pentateuch." In *Chambers Encyclopaedia.* London & Edinburgh, 1935. 9:
[201].

2502. **Patte, D.** "An Analysis of Narrative Structure and the Good Samaritan." *Semeia* 2 (1974): 1-26. [NTAb (1975) 19:183].
[1502/ 1502.3].

2503. —————. "Comment on the Article of J. D. Crossan." *Semeia* 2 (1974): 117-121.
[1502/ 1502.3].

2504. —————. "Structural Network in Narrative:The Good Samaritan." *Soundings* 58 (1975): 221-242.
[1502.3].

2505. **Paul, A.** Reviewer. **Albrecht Wirth,** "Aus orientalischen Chroniken." *BZ* 4 (1985): 23-29.
[107/ 1600/ 1601].

2506. —————. "Écrits de Qumran et sectes juives aux premiers siècles de l'Islam." In *Recherches sur l'origine du Qaraisme.* Paris, 1969.
[1003.3/ 1005].

2507. **Paulus, H. E. G.** *Commentatio critica exhibens Bibliotheca Oxoniensi Bodleiana specimina versionum Pentateuchi septem Arabicarum nondum editarum cum versionibus.* Jenae, 1789.
[2300/ 2302].

2508. —————. "Zur Geschichte des samaritanisch-arabischen Pentateuchs." *Neues Repertorium für Biblische und morgenländische Literatur.* Jenae, 1791. 171-180.
[2302].

2509. **Payne-Smith, R.** "The Samaritan Chronicle of Abu'l Fatch, the Arabic Text from the MS in the Bodleian Library, with a Literal English Translation." *DVJ* 2 (1863): 304-432.
[1601].

2510. **Pazdan, M. M.** "Nicodemus and the Samaritan Woman: Contrasting Models of Discipleship." *Biblical Theological Bulletin* 17.1 (1987): 145-148.
[1502.1].

2511. **Pearson, B. A.** Reviewer. **J. Fossum,** "The Name of God and the Angel of the Lord." *Religious Studies Review* 12.3/4 (July-October, 1986): 297a.
[107/ 1101].

2512. **Pearson, J. D.** *Oriental Manuscript Collections in the Libraries of Great Britain and Ireland.* London, 1954. 19-29. [Also available as a microfiche, IDC Leiden].
[101/ 103].

2513. —————. *Oriental Manuscripts in Europe and North America.* Bibliotheca Asiatica 7. Zug: IDC-Interdocumentation, 1971.
[101/ 103].

2514. **Pearson, J. D., Noel Matthews and M. Doreen Wainwright.** *A Guide to Manuscripts and Documents in the British Isles Relating to the Middle East and North Africa.* Oxford: OUP, 1980. pp. 40, 102, 124, 149, 213, 385.
[100].

2515. **Pedersen, Johannes.** *Inscriptiones Semiticae Collectionis Ustinowianae.* Oslo: Symbolae Osloenses, 1928. Fasc. Sup. 2: 15-25.
[2500/ 2510.1].

2516. **Penna, A.** Reviewer. J. Macdonald, "The Samaritan Chronicle II." *Revista Biblica Dell' Assoc. Bib. Ital.* 18 (1970): 410-411.
[107/ 1603].

2517. **Pérez Castro, F.** "Das Kryptogramm des Sefer Abischa." *VT Supplement* 7 (1960): 52-60. [Reprinted in Dexinger and Pummer, *Die Samaritaner* 220-229].
[2301].

2518. —————. "El criptograma del Séfer Abisa." *Sefarad* 19 (1959): 384-391.
[2301].

2519. —————. "El Séfer Abisa el antiguo y célèbre rollo del Pentateucho Samaritano de Nablus." *Sefarad* 13 (1953): 119-129.
[2301].

2520. —————. "Fragmento inédito del Séfer Abisa." *Sefarad* 21 (1961): 3-8.
[2301].

2521. —————. *Séfer Abisa, edición del fragmento antiguo.* Madrid-Barcelona: Seminario Filológico Cardinal Cisneros, 1959. 2:
[2301].

2522. **Perles, F.** Reviewer. A. Cowley, "Samaritan Liturgy." *OLZ* 15 (1912): 212-220.
[107/ 2100].

2523. —————. Reviewer. J. A. Montgomery, "The Samaritans." *OLZ* 10 (1907): 632-634.
[107/ 200].

2524. **Perles, J.** "La légende d'Asnath." *REJ* 22 (1891): 87-92.
[1800/ 3005].

2525. **Perrot, C.** "Petuhot et Setumot. Étude sur les Alinéas du pentateuque." *RB* 76 (1969): 50-91.
[2306.1].

2526. **Pertsch, Wilhelm.** *Die orientalischen Handschriften der Herzoglichen Bibliothek zu Gotha, mit ausnahme der Persichen, Turkischen und Arabischen.* Gotha, 1893.
[Nos. 30 & 57].
[101/ 103].

2527. **Petal, M.** "Samaritan Origins." (Hebrew) in *Avodat (Student resource book)*. Tel
Aviv, 1972.
[801.1].

2528. **Petermann, Julius Heinrich.** *Brevis linguae samaritanae grammatica, literatura,
chrestomathia cum glossario.* Carlsruhe & Leipzig: Porta Linguarum
Orientalium, 1873. [Reprinted, Berlin 1873].
[2602].

2529. ———. *Reisen im Orient, 1852-1855.* Leipzig, 1860-61. 2 vols: 269-292.
[Reprinted 1865 and Amsterdam, Philo Press 1976—one of the more
intelligent travel accounts. Describes the Passover of 1853].
[202/ 308/ 1404].

2530. ———. "Samaria und die Samaritaner." *Realencyklopädie für protestantische
Theologie und Kirche* 13 (1884): 340-355.
[201].

2531. ———. *Versuch einer hebräischen Formenlehre nach der Aussprache der
heutigen Samaritaner nebst einer darnach gebildeten Transscription der
Genesisund einer Beilage enthaltend die von dem recipirten Texte des Pentateuchs
abweichenden Lesarten der Samaritaner, von H. Petermann. Leipzig, 1868.*
Leiden: AKM, 1866. 5: 1-327. [Reprinted, 1868, 1876. Kraus reprints 1966,
Philo Press 1969].
[2300/ 2600].

2532. **Petermann, Julius Heinrich and B. Pick.** "Samaria and Samaritans." In P. Schaff,
editor, *A Religious Encyclopedia.* New York: Funk & Wagnalls, 1891. 4: 2101-
2104.
[201].

2533. **Petermann, Julius Heinrich and K. Vollers.** *Pentateuchus Samaritanus ad fidem
librorum manuscriptorum apud Nablusianos repertorum, editit et varios lectiones
adscripsit.* Berlin: Moeser, 1872-1891. [Genesis and Exodus ed. Petermann,
1872 & 1882; Leviticus, Numbers & Deuteronomy ed. Vollers, 1883, 1885 &
1891].
[2300].

2534. **Peters, N.** "Eine kritische Ausgabe des hebräischen Pentateuchs der Samaritaner."
BZ 13 (1915): 97-105.
[2300].

2535. **Petit, Samuel.** *Eclogae Chronologicae, in quibus de variis annorum Judaeorum,
Samaritarum etc. Eclogas Chronologicas "Samaritanorum".* Paris, 1632.
[700].

2536. **Petrozzi, M. T.** "I Samaritani." *TS* 50 (1974): 101-107.
[200].

2537. ———. *Samaria.* Jerusalem, 1973.
[410].

2538. **Pettigrew, Thomas J.** *Bibliotheca Sussexiana—A Descriptive Catalogue.* London: Longman & Co., 1827. Vol. 1: part 2.
[101/ 103].

2539. **Pharr, C.**, editor. "Shipmasters" (13:5:18) "Jews Caelicolists and Samaritans" (16:8) "Jews, Samaritans, Heretics and Pagans" (N.Th.3:1)." *The Theodosian Code.* Princeton: Princeton University Press, 1952. 394; 467-471; 488-490.
[305.4/ 808/ 1003.1].

2540. **Philaster.** "Liber de Haeresibus (iv. Dositheus) (vii. Samaritani) (xxix. Simon Magus) (xxx. Menander)." *PL* 12 1118, 1120-1121; 1142. [Notes by J. Fabrici].
[305.5/ 1500/ 1503/ 1506.1/ 1506.2].

2541. **Phocas, J. A.** Stewart, editor, *Pilgrimage in the Holy Land, 1185 A.D.* London: Palestine Pilgrims Text Society, 1896.
[306.2/ 400].

2542. **Photius.** "Ad Amphilocium Quaestiones." *PG* 101 455-466.
[305.5/ 1500/ 1503].

2543. ————. "Myriobiblon sive Bibliotheca." *PG* 103 399-406.
[305.5/ 1500/ 1503].

2544. **Pick, B.** "Horae Samaritanae. Collection of the Various Readings of the Samaritan Pentateuch Compared with the Hebrew and Other Ancient Versions." *BS* (1876-1878): 76f; 309f.
[2300].

2545. ————. "Samaritan Pentateuch ", "Samaritan Versions ", "Samaritan Language ", "Samaritan Liturgy", "Samaritan Literature ", "Samaritan Sects." In J. McClintock and J. Strong, editors, *Cyclopaedia of Biblical, Theological and Ecclesiastical Literature.* New York, 1885. 9:
[201].

2546. **Pickard, J. G.** "The Samaritan Stone at Gaza." *PEFQS* (1873): 157-158.
[2508].

2547. **Pik, H.** Reviewer. I. Ben-Zvi, "Sepher Hashomronim." (Hebrew) *QS* 12.924 (1935-1936): 282.
[107/ 200].

2548. **Pilcher, E. J.** "A Samaritan Periapt." *JRAS* 3 (July 1920): 343-346. [A small amulet with a bilingual Greek-Samaritan inscription].
[601/ 2501].

2549. **Pinchas, M. ben.** *Order of the Samaritan Passover on the Gerizim Mountain at Nablus.* Jerusalem: Greek Convent Press, 1936.
[1404/ 2102].

2550. **Pinchinat, Barthélemy.** *Dictionnaire chronologique, historique, critique, sur l'origine de l'idolatrie, des sectes des Samaritains, des Juifs...* Paris: Pralard, 1736. 526 pp.

4?.
[201].

2551. **Pines, Y. M.** "The Samaritan Passover Sacrifice." (Hebrew) in **Y. L. Baruch and Yom Tov Levinski,** editors, *Sepher Hamo'adim.* 2nd edn. Tel Aviv: Dvir, 1952. 404-407.
[1404].

2552. **Pingree, D.** Reviewer. **S. Powels,** "Der Kalender der Samaritaner." *BO* 38 (1981): 563.
[107/ 1400].

2553. **Planas, Francisco.** "Jesús, judío, y la Samaritana." *CB* 12 (1922): 225-228. [John 4:9 etc.].
[1502.1].

2554. **Plumptre, E. H.** "The Samaritan Element in the Gospel and Acts." *The Expositor* 7.1st series (1878): 22-40.
[1003.1/ 1502].

2555. **Pococke, E.,** editor. (Arabic & Latin) *Abu'l Faragii Specimen Historiae Arabum.* Oxford, 1650.
[1600].

2556. —————. *Eutychius Patriarchae Alexandrinae, Annales.* Oxford, 1658. 2 vols.:
[1600].

2557. **Podolski, B.** "Research in Russia on the Samaritans." *A–B* 275 (1/4/80): 8.
[106].

2558. **Poffet, Jean Michel.** La méthode éxégetique d'Héracléon et d'Origène commentateurs de Jn.4: Jésus, la samaritaine et les samaritains.(Ph.D.) Freiburg: 1984. [Published, Freiburg, Paradosis 28, 1985, 304 pp.].
[1502.1].

2559. **Pohl, Heinz.** Reviewer. **H. Kippenberg,** "Garizim und Synagoge." *JBL* 91 (1972): 409-412.
[107/ 800/ 807].

2560. —————. Reviewer. **H. Kippenberg,** "Garizim und Synagoge." *JNES* 33 (1974): 165-166.
[107/ 800/ 807].

2561. —————. Reviewer. **Sergio Noja,** "Kitab al Kafi." *TLZ* 98 (1973): 830-834.
[107/ 2203].

2562. —————. *Kitab al Mirat. Das Buch der Erbschaft des samaritaners Abu Ishaq Ibrahim.* Berlin: Walter de Gruyter, 1974.
[2204].

2563. —————. "Les manuscrits Sassoon 731 et Rylands Sam. 172-deux exemples de manipulations par les copistes dans les apographes modernes." In **Rothschild**

and Sixdenier, editors, *Etudes samaritaines.* Louvain-Paris, 1988. 271-275.
[103].

2564. —————. "Report on the Manuscripts of Dalil as-Sa'il and Kashif al-
Ghayahib." In A. Tal & M. Florentin, editors, *Proceedings of the First
International Congress of the Société d'Études Samaritaines.* Tel Aviv: Chaim
Rosenberg School for Jewish Studies, University of Tel Aviv, 1991. 245-248.
[103].

2565. —————. "Zu einer Besprechung R. Degen's *die Welt des Orients* 6 (1971),
pp.63-79." In *Christentum am Roten Meer.* 1973. II: 359-367.
[107/ 1502].

2566. Poliakov, Léon. *Les Samaritains: suivi d'une étude de Gilles Firmin: A propos du
Pentateuque samaritain.* Paris: Editions du Seuil, 1991. [183 pp.].
[200].

2567. —————. Reviewer. A. D. Crown, "The Samaritans." *Revue historique de droit
français et étranger* 68.3 (1990): 391-393.
[107/ 200].

2568. Pollard, T. E. "Jesus and the Samaritan Woman." *ET* 92.5 (1981): 147-148.
[1502.1].

2569. Poloner, J. "Description of the Holy Land (c.1421AD)." Aubrey Stewart,
Translator, London: Palestine Pilgrim Text Society, 1894.
[306.2/ 400].

2570. Poncet, M. *Nouveaux éclaircissemens sur l'origine et le Pentateuque des Samaritains.
Par un religieux Bénédictin de la Congrégation de S. Maur.* François Clément.
Paris, 1760. [BL 3128.d.47].
[801.1/ 2300].

2571. Porath, E. "Die Passivebildung des Grundstammes im Semitischen." *MGWJ* 70
(1926): 180-193.
[2602].

2572. Porter, J. L. *Through Samaria to Galilee and the Jordan.* London, Edinburgh and
New York, 1889. 29-34.
[308].

2573. Postel, Guillaume. *De Foenicum Literis.* Paris: Martin Iuuen, 1552.
[105].

2574. —————. *Linguarum duodecim characteribus differentium alphabetum introducto
ac legendi Modus.* Paris: Petrus Vernoliensias, 1538. [The first printed
Samaritan alphabet in northern Europe. Reprinted, IDC fiche no. AR-1487].
[105].

2575. Potin, J. "Jésus chez les samaritains." *BTS* 44 (1962): 4-5.
[1502.1].

2576. **Powels, Sylvia.** Reviewer. **A. D. Crown,** "A Bibliography of the Samaritans." *AN* 26 (1988): 115-121.
[101/ 107].

2577. —————. *Der Kalender der Samaritaner anhand des Kitab Hisab as-Sinin und anderer Handschriften.* Studia Samaritana 3. Berlin: Walter de Gruyter, 1977.
[1400].

2578. —————. "Relations Between Samaritan and Arabic Astronomical Calculations." *AN* 25 (1987): 92-142.
[700/ 1400].

2579. —————. "Relations entre le méthodes de calcul astronomique chez les Samaritains et les Arabes." In **Rothschild and Sixdenier,** editors, *Études samaritaines.* Louvain-Paris, 1988. 277-286.
[700/ 1400].

2580. —————. "The Samaritan Calendar and the Roots of Samaritan Chronology." In **A. D. Crown,** editor, *The Samaritans.* Tübingen: Mohr, 1989. 691-742.
[700/ 1400].

2581. —————. "Samaritan Proverbs." *AN* 28 (1990): 76-95.
[1800].

2582. —————. "Samaritan Proverbs." In **A. Tal and M. Florentin,** editors, *Proceedings of the First International Congress of the Société d'Études Samaritaines.* Tel Aviv: Chaim Rosenberg School for Jewish Studies, University of Tel Aviv, 1991. 249-260.
[2101].

2583. **Poznanski, S.** "Festivals and Fasts (Jewish)." *ERE* 1912. 5: 879-881.
[201].

2584. —————. "Ibn Hazm über Jüdische Sekten." *JQR* 16 (1904): 765-771.
[1500].

2585. —————. Reviewer. "Ibrahim ibn Jakub on Leviticus 23." *JQR* 17 (1905): 187-189.
[107/ 2305].

2586. —————. "Karaites." *ERE* 1914. 7: 662-672.
[1004].

2587. —————. Reviewer. **M. Klumel,** "Mischpatim." *JQR* 16 (1904): 402-408.
[107/ 2200].

2588. —————. "Zur Jüdisch-arabischen literatur." *OLZ* 7 (1904): 85f.
[1550].

2589. **Prawer, Joshua.** *Histoire du Royaume Latin de Jerusalem.* Paris: CNRS, 1975. 2 vols.
[810].

2590. Preiss, Ludwig and Paul Rohrbach. *Palestine and Transjordania.* London, 1926.
[308/ 400].

2591. Prest, Loring A. "The Samaritan Woman." *The Bible Today* 30.6 (1992): 367-371.
[1502.1].

2592. Prete, B. "La samaritana (Giov.4, 1-42)." *Sacra Doctrina* 9 (1964): 252-268.
[1502.1].

2593. Price, M. J. and Bluma L. Trell. *Coins and Their Cities.* Detroit, 1977. See especially p. 175 and fig. 302.
[602].

2594. Prijs, Joseph. *Die Basler Hebräischen Drucke (1492-1866).* Freiburg: Urs Graf-Verlag, 1964. [Lists the following Samaritan type specimens Johann Pistorius, of 1710 (no. 285); Leusden, Basel specimen of 1739 (no. 291); Lord's Prayer from Basel, 1830 (no. 315); Samaritan specimen for Lord's Prayer, Basel, 1830 (no. 315).
[105].

2595. Prime, William C. *Tent Life in the Holy Land.* New York, 1857. 326-328. [Reprinted New York, Arno Press 1977].
[308/ 400].

2596. Pritchett, Mr. "Note on the Newly Discovered Samaritan Stone." *PEFQS* (1873): 118.
[2508].

2597. Procopius. H. B. Dewing, editor and translator, *Buildings.* London: Loeb Classical Library, 1954.
[305.4/ 808].

2598. Procopius of Gaza. "Commentary on Isaiah." *PG* 87 1951-1954; 1975-1978; 2011-2018.
[1003.1].

2599. Prosper, A. "Simon (dit le magicièn) Dieu Sauveur des samaritains." *CCER* 5 (1955).
[1107/ 1506.2].

2600. Protopopov, V. *Reise zu den Samaritanern. Das samaritanische Passah auf dem berg Garizim.* 1912.
[308/ 1404].

2601. ————. *V oblasti samarjanskoj literatury. Samarjanskie Khroniki Novaja samarjanskaja khronika izdannaja Adlerom i Zeligsonom.* Kazan, 1913.
[1600/ 1602].

2602. ————. *V oblasti samarjanskoj literatury. Samarjanskaya Kniga Iisusa Navina.* Kazan, 1913.
[1604/ 1605].

2603. **Provera, M.** "Le bon samaritain (Lc.10, 25-37)." *TS(F)* 11 (1974): 289-294. [1502.3/ 1502.4].

2604. —————. "Os Samaritanos de Naplusa." *RCB* 3.6-7 (1966): 61-72. [200].

2605. **Puech, Emile.** "Une nouvelle amulette samaritaine." **Arthur Segal Michael Heltzer and Daniel Kaufman,** editors, *Studies in the Archaeology and History of Ancient Israel; in Honor of Moshe Dothan.* Haifa: Haifa University Press, 1993. 153-162. [600/ 601/ 2500].

2606. **Pummer, Reinhard.** "Antisamaritanische Polemik in jüdischen Schriften aus der intertestamentarischen Zeit." *BZ* NF 26.2 (1982): 224-242. [1003.4/ 1001/ 2205].

2607. —————. "Argarizin–A Criterion for Samaritan Provenance." *JSJ* 18 (1987-1988): 18-25. [2000].

2608. —————. "Aspects of Modern Samaritan Research." *E et T* 7.2 (1976): 171-188. [*NTAb* 21 (1977): 283]. [106].

2609. —————. "The Book of Jubilees and the Samaritans." *E et T* 10 (1979): 147-148. [1003.4/ 2007].

2610. —————. Reviewer. J. S. Isser, "The Dositheans; A Samaritan Sect in Late Antiquity." *JAOS* 99 (1979): 388-389. [107/ 1503].

2611. —————. "Einführung in den Stand der Samaritanerforschung." In **F.Dexinger and R. Pummer,** eds., *Die Samaritaner.* Darmstadt: Wissenschaftliche Buchgesellschaft, 1992. 1-66. [106].

2612. —————. "Genesis 34 in Jewish Writings of the Hellenistic and Roman Periods." *HTR* 75 (1982): 177-178. [2000/ 2304].

2613. —————. "Inscriptions." In **A. D. Crown,** editor, *The Samaritans.* Tübingen: Mohr, 1989. 190-194. [2500].

2614. —————. Reviewer. **R. Egger,** "Josephus Flavius und die Samaritaner." *JBL* 107 (1988): 768-772. [107/ 303.5].

2615. —————. "Nablus und Tel Aviv—Tradition und Moderne." In *Festschrift Prof. Manfred Büttner.* Abhandlungen zur Geschichte der Geowissenschaften und Kosmologie, forthcoming. [200/ 500/ 1504].

2616. ————. "New Evidence for Samaritan Christianity?" *CBQ* 41.1 (1979): 98-
117.
[1003.1/ 1502].

2617. ————. "The Present State of Samaritan Studies I." *JSS* 21 (1976): 39-61.
[Reprinted in *A–B Samaritan News* nos. 211-217 (1978)].
[106].

2618. ————. "The Present State of Samaritan Studies II." *JSS* 22 (1977): 27-41.
[Reprinted in *A–B-Samaritan News* (1978-1979)].
[106].

2619. ————. Reviewer. **S. Lowy,** "The Principles of Samaritan Bible Exegesis."
JAOS 102 (1982): 186-187.
[107/ 2305].

2620. ————. "Samaritan Amulets from the Roman-Byzantine Period and Their
Wearers." *RB* 94 (1987): 251-263.
[601/ 808].

2621. ————. "Samaritan Manuscripts in Toronto." *RUO* 46.3 (1976): 345-363.
[103].

2622. ————. "The Samaritan Manuscripts of the Chester Beatty Library."
Proceedings of the Irish Biblical Association 6 (1982): 103-115. [Reprinted from
Studies: An Irish Quarterly Review].
[103].

2623. ————. "A Samaritan Manuscript in McGill University." *Fontanus* 5 (1992):
161-172.
[103].

2624. ————. *Samaritan Marriage Contracts and Deeds of Divorce. Volume I.* XI+380
pages and 37 plates. Wiesbaden: Otto Harrassowitz, 1993.

2625. ————. "Samaritan Material Remains and Archaeology." In **A. D. Crown,**
editor, *The Samaritans.* Tübingen: Mohr, 1989. 135-177.
[600].

2626. ————. "The Samaritan Pentateuch and the New Testament." *NTS* 22.4
(1976): 441-443. [*NTAb* 21 (1977): 284].
[1003.1/ 2300].

2627. ————. "Samaritan Rituals and Customs." In **A. D. Crown,** editor, *The
Samaritans.* Tübingen: Mohr, 1989. 650-690.
[1200].

2628. ————. Reviewer. **A. Tal,** "The Samaritan Targum of the Pentateuch I."
JAOS 101 (1981): 447-448.
[107/ 2401].

2629. ————. *The Samaritans*. Leiden: E. J. Brill, 1987. Studies in the Iconography of Religions xxiii, 5.
[102].

2630. ————. Reviewer. **R. J. Coggins**, "Samaritans and Jews." *JSS* 23 (1978): 125-127.
[107/ 801.1].

2631. ————. "The Samaritans—A Jewish Offshoot or a Pagan Cult?" *Bible Review* 7.5 (1991): 22-29; 40.
[200].

2632. ————. "Were There Samaritan Christian Churches?" In **A. Tal and M. Florentin,** editors, *Proceedings of the First International Congress for Samaritan Studies.* April 10-14 1988. Tel Aviv: University of Tel Aviv and the Société d'Études Samaritaines, 1991. 123-138.
[1301].

2633. **Pummer, Reinhard and F. Dexinger,** editors. *Die Samaritaner.* Wege der Forschung, 604. Darmstadt: Wissenschaftliche Buchgesellschaft, 1992.
[200].

2634. **Pummer, Reinhard and P. E. Dion.** "A note on the 'Samaritan Christian Synagogue' in Ramat Aviv." *JSJ* 11 (1980): 217-222.
[1003.1/ 1304/ 1502].

2635. **Pummer, Reinhard, A. D. Crown and A. Tal,** editors. *Companion to Samaritan Studies.* Tübingen: J.C.B.Mohr, 1993.
[202].

2636. **Pummer, Reinhard, and M. Roussel.** "A Note on Theodotus and Homer." *JSJ* 13 (1983): 177-182.
[2005].

2637. **Purchas, James.** *Purchas, His Pilgrimes.* Hakluyt Society Voyages. London, 1625. Discusses the origin of the Samaritan script.
[105/ 2501].

2638. **Purvis, James D.** "Ben Sira and the Foolish People of Shechem." *JNES* 24 (1965): 88-94.
[804/ 2007].

2639. ————. Reviewer. **J. S. Isser,** "The Dositheans." *JBL* 97.2 (1978): 290-291.
[107/ 1503].

2640. ————. "The Fourth Gospel and the Samaritans." *NT* 17 (1975): 161-198.
[1502.1].

2641. ————. "Israel's Samaritan Sect." *Jewish Digest* 23 (1978): 53-55.
[200].

2642. ————. "Joseph in the Samaritan Traditions." In **G. W. E. Nickelsburg,** editor, *Studies on the Testament of Moses.* Septuagint and Cognate Studies 5.

Missoula, 1975. 147-153.
[1003.4/ 1800/ 2007].

2643. ————. Reviewer. **J. Macdonald,** "Memar Marqah." *JNES* 25 (1966): 152-153.
[107/ 1803].

2644. ————. "New Light on the Early History of the Samaritans." *Hebrew Studies in America* 3 (1973): 23-31.
[800/ 801].

2645. ————. The Origin of the Samaritan Sect.(Ph.D.) Harvard: Harvard University, 1963.
[801.1].

2646. ————. "The Palaeography of the Samaritan Inscription from Thessalonica." *BASOR* 221 (1976): 121-123.
[2501.1/ 2513].

2647. ————. Reviewer. **L. F. Giron Blanc,** "Pentateucho Hebreo Samaritano." *JBL* 97.3 (1978): 441-443.
[107/ 2300].

2648. ————. *The Samaritan Pentateuch and the Origin of the Samaritan Sect.* Cambridge (Mass.): Harvard University Press, 1968.
[801.1/ 2300].

2649. ————. "The Samaritan Problem: A Case Study in Jewish Sectarianism in the Roman Era." In **B. Halpern and J. D. Levenson,** editors, *Tradition in Transformation (F. M. Cross Festschrift).* Indiana, 1981. 350-383.
[807].

2650. ————. "Samaritan", "Samaritan Pentateuch." In *IDB.* Nashville: Abingdon, 1976. Supplementary: 772-777. [Reprinted in Dexinger and Pummer, *Die Samaritaner,* 408-417].
[201].

2651. ————. "Samaritan Traditions on the Death of Moses." In **G. W. E. Nickelsburg,** editor, *Studies on the Testament of Moses.* Septuagint and Cognate Studies 4. Cambridge, Mass.: Seminar papers, 1973. 93-117.
[1800/ 2007/ 3008].

2652. ————. "Samaritan version of the Torah." (Hebrew) in *EM.* , 1982. 8: 173-182.
[2300].

2653. ————. "The Samaritans." In **W. D. Davies and Louis Finkelstein,** editors, *Cambridge History of Judaism.* Cambridge: CUP, 1989. 591-613.
[801].

2654. ————. Reviewer. **R. J. Coggins,** "Samaritans and Jews." *JTS* 27 (1976): 163-175.
[107/ 800].

2655. —————. "The Samaritans and Judaism." In **R. A. Kraft and George Nickelsburg**, editors, *Early Judaism and its Modern Interpreters.* Philadelphia, Atlanta: Fortess & Scholars Press, 1986. 81-98.
[801.1/ 805/ 806/ 1002].

2656. —————, Reviewer. "Studies in Samaritan Manuscripts and Artifacts." **R. T. Anderson,** *BASOR.* 1982. 248: 75-76.
[101/ 103/ 107].

2657. —————. "Studies on Samaritan Materials in the W.E.Barton Collection in the Boston University Library." In *Proceedings of the Fifth World Conference of Jewish Studies.* 1965. Jerusalem: World Union of Jewish Studies & Magnes Press, 1972. 134-143.
[101/ 106].

2658. —————. Reviewer. **J. Macdonald,** "The Theology of the Samaritans." *JNES* 25 (1966): 213-216.
[107/ 1100].

Q

2659. Qimron, E. "Did "Phillippi's Law" occur in Samaritan Hebrew?" (Hebrew) in A. Tal and M. Florentin, editors, *Proceedings of the First International Congress of the Société d'Études Samaritaines.* Tel Aviv: Chaim Rosenberg School for Jewish Studies, University of Tel Aviv, 1991. 13*-18*. [2602].

2660. Qimron, Elisha. "On the Language of the Torah: The Samaritans in 1979." *A–B* (10/4/80): 30-33. [2300].

2661. —————. "Medial Aleph in the Hebrew and Aramaic of Qumran with the Hebrew and Aramaic of Other Sources." *Leshonenu* 39 (1975): 133-146. [2600/ 2602].

2662. Quispel, Gilles. *Gnosis als welt Religion.* Zurich, 1951. 45-70. [1506].

2663. Quispel, Gilles. "Simon en Helena." *NTT* 5 (1950-1951): 339-346. [1506.2].

R

2664. Rabello, Alfredo M. *Giustiniano, Ebrei E Samaritani alla luce delle Font Storico-Letterarie Ecclesiastiche e Giuridiche.* 2 vols. Milano: A Giuffré, 1987-1988. [808/ 808.1].

2665. ————. "The Samaritans in Justinian's Code I, 5." In **A. Tal and M. Florentin**, editors, *Proceedings of the First International Congress of the Société d'Études Samaritaines.* Tel Aviv: Chaim Rosenberg School for Jewish Studies, University of Tel Aviv, 1991. 139-146. [808].

2666. Rabi, Y. "Meet the Samaritans." *Jewish Digest* (26 April 1981): 53-54. [200].

2667. Rabinowitz, L. "Mt. Gerizim and Mt. Ebal." *Mahanaim* 116 (1968): 162-165. [404/ 406].

2668. Radé, M. "Das samaritanische Buch Josua." *Christliche Welt* 22 (1908): 868-870. [1604/ 1605].

2669. Raffaeli (Raffalovitch), S. "A Recently Discovered Samaritan Charm." *JPOS* 1 (1920-21): 143-144. [601].

2670. ————. "Ursprung und Entwicklung de Jüdischen Sekte der Samaritaner." *Luah Eretz Israel* 16 (1910): 49-71. [Also has the Hebrew title "Ephraim vekat Hashomronim"]. [801/ 801.1].

2671. Rahlfs, Alfred. "Ein weiteres Fragment der griechischen Übersetzung des samaritanischen Pentateuchs." *NKGW phil-hist. Klasse* 2 (1911): 263-266. [Reprinted, Berlin 1911]. [2309/ 2400].

2672. Rainey, Anson F. "Semantic Parallels to the Samaria Ostraca." *PEQ* 102 (1970): 45-51. [410/ 606.1].

2673. ————. "The *Sitz im leben* of the Samaria Ostraca." *TA* 6.1/2 (1979): 91-94. [410/ 606.1].

2674. Ramaroson, L. "Comme 'le bon Samaritain', ne chercher qu'à aimer (Lc.10, 29-37)." *Biblica* 56 (1975): 533-536. [1502.3/ 1502.4].

2675. Randall, R. *Jordan and the Holy Land.* London, 1968. [903].

2676. Rappaport, Uriel. "The Samaritans in the Hellenistic Period." (Hebrew) *Zion* 55.4 (1990): 373-398. English summary, p. xv. [804].

2677. **Rappoport, S.** "Deux hymnes samaritains." *JA* 16.9th series (1900): 289-314. [Reprinted, Imprimerie Nationale, 1900]. [2100].

2678. —————. *La liturgie samaritaine. Office du soir des fêtes. (Texte samaritain et traduction arabe) précédé d'une étude sur la liturgie samaritaine, son origine et son rapport avec celle des Juifs, des Caraites, des Chrétiens et des Musulmans.* Paris, 1900. [First presented as a Ph.D., Basel. 76pp]. [2100].

2679. **Rappoport, S. and B. Beer.** "Der Berg des Ostens bei den Samaritanern." *ZDMG* 12 (1858): 730-733. [2305].

2680. **Rasche, Johann Christoph.** *Lexicon Universale rei numariae veterum et precipue Graecorum ac Romanorum.* Lipsae, 1785-1805. 4: 1720-1772. [s.v. Samaritico caractere inscriptos Ebraeorum numos etc.]. [603].

2681. **Ratjen, H.** "Handschriften der Kieler Universitäts-Bibliothek." *Serapeum* 273-283 (1870): [For the Samaritan MSS see pp. 274-275]. [101/ 103].

2682. **Raue, Christian.** *A Discourse of the Orientall Tongues, etc. Ebrew, Samaritan.* London, 1649. 92 pp. [2600].

2683. —————. *A generall grammar for the ready attaining of the Ebrew, Samaritan, etc.* London, 1650. [149 pp. Often printed together with his *A Discourse...*]. [2600].

2684. —————. *Orthographiae et analogiae ebraicae delineatio...Ebraea. Chaldae. Syra. Samaritica.* Amsterdam, 1646. [2600].

2685. **Rau(e), Sebald.** *Sebaldii Ravii exercitationes Philologicae Car.Franc. Hubigantii Prolegomena in Scripturam Sacram.* Lugdunum Batavorum, 1785. [Also known as Specimen observationum ad C.F. Houbigant Prolegomena II: ii, Bremae, 1774]. [2300].

2686. —————. *Specimen philologicum continens descriptionem codicis MS Bibliotheca Lugduno Batavae partemque inde excerptam versionis Samaritano Arabicae Pentateuch.* Lugduni Batavorum: Luchtmans, 1803. [2300].

2687. **Ravina (Rabinowitz), M.** "Organum and the Samaritans." (English edition, translated by Alan Marbé.) Tel Aviv: Israel Music Institute, 1963. 62 pp. [3303].

2688. **Ravio, S. F. J. and G. van Vloten.** *Specimen Philologicum. Diss. de cod. vers. Samarit. Arab. Pentateucho.* Leiden, 1803. [The volume is the defense of van

Vloten's thesis; 94 pp.].
[2302].

2689. **Raynor, Joyce Toby.** Social and Cultural Relationships in Scythopolis/Beth Shean in the Roman and Byzantine Periods. (Ph.D.) Durham, N.C.: Duke University, 1982.
[411/ 808].

2690. **Reed, Samuel Courtney.** The Abrahamic Section of Genesis (11:27-25:11): A New Translation with Essays and Notes on the Text and the Theory of Biblical Translation.(Ph.D.) The University of Texas at Austin: 1980.
[1005/ 2300].

2691. **Reeg, Gottfried.** "Zu den samaritanischen Synagogen in Israel bis zur Zeit des Arabereinfalls." *IJUT*.149-154 (1971/72):
[809/ 1304].

2692. **Rees, Abraham.** "Samaria", "Samaritans." In *The Cyclopaedia or Universal Dictionary.* London, 1819. 31.
[201].

2693. **Rehlingius, Joannes.** *Dissertatio Critica de Samaritanismo et Hebraismo Justini M...disputationi subjiciet Joannes Rehlingius.* Wittenbergae, 1729.
[1502].

2694. **Reich, Rony.** "A Note on Samaritan Ritual Baths." (Hebrew) in **Jacoby and Tsafrir,** editors, *Jews, Samaritans and Christians in the Byzantine Period.* Jerusalem, 1988. 242-244.
[606].

2695. ————. "A Samaritan Amulet from Nahariya." *RB* 92 (1985): 383-388.
[601].

2696. **Reicke, B.** "Der barmherzige Samariter." In **O. Bocher and K. Haacker,** editors, *Verborum Veritas. Festschrift für Gustav Stählin.* Wüppertal, 1970. 103-109.
[1502.3].

2697. **Reifenberg, A.** "Mt. Gerizim." (Hebrew) *EI* 1 (1951): 74-76.
[406].

2698. **Reinach, S.** Reviewer. **A. S. Yahuda,** "Zum samaritanischen Josua. Eine Erklärung." *Revue Archéologique* 13 (1909): 136-137.
[107/ 1604/ 1605].

2699. **Reinicke, Karl.** "Reiseskizzen aus dem heiligen Lander." *Neueste Nachtrichten aus dem Morgenlände* 24 (1888): 118-129.
[308/ 400].

2700. **Reisner, G. A.** "The Harvard Expedition to Samaria." *HTR* 3 (1910): 248-263.
[600].

2701.   **Reisner, G. A., C. S. Fisher and D. G. Lyon.** *Harvard Excavations at Samaria.*
        Cambridge (Mass), 1924.
        [410/ 600].

2702.   **Reland, Hadrian.** "Antiquitates Sacrae." In **B. Ugolini,** *Thesaurus.* Venice, 1741.
        2: 303f.
        [200].

2703.   —————. *Dissertatio altera de inscriptione nummorum quorundam samaritanorum*
        ad...Jacobum de Wildein qua Amphora Mannae nummis illis inscripta etc. Trajecti
        ad Rhenum, 1704. Plates opposite last page. [Reprinted, B. Ugolini,*Thesaurus,*
        Venice 1765, 28:1077-1216].
        [603/ 2501].

2704.   —————. *Dissertatio de inscriptione nummorum quorundam samaritanorum*
        ad...Jacobum de Wilde. Amstelodami, 1702.
        [603].

2705.   —————. "Dissertatio de Monte Garizim." In *Dissertationum Miscellanearum*
        Pars Prima. Trajecti ad Rhenum, 1706. 3: 121-162. [Reprinted in B. Ugolini,
        Thesaurus, Venice (1747) 8:716-737].
        [406].

2706.   —————. "Dissertatio de Samaritanis." In *Dissertationum Miscellanearum Pars*
        Altera. Trajecti ad Rhenum, 1707. 7: 3-94. [Reprinted in B. Ugolini, *Thesaurus,*
        Venice (1759) 22:554-602].
        [200/ 800].

2707.   —————. *Dissertatio Tertia de Numis Samaritanis ad Johann. Baptist Ottium.*
        Trajecti ad Rhenum, 1704.
        [603].

2708.   —————. "Dissertation de nummis Samaritanis I; Dissertatio Altera:
        Dissertatio Tertia; Dissertatio Quarta; Dissertation Quinta; Epistola de
        Nummis Samaritanis." In **B. Ugolini,** *Thesaurus.* Venice, 1765. 28: 1178-1198;
        1199-1216; 1231-1242; 1247-1257; 1257-1282; 1287-1292.
        [603].

2709.   —————. "Joh. Bapt. Ottii Epistola de Numis quibusdam Samaritanis ad
        Adrianum Relandum cum Hujus Responso." In **A. Reland,** *Dissertation Altera*
        de Inscriptione Nummorum quorundam Samaritanorum. Trajecti ad Rhenum:
        Guil. Broedelet (Bibliopolam), 1709.
        [603].

2710.   —————. *Palaestina ex monumentis veteribus illustrata.* Trajecti ad Rhenum,
        1714. [Two parts in one vol. 1068 pp. Maps and plans of the early 18th
        century].
        [400/ 401].

2711.   —————. "Réponse à ce que M. Gagnier a objecté contre son explication de
        quelques médailles samaritaines." In *Mémoires de Trevoux.* Nov 1705. 1997-
        2004. [Reprinted, B. Ugolini, *Thesaurus,* Venice 1765, 28:1287-1292].
        [603/ 2501].

2712. **Renwick, David Alistair.** Paul, the Temple and the Presence of God. (Ph.D.)
Union Theological Seminary in Virginia: 1988.
[1502].

2713. **Rettig, David.** Memar Marqa; ein samaritanischer Midrasch zum Pentateuch.
(Ph.D.) Bonn: Bonn University, 1934.
[1803].

2714. —————. *Memar Marqa; ein samaritanischer Midrasch zum Pentateuch
untersucht.* 74pp Stuttgart: Bonner orientalische Studien, 1934. 8:
[1803].

2715. **Revel, Bernard.** The Karaite Halachah and its Relation to the Sadducean,
Samaritan and Philonean Halachah. (Ph.D.) Philadelphia: Dropsie College,
1912.
[2200].

2716. —————. *The Karaite Halachah and its Relation to the Sadducean, Samaritan
and Philonean Halachah.* Philadelphia, 1913. [Reprinted in P. Birnbaum,
Karaite Studies, New York 1971:1-98; also printed in *JQR,* NS 2 (1911):517-
544; 3 (1912-1913):337-396].
[2200].

2717. **Riaud, Jean.** "Les samaritains dans les 'Paralipomena Jeremiae'." *Littérature
intertestamentaire* (octobre 1983)(1985): 133-152.
[801.1].

2718. **Riaut, Comte.** "Voyage en Terre Sainte d'un maire de Bordeaux au XIVᵉ siècle."
AOL 2 (1884): 378-384.
[306.3/ 401].

2719. **Ricciotti, Giuseppe.** *Storia d'Israele.* Torino, 1947. 4th edn. [Other edns. French,
1939, English, 1955, German, 1955].
[200/ 400].

2720. **Richard, Earl.** "Acts 7: An Investigation of Samaritan Evidence." *CBQ* 39.2
(1977): 190-208.
[1502.2/ 1502.3].

2721. —————. "The Polemical Character of the Joseph Episode in Acts 7." *JBL* 98
(1979): 255-267.
[1502.2].

2722. **Richter, G.** *Verzeichnis der orientalischen Handschriften der Staats-und
Universitätsbibliothek, Breslau.* Leipzig, 1933.
[101/ 103].

2723. **Rieser, Ursula.** Reviewer. A. D. Crown, "The Samaritans." *Études Théologiques et
Religieuses* 2 (1993): 271-272.
[200/ 107].

2724. **Rieu, Charles.** *Catalogus Codicum Manuscriptorum Orientalium qui in Museo
Britannico Asservantur.* London, 1846-1871. [Pars secunda nos. 639-642, pp.

517-520].
[101/ 103].

2725. **Rieu, Charles.** *Supplement to the Catalogue of the Arabic Manuscripts in the British Museum.* London, 1894.
[101/ 103].

2726. **Rigg, Horace.** "Thallus, the Samaritan?" *HTR* 34 (1941): 111-119.
[2000/ 3010.1].

2727. **Rinaldi, G.** Reviewer. E. Robertson, "Catalogue of Samaritan Manuscripts: The Gaster Manuscripts." *BO* 7 (1965): 40-41.
[101/ 103/ 107].

2728. —————. Reviewer. R. Macuch, "Grammatik das samaritanisch Hebräisch." *BO* 12 (1970): 141-142.
[107/ 2600].

2729. —————. Reviewer. S. Noja, "Kitab al Kafi." *BO* 14 (1972): 224.
[107/ 2203].

2730. —————. Reviewer. A. Murtonen, "Materials for a non-Masoretic Grammar I." *BO* 4 (1962): 192.
[107/ 2602].

2731. **Ritter, Carl.** "Samaria." In W. L. Gage, translator, *The Comparative Geography of Palestine and the Sinaitic Peninsula.* Edinburgh: T & T Clark, 1866. 4: chapter 4: 287-331.
[410/ 800].

2732. **Rivera, C. F.** Reviewer. J. Bowman, "Samaritan Problem." *RbiCalz* 30 (1968): 246.
[107/ 1502/ 1503].

2733. **Robert, Jean and Robert Louis.** "Bulletin épigraphique no 369. Une synagogue samaritaine à Thessalonique." *Revue des Études Grecques* 82 (1969): 4717-4718.
[512/ 600/ 1304].

2734. **Roberts, B. J.** Reviewer. Edward Robertson, "Catalogue of Samaritan Manuscripts II. The Gaster Manuscripts." *JTS* 14 (1963): 571-572.
[103/ 107].

2735. **Roberts, Bleddyn J.** "The Divergences in the Pre-Tiberian Massoretic Text." *JJS* 1 (1949): 147-155.
[2300].

2736. —————. Reviewer. J. D. Purvis, "The Samaritan Pentateuch and the Origin of the Samaritan Sect." *JTS* 20 (1969): 569-571.
[107/ 801.1/ 2300].

2737. —————. "The Samaritan Version." In *The Old Testament, Text and Version.* Cardiff: University of Wales Press, 1951. 188-196.
[2300].

2738. ——————. "Text, O.T.", "Samaritan Pentateuch." In *IDB*. Nashville: Abingdon, 1962. 4: 90, 580-594.
[2300].

2739. **Robertson, Edward**. "The Ancient Scroll of the Samaritans." In **Bruno Schindler**, editor, *The Gaster Centenary Publication*. London, 1958. 1-7.
[2301].

2740. ——————. "The Astronomical Tables and Calendar of the Samaritans." *Melilah* 3-4 (1950): 311-327.
[1400].

2741. ——————. *Catalogue of the Samaritan Manuscripts in the John Rylands Library*. Manchester: John Rylands Library, 1938, 1962. 2 volumes: [Volume 2 = The Gaster Manuscripts].
[101/ 103].

2742. ——————. "Ibrahim Al 'Ayyah, a Samaritan Scholar of the Eighteenth Century." In **I. Epstein, E. Levine and C. Roth**, editors, *Essays in Honour of the Very Rev. Dr. J. H. Hertz*. London: Edward Goldston, 1943. 341-350. [70th birthday Festschrift: the title on the cover differs =*Essays Presented to J .H. Hertz, Chief Rabbi*].
[3005].

2743. ——————. "Law and Religion Among the Samaritans." In **E. Rosenthal**, editor, *Judaism and Christianity: III. Law and Religion*. London, 1938. 69-88.
[Reprinted as one volume, Ktav, New York, 1969].
[1100].

2744. ——————. "Notes and Extracts from the Semitic MSS in the John Rylands Library, Manchester. 1. Concerning the Abisha Scroll. 2. The Samaritans and the Sabbatic River. 3. Samaritan Pentateuch Manuscripts with a Description of Two Codices 4. Zainab-as Safawiyah, a Samaritan Poetess. 5. In Samaritan Nablus Two Centuries Ago. 6. The Astronomical Tables and Calendar of the Samaritans." *BJRL* 1=19: 412-437. 2=20: 354-378. 3=21: 244-272. 4=21: 425-444. 5=22: 223-242. 6=23: 458-486 (1934-1939).
[101/ 903/ 1400/ 1800/ 2300/ 2301/ 3000].

2745. ——————. *The Old Testament Problem*. Manchester: Manchester University Press, 1950.
[801.1].

2746. ——————. *The Period of the Judges; A Mystery Period in the History of the Judges*. Manchester: Manchester University Press, 1946.
[801.1].

2747. ——————. "The Relationship of the Arabic Translation of the Pentateuch to that of Saadyah." In **E. I. J. Rosenthal**, editor, *Saadyah Studies*. Manchester: Manchester University Press, 1943. 166-177.
[2302].

2748. ——————. Reviewer. **F. Pérez Castro**, "Séfer Abisha." *VT* 12.2 (1962): 228-235.
[107/ 2301].

226 Bibliography of the Samaritans

2749. **Robertson, James.** *Grammatica linguae Hebraeae...de antiquitate Quadrati et Samaritani characteris.* Edinburgh, 1758. Second edn. London, 1768. [2600/ 2602].

2750. **Robinson, J. A. T.** "The 'Others' of John 4: 38." In *Twelve New Testament Studies.* Studies in Biblical Theology. London: SCM Press, 1962. 61-66. [1502.1].

2751. **Robinson, Edward.** "Abriss einer Reise in Palästina im Jahre 1852 von E. Robinson, E. Smith und andern." *ZDMG* 7 (1853): 37-78. [400/ 408].

2752. ——————. *Biblical Researches in Palestine, Mount Sinai and Arabia Petraea.* London, 1841. Vol. 3:97-107; 115-134. [106/ 400].

2753. ——————. *Later Biblical Researches in Palestine.* Boston, 1856. [Reprinted, Arno Press, New York 1977]. [308/ 412].

2754. ——————. *Palästina und die südlich angrenzenden Länder.* Halle, 1841. Vol. 3:317-361. [400].

2755. **Rödiger, E.** "Geschichte und Literatur der Samaritaner." *Der Orient* 9.49 (1848): 762-767; 778-780; 788-793. [102/ 801.1/ 1550].

2756. ——————. "Schlussbemerkung über die samaritanischen Inschriften." *ZDMG* 14 (1860): 632-634. [2500].

2757. **Rödiger, E. and E. G. Schlutz.** "Biblische Geographie." *Hallesche Allgemeine Literaturzeitung* (1845): 649-651, 657-671, 678-680. Illustrated. [400].

2758. **Roger, Louis.** "Examin de la la conjecture du père Tournemine sur la difference du text hébreux-samaritain et grecque touchant les annés des patriarchs." In *Memoirs de Trévoux.* , 1703. [700/ 2300].

2759. **Rogers, E. T.** *Notices of the Modern Samaritans Illustrated by Incidents in the Life of Jacob esh-Shelaby Gathered From Him and Translated.* London: Sampson Low & Sons, 1855. [903/ 3006].

2760. **Rogers, Mary Eliza.** *Domestic Life in Palestine.* London, 1863. :244-281. [French version, Paris, 1865:316-346, 498-499]. [813/ 903/1404].

2761. ——————. "Samaria and the Plain of Esdraelon." In C. **Wilson,** editor, *Picturesque Palestine.* Cincinnati, London, Melbourne and Sydney, 1865. 2: [102/ 410].

2762. **Rogers, Robert William.** "A Catalogue of Manuscripts (Chiefly Oriental) in the Library of Haverford College." *Haverford College Studies* 23.4 (1890): 28-50. [The catalogue is also known as the Rendel Harris Catalogue]. [101/ 103].

2763. **Rohrbach, Paul.** "Die Samaritaner." *Gartenlaube* (1908): 341-343. [102/ 200].

2764. **Rohricht, R.** "Le pèlerinage du moine Augustin Jacque de Verone." *ROL* 3 (1895): 115-302. [306.2/ 401].

2765. **Roll, I. and E. Ayalon.** "Roman Roads in Western Samaria." *PEQ* 118.2 (1986): 113-134. [400.2].

2766. **Romanoff, Paul.** "Onomasticon of Palestine." *AAJR* 7 (1935-1936): 147-227. [Reprinted, 1936; 81 pp.]. [400].

2767. **Ronzevalle, N.** "Concerning Samaritan Inscriptions Discovered in Damascus." *AIBL* (1903): 92. [2506].

2768. **Rosen, Georg.** "Alte Handschriften des samaritanischen Pentateuch." *ZDMG* 18 (1864): 582-589. [101/ 2300].

2769. ————. "Über Nablus und Umgegend." *ZDMG* 14 (1860): 634-639. [Population statistics for 1860]. [408/ 903].

2770. ————. "Über samaritanische Inschriften." *ZDMG* 14 (1860): 622-631. [2500/ 2510.1].

2771. **Rosen, Gladys L.** The Joseph Cycle (Gen. 37-45) in the Samaritan Arabic Commentary of Meshalmah ibn Murjan. (Ph.D.) New York: Columbia University, 1951. [2305/ 3008.1].

2772. **Rosenberg, J.** *Argarizim. Lehrbuch der samaritanischen Sprache und Literatur. Die Kunst der Polyglottie.* Bibliothek der Sprachenkunde 71. Wien, Pest and Leipzig: Hartleben, 1901. [2600].

2773. **Rosenberg, S. E.** "Reunion of the Samaritans in Modern Israel." *United Synagogue Review (USA)* 21 (Oct. 1968): 14-15. [903].

2774. **Rosenfeld, M.** *Der Midrasch über den tod Moses.* Berlin, 1889. [1802/ 3008].

2775. **Rosenfeld, S.** "Jewish Sects Today." *Midstream* 31 (November, 1985): 37-39.
[200].

2776. **Rosenthal, Franz.** "Samaritans." In *An Aramaic Handbook.* Wiesbaden:
Harrassowitz, 1967. II: 1-12.
[2800].

2777. **Roshwald, M.** "Marginal Jewish Sects in Israel II." *IJMES* 4 (1973): 328-354. [See
328-343 and the summary p. 354].
[200/ 1205].

2778. **Ross, J. F. and L. E. Toombs.** "Les découvertes effectuées au cours des dernières
campagnes de fouilles à Sichem." *BTS* 44 (1962): 6-15.
[412/ 600].

2779. —————. "Six Campaigns at Biblical Shechem." *ADHL* (1967): 119-128.
[412/ 600].

2780. —————. "Three Campaigns at Biblical Shechem." *Archaeology* 14 (1961): 171-
179.
[412/ 600].

2781. **Roth, Cecil.** "Catalogue of Manuscripts in the Roth Collection." In **Saul
Lieberman**, editor, *Alexander Marx Jubilee Volume.* New York, 1950. 503-535.
[103].

2782. **Rothschild, Jean-P.** "Autor du Pentateuque samaritain: voyageurs, enthousiastes et
savants." In **J. R. Armogathe**, editor, *Le grand Siècle et la Bible.* Paris:
Beauchesne, 1989. 61-74.
[308/ 2300].

2783. —————. *Catalogue des manuscrits samaritaines.* Paris: Bibliothèque Nationale,
1985.
[101/ 103].

2784. —————. "La liturgie samaritaine; projet d'un repertoire d'hymnes." In **A. Tal
and M. Florentin**, editors, *Proceedings of the First International Congress of the
Société d'Études Samaritaines.* Tel Aviv: Chaim Rosenberg School for Jewish
Studies, University of Tel Aviv, 1991. 261-274.
[2100].

2785. —————. Reviewer. **L.Vilsker,** "Manuel d'Araméen Samaritain." *REJ* 141
(1982): 237-239.
[107/ 2800].

2786. —————. "Manuscrits samaritains." *Revue d'Histoire des Textes* 11 1981 (1983):
419-429.
[101].

2787. —————. "Le premier congrès général d'études des samaritains (Tel-Aviv-
Jerusalem, 11-13 Avril 1988)." *REJ* 148.3-4 (1989): 493-496.
[106].

2788. ——————. Reviewer. **J. M. Cohen**, "A Samaritan Chronicle." *REJ* 140 (1981): 210-214.
[107/ 1603].

2789. ——————. "Samaritan Manuscripts." In **A. D. Crown**, editor, *The Samaritans*. Tübingen: Mohr, 1989. 771-794.
[101/ 103].

2790. ——————. Reviewer. **A. Broadie**, "A Samaritan Philosophy." *REJ* 143.1-2 (1984): 158-160.
[107/ 1803].

2791. ——————. Reviewer. **Bruce Hall**, "Samaritan Religion from John Hyrcanus to Baba Rabba." *REJ* 148 (1989): 162.
[107/ 1002/ 1003.4].

2792. ——————. Reviewer. **A. D. Crown**, "The Samaritans." *REJ* 149.1-3 (1990): 198-200.
[107/ 200].

2793. ——————. Reviewer. **R. T. Anderson**, "Studies in Samaritan Manuscripts." *REJ* 142.1 (1983): 171-173.
[101/ 103/ 107].

2794. ——————. "Trois manuscrits liturgiques samaritains." *REJ* 148.1-2 (1989): 93-102.
[101/ 2100].

2795. ——————. "Une variante de la 'Chronique Adler': le manuscrit sam. 38 de la Bibliothèque Nationale de Paris." In **Rothschild and Sixdenier**, editors, *Études samaritaines*. Louvain-Paris, 1988. 181-192.
[101/ 1602].

2796. **Rothschild, Jean-P. and G. D. Sixdenier.** editors, *Études samaritaines Pentateuque et Targum, exégèse et philologie, chroniques Actes de la Table Ronde: "Les manuscrits samaritains. Problèmes et méthodes" (Paris, Institut de Recherche et d'Histoire des Textes, 7-9 Octobre 1985).*
Louvain-Paris: E.Peeters, 1988.
[100/ 101/ 103/ 106/ 2300/ 2600].

2797. **Rothstein, D. J. W.** Reviewer. **A. F. Von Gall**, "Der hebräische Pentateuch der Samaritaner." *DL* 36 (1915): 125-134.
[107/ 2300].

2798. ——————. *Juden und Samaritaner. Die grundlegende Scheidung von Judentum und Heidentum.* Leipzig: J. C. Hinrichs, 1908.
[801.1/ 802].

2799. **Rouchau, V.** "La Samarie." *TS* (1974): 278-282.
[410].

2800. **Roustang, F.** "Les moments de l'acte de foi et ses conditions de possibilité. Essai d'interprétation du dialogue avec la Samaritaine." *RSR* 46.3 (1958): 344-378.

[*NTAb* 3 (1958): 379].
[1502.1].

2801. **Rowley, Harold Henry.** Reviewer. John Macdonald, "Memar Marqah." *ET* 76 (1964-65): 135.
[107/ 1803].

2802. ——————. Reviewer. John Bowman, "Samaritan Problem." *ET* 81 (1969-1970): 159.
[107/ 1500].

2803. ——————. "The Samaritan Schism in Legend and History." In **B. W. Anderson** and **W. Harrelson**, editors, *Israel's Prophetic Heritage (Essays in Honour of James Muilenberg)*. London, 1962. 208-222.
[802.1].

2804. ——————. "Sanballat and the Samaritan Temple." *BJRL* 38 (1955): 166-198. [Reprinted in *Men of God* (Studies in Old Testament History and Prophecy) London and Edinburgh, 1963:246-276].
[802.1].

2805. ——————. "Sanballat et le temple samaritain." (Études presentées au VIes journées bibliques de Louvain) *L'Ancien Testament et l'Orient*. 11-13 September, 1954. Louvain, 1957.
[802.1].

2806. **Rubin, Zev.** "Christianity in Byzantine Palestine." *Jerusalem Cathedra* 3 (1983): 97-113.
[808].

2807. **Rubinstein, Solomon Joseph.** Zur Geschichte der Entstehung der samaritanischen Gemeinde.Kritisch-Historische untersuchung.(Ph.D.) Libau: University of Bern, 1906.[Holding Library: Annenberg Research Institute].
[802.1].

2808. **Rudolph, K.** Reviewer. H. Kippenberg, "Garizim und Synagoge." *TR* 37 (1972): 338-341.
[107/ 806/ 808].

2809. ——————. Reviewer. H. Kippenberg, "Garizim und Synagoge." *TLZ* 97 (1972): 576-579.
[107/ 806/ 808].

2810. ——————. "Simon—Magus oder Gnosticus?" *TR* 42 (1977): 279-359.
[1506.2].

2811. **Rule, W. H.** "Assyria—The Samaritan Pentateuch." In *Oriental Records: Historical Confirmations of the Old and New Testament Scriptures*. London, 1877. 76-82.
[2300].

2812. **Rutherforth, Thomas.** *A Letter...to Dr Kennicott in Which His Defence of the Samaritan Pentateuch Is Examined*. Cambridge, 1761.
[2300].

2813. **Rutherforth, Thomas.** *A Second Letter...to Dr Kennicott in Which His Defence of His Second Dissertation Is Examined.* Cambridge, 1762.
[2300].

2814. **Rybinski, W.** *Samarjane. Obzor istochnikov dlya izucheniya samaryanstva.* Kiev, 1913.
[106/ 200].

S

2815. **S. A.** "Jacob's Well." *PEFQS* (1877): 72-75.
[407/ 1502.1].

2816. **Sabugal, S.** "El Título Mesías-Cristos en el contexto del relato sobre la actividad de Jésus en Samaría: Jn 4, 25, 29." *Augustinianum* 12.1 (1972): 79-105. [*NTAb* 17 (1973):577].
[1502.1].

2817. **Sacchi, P.** "Studii Samaritani—I. Samaritani nell'AT." *Rivista di storia e letteratura religiosa* 5.2 (1969): 414-440.
[200/ 800].

2818. **Sacerdote, Gustavo.** *Catalogo dei codici ebraici della Biblioteca Casanatense (= Catloghi dei codici orientali di alcure biblioteche d'Italia, Fasc. 6).* Firenze, 1897. 657-658, nos. 226-230.
[103].

2819. **Sachs, L. and M. Bat-Miriam.** "The Genetics of Jewish Population. I. Finger-print Patterns in Jewish Population in Israel." *AJHG* 9 (1957): 117-126.
[2901/ 3500].

2820. **Safrai, Shmuel.** (Hebrew) *Pilgrimage at the Time of the Second Temple.* Tel Aviv: Am Hasefer, 1965. [See especially chapter 2 on the Samaritan Temple].
[805/ 1305].

2821. **Safrai, Ze ev.** "The Division of Samaria into Toparchies." (Hebrew) in *Borders and Authority in Israel in the Mishnaic and Talmudic Periods.* Tel Aviv, 1983.
[410/ 806].

2822. —————. The Land of Samaria: Its Geography and History in the Romano Byzantine Period.(Hebrew) Jerusalem: Hebrew University, 1978.Ph.D.
[400/ 808].

2823. —————. "The List of Men Appointed by Baba Rabbah." (Hebrew) in Z. **Ehrlich,** editor, *Samaria and Benjamin.* Jerusalem, 1987. 131-140.
[808/ 1601/ 3003].

2824. —————. "Marginal Notes on the Rehob Inscription." (Hebrew with English summary) *Zion* 42.1-2 (1977): 1-23.
[808].

2825. —————. "Samaritan Synagogues in the Romano-Byzantine Period." (Hebrew) *Cathedra* 4 (1977): 84-112.
[808/ 1304].

2826. —————. "Was there a 'Samaritan Church' at Tell Qasile?" *Qadmoniot* 11.4 (44) (1978): 129.
[1502].

2827. **Saggie, Eli.** "Israel's Economic Policy in Judaea and Samaria." *IEJ* (1975): 111-128.
[903].

2828. **Said, Edward.** *Orientalism.* London: Routledge & Kegan Paul, 1978.
[1700].

2829. **Sailman, M.** *The Researches in the East or an important account of the...ten tribes of Israel.* London: E. Justini for the author, 1818.
[200].

2830. **Sainthill, Richard.** "The Use of the Samaritan Language by the Jews Until the Reign of Hadrian Deduced from the Coins of Judaea." *Numismatic Chronicle* 14 (1852): 89-104.
[603/ 2501].

2831. **Saley, R. J.** Reviewer. J. Macdonald, "The Samaritan Chronicle II." *JAAR* 41 (1973): 650-652.
[107/ 1603].

2832. **Saller, S. J.** *The Memorial of Moses on Mt. Nebo.* Jerusalem: Franciscan Press, 1941-1950. 3 volumes.
[409/ 508/ 3008].

2833. ——————. *A Revised Catalogue of the Ancient Synagogues of the Holy Land.* Jerusalem: Franciscan Press, 1969. [Reprinted as the *Second Revised Catalogue*, Jerusalem 1972].
[1304].

2834. **Salles, A.** "Simon le magicien ou Marcion." *VC* 12 (1958): 197-224.
[1506.2].

2835. **Salles-Dabadie, J. M. A.** *Recherches sur Simon le Mage I. L'*"*Apophasis Megàle*'. Paris: Gabalda, 1969. [CRB 10].
[1506.2].

2836. **Salonen, A.** Reviewer. A. Murtonen, "Materials for a Non-Masoretic Hebrew Grammar." *Teologinen Aikakauskirja* 63 (1958): 174-178.
[107/ 2600].

2837. **Samburski, Samuel.** "Proculus, the President of the Platonic Academy and his Successor, Marinus the Samaritan." (Hebrew) *Proceedings of IASH.* Jerusalem: IASH, 1986. 145-159.
[2000/ 3007/ 3010].

2838. **Sampey, J. R.** "The Samaritans." *Biblical World* (1899): 188f.
[200].

2839. **Samuel ben David, the Karaite.** "The Travels of Samuel ben David the Karaite from Crimea." (Hebrew) in A. Ya'ari, editor, *Travellers to the Holy Land.* Ramat Gan: Masada, 1976. 221-266.
[309/ 407/ 407.1/ 407.2].

234   Bibliography of the Samaritans

2840. San Aquilino, A. *Pentateuchi Hebraeo-Samaritani praestantia in illustrando et emendando textu masorethico.* Heidelberg, 1783.
[2300].

2841. Sanchez, R. "Versiones Arabes del Pentateucho Samaritano." In *Enciclopedia de la Biblia.* 1965. 5: 1008-1009.
[2300].

2842. Sanchis, D. "Samaritanus ille. L'exégèse augustinienne de la parabole du bon samaritain." *RSR* 49.3 (1961): 406-425. [*NTAb* 6 (1962):471].
[1502.3].

2843. Sanderson, Judith. "The Contribution of 4QpaleoExod^m to Textual Criticism." *RQ* 13 (1988): 547-560.
[2307].

2844. —————. *An Exodus Scroll From Qumran:4QPaleo Exod^m and the Samaritan Tradition.* Atlanta: Scholars Press, 1986. Harvard Semitic Studies.
[2307].

2845. —————. "The Old Greek of Exodus in the Light of 4QPaleoExod^m." *Textus* 14 (1988): 87-104.
[2307].

2846. Sandys, George. *Description of the Turkish Empire.* London, 1615.
[306.3/ 400].

2847. Santi Mattei, P. "Miscellen (Ein fragment des hebräischen-samaritanischen Pentateuchs)." *Hebräische Bibliographie: Blätter für neuere und altere literature des Judenthums* 79 (1874): 19.
[2300].

2848. Sanuto, M. *Marino Sanuto's Secrets for True Crusaders to Help Them to Recover the Holy Land.* London, 1896.
[810].

2849. Sasagu, Arai. "Zum 'Simonianischen' in Authlog und Bronte." In M. Krause, editor, *Gnosis and Gnosticisim.* Leiden: Brill, 1981. 3-15.
[1506.2].

2850. Sasson, Victor. "*Smn rhs* in the Samaria Ostraca." *JJS* 26.1 (1981): 1-5.
[410/ 606.1].

2851. Sassoon, David Solomon. *Ohel David: A Descriptive Catalogue of the Hebrew and Samaritan Manuscripts in the Sassoon Library.* London, 1932. [Vol.2: 580-603. Reprinted, Ktav].
[101].

2852. Sbath, Paul. "Manuscrits orientaux de la bibliothèque de R. P. Sbath." *Echos d'Orient* 27 (1928): 487.
[101/ 103].

2853. **Scaliger, Joseph.** *Animadversiones in Chronologia Eusebii.* Lugduni Batavorum, 1606. [Notes to the *Thesaurus*].
[800].

2854. ——————. *Opus de Emendatione Temporum.* Paris, 1583. [The 2nd edn. Leiden 1598, is important for the history of Samaritan typefounding. Other editions Geneva 1614 and Cologne 1629].
[105/ 1400].

2855. **Schaaf, Carolo.** *Lexicon Syriacum Concordentiale. Syriacas et linguarum affinium dictiones.* Leiden, 1709. [Draws on Samaritan examples].
[105/ 2800].

2856. **Schachter, I.** "A Bibliographical Project of 5000 Entries on the Samaritans." (Hebrew) *A–B* (1979): 226.
[100].

2857. **Schaik, A. van.** Reviewer. J. Fossum, "The Name of God and the Angel of the Lord." *Tijdschrift voor Theologie* 26.3 (1986): 298.
[107/ 1101/ 1110].

2858. **Schalit, A.** "Die Denkschrift der Samaritaner an König Antiochos Epiphanes zu Beginn der grossen Verfolgung der jüdischen Religion im Jahre 167 v Chr. (Josephus AJ, xii, §258-264)." *ASTI* 8 (1972): 131-183.
[1109.1].

2859. ——————. "The Sectarian Wars in Jerusalem at the end of the Fifth Century and the Beginning of the Fourth Century BCE." (Hebrew) in **M. Schwab and J. Guttman**, editors, *Sefer Jonathan Levi.* Jerusalem, 1949. 252-272.
[802/ 802.1].

2860. **Schalit, M. A.** *Travelled Roads. Memoirs of a Doctor who Lived in the Land of Israel.* New York, 1954. 316-357.
[813.2/ 903].

2861. **Scharlemann, M. H.** *Stephen: A Singular Saint.* Analecta Biblica 34. Rome: Pontifical Biblical Institute, 1968.
[1502.2].

2862. **Scheba, Ch et al.** "Epidemiologic Surveys of Deleterious Genes in Different Population Groups in Israel." *American Journal of Public Health* 52.7 (1962): 1101-1106.
[2901/ 3500].

2863. **Schechter, Solomon.** *Documents of Jewish Sectaries and Fragments of a Zadokite Work.* Cambridge: CUP, 1910. [Reprinted, Ktav, New York 1970].
[1003.4].

2864. **Schefer, Charles.** "Abou'l Hassan Aly el Herewy: Indications sur les lieux de pèlerinage." *AOL* 1 (1881): 587-609.
[307/ 400].

2865. **Scheftelowitz, J.** Reviewer. **Moses Gaster,** "The Asatir." *OLZ* 31 (1928): 1101f.
[107/ 1801].

2866. **Scheidius, Everard.** "Varietas lectionum selectarum ex Pentateucho Samaritano."
In *Specimen I. Thesium Philologico-exegeticarum ad Vetus Testamentum.* 14 pp.
Harderovici Gelrorum, 1776.
[2300].

2867. **Schenke, H. M.** "Jacobsbrunnen—Josephsgrab-Sychar. Topographische
Untersuchungen und Erwägungen in der Perspektive von Joh., 4.5.6." *ZDPV*
84 (1968): 159-184.
[407/ 407.1/ 413/ 1502.1].

2868. **Scher, Addai.** "Histoire Nestorienne." *PO* 4 (1908): chapter 30.
[305.6].

2869. **Schettler, P. A., G. A. Smith, L. Snow, et al.** *Correspondence of Palestine Tourists.*
New York, 1872-1873. [Reprinted, New York, Arno Press 1977].
[308].

2870. **Schiby, J.** "A Samaritan Synagogue in Salonica." (Hebrew) *Zion* 42.1-2 (1977):
103-109. [English summary. The Hebrew title is "A Samaritan
Community..."].
[512].

2871. **Schiemenz, G. P.** "Jacobsbrunnen im tiefen Tal." In *Collectanea Byzantina.*
Orientalia Christiana Analecta 204. Roma, 1977. 147-180.
[407].

2872. **Schiffer, S.** *Keilinschriftliche Spuren der in der zweiten Hälfte des 8 Jahrhunderts von
den Assyrern nach Mesopotamien deportierten Samarier.* 1. Berlin: Beihefte Zur
Orientalischen Literaturzeitung, 1907.
[801.1].

2873. **Schiffman, L. H.** "The Samaritans in Tannaitic Halakhah." *JQR* 75.4 (1985): 323-
350.
[1003.4/ 1106].

2874. **Schiller, Ely.** *The Holy Land in Old Engravings and Illustrations.* Jerusalem: Ariel
Publishing House, n.d. (1980s?).
[102].

2875. **Schindler, Bruno,** editor. "Bibliography of Moses Gaster." In *Gaster Centenary
Publication.* London: Lund, Humphries, 1958.
[100].

2876. **Schlogl, N.** Reviewer. **Leah Goldberg,** "Das samaritanische Pentateuchtargum."
WZKM 53 (1936): 301.
[107/ 2401].

2877. **Schmelz, Oskar U.** "Population Changes in Judaea and Samaria." *JQ* 4 (1977): 95-
110.
[813/ 903].

2878. **Schmid, Lothar.** "Die Komposition der Samaria-Szene in Joh. 4, 1-42." *ZNW* 28 (1929): 148-158.
[1502.1].

2879. **Schmidt, N.** "Sects (Samaritan)." *ERE.* 1920. 11: 343-345.
[201/ 1500].

2880. **Schmidt, W.** "Zum Baumbestand auf dem Garizim." *ZDPV* 78 (1962): 89-90.
[400.1/ 406].

2881. **Schmieder, Carl Christoph.** *Handwörterbuch der gesammten Munzkunde.* Halle and Berlin, 1811.
[603].

2882. **Schmitt, Hans C.** Reviewer. J. Sanderson, "An Exodus Scroll from Qumran: 4QPaleo Exod^m." *ZAW* 100.1 (1988): 151.
[107/ 2307].

2883. **Schneider, A. M.** "Romische und byzantinische Bauten auf dem Garizim." *ZDPV* 68 (1951): 211-234.
[600/ 808].

2884. **Schneider, G.** "Stephanus, die Hellenisten und Samaria." In J. Kremer, editor, *Les Actes des Apôtres: Traditions, rédaction, théologie.* Gembloux: Leuven University Press, 1979. 215-240.
[1502.2].

2885. **Schneider, Th.** "Die Amwas-Inschrift und Irenaus, Elenchos IV, 23, 3." *ZNW* 29 (1930): 155-158.
[808/ 1003.1/ 2502].

2886. **Schnurrer, C. F.** "Noch eine Probe aus dem samaritanischen Chronikon des Abu'l Phathach." In H. E. G. Paulus, editor, *Memorabilien.* 1792. 2: 54-101.
[1601].

2887. —————. *De Pentateucho arabico polyglotto disputatio philologica etc.* Tübingae, 1780.
[2302].

2888. —————. "Probe aus dem samaritanischen Chronikon des Abu'l Phathach." *RBML* (1790): 117-159.
[1601].

2889. —————. "Probe eines samaritanischen biblischen Commentars über I.B. Moses XLIX." *RBML* 15/16 (1784-5): 154-199.
[2304].

2890. —————. "Samaritanischer Briefwechsel." *RBML* 9 (1781): 1-46.
[1700].

2891. **Schnurrer, D.** "Die Samariter." *Mines d'orient.* Vienne, 1809. 438-448.
[200].

2892. **Schoeps, H. J.** "Simon Magus in der Haggadah?" *HUCA* 21 (1948): 257-274.
[1506.2].

2893. **Schofield, J. N.** "The Samaritan Passover." *PEFQS* (1936): 93-96.
[1404].

2894. **Schonfield, Hugh J.** "The Samaritan Hope." *Search* (Jan. 1933): 20-35.
[200].

2895. **Schottroff, L.** "Johannes 4, 5-15 und die Konsequenzen des johanneischen
Dualismus." *ZNW* 60.3-4 (1969): 199-214.
[1502.1].

2896. **Schreiner, J.** Reviewer. J. **Macdonald,** "Memar Marqah." *BZ* 11 (1967): 274.
[107/ 1803].

2897. **Schreiner, M.** "Zur Geschichte der Aussprache des Hebräischen." *ZAW* 6 (1886):
213-259.
[2600].

2898. **Schrijver, Emil G. L.** Reviewer. A. D. **Crown,** "The Samaritans." *Studia
Rosenthaliana* 24.1 (1990): 84-85.
[107/ 200].

2899. **Schrire, T.** *Hebrew Amulets, Their Decipherment and Interpretation.* London:
Routledge & Kegan Paul, 1966. [9, 10, 46].
[601].

2900. —————."A Kabbalistic Samaritan Amulet." *IEJ* 20 (1970): 109-112. [Plate 28
D-E].
[601].

2901. —————. "Samaritan Amulets 'Yat' and Exodus 14:20." *IEJ* 22 (1972): 153-
155.
[601].

2902. **Schröder (Dr).** "Die samaritanische Inschrift von es-Sindiäne." *ZDPV* 31 (1908):
249-253. [An appendix to Graf E. von Mülinen,"Beiträge zur Kenntnis des
Karmels"].
[2505].

2903. **Schudt, J.** *Deliciae Hebraeo-Philologicae sive Tractatus de Studio linguae et Philologie
Hebraicae.* Francofurti ad Moenum, 1700. [A Samaritan script on p. 72].
[105/ 2501].

2904. **Schühlein, Fr.** "Samaritan Language and Literature","Samaria, Samaritans." In
The Catholic Encyclopedia. New York, 1912. 13: 417-420.
[201/ 1550/ 2600].

2905. **Schuller, Eileen.** "4Q372 1: A Text About Joseph." *RQ* 14.3 (January 1990): 349-
376.
[1005/1305/3006.2].

2906. **Schultens, A.** "Vita et res gestae...Saladini...auctore Bohadino...Nec non excerpta ex Historia Universali Abu'l Fedae." Lugdunum Batavorum, 1732. [307.2/ 700].

2907. **Schultzen, Benjamin.** *Orientalisch und Occidentalisches Sprachmeister...hundert Alphabete nebst ihrer Aussprache auch einigen Tabulis Polyglottis.* Leipzig, 1748. [105/ 2600].

2908. **Schulz, Johann Christoph.** *De implacabili Judaeorum...in Samaritas odio...gentis Samaritanae historia et religio...* 134 pp. Wittenberg, 1756. [Holding library: Chicago]. [800/ 2205].

2909. **Schur, Nathan.** "Data on the Samaritans in Western Christian Pilgrims' Journals from the Fourteenth Century to the End of the Eighteenth Century." (Hebrew) *Cathedra* 13 (1980): 177-199 + chart. [306/ 306.1/ 306.2].

2910. —————. "The History of the Jews of Shechem in the Medieval and Modern Periods." (Hebrew) in **Shimon Dar and Zeev Safrai,** editors, *Samaria Studies.* Tel Aviv: Hakibutz Hameuchad, 1986. 229-301. [811/ 813/ 903].

2911. —————. "The Modern Period (from 1516 A.D)." In **Alan D. Crown,** editor, *The Samaritans.* Tübingen: Mohr, 1989. 113-134. [813/ 813.1/ 813.2/ 903].

2912. —————. "Numerical Relationships Between Households and Inhabitants in the Towns of Eretz Israel in the Ottoman Period." (Hebrew) *Cathedra* 17 (1981): 102-106. [813/ 903].

2913. —————. *The Samaritans.* Beiträge zur Erforschung des Alten Testamentes und des Antiken Judentums 18. Frankfurt am Main: Peter Lang, 1989. [Second ed. 1992]. [200].

2914. —————. "The Samaritans as Described in Christian Itineraries (14th-18th Centuries)." *PEQ* 118 (July-December 1986): 144-155. [306/ 306.1/ 306.2].

2915. —————. "The Samaritans in the Ottoman Period (1516-1918)." In **A. Tal & M. Florentin,** editors, *Proceedings of the First International Congress of the Société d'Études Samaritaines.* Tel Aviv: Chaim Rosenberg School for Jewish Studies, University of Tel Aviv, 1991. 147-152. [813.1].

2916. **Schwab, M.** "Les manuscrits et incunables hébreux de la bibliothèque de l'Alliance Israélite." *REJ* 49 (1904): 74-88, 270-296. [101/ 103].

2917. ——————. Reviewer. A. S. Yahuda, "Zum samaritanischen Josua: eine
      Erklärung." *REJ* 57 (1909): 149-152.
      [107/ 1604/ 1605].

2918. Schwank, B. "'Wer ist mein Nächster?' (Lk.10, 29). Eine erklärung des
      Evangeliums des 12 sonntags nach Pfingsten." *Benediktinische Monatsschrift* 33
      (1957): 292-295. [*NTAb* 2 (1957): 62].
      [1502.4].

2919. Schwartz, Daniel R. "On Some Papyri and Josephus Sources and Chronology for
      the Persian Period." *JSJ* 21.2 (1990): 175-199.
      [303.5/ 802.1/ 804].

2920. Schwartz, Seth. "The 'Judaism' of Samaria and Galilee in Josephus' Version of the
      Letter of Demetrius I to Jonathan (Antiquities 13.48-57)." *HTR* 82.4 (1989):
      377-391.
      [303.5/ 804].

2921. Schwarz, Fr. Imm. *Exercitationes historico-criticae in utrumque Samaritanum
      Pentateuchum.* Wittenberg, 1756.
      [2300].

2922. Scobie, C. H. H. "The Origins and Developments of Samaritan Christianity."
      NTS 19.4 (1973): 390-414.
      [1502].

2923. ——————. "The Samaritan Ministry." In *John the Baptist.* 1964. 163-177.
      [1502].

2924. ——————. "The Use of Source Material in the Speeches of Acts III and VII."
      NTS 25 (1979): 399-421.
      [1502.2].

2925. Scott, Ernest F. "Gnosticism." *ERE.* 1913. 6: 231-242.
      [1506].

2926. Scott, J. R. and N. J. D. White. *Catalogue of the manuscripts Remaining in Marsh's
      Library, Dublin.* Dublin, 1913.
      [101/ 103].

2927. Scott, R. B. Y. "Another Griffin Seal from Samaria." *PEQ* 86 (1954): 87-90.
      [607].

2928. Scroggs, V. R. "The Earliest Hellenistic Christianity." In J. Neusner, editor,
      Religions in Antiquity. Essays in Memory of E. R. Goodenough. Leiden: Brill,
      1968. 176-206.
      [1002].

2929. Séd, N. "Le Memar (Marqah) samaritain, le Sefer Yesirah et les trente-deux sentiers
      de la Sagesse." *RHR* 170 (1966): 159-184.
      [1803].

2930. **Seebass, H.** "Garizim und Ebal als Symbols von Segen und Fluch." *Biblica* 63.1 (1982): 22-37.
[801].

2931. **Seeligmann, I. L.** "Indications of Editorial Alteration and Adaptation in the Massoretic Text and the Septuagint." *VT* 11 (1961): 201-221.
[2300/ 2400].

2932. **Segal, J. B.** *The Hebrew Passover From the Earliest Times to AD 70.* Oxford: OUP, 1963.
[1404].

2933. **Segal, M. H. (Z).** "The Marriage of the High Priest to the Daughter of Sanballat and the Building of the Temple on Gerizim." (Hebrew) **Cassutto, Klausner and Guttman,** editors, *Asaph Festschrift on his Sixtieth Birthday.* Jerusalem, 1952-53. 404-414. [Reprinted in Dexinger & Pummer, *Die Samaritaner.* 198-219].
[802.1].

2934. —————. "The Samaritan Pentateuch." (Hebrew) In *Mevo Hamiqra.* Jerusalem, 1972. 911-921. [Reprint edn.].
[2300].

2935. **Segalla, Giuseppe.** "Tre personaggi in cerca di feda un guideo, una Samaritana, un pagano (Gv 3-4)." *Parole di Vita* 16 (1971): 29-49.
[1502.1].

2936. **Segert, S.** Reviewer. R. Macuch, "Grammatik des samaritanischen Aramäisch." *WZKM* 75 (1983): 209-213.
[107/ 2800].

2937. —————. Reviewer. **A. Murtonen,** "Materials for a Non-Masoretic Grammar I." *AO* 17 (1959): 347-348.
[107/ 2600].

2938. **Segre, A. S.** "Manoscritti ebraici e Samaritani della collezione D. D. Sassoon." *RMI* 42 (1976): 168-173.
[103].

2939. **Séjourne, P.** "Concerning a Samaritan Inscription Discovered at Gaza." *AIBL* (1905): 539-540.
[2508].

2940. —————. "Nouvelle découverte d'une église de l'époque franque au Puits de la Samaritaine." *RB* 4 (1895): 619-622.
[407/ 1301].

2941. **Sell, Charles Edward.** *The Samaritans and Other Jewish Sects.* London & Madras: SPCK, 1927. 95pp.
[200].

2942. **Sellers, O. R.** "Coins of the 1960 Excavation at Shechem." *BA* 25 (1962): 87-96.
[412/ 600/ 603].

2943. **Sellin, E.** "Balata." *QDAP* 1 (1932): 1-4.
[412/ 600].

2944. ——————. "Die Masseben des el-Berith in Sichem." *ZDPV* 51 (1928): 119-123.
[Plates 8-12].
[412/ 600/ 604].

2945. ——————. "Wann wurde das Moselied Dtn. 32 gedichtet?" *ZAW* 43.NF 2
(1925): 161-173.
[2300/ 3008].

2946. **Sellin, E. and F. M. Böhl.** "Die Ausgrabungen von Sichem." *ZDPV* 49-50 (1926-
1927): 49:229-236, 304-320 50: 205-211, 265-274.
[412/ 600/ 604].

2947. **Sellin, E. and H. Steckweh.** "Sichem." *ZDPV* 64 (1941): 1-20. [Plates 1-4, 1 fig.].
[412/ 600].

2948. **Sellin, G.** "Lukas als Gleichniserzähler; die Erzählung vom barmherzigen Samariter
(Lk.10, 25-37)." *ZNW* 65-66 (1974-1975): 166-189; 19-60.
[1502.3].

2949. **Seltzer, Carl C.** "The Samaritans and the Near East." In *Contributions to the Racial
Anthropology of the Near East (Papers of the Peabody Museum xvi/2).* 1940. 23-
29. [Plate 3].
[200/ 2901].

2950. **Sennert, A.** *Schediasma de linguis orientalibus.* Wittenberg, 1681. [Typis &
sumptibus C. Schrödteri. Section 6 is on the Samaritan and includes a
Samaritan type face.].
[105/ 2600].

2951. **Serarius, Nicolaus.** *Rabbine et Herodes seu de tora Rabbinorum gente et de Herodis
Naturalibus.* Moguntiae, 1607. See the section "Maior in Hebraeis literis erando
quam in aliis occasio propter literarum simuludinem praesertim post
Samariticas".
[105/ 806].

2952. **Shalish, J.** "Hamesh Me'ot Ha'aharonim." *Qol Tel Aviv Vehamerkaz* (13/11/81):
23.
[3000].

2953. **Shanks, Herschel.** "Glorious Beth Shean." *BAR* 16.4 (1990): 16-31.
[411/ 808].

2954. **Sharf, Andrew.** *Byzantine Jewry from Justinian to the Fourth Crusade.* London:
Routledge & Kegan Paul, 1971.
[808/ 808.1/ 809].

2955. **Sharp, Thomas.** *Discourses Touching the Antiquity of the Hebrew Tongue and
Character.* London, 1755.
[2600].

2956. **Shea, William H.** "The Date and Significance of the Samaria Ostraca." *IEJ* 27 (1977): 16-27.
[301/ 2500].

2957. **Shears, Edward.** "The Samaritan Pentateuch." *The Guardian* (3 August 1892): 1169.
[2300].

2958. **Shehadeh, Haseeb.** The Arabic Translation of the Samaritan Pentateuch.(Ph.D., Hebrew & Arabic) Jerusalem: Hebrew University, 1977.
[2302].

2959. —————. "The Arabic Translation of the Samaritan Pentateuch." *Tarbiz* 52.1 (1982): 59-82.
[2302].

2960. —————. (Hebrew, Arabic and English) *The Arabic Translation of the Samaritan Pentateuch: Edited from Manuscripts with an Introductory Volume.* Jerusalem: Israel Academy of Sciences and Humanities, 1989. 1: Genesis-Exodus:
[2302].

2961. —————. "The Arabic Translation of the Samaritan Pentateuch." In **A. D. Crown**, editor, *The Samaritans.* Tübingen: Mohr, 1989. 481-516.
[2302].

2962. —————. "The Classification of the versions of the Samaritan Arabic Translation of the Pentateuch and Identifying Nomenclature of the Fauna." *Leshonenu* 48-49.1 (1984): 35-48. Hebrew with an English summary.
[2302/ 2700].

2963. —————. "Contribution of 'Aille Torah' to Understanding of the Arabic Translation of the Samaritan Torah." *A–B* 253 (1/2/80): 3-5.
[2302].

2964. —————. "The Groups of the Samaritan Manuscripts of the Arabic Translation of the Pentateuch." In **Rothschild and Sixdenier,** editors, *Études samaritaines.* Louvain-Paris, 1988. 205-218.
[103/ 2302].

2965. —————. "A New Group of Manuscripts including an Arabic translation of the Samaritan Pentateuch (ATSP)." In **A. Tal & M. Florentin,** editors, *Proceedings of the First International Congress of the Société d'Études Samaritaines.* Tel Aviv: Chaim Rosenberg School for Jewish Studies, University of Tel Aviv, 1991.
[103/ 2302].

2966. —————. "A New Unknown Version of the Arabic translation of the Samaritan Pentateuch." In **M. Macuch, C. Müller-Kessler and B. G. Fragner,** editors, *Studia Semitica Necnon Iranica Rudolpho Macuch Septuagenario ab Amicis et Discipulis Dedicata.* Wiesbaden: Harrassowitz, 1989. 303-328.
[2302].

2967. —————. (Hebrew) *Prolegomenon to the Samaritan Arabic Version of the Pentateuch.* Jerusalem: Hebrew University, 1979.
[2302].

2968. —————. "*Pt=Pr,* a non-Moslem Word." *Studia Orientalia* 55.17 (1984): 341-355.
[2700].

2969. —————. "The Samaritan Arabic Version." (Hebrew) *Tarbiz* 52.1 (1983): 59-82.
[2302].

2970. —————. *The Samaritan Pentateuch: Original and Translation.* Jerusalem: Akademon, Hebrew University, 1985. Seminar papers.
[2300].

2971. —————. "When Did Arabic Replace Samaritan Aramaic?" (Hebrew) in **M. Bar Asher,** editor, *Mekhkare Lashon. On the Seventieth Birthday of Prof. Z. Ben-Hayyim.* Jerusalem: Magnes Press, 1983. 515-528.
[2700/ 2800].

2972. **Shelton, J. C.** *Commentary and Indexes to Michigan Papyri Vol. IV.* Cologne, 1976-1977. [See item 2752].
[303.2].

2973. **Shepstone, H. J.** "A Biblical Survival: The Samaritan Midnight Passover on Mt. Gerizim." *ILN* 157.4246 (September 1920): 358-364.
[102/ 1404].

2974. **Shmueli, H.** "Sanballat the Horonite, His Son-in-Law and the Establishment of the Temple at Mt. Gerizim." (Hebrew) *Sefer S. Dim.* Jerusalem: Kiryath Sefer, 1957. 313-341.
[802.1].

2975. **Shotwell, W. A.** *The Biblical Exegesis of Justin Martyr.* London, 1965.
[1003.1/ 1502].

2976. **Shunnar, Zuhair.** *Katalog samaritanischer Handschriften.* Berlin, 1974.
[101/ 103].

2977. —————. "The Number of Commandments in the Torah." (Hebrew) *A-B* 8.197 22-27.
[1106/ 2300].

2978. —————. "Zweisprachiges samaritanisches Lobspreisgedicht auf Moses." In **R. Stiehl and H. E. Stier,** editors, *Beiträge zur Alten Geschichte und deren Nachleben. Festschrift für Franz Altheim zum 6. 10. 1968.* Berlin: Walter de Gruyter, 1970. 176-191.
[1801/ 1802/ 1803].

2979. **Shvut, Abraham.** "The Vines of Samaria." (Hebrew) in **Z. Ehrlich,** editor, *Samaria and Benjamin.* Jerusalem, 1987. 141-146.
[400.1].

2980. **Sidersky, D.** "Le décalogue samaritain." *JA* 7.11th series (1916): 171-176.
[1103].

2981. —————. "Note sur la chronologie samaritaine." *JA* 10.11th series (1917): 513-532.
[700].

2982. —————. "Le sacrifice pascal des samaritains." *RHR* 98 (1928): 193-200.
[1303/ 1404].

2983. **Siegfried, C.** Reviewer. **N. Cohn,** "Die Zaraath-Gesetze." *TLZ* 16 (1899): 457-458.
[107/ 1106/ 1109].

2984. —————. Reviewer. **L. Wreschner,** "Samaritanische Traditionen." *TLZ* 13 (1888): 546.
[107/ 1100/ 1200/ 3009].

2985. **Sifton, Paul G.** "News Notes." *Manuscripts* 35.1 (1983): 35-36. [On Samaritan manuscripts at Columbia University].
[103].

2986. **Sigal, Phillip.** *Judaism, the Evolution of a Faith.* Grand Rapids: Eerdmans, 1988.
[See especially, pp. 62-65].
[800].

2987. **Silva, R.** "La Parábola del buen Samaritano." *CB* 23 (1966): 234-240.
[1502.3].

2988. **Silvestre, M. J. B.** With **F. Madden,** translator, *Universal Palaeography.* London, 1850. 1: 58-61.
[2501].

2989. **Simon, H.** Reviewer. **S. Powels,** "Der Kalender der Samaritaner." *OLZ* 75 (1980): 259-263.
[107/ 1400].

2990. **Simon, Marcel.** *St. Stephen and the Hellenists in the Primitive Church.* London & New York: Longmans Green & Co., 1958.
[1502.2].

2991. —————. "Stephen and the Jerusalem Church." *JEH* 2 (1951): 127-141.
[1502.2].

2992. **Simon, Richard.** *Antiquitates Ecclesiae Orientalis.* London, 1682.
[2300].

2993. —————. *Cérémonies et coutumes qui s'observent aujourd'hui parmi les juifs.* Paris, 1674. [This is a translation of Leon di Modena's work].
[200/ 813].

2994. ————. *A Critical History of the Old Testament.* London, 1682. [Various other editions of the French original and the translation].
[2300].

2995. Simonod, E. "Quelques textes sur la Samaritaine." *Messager Orthodoxe* 83 (1979): 6-56.
[1502.1].

2996. Simsar, Muhammad A. *Oriental Manuscripts of the John Frederick Lewis Collection in the Free Library of Philadelphia.* Philadelphia, 1937.
[101/ 103].

2997. Sirat, Colette. "Paléographie hébraïque et paléographie samaritaine." In Rothschild and Sixdenier, editors, *Études samaritaines.* Louvain-Paris, 1988. 45-55.
[2501].

2998. Six, E. "Chez les samaritains. Au pied du Mont Garizim." *BTS* 4 (1957): 2ff.
[200].

2999. Sixdenier, Guy D. "Aspects des relations des samaritains avec leur voisins du Nord." In A. Tal & M. Florentin, editors, *Proceedings of the First International Congress of the Société d'Études Samaritaines.* Tel Aviv: Chaim Rosenberg School for Jewish Studies, University of Tel Aviv, 1991. 153-172.
[1002].

3000. ————. "Elements of Samaritan Numismatics." In A. D. Crown, editor, *The Samaritans.* Tübingen: Mohr, 1989. 178-189.
[603].

3001. ————. "La langue du Targum samaritain; observations sur son évolution." *JA* 272.3/4 (1984): 223-235.
[2401/ 2800].

3002. ————. Reviewer. I. R. M. Bóid, "Principles of Samaritan Halachah." *JSJ* 21.2 (1990): 253-254.
[107/ 1106/ 2200].

3003. ————. "Remarques sur la paléographie samaritaine." *JA* 248.2 (1960): 189-197.
[2501.1].

3004. ————. "Le Targum samaritain du pentateuque: examen comparé de quelques variantes à témoins rares des versions de l'Exode." In Rothschild and Sixdenier, editors, *Études Samaritaines.* Louvain-Paris, 1988. 131-137.
[2401/ 2800].

3005. Skehan, Patrick W. "The Biblical Scrolls from Qumran and the Text of the Old Testament." *BA* 28 (1968): 87-100.
[2307].

3006. ——————. "Exodus in the Samaritan Recension from Qumran." *JBL* 74 (1955): 182-187.
[2307].

3007. ——————. "The Period of the Biblical Texts from Khirbet Qumran." *CBQ* 19 (1957): 435-440.
[2307].

3008. ——————. "Qumran and the Present State of Old Testament Text Studies: The Masoretic Text." *JBL* 78 (1959): 21-25.
[2307].

3009. ——————. "The Qumran Manuscripts and Textual Criticism." *VTSup* 4 (1957): 148-160.
[2307].

3010. ——————. Reviewer. J. Macdonald, "The Samaritan Chronicle II." *CBQ* 32 (1970): 616-617.
[107/ 1603].

3011. ——————. "The Scrolls and the Old Testament Text." In **D. N. Freedman and J. C. Greenfield**, editors, *New Directions in Biblical Archaeology*. Garden City, NY: Doubleday, 1971. 99-112.
[2307].

3012. **Skinner, J. D.** "Notes on a Newly Acquired Samaritan Manuscript." *JQR* 14 (1902): 26-36. Plate 1.
[103/ 2300].

3013. **Smedley, E. and H. J. Rose.** "Religion of the Samaritans." In *Encyclopaedia Metropolitana*. London, 1845. 10: 595-596.
[201/ 1000].

3014. **Smend, R.** "Ueber die Genesis des Judenthums." *ZAW* 2 (1882): 94-151.
[801.1].

3015. **Smend, R. junior.** Reviewer. F. Pérez Castro, "Sefer Abisha." *ZDPV* 76 (1960): 771-772.
[107/ 2301].

3016. **Smith, D. R. and D. Goldstein.** *Second Supplementary Catalogue of Hebrew Printed Books in the British Library 1893-1960 (letters N–Z)*. London: British Library, 1989.
[100].

3017. **Smith, Morton.** "The Account of Simon Magus in Acts 8." In *Harry Austryn Wolfson Jubilee Volume*. Jerusalem: AAJR, 1965. 2: 735-749.
[1506.2].

3018. ——————. "Aramaic Studies and the Study of the New Testament." *JBL* 57 (1958): 304f.
[2800].

3019. —————. *Palestinian Parties and Politics That Shaped the Old Testament.* New York: Columbia University, 1971. 148-201. [Pp. 193-201 are "Alt's Account of the Samaritans". Second corrected edn. SCM Press, 1987, with differing pagination].
[801/ 801.1/ 802].

3020. —————. Reviewer. **James Purvis,** "The Samaritan Pentateuch and the Origin of the Samaritan Sect." *ATR* 53 (1971): 127-129.
[107/ 801.1/ 2300].

3021. —————. Reviewer. **J. A. Montgomery,** "The Samaritans." (Reprint edition) *ATR* 53 (1971): 127-129.
[107/ 200].

3022. —————. Reviewer. **M. Gaster,** "Studies and Texts." (Reprint edition) *JBL* 911 (1972): 130-132.
[107/ 200/ 1800].

3023. **Smith, R. E.** Reviewer. **R. Coggins,** "Samaritans and Jews." *Southwestern Journal of Theology* 18 (1975): 89.
[107/ 801/ 801.1].

3024. **Smith, T. C.** "The Charity of the Good Samaritan." *BT* 6 (1963): 361-366.
[1502.3].

3025. —————. "The Parable of the Samaritan." *R.Ex* 47 (1950): 434-441.
[1502.3].

3026. **Smith, W. R.** "Samaritans." *Encyclopaedia Britannica.* 9th. London & New York, 1886. 21: 244-246.
[201].

3027. **Smith, W. R. and T. K. Cheyne.** "Samaritans." In *Encyclopaedia Britannica.* 15th. London & New York, 1974.
[201].

3028. **Smitskamp, R.,** editor. *Philologia Orientalis.* Leiden: E.J.Brill, 1992. [A limited, cased edition of 150 copies of the three fascicles published previously. Deals extensively with early printings of Samaritan interest and the Samaritan font.].
[105].

3029. **Snaith, N. H.** Reviewer. **J. Macdonald,** "Theology of the Samaritans." *SJT* 18 (1965): 103.
[107/ 1100].

3030. **Sobernheim, Moritz.** "Samaritanische Inschriften aus Damascus." *MNDPV* 8 (1902): 70-80. Illustrated.
[2506].

3031. **Sofer, Zvi.** "Samaritan Music." (Hebrew) *Proceedings of the Israel Institute for Religious Music* 3 (1962): 99-102.
[3300].

3032. —————. (Hebrew) *The Samaritan Passover.* Haifa, 1952. [26 pp. + ill.].
       [102/ 1404].

3033. **Soggin, J. Alberto.** "Bemerkungen zur alttestamentlichen Topographie Sichems
       mit besonderen Bezug auf Jdc.9." *ZDPV* 83 (1967): 183-198.
       [400.4/ 412].

3034. —————. Reviewer. **R. Macuch,** "Grammatik des samaritanischen Aramäisch."
       Protestantesimo 23 (1972): 180-181.
       [107/ 2800].

3035. —————. "Zwei umstrittene Stellen aus dem überlieferungskreis um Shechem."
       ZAW 73 (1961): 78-87.
       [801].

3036. **Sommelius, Gustaf.** *De lingua et literis Samaritanis...* Londini Gothorum, 1766.
       Vol. 1.
       [2501/ 2600].

3037. **Soubigou, L.** "As conversas de Jesus em Sicar, na Samaria (Jo.4, 1-42)." In **S.
       Voigt,** editor, *Atualidades Bíblicas.* Petropolis, 1971. 510-518.
       [1502.1].

3038. **Souciet, Étienne.** "Dissertation sur les médailles hébraïques appelées
       communément samaritaines." *Recueil des Dissertations Critiques* 1 (1715): 1-
       154.
       [603].

3039. **Spanheim, Ezekiel.** "Agit de formis literarum Phoenicum Hebraeorum,
       Samaritanorum." In *Dissertationes de Praesantia et usu numismatum
       Antiquorum.* 2nd edn. Amsterdam: Daniel Elsevier, 1671.
       [105/ 2501].

3040. **Spector, Joanna.** "Samaritan Chant." *International Folk Music Journal* 16-17 (1964-
       65): 66-69.
       [3300].

3041. —————. "The Significance of the Samaritan Neumes and Contemporary
       Practice." *St. Musicolgia* 7 (1965): 141-153.
       [3300/ 3301].

3042. —————. "Sources of Ancient Israelite Religious Music (The Samaritan,
       Karaite, Kurdistan Jewish, Persian and Greek Orthodox Traditions)."
       (Hebrew) *Proceedings of the Israel Institute for Religious Music* 3 (1962): 90-99.
       [3300].

3043. —————. "Written Tradition and Contemporary Practice in the Biblical
       Cantillation of the Samaritans." (English section) *Fourth World Congress of
       Jewish Studies.* 1965. Jerusalem, 1968. 2: 153-166. [Abstract in Hebrew:478].
       [2308/ 3302].

3044. **Spencer, F. Scott.** "2 Chron. 25:5-15 and the Parable of the Good Samaritan."
　　　 WTJ 46.2 (1984): 317-349.
　　　 [1502.3].

3045. ──────. "Philip and the Samaritans/ Philip and Simon Magus." = chapters 2-
　　　 3 *The Portrait of Philip in Acts. JSNT* Sup. series 67. Sheffield: Sheffield
　　　 Academic Press, 1992. 26-127.
　　　 [1502.2/ 1506/ 1506.2].

3046. **Sperber, Alexander.** "Hebrew Based on Greek and Latin Transliterations." *HUCA*
　　　 12-13 (1937-38): 103-274. [The Israelite nature of the Samaritan recension:
　　　 149-153].
　　　 [2300/ 2604].

3047. ──────. "Hebrew Based upon Biblical Passages in Parallel Transmission."
　　　 HUCA 14 (1939): 153-249. [Samaritan orthography and pronunciation].
　　　 [2300/ 2604].

3048. ──────. *A Historical Grammar of Biblical Hebrew: A Presentation of Problems
　　　 with Suggestions for Their Solution.* Leiden: Brill, 1966.
　　　 [2300/ 2602/ 2603/ 2604].

3049. ──────. "New Testament and Septuagint." *JBL* 59 (1940): 242-246.
　　　 [2400].

3050. ──────. *The Pre-Masoretic Bible Discovered in Four Manuscripts Representing
　　　 a Unique Tradition.* Copenhagen, 1968.
　　　 [2300/ 2307].

3051. **Spicq, Ceslaus.** "The Charity of the Good Samaritan—Luke 10:25-37." In
　　　 Contemporary New Testament Studies. 1965. 218-224.
　　　 [1502.3].

3052. **Spinka, M. and G. Downey.** *The Chronicle of John Malalas, Books 8-18.* Chicago,
　　　 1940.
　　　 [305.4].

3053. **Spiro, Abraham.** "When Was the Samaritan Temple Built." *JBL* (proceedings) 70
　　　 (1955): 11.
　　　 [1305].

3054. ──────. "Samaritans, Tobiads and Judahites in Pseudo-Philo." *PAAJR* 20
　　　 (1951): 279-355.
　　　 [2205/ 2305].

3055. ──────. "Stephen's Samaritan Background." In **J. Munck**, editor, *The Acts of
　　　 the Apostles.* New York: Doubleday, 1967. 31: Appendix v: 285-300.
　　　 [1502.2].

3056. **Spiro, Jean.** "Étude sur le peuple samaritain." *Revue Chrétienne* 5 (1897): 263-280.
　　　 [200].

3057. **Spoer, Hans H.** "Description of the Case Roll of a Samaritan Pentateuch." *JAOS* 27 (1906): 105-107. [1 plate].
[606.1/ 2309.1].

3058. ——————. "Notes on Some New Samaritan Inscriptions." *PSBA* 30 (1908): 284-291.
[2500].

3059. **Springer, J. A.** "Simon." In C. F. **Pfeiffer et al.**, editors, *Wycliffe Bible Encyclopedia.* Chicago, 1975. 2: 1593.
[1506.2].

3060. **Spyridon, S. N.** (Hebrew and English) *Extracts from Annals of Palestine, 1821-1841.* Jerusalem, 1979. [Reprinted from *JPOS* (1938). 18. The Hebrew section (38pp) is rather different from the English].
[306.3].

3061. **Spyridonidis, C. K.** "The Church over Jacob's Well." *PEFQS* (1908): 243-253.
Figs. 1-3.
[407].

3062. **St. Clair, G.** "The Samaritans: The Ancient Copy of the Law." *PEFQS* (1888): 50-51.
[2301].

3063. **Stafford, Roland G.** "The Samaritan Passover." *PEFQS* (1903): 90-92.
[1404].

3064. **Stanley, Arthur Penrhyn.** "The Samaritan Passover." In *Sermons Preached Before His Royal Highness the Prince of Wales During His Tour in the East.* London: John Murray, 1863. 175-184. [Considers the Passover of 1862].
[308/ 1404].

3065. ——————. *Sinai and Palestine.* London: John Murray, 1883. [Numerous earlier and later editions. This edition is the best].
[200/ 400].

3066. **Stanley, David M.** "Interlude samaritain." *BTS* 28 (1960): 2-3.
[1502.1].

3067. ——————. "Samaritan Interlude (Jn. 4:1-42)." *Worship* 34 (1964): 137-144.
[1502.1].

3068. **Stanton, G.** "Samaritan Incarnational Christology." In M. **Goulder,** editor, *Incarnation and Myths, the Debate Continued.* London and Grand Rapids: SCM and Eerdmans, 1979. 243-246.
[1100].

3069. **Stave, Erik.** *Israels land och dess historia intill Jesu och apostlarnes dagar.* Stockholm, 1918. 118-156.
[1003.1/ 1502].

3070. **Steinmeyer, F. L.** *Beiträge zum Verständniss des Johanneischen Evangeliums II Das Gespräch Jesu mit der Samariterin.* Berlin: Wiegandt & Grieben, 1887. [1502.1].

3071. **Steinschneider, Moritz.** Reviewer. **Esriel Munk,** "Des Samaritaners Marqah." *DL* 13 (1892): 1135f. [107/ 1803].

3072. —————. Reviewer. **Esriel Munk,** "Des Samaritaners Marqah." *TLZ* 17 (1892): 403f. [107/ 1803].

3073. —————. *Die arabische Literatur der Juden.* Frankfurt, 1902. [Reprinted Georg Olms, Hildesheim, 1964. See 319-334]. [1550].

3074. —————. "Polemische und apologetische Literatur in arabischen Sprache zwischen Muslimen, Christen und Juden." *AKM* 6.3 (1877): 1-456. [2205].

3075. —————. "Samaritanische Ärzte." *Hebräische Bibliographie* 88 (1875): 84-86. [3500].

3076. —————. "Supplément aux catalogues des manuscrits hébreux et samaritains de la Bibliothèque Impériale." *ZHB* (1902): 6. [Reprinted, Frankfort, J. Kaufman, 1903]. [101/ 103].

3077. **Stemberger, Günter.** Reviewer. **A. M. Rabello,** "Giustiniano Ebrei E Samaritani I." *JSJ* 19.2 (1988): 254-256. [107/ 808].

3078. —————. Reviewer. **A. M. Rabello,** "Giustiniano, Ebrei E Samaritani II." *JSJ* 21. 2 (1990): 269-271. [107/ 808].

3079. —————. "Stephanusrede und jüdische Tradition." In **A. Fuchs,** editor, *Jesus in der Verkündigung der Kirche.* Linz: STNU, 1976. 154-174. [1502.2].

3080. **Stenhouse, Paul L.** Kitab al-Tarikh of Abu'l Fath. (Ph.D.) Sydney: University of Sydney, 1981. [1601].

3081. —————. *Kitab al-Tarikh of Abu'l Fath.* Sydney: Mandelbaum Judaica Series 1, 1985. [1601].

3082. —————. "Origins and History of the Samaritans." *Compass* 10.2 (1976): 33-36. [200].

3083. —————. "The Reliability of the Chronicle of Abu'l Fath with Special Reference to the Dating of Baba Rabba." In **Rothschild and Sixdenier,** editors, *Études samaritaines.* Louvain-Paris, 1988. 235-257.
[700/ 800/ 1601].

3084. —————. "Samaritan Arabic." In **A. D. Crown,** editor, *The Samaritans.* Tübingen: Mohr, 1989. 585-623.
[2700].

3085. —————. "Samaritan Chronicles." In **A. D. Crown,** editor, *The Samaritans.* Tübingen: Mohr, 1989. 218-265.
[1600].

3086. —————. "Samaritan Chronology." In **A. Tal and M. Florentin,** editors, *Proceedings of the First International Congress of the Société d'Études Samaritaines.* Tel Aviv: Chaim Rosenberg School for Jewish Studies, University of Tel Aviv, 1991. 173-188.
[700].

3087. —————. Source and Purpose of the Chronicle Sections of the John Rylands Hillukh MSS 182, 183. (M.A. thesis) Sydney: University of Sydney, 1972.[Unpublished].
[1600/ 2201].

3088. **Sterling, Gregory E.** "The Hellenistic Jewish Historians." = chapter 5 in *Historiography and Self-Definition.* 137-222 *NTSupp* 64. Leiden, New York and Köln: Brill, 1992.
[303/ 303.5 /2001/2004].

3089. **Stern, Ephraim.** "Achaemenian Tombs at Shechem." *Qadmoniot* 13.3-4 (1980): 101-103. [Persians in Samaria].
[600/ 803].

3090. —————. Reviewer. **Y. Meshorer and S. Qedar,** "Coins from Samaria." *Qadmoniot* 25.1-2 (1992): 97-98.
[107].

3091. —————. "New Evidence on the Administrative Division of Palestine in the Persian Period." In **Heleen Sancisi-Weerdenburg and Amélie Kuhrt,** editors, *Achaemenid History IV: Centre and Periphery.* Leiden: Nederlands Instituut voor het Nabije Oosten, 1990. Proceedings of the Groningen 1986 Achaemenid History Workshop: 221-226.
[803].

3092. **Stern, Ephraim and Y. Magen.** "A Persian Period Pottery Assemblage from Qudum." *EI* 16 (1982): 182-197. [Plates 19-23].
[606.1].

3093. —————. "A Pottery Group of the Persian Period from Qadum in Samaria." *BASOR* 253 (1984): 9-27.
[600/ 606.1/ 803].

3094. **Stern, Menahem.** "The Conflict Between the Samaritans and the Jews Under Cumanus According to Josephus and Tacitus." In **S. Safrai** and **M.Stern,** editors, *Compendium Rerum Judaicarum ad Novum Testamentum.* Van Gorcum: Assen & Philadelphia, 1974. Appendix II, vol. 1:1: 374-376. [303.5/ 807].

3095. ——————. *Greek and Latin Authors on Jews and Judaism.* Jerusalem: IASH, 1976, 1980, 1984. 3 volumes. [300/ 303/ 305.5].

3096. ——————. "Jewish and Samaritan Scholars and Philosophers in the Time of Isadorus of Damascus." (Hebrew) *Studies in the History of Israel and the Jewish People* 3 (1974/5): 85-97. [2000].

3097. **Sternheim, Hans.** "Die Samaritaner von Nablus. Ein Kriegsbrief (30.8.1918)." *Mitteilungen des Bundes der Asienkämpfer* 7 (1925): 160-161. [813.2/ 903].

3098. **Stertz, S. A.** "Christianity in the *Historia Augusta." Latomus* 36.3 (1977): 694-715. [805].

3099. **Steuernagel, C.** Reviewer. **D. J. W. Rothstein,** "Juden und Samaritaner." *TLZ* 34 (1909): 67-68. [107/ 800/ 801.1].

3100. ——————. Reviewer. **J. A. Montgomery,** "The Samaritans." *TLZ* 33 (1908): 452-455. [107/ 200/ 800].

3101. **Stewart, A.,** editor. *Anonymous Pilgrims (11th and 12th Centuries).* London: PPTS, 1894. [306.2/ 306.3/ 401].

3102. ——————, editor. *Burchard of Mt.Zion.* London: PPTS, 1896. 22-54. [306.2/ 306.3/ 401].

3103. ——————, editor. *Description of the Holy Land by John of Wurzburg.* London: PPTS, 1896. [306.2/ 306.3/ 401].

3104. ——————, editor. *John Poloner's Description of the Holy Land.* London: PPTS, 1894. [306.2/ 306.3/ 401].

3105. ——————, editor. *Ludolph von Suchem's Description of the Holy Land.* London: PPTS, 1895. [306.2/ 306.3/ 401].

3106. ——————, editor. *Marino Sanuto's Secrets for True Crusaders to Help Them Recover the Holy Land.* London: PPTS, 1896. 19-30. [306.2/ 306.3/ 401].

3107. ————, editor. *The Pilgrimage of Joannes Phocas to the Holy Land.* London: PPTS, 1896.
[306.2/ 306.3/ 401].

3108. ————, editor. *Theoderic's Description of the Holy Places.* London: PPTS, 1896.
[306.2/ 306.3/ 401].

3109. **Stiehl, Ruth.** "Erwägungen zur Samaritanerfrage." In **F. Altheim and R. Stiehl,** *Die Araber in der Alten Welt.* Berlin, 1967. Vol. 4: 204-224.
[307/ 1003/ 1003.3].

3110. ————. Reviewer. **R. Macuch,** "Grammatik des samaritanischen Hebräisch." *WZKM* 63.4 (1972): 300-302.
[107/ 2600].

3111. **Stoehr, H.** *Theoria et praxis linguarum sacrarum scilicet Samaritanae, Hebraeae et Syriacae, earumque harmonia.* Augsburg: 1796.
[2600].

3112. **Stone, Michael and E. W. Nickelsburg,** editors. "The Samaritans." In *Faith and Piety in Early Judaism: Texts and Documents.* Philadelphia: Fortress Press, 1983. 11-19. [Extracts from Chronicle II].
[309.1].

3113. **Strack, H.** Reviewer. **M. Heidenheim,** "Bibliotheca Samaritana I." *LZ* 35 (1885): 1728-1731.
[107/ 2300].

3114. **Strack, H. and P. Billerbeck.** *Kommentar zum Neuen Testament aus Talmud und Midrasch.* München, 1922-28.
[1003.1/ 1502].

3115. **Strahan, James.** "Samaria." In **J. Hastings,** *Dictionary of the Apostolic Church.* Edinburgh: T & T Clark, 1918.
[201/ 410].

3116. **Stratos, A. N.** *Byzantium in the Seventh Century.* Amsterdam, 1972. [Translation of the Greek edition, Athens 1965].
[808].

3117. **Strizower, Schifra.** "The Samaritans." *Exotic Jewish Communities.* Popular Jewish Library. London & New York: Yoseloff, 1962. chapter 5. 140-157.
[200].

3118. **Strong, James.** "The Modern Samaritans." In *McClintock and Strong Cyclopaedia.* 1880. Vol. 9: 132-138.
[201/ 813].

3119. **Strugnell, John.** "Quelques inscriptions samaritaines." *RB* 74 (1967): 550-580. 2 figs.
[1103/ 2500].

3120. —————. "The Qumran Scrolls, a Report on Work in Progress." In S. Talmon, editor, *Jewish Civilization in the Hellenistic-Roman Period.* Sheffield: Sheffield Academic Press, 1991. 95-106.
[2307].

3121. Strugnell, John and James Purvis. "An Early Samaritan Decalogue Inscription in the Israel Museum." *Israel Museum News* 2 (1976): 87-91.
[1103/ 2504].

3122. Sukenik, E. L. *Ancient Synagogues in Palestine and Greece.* London: OUP, 1934.
[1304].

3123. —————. "The Date of the Samaritan Inscription from Shechem." (Hebrew) *Yediot* 4 (1936-37): 130-131.
[412/ 2510.1].

3124. —————. "Inscribed Hebrew and Aramaic Potsherds from Samaria." *PEFQS* (1933): 152-156.
[410/ 606.1].

3125. —————. "Ruins of the Samaritan Temple Sha'albim (Salbit)." (Hebrew) *Bulletin of the Antiquities Division of the State of Israel* 2 (1950): 31-32.
[411.1/ 1304/ 1305].

3126. —————. "A Samaritan Inscription of the Ayyubid Period from Bet Chanin." *BJPES* 12 (1946).
[2502].

3127. —————. "The Samaritan Synagogue at Salbit, Preliminary Report." *BR* 1 (1949): 25-30. [Fig. 8].
[411.1/ 2510.2/ 1304].

3128. Sukenik, E. L. and M. N. Todin. "On the Greek Inscription in the Samaritan Synagogue at Salbit." *BR* 2 (1951): 27-28. Plate 12.
[411.1/ 2510.2/ 1304].

3129. Sundberg, A. C. "The Samaritan Pentateuch." In *The Old Testament of the Early Church.* 1964. 107-112.
[2300].

3130. Suriano, Fra Francesco. With Theophilus Bellorini, translator, *Treatise on the Holy Land.* Jerusalem: Franciscan Press, 1949. [2nd ed. 1983].
[308/ 400].

3131. Sussman, Varda. "Samaritan Cult Symbols as Illustrated on Oil Lamps from the Byzantine Period." (Hebrew) *Israel People and Land, Eretz Israel Museum Yearbook* 4.(22) New series (1986-7): 133-146. English summary pages 13* & 14*.
[604/ 605/ 808/ 1300].

3132. —————. "Samaritan Lamps of the 3rd-4th Centuries AD." *IEJ* 28.4 (1978): 238f.
[605].

3133. ——————. "The Samaritan Oil Lamps from Apollonia-Arsuf." *Tel Aviv* 10.1 (1983): 71-96.
[605].

3134. **Swarsensky, Manfred.** Die Begräbnis und Trauerliturgie der Samaritaner nach zwei Handschriften der preussichen Staatsbibliothek. (Ph.D.) Berlin: University of Wurzburg, 1930.
[1203/ 2103].

3135. ——————. "Die Samaritaner." *Berliner Jüdische Gemeindeblatt* 21st year (1931): 126-128. Illustrated.
[102/ 200].

3136. **Swinton, John.** *Inscriptiones Citieae...Accedit de nummis quibusdam Samaritanis et Phoeniciis dissertatio.* Oxonii, 1750. 45-87. [With a letter of Joh. Hen. Brucker].
[603/ 2501].

3137. ——————. *Inscriptiones Citieae sive in binas alias inscriptiones...de nummis quibusdam Samaritanis.* Oxonii, 1753.
[603/ 2501].

3138. **Sylva, Denis D.** "The Meaning and Function of Acts 7:46-50." *JBL* 106 (1987): 261-275.
[1502.2].

3139. **Szpidbaum, H.** "Die Samariter." *Mitteilungen der Anthropologischen Gesellschaft in Wien* 57 (1927): 137-158.
[2901].

3140. ——————. "Samaritaner in anthropologischer Beziehung." *Sprawozdanie z czyyoki tow. Naukowego Warszawa (Compte rendus des séances de l'Académie des Sciences et des Lettres de Varsovie)* 19 (1926): 355-364.
[2901].

3141. ——————. "Typy Antropologiczne Verod Samarytan." *Przeglad anthropolgyozny, Posnan* 2 (1927): 9-18. [French summary: 41-42].
[2901].

3142. **Sztern, S. N.** Essai sur les origines et l'histoire de la communauté samaritaine. (Ph.D.) Paris: Sorbonne, 1945.
[800/ 801.1].

3143. **Szuster, Icko.** Marqa-Hymnen aus der samaritanischen Liturgie übersetzst und bearbeitet.(Inaugural dissertation) Berlin: Bonn University, 1936.
[803/ 2102.1].

3144. **Szyszman, S.** "Centenaire de la Mort de Firkowicz." *VT Sup.* 28 (1975): 196-216.
[103].

3145. ——————. "Les passionnants manuscrits d'Abraham Firkowicz." *Archaeologia* 78 (1975): 61-69.
[103].

T

3146. **T. W. N.** "The Samaritan Pentateuch." *The Guardian* (20th July 1892): 1087.
[2300].

3147. **Tadmor, H.** "Fragments of an Achaemenid Throne from Samaria." *IEJ* 24 (1974): 37-43.
[600/ 803].

3148. ——————. "Some Aspects of the History of Samaria During the Biblical Period." (Hebrew) *Jerusalem Cathedra* 3 (1983): 1-11.
[801].

3149. ——————. "Towards a History of Samaria from Its Foundation to the Macedonian Conquest." (Hebrew) *Eretz Shomron.* Jerusalem: IES, 1973. 67-74.
[801].

3150. **Tadmor, H. and S. Ahituv.** "Shomron." (Hebrew) in *EM.* 1982. 8: 142-148.
[410/ 801].

3151. **Taglicht, Israel.** *Die Kuthäer als Beobachter des Gesetzes nach talmudischen Quellen nebts Berücksichtigung der samaritanischen Correspondenz und Liturgie.* Erlangen, Berlin, 1888.
[304.2/ 801.1].

3152. **Tal, Abraham.** "Berurim ba-Aramit shel Erets Israel." (Hebrew) *Leshonenu* 1.1979 (44): 43-65.
[2600].

3153. ——————. "Between Hebrew and Aramaic in the Samaritan Forms." (Hebrew) *Transactions of the Academy of Humanities* 7.10 (1987): 239-255.
[2600/ 2800].

3154. ——————. "The Contribution of Samaritan Aramaic to the Understanding of the Hebrew of the Earlier Payetanim." (Hebrew) in M. A. Friedman, A. Tal and G. Brin, editors, *Researches in Talmudic Literature.* Tel Aviv: University of Tel Aviv, 1983. 167-169.
[2600 / 2800].

3155. ——————. "Un fragment inédit du Targum Samaritain." In D. Muñoz León, editor, *Salvación en la palabra en Memoria del Prof. A. Díez Macho.* Madrid: Ediciones Cristianou, 1986. 533-540.
[2401].

3156. ——————. "L'exégèse samaritaine à travers les manuscrits du Targum." In Rothschild and Sixdenier, editors, *Études samaritaines.* Louvain-Paris, 1988. 139-148.
[103/ 2305].

3157. ——————. "The Lexicon of Samaritan Aramaic and its Problems." In A. Tal and M. Florentin, editors, *Proceedings of the First International Congress of the*

Société d'Études Samaritaines. Tel Aviv: Chaim Rosenberg School for Jewish Studies, Tel Aviv University, 1991. 347-355.
[2800].

3158. —————. "Modern Manuscripts of the Samaritan Targum of the Pentateuch." *IOS* 9 (1979): 129-146.
[103/ 2401].

3159. —————. "The Need for a New Lexicon of Samaritan Aramaic." (Hebrew) in *Proceedings of the Eighth World Congress of Jewish Studies.* Jerusalem: World Union of Jewish Studies, 1982. Div.D: 15-19.
[2603].

3160. —————. "Samaritan Literature." In **Alan D. Crown,** editor, *The Samaritans.* Tübingen: Mohr, 1989. 413-467.
[1550].

3161. —————, editor. (Hebrew, Aramaic and English) *The Samaritan Targum of the Torah.* Tel Aviv: Tel Aviv University Press, 1980-1983. 3 vols. [A critical edition with a substantial introduction].
[2401].

3162. —————. "The Samaritan Targum of the Pentateuch." In **Martin Jan Mulder and Harry Sysling,** editors, *Mikra.* Assen/Maastricht/Philadelphia: Van Gorcum/Fortress, 1988. 189-216.
[2400].

3163. —————. "The Samaritan Targum to the Pentateuch, Its Distinctive Characteristics and Its Metamorphosis." *JSS* 21. 26-38 (1976):
[2401].

3164. —————. "The Samaritan Targum to the Torah—Its Unity and Metamorphosis." (Hebrew) *Proceedings of the Sixth World Congress of Jewish Studies.* 1973. Jerusalem: World Union of Jewish Studies, 1977. 1: 111-117.
[2401].

3165. —————. "The Samaritan Targumic Version of the 'Blessing of Moses' (Deut.33) According to an Unpublished Ancient Fragment." *AN* 24 (1986): 178-195.
[2300/ 2401].

3166. —————. "Targumic Fragments in an Old Samaritan Prayerbook." In **M. Macuch, C. Müller-Kessler and B. G. Fragner,** editors, *Studia Semitica Necnon Iranica Rudolpho Macuch Septuagenario ab Amicis et Discipulis Dedicata.* Wiesbaden: Harrassowitz, 1989. 329-342.
[2102/ 2401].

3167. —————. "Towards a Critical Edition of the Samaritan Targum of the Pentateuch." *IOS* 8 (1978): 107-128. [Abstracted, *A–B*, 255-257, 1/1/80-1/4/80].
[2401].

3168. **Tal, Abraham and M. Florentin,** editors. *Proceedings of the First International Congress of the Société d'Études Samaritaines. Tel Aviv.* Tel Aviv: Chaim Rosenberg School for Jewish Studies, University of Tel Aviv, 1991.
[200].

3169. **Tal, Abraham, A.D.Crown and R.Pummer,** editors. *A Companion to Samaritan Studies.* Tübingen: Mohr, 1993.
[200].

3170. **Talmon, Shemaryahu.** "The Abisha Scroll of Pinhas the Priest." (Hebrew) *Molad* 18 (1961): 580-581.
[2301].

3171. —————. "Approaches to the Study of the Samaritan Pentateuch Version." (Hebrew) *Tarbiz* 22 (1951): 124-128.
[2300].

3172. —————. "Aspects of the Textual Transmission of the Bible in the Light of the Qumran Manuscripts." *Textus* 4 (1964): 95-132.
[1005/ 2307].

3173. —————. "Biblical Traditions on the Early History of the Samaritans." (Hebrew) in *Eretz Shomron: The 30th Archaeological Convention.* Jerusalem: IES, 1973. 19-33.
[801.1].

3174. —————. "Die Samaritaner." *Süddeutsche Zeitung am Wochenende* 22/23 (1976): 129-130.
[200].

3175. —————. "Die Samaritaner in Vergangenheit und Gegenwart." In *Frankfurter Universitätsreden.* Frankfurt am Main: Klostermann Verlag, (1969) 1972. 42: 71-83. [Reprinted in Dexinger and Pummer, *Die Samaritaner,* 379-392].
[200/ 800/ 813].

3176. —————. "Editorial note." (Hebrew) in **I. Ben Zvi,** *Sefer Hashomronim.* Reprint edition. Jerusalem, 1970, 1973.
[200].

3177. —————. "Fragments of Scrolls from Masada." *EI* 20 (1990): 278-276. [On the name Har Gerizim].
[2600].

3178. —————. "The Internal Diversification of Judaism in the Early Second Temple Period." In **S. Talmon,** editor, *Jewish Civilization in the Hellenistic-Roman Period.* Suppl.JSP. Sheffield: JSOT, 1991. 16-43.
[801/ 802].

3179. —————. "Los samaritanos; pasado y presente." *Helmantica* 30.92/93 (1979): 317-330.
[200].

3180. —————. Reviewer. "Observations on the Samaritan Pentateuchal Version."
       (Hebrew) *Tarbiz* 22 (1951): 124-128. [Review of G. Gerleman, *Synoptic
       Studies in the Old Testament,* (Lund, 1948)].
       [107/ 2300].

3181. —————. "The Samaritan Pentateuch." *JJS* 2.3 (1951): 144-150.
       [2300].

3182. —————. "The Samaritans." *Scientific American* 236 (June, 1977): 100-108.
       [200].

3183. —————. Reviewer. F. Pérez Castro, "Séfer Abisa." *Erasmus* 14 (1961): 24-28.
       [107/ 2300/ 2301].

3184. —————. (Hebrew) *Selections from the Pentateuch in the Samaritan Version.*
       Jerusalem: Dept of Bible Studies, Hebrew University, 1956-57. [Another edn.
       1959].
       [2300].

3185. —————. "Some Unrecorded Fragments of the Hebrew Pentateuch in the
       Samaritan Version." *Textus* .3 (1963): 60-73.
       [2300].

3186. —————. Chaim Rabin, "Synonymous Readings in the Old Testament."
       Scripta Hierosolymitana 8 (1961): 335-383. [Discussion of some Samaritan
       readings].
       [2300].

3187. —————. "Three Books Found in Ezra." (Hebrew) *Segal Festschrift.* Jerusalem:
       Society for Biblical Research, 1965.
       [801/ 802].

3188. —————. "Typen der Messiaserwartung um die Zeitenwende." In H. Wolff,
       editor, *Probleme biblischer Theologie (Von Rad Festschrift).* München, 1971.
       571-588. [Reprinted as, 'Types of Messianic Expectation at the Turn of the
       Era' *CCAR* (Spring, 1976). 23:1-11].
       [1107].

3189. Talshir, David. Nomenclature of the Fauna in the Samaritan Targum. (Hebrew,
       Ph.D. thesis) Jerusalem: Hebrew University, 1981.
       [2401].

3190. —————. "Remnants of Hebrew in Samaritan Aramaic." (Hebrew) in A. Tal
       and M. Florentin, editors, *Proceedings of the First International Congress of the
       Société d'Études Samaritaines.* Tel Aviv: Chaim Rosenberg School for Jewish
       Studies, University of Tel Aviv, 1991. 1*-6*.
       [2800].

3191. Tamani, Giuliano. *Catalogo dei Manoscritti Ebraici della Bibliotheca Marciana di
       Venezia.* Firenze, 1972.
       [101].

3192. **Tamaro, B. F.** *Inscriptiones Italiae.* Roma, 1947. 5: 91-92. [Possible Samaritan tomb inscriptions].
[305.5/ 1203/ 2500].

3193. **Tannehill, Robert C.** "Comments on the Articles of D. Patte and J. D. Crossan." *Semeia* 2 (1974): 113-116.
[1003.1/ 1502].

3194. **Tappy, Ron E.** *The Archaeology of Israelite Samaria.* Atlanta, Georgia: Scholars Press, 1992. Vol. 1. Early Iron Age through Ninth Century BCE.
[600].

3195. **Tattam, (Archdeacon).** "The Abisha Scroll." *Parthenon* 4. (May 24, 1862).
[2301].

3196. **Taurinensis, S. Maximi.** "Homilia." *PL* 57 478-480; 740.
[305.5].

3197. **Taylor, Joan E.** Reviewer. **A. D. Crown,** "The Samaritans." *BAIAS* 8 (1989-1990): 64-65.
[107/ 200].

3198. **Taylor, W. M.** *Jesus at the Well; John IV, 1-42.* New York: Randolph & Co., 1884.
[1502.1].

3199. **Taylor, W. R.** "A New Samaritan Inscription." *BASOR* 81 (Feb.1941): 1-6. [With a note by W. F. Albright. Also reprinted separately].
[2500/ 2508].

3200. —————. "Recent Epigraphic Discoveries in Palestine." *JPOS* 10 (1930): 16-22. [2 plates].
[2500/ 2501/ 2508].

3201. —————. "Samaritan Inscription from Gaza." *JPOS* 16 (1936): 131-137. [Plates 6 & 7].
[2508].

3202. **Tchernowitz, Chaim (Rav Tsair).** "Roots of the Samaritan Schism." (Hebrew) *Bitzaron* 1 (1939-40): 201-206.
[801.1].

3203. **Teeple, H. M.** *The Mosaic Eschatological Prophet.* Philadelphia: Society of Biblical Literature, 1957. Monograph X.
[1105/ 3008].

3204. **Temple, R. C.** Reviewer. **M. Gaster,** "The Asatir." *JRAS* (1928): 454-458.
[107/ 1801].

3205. **Tenckinck, Egbertus H.** *Resp. Dissertatio Critica qua lectio Hebraei Codicis in...Deut xxvii:4 defenditur et ea Samaritani tanquam spuria rejicitur.* Franequerae, 1767.
[1107].

3206. Tentzelius, W. E. *Exercitatio Philologico de Proseuchis Samaritanoram.* Wittenberg, s.d. (1682?). [2600].

3207. Ternant, D. "Le bon samaritain, Lc.10, 25-37." *ASeign* 46 (1974): 66-77. [1502.3].

3208. Testa, E. "La mitica rigenerazione della vita in un amuleto samaritano-cristiano del IV secolo." *SBFLA* 23 (1973): 286-317. [601].

3209. Theodoretus. "Quaestiones in libros Regum." *PG* 80 712, 720-722. [305.4].

3210. Theodosius. "Selecta de Religione Decreta." *PL* 13 539-542. [305.5].

3211. ————. "De Terra Sancta." *SPTROL.* Paris, 1879. 71-72. [C. AD 530]. [305.5].

3212. Theodosius Secundum. "De Situ Terra Sancta." *SPTROL.* Paris, 1879. 81-83. [305.5].

3213. Theodotos. A. Ludwich, editor, *De Theodoti carmine graeco-judaico commentatio...* Hartungiana: Acad. Alb. Regim. 2, 1899. [2005].

3214. Theophanes. "Chronographia." *PG* 108 407-414. [Other edns., e.g.C. de Boor, Hildesheim, 1963]. [305.4].

3215. Theophanes Cerameus. "Homilies." *PG* 132 719-746. [305.4].

3216. Theophylactus. "Enarratio in Evangelium Lucae." *PG* 123 843-850; 987-990. [305.4].

3217. ————. "Enarratio in Evangelium Joannis." *PG* 123 1223-1258. [305.4].

3218. ————. "Enarratio in Evangelium S. Matthaei." *PG* 123 235-238, 307-410. [305.4].

3219. Thomas, D. Winton. Reviewer. R. Macuch, "Grammatik des samaritanischen Hebräisch." *BL* (1970): 83-84. [107/ 2602].

3220. ————. Reviewer. A. Murtonen, "Materials for a Non-Masoretic Grammar III: A Grammar of the Samaritan Dialect of Hebrew." *JSS* (1961): 273-275. [107/ 2602].

3221. ————. "The Textual Criticism of the Old Testament." In H. H. Rowley, editor, *The Old Testament and Modern Study.* Oxford: OUP, 1951. 238-263.

[2nd edn. 1961].
[2300].

3222. ——————. Reviewer. J. Macdonald, "The Theology of the Samaritans." *ET* 76 (1964): 79-80.
[107/ 1100].

3223. **Thomas, Joseph.** *Le mouvement baptiste en Palestine et Syrie (150 av J-C—300 ap. J-C).* Gembloux, 1935.
[1002].

3224. **Thomassin, Louis.** "Agitur de Literis Samaritans." In *La méthode d'étudier et d'enseigner Christienement et utilement la grammaire ou les langues par report à l'écriture Sainte en les reduisant toutes à l'Hébreu.* Paris, 1690.
[2600].

3225. **Thompson, George et al.** *A View of the Holy Land.* Wheeling, W. Va.: James Rossell, 1850. 234-239.
[308].

3226. **Thompson, J. A.** "Samaritan Evidence for 'all of them in the Land of Shinar' (Gen.10:10)." *JBL* 90 (1971): 99-102.
[2300].

3227. **Thomson, J. E. H.** "The Pentateuch of the Samaritans: When they Got It, and Whence." *JTVI* 52 (1920): 142-176.
[2300].

3228. ——————. "The Samaritan Passover." *PEFQS* (1902): 82-89.
[1404].

3229. ——————. "The Samaritans." *ET* 11 (1900): 375-377.
[200].

3230. ——————. *The Samaritans: Their Testimony to the Religion of Israel.* Edinburgh and London: Oliver and Boyd, 1919. [The Alexander Robertson Lectures (delivered before the University of Glasgow, 1916). Reprinted, New York, 1976].
[200].

3231. **Thomson, William M.** *The Land and the Book.* London & New York: Nelson and Sons, 1846. [Other edns.].
[400].

3232. **Thornton, T. C. G.** "The Samaritan Calendar: A Source of Friction in New Testament Times." *JTS* 42.2 (1991): 577-580.
[1400].

3233. **Tigay, Jeffrey H.** "Conflation as a Redactional Technique." In *Empirical Models for Biblical Criticism.* Philadelphia: University of Pennsylvania Press, 1985. 53-89. [See also appendix A for Samaritan Exodus 18].
[2300].

3234. —————. "An Empirical Basis for the Documentary Hypothesis." *JBL* 94.3 (1975): 329-342.
[2300].

3235. —————. "An Empirical Model of the Samaritan Pentateuch for Literary Research." (Hebrew) *BM* 22 (1977): 348-361.
[2300].

3236. **Tisserant, Eugene.** Reviewer. **A. von Gall**, "Der hebräische Pentateuch der Samaritaner (Exodus-Deuteronomy)." *RB* 30.2 (1921): 616-617.
[107/ 2300].

3237. —————. Reviewer. **A. von Gall**, "Une nouvelle édition du pentateuque Samaritain—édition von Gall, prolegomena, Genèse." *RB* 11.4 (1914): 542-549.
[107/ 2300].

3238. —————. "Specimena codicum Orientalium." In **Iohannis Lietzmann,** *Tabulae in usum scholarum editae sub cura Iohannis Lietzmann, 8.* Bonn, 1914. [A description of the Barberini Triglot].
[103/ 2300].

3239. **Tobler, Titus.** *Bibliographia Geographia Palestinae.* Amsterdam, 1954 (reprint).
[400].

3240. **Tollerson, James William.** The Rôle of the Samaritans in the Ministry of Jesus. (Ph.D.) New Orleans: New Orleans Baptist Theological Seminary, 1979.
[1502].

3241. **Toombs, Lawrence E.** "Daily Life in Ancient Shechem." *Drew Gateway* 32 (Spring, 1962): 127-134.
[801].

3242. —————. "Shechem— Problems of the Early Israelite Era." In **F. M. Cross,** editor, *Symposia Celebrating the Seventy-fifth Anniversary of the Founding of the American Schools of Oriental Research.* Cambridge, Mass.: American Schools of Oriental Studies, 1979. 69-83.
[412/ 801].

3243. —————. "The Stratification of Tell Balatah (Shechem)." *BASOR* 223 (1976): 57-59.
[412/ 600].

3244. **Toombs, Lawrence E. and G. E. Wright.** "The Fourth Campaign at Balatah (Shechem)." *BASOR* 169 (1963): 1-60.
[412/ 600].

3245. —————. "The Third Campaign at Balatah (Shechem)." *BASOR* 161 (1961): 11-54.
[412/ 600].

3246. **Torrey, C. C.** *Ezra Studies.* Chicago: University of Chicago Press, 1910.
       [Reprinted, New York, 1970].
       [802/ 802.1].

3247. —————. "Sanballat 'the Horonite'." *JBL* 47 (1928): 380-389.
       [802.1].

3248. **Torris, J.** "Qui des deux fut schismatique, le samaritain ou le juif?" *La pensée et les
       hommes* 18 (1974): 77-80.
       [801.1/ 1003.4].

3249. **Tournay, R.** Reviewer. E. Robertson, "Catalogue of the Samaritan Manuscripts in
       the John Rylands Library II." *RB* 70 (1963): 314-315.
       [107/ 2300].

3250. —————. Reviewer. **S. Talmon,** "Quatre fragments." *RB* 71 (1964): 427-428.
       [Review of the article in *Textus* III (1963)].
       [107/ 2300].

3251. —————. "Quelques relectures bibliques antisamaritaines." *RB* 71 (1964): 504-
       536.
       [801].

3252. —————. Reviewer. **J. Bowman,** "Transactions—Bowman." *RB* 67 (1960):
       611.
       [107/ 801].

3253. **Tov, Emanuel.** "Hebrew Biblical Manuscripts from the Judaean Desert: Their
       Contribution to Textual Criticism." In **S. Talmon,** editor, *Jewish Civilization in
       the Hellenistic-Roman Period.* Sheffield: Sheffield Academic Press, 1991. 107-
       137.
       [2307].

3254. —————. "Une inscription grecque d'origine samaritaine trouvée à
       Thessalonique." *RB* 81.3 (1974): 394-399.
       [2513].

3255. —————. "A Modern Textual Outlook Based on the Qumran Scrolls." *HUCA*
       53 (1982): 11-27.
       [1005/ 2300/ 2307].

3256. —————. "The Nature and Background of Harmonizations in Biblical MSS."
       JSOT 31 (1985): 3-29.
       [2300].

3257. —————. "A New Understanding of the Samaritan Pentateuch in the Wake of
       the Discovery of the Dead Sea Scrolls." In **A. Tal & M. Florentin,** editors,
       *Proceedings of the First International Congress of the Société d'Études
       Samaritaines.* Tel Aviv: Chaim Rosenberg School for Jewish Studies, University
       of Tel Aviv, 1991. 293-304.
       [2307].

3258. —————. "Pap. Giessen 13, 19, 22, 26: A Revision of the LXX?" *RB* 78 (1971): 355-383.
[2309/ 2400].

3259. —————. "The Proto-Samaritan Texts and the Samaritan Pentateuch." In **A. D. Crown,** editor, *The Samaritans.* Tübingen: Mohr, 1989. 397-407.
[2300/ 2307].

3260. —————. "The Relationship Between Witnesses to the Scripture Versions in the Light of the Dead Sea Scrolls." (Hebrew) *BM* 77 (1978/1979): 161-170.
[2300/ 2307].

3261. —————. "The Samaritan Pentateuch and the So-Called 'Proto-Samaritan' Texts." (Hebrew) in **M. H. Goshen-Gottstein, Shlomo Morag and Simcha Kogut,** editors, *Shai le Chaim Rabin: Studies on Hebrew and Other Semitic Languages.* Jerusalem: Academon Press, 1990. 136-146.
[2300/ 2307].

3262. —————. "The Textual Appearance of the Leviticus Scroll from Qumran Cave 11." (Hebrew) *Shnaton* 3 (1978): 238-244.
[2300/ 2307].

3263. **Tov, Emanuel and J. Cook.** "A Computerised Database for the Qumran Biblical Scrolls with an Appendix on the Samaritan Pentateuch." *JNSL* 12 (1984): 133-137.
[1005/ 2300/ 2307].

3264. **Townsend, John T.** "The Speeches in Acts." *ATR* 42 (1960): 150-159.
[1502.2].

3265. **Trinitate, S. S. (F. Dominicus à Philippus).** "Samaritan." In *Bibliotheca Theologica.* Rome, 1667. Vol II.
[105/ 200].

3266. **Tristram, H. B.** *The Land of Israel: A Journal of Travels in Palestine.* 2nd. London, 1886. 141-160.
[200/ 308].

3267. **Trotter, John F.** A Critical Study of the Ideological Background of the 14th Century Samaritanism with Special Reference to the Works of Abisha b. Pinchas, Abdallah b. Solomon and ben Manir. (Ph.D. thesis) Leeds: University of Leeds, 1961.
[1550/ 2100].

3268. —————. *Did the Samaritans of the Fourth Century Know the Epistle to the Hebrews?* Leeds: LUOS, 1961.
[1502/ 1506/ 1803].

3269. —————. *Gnosticism and the Memar Marqah.* Leeds: LUOS, 1964.
[1506/ 1803].

3270. **Troupeau, Gérard.** *Catalogue des MSS arabes 1. Manuscrits Chrétiens.* Paris, 1972.
[101].

3271. **Trudinger, L. P.** "Once Again 'Now Who Is My Neighbour?'." *EQ* 48 (1976): 160-163.
[1502].

3272. **Trumbull, H. C.** "The Samaritan Passover." In *Studies in Oriental Social Life.* Philadelphia, 1894 & London, 1895. 371f.
[1404].

3273. **Trumbull, H. C. and E. W. G. Masterman.** "Jacob's Well." *PEFQS* (1900): 61-65.
[407].

3274. **Tsafrir, Yoram.** (Hebrew) *The Land of Israel from the Destruction of the Second Temple to the Muslim Conquest.* Jerusalem: Yad Ben Zvi, 1985.
[808].

3275. —————. "A New Reading of the Samaritan Inscription from Tell Qasile." *IEJ* 31.3-4 (1981): 220-222.
[414/ 2512].

3276. —————. "On the Samaritan Church at Tell Qasile." *Qadmoniot* 12.1 (1979): 30-31.
[414/ 1301].

3277. **Tsedaka, A.** (Hebrew) *The Celebration of Passover by the Samaritans.* Holon, 1962.
[14 pp. English title page; Library of Congress].
[1404].

3278. —————. "On the History of the Samaritans, Their Beliefs and Religion." (Hebrew) in **M. Zohary, A. Tartakover, M. Zand, et al.,** editors, *Hegot Ivrit Be'artsot Ha'Islam.* Jerusalem, 1980.
[200].

3279. —————. "Notes on Samaritan History and Customs." (Hebrew) *Bulletin of the Museum Ha'aretz* 10 (1968): 51-55.
[200/ 1200].

3280. —————. (Hebrew) *The Samaritan Passover.* Holon, 1962. [14 pp.].
[1404].

3281. —————. "The Samaritans." (Hebrew) *Gesher* 13 (1966): 115-124.
[200/ 1200].

3282. —————. (Hebrew) *The Sefer Hayerushot Haisraeli Hashomroni.* Holon, 1969.
[2207].

3283. —————. (Hebrew) *The Sefer Hayerushot of Abi Yitzhak Elmantsef According to a Manuscript of A. N. Tsedaka.* Holon, 1969.
[2207].

3284. —————. (Hebrew) *Zevah Hapesach Etsel Hashomronim.* Holon, February, 1968. [44 pp.].
[1404].

3285. **Tsedaka, Abraham ben Marhiv.** (Hebrew) *The Little Molad Moshe.* Holon, n.d. [39pp]. [1802].

3286. —————. (Hebrew) *Molad Mosheh ben Amram.* Holon, 1964. [The abridged version of the text of Pinhas b. Isaac]. [1802].

3287. —————. (Hebrew) *Songs in Praise of Moses ben Amram the Prophet.* Holon: Committee for Samaritan Publications, 1956. [2101/ 3008].

3288. **Tsedaka, A. and R. Tsedaka.** (Hebrew) *The Book of Rejoicing.* Holon, 1964. 2 vols. [25 cms.]. [2103].

3289. —————. (Hebrew) *Prayer Book for the Sabbath of the Decalogue.* Holon, 1962. [155 pp.]. [1405/ 2104].

3290. —————. (Hebrew) *Prayer Books for the Two Sabbaths of the First Month.* Holon, 1961. [103 pp.]. [1405/ 2104].

3291. **Tsedaka, Binyamim.** Editor, *A–B Samaritan News* (1/12/69 onwards). [104].

3292. —————. "Birth, Among the Samaritans." (Hebrew) *Bama'aracha* 9.100 (1969): 8-9, 19. [1200].

3293. —————. "A Case for a Samaritan Torah from the year 1565 in the Jewish Museum in New York." (Hebrew) *A–B* 367-377 (1985). [2309.1/ 3100].

3294. —————. "The Correlation Between the State of the Samaritan Manuscripts and the State of the Samaritan Community: Past and Present." In **Rothschild and Sixdenier,** editors, *Études samaritaines.* Louvain-Paris, 1988. 289-292. [103/ 903].

3295. —————. "Death, Among the Samaritans." *Bama'aracha* 10.120 (1971): 18-21. [1203].

3296. —————. "Divorce, Samaritan Style." (Hebrew) *Bama'aracha* 10.118 (1971): 10-11. [1205].

3297. —————. "Introduction to Samaritan History." (Hebrew) *Shevet Va'am (2nd series)* 1.6 (1971): 283-295. [Reprinted, Jerusalem 1971, with an errata page]. [800].

3298. —————. "Journey to Leiden." (Hebrew) *A–B* 385/386 (1985): 15-21. [103].

3299. —————. "Passages in the History of the Samaritans." (Hebrew) *A–B* 251-254 (1/1/80-15/2/80):
[800].

3300. —————. "Passover on Mt. Gerizim." (Hebrew) *Bama'aracha* 9.96 (1969): 22-24.
[1404].

3301. —————. "Pathways in Samaritan Tradition." (Hebrew) *Bama'aracha* 9.104 (1969): 16-18.
[1800].

3302. —————. "President I. Ben Zvi 'The Good Samaritan'." (Hebrew) *Bama'aracha* 9.97 (1969): 16-17.
[1003.4].

3303. —————. "Samaritan Festivals." *EJ.* 14: 741-748.
[1400].

3304. —————. "The Samaritan High Holydays." (Hebrew) *Bama'aracha* 9.101 (1969): 8-10, 22.
[1401/ 1403].

3305. —————. "Samaritan History, 1300-1970." In *EJ.* 14: 734-738.
[201/ 811/ 813].

3306. —————. "Samaritan Leader Disputes Altar." *BAR* 2.13 (March-April 1987): 67-68.
[404/ 1303].

3307. —————. "The Samaritan Synagogue." *Davar* (2/9/79):
[1304].

3308. —————. Reviewer. **Z. Safrai,** "Samaritan Synagogues in the Roman-Byzantine Periods." (Hebrew) *A–B* 191.8 (1977): 22-23.
[107/ 808/ 1304].

3309. —————. Reviewer. **M. Cohen,** "Samaritan Writing." *A–B* 156 (1976): 5-6.
[107/ 2300].

3310. —————. "Shavuot Among the Samaritans." (Hebrew) *Bama'aracha* 9.96 (1969): 10-11.
[1407].

3311. —————. "Special Samaritan Traditions in Non-Samaritan Sources." In **A. Tal & M. Florentin,** editors, *Proceedings of the First International Congress of the Société d'Études Samaritaines.* Tel Aviv: Chaim Rosenberg School for Jewish Studies, University of Tel Aviv, 1991. 189-204.
[300].

3312. —————. "Succoth Among the Samaritans." (Hebrew) *Bama'aracha* 9.102 (1969): 22-23, 25.
[1409].

3313. —————. "The Uniqueness and Hardship of a Samaritan Journal." *Our Press— World Federation of Jewish Journalists.* 1989. 3: 13-18. [About *A–B.-The Samaritan News* edited by Benyamim Tsedaka and Yefet b. Ratson Tsedaka]. [104/ 3011].

3314. Tsedaka, Binyamim and Yefet Tsedaka. *The Samaritans in 1988: A–B Echos.* N.P. (Holon?): A–B?, n.d.(1989?).
[200/ 903].

3315. Tsedaka, I. and A. b. N. Tsedaka. (Hebrew) *The Prayers for the End of Shabbat.* Holon: Committee for Samaritan Publications, 1957. [29 pp.].
[1405/ 2104].

3316. Tsedaka, I., A. b. N. Tsedaka, R. Tsedaka. (Hebrew) *The Samaritan Prayer Book for the Weeks Between Passover and Pentecost.* Holon: Committee for Samaritan Publications, 1956.
[1406/ 2102].

3317. Tsedaka, Israel. (Hebrew) *Book of Festivals for Sabbaths and Every Festival of Joy.* Holon, 1963. [299 pp.].
[1405/ 2104].

3318. —————. (Hebrew) *Prayer Book for Hag Hammazot.* Holon (?), n.d. [92 pp. 17 x 12 cm.].
[1404/ 2102].

3319. —————. (Hebrew) *Prayer Book for Shavuot.* Holon (?), n.d. [92 pp. 17 x 13 cm.].
[1407/ 2102].

3320. —————. (Hebrew) *Prayer Book for the Eve of Sabbath and the Daily Evening Prayers.* Holon (?), n.d. [174 pp. 25 x 17 cm.].
[1405/ 2102/ 2104].

3321. —————. (Hebrew) *Prayer Book for the Sabbath of Succoth.* Holon (?), n.d. [170 pp. 24 x17 cm.].
[1405/ 1409/ 2104].

3322. —————. (Hebrew) *Prayer Book for the Intermediate Days of Passover and the Seventh Day of Passover.* Holon, 1964. [154 pp. 17 cm.].
[1404/ 2102].

3323. —————. (Hebrew) *Prayers for Passover and Mazzoth.* Holon, 1964. [340 pp. 25 cm.].
[1210/ 1404].

3324. —————. (Hebrew) *Prayers for Tabernacles, Mornings and Evenings on Mt Gerizim.* Holon, 1963. [90 pp. 17 cm.].
[1409/ 2102].

3325. —————. (Hebrew) *Sabbath Prayers—Noon and the End of Sabbath with Various Piyyutim.* Holon, 1961. [187 pp.].
[1405/ 2104].

3326. —————. "The Samaritans Outside Shechem." (Hebrew) in G.Kressel, editor, *Hol Veruah.* Tel Aviv, 1964. 225-227.
[500].

3327. —————. (Hebrew) *Sefer Hatorah.* Holon, 1967. [Based on the Barberini Triglot and BL Or 7562].
[2300].

3328. Tsedaka, Japhet, Isaac Yehoshua, Barukh Tsedaka, editors. *Gerizim.* 3/1970 - 1971. [An incomplete set in the Oxford Centre for Postgraduate Hebrew Studies library].
[104].

3329. Tsedaka, Japhet, Meir Shoshani and I. Yehoshua, editors. *Shevuaim.* Bi-weekly, 1970. [An incomplete set in the Oxford Centre for Postgraduate Hebrew Studies library].
[104].

3330. Tsedaka, R. ben Binyamim. *Shirat Ha'otot Vehamofetim.* Shechem/Holon, 1977.
[2100].

3331. Tsedaka, Raçon. (Hebrew) *Genesis, the Samaritan Version with a Translation into Aramaic and Arabic.* Holon, 1966.
[2300/ 2302/ 2401].

3332. —————. (Hebrew) *Liturgy for Yom Kippur.* Tel Aviv, 1960. [183 pp. 25 cm.].
[1401/ 2102].

3333. —————. (Hebrew & Arabic) *Memar Marqah.* Holon (?), n.d. [417 pp. 25 x 17cm.].
[1803].

3334. —————. (Hebrew) *The Minor Molad Moshe and Piyyutim by Abraham b. Marhiv Tsedaka.* Holon (?), n.d. [39 pp. 25 x 17cm.].
[1802].

3335. —————. (Hebrew) *Molad Mosheh.* Holon (?), s.d. [Reprinted, 1960 with a different title page; 25 x 17 cm.].
[1802].

3336. —————. (Hebrew) *Prayer Book for the Zimmuth of Succoth, New Year, and the Ten Penitential Days.* Holon (?), s.d. [377 pp. 17 x 25 cm.].
[2102].

3337. —————. (Hebrew) *Prayer Book for the Sabbaths of Shavuot.* Holon, 1968.
[1405/ 1407/ 2104].

3338. —————. (Hebrew) *Sefer Tahannune Israel—Piyyutim Shomroniyim.* Holon, 1976. 2 vols.
[2101].

3339. Tsedaka, Raçon and B. Tsedaka. (Hebrew) *Songs and Piyyutim for the Evening of Atonement with Explanation of Samaritan Laws and Customs.* Holon (?), n.d.

[403 pp.].
[1401/ 2102].

3340. **Tsedaka, Raçon (Hassafary).** (Hebrew & Arabic) *Kitab al Tassabich = (Book of Commendations).* Holon, 1970.
[1550/ 2603].

3341. **Tsedaka, Raçon with Dov Noy,** editors. (Hebrew) *Samaritan Legends.* Haifa: Israel Folklore Archives publication series, 8, 1965. [English summaries: 86-89 + preface].
[1800].

3342. **Tsedaka, Raçon and A. Tsedaka,** editors. (Hebrew) *The Jewish and Samaritan Versions of the Pentateuch.* Tel Aviv, 1961-1965. [Available five parts separatum or in one volume. The two versions are printed in parallel columns with differences in larger characters].
[2300].

3343. **Tsedaka, Raçon and A. b. N. Tsedaka.** (Hebrew) *Memar Marqah.* Holon, 1962.
[1803].

3344. **Tsedaka, Raçon and Tsedaka,B.** (Hebrew) *Shirat Ha'otot wehaMofetim de Levi ben Abisha haCohen haLevi.* Holon, 1977. [25 pp.].
[2101].

3345. **Tsereteli, K.** *Materialy po Aramejskoj dialekologii.* Tbilissi, 1965.
[2800].

3346. **Tshelebi, E.** *Travels in Palestine, 1648-1650.* Jerusalem, 1980. [Reprint from *QDAP* (1935) 4 onwards].
[304.4].

3347. **Tur Sinai, N. H.** "Evolution of the Final Letters." *Halashon Vehasefer* 2 (1953): 3-34.
[2501].

3348. **Turaev, B.** *Koptiskiia, Siriskiia, Samaritanskiia, Rukopisi.* Azia Tskii Muzeii, 1920.
[2600].

3349. **Turner, G. C.** A Classed Inventory of the Oriental Manuscripts in the British Museum, 1886.London: British Library, 1886.[An unpublished, handwritten checklist of the Oriental MSS including the Samaritan manuscripts, from the British Library].
[100/ 103].

3350. **Tushingham, A. D.** "A Hellenistic Inscription from Samaria-Sebaste." *PEQ* 104 (1972): 59-63.
[410/ 2500].

3351. **Tweedy, Owen.** "The Samaritan Passover." *Atlantic Monthly* 141 (1928): 550-555.
[1404].

3352. **Tychsen, Oluf Gerhard.** "Commentatio de Numis HebraeoSamaritanis ignotus characteribus inscriptis." *Commentationes Societatis Gottingen* 8 (1784): 122f. [603/ 2501].

3353. —————. *Die Unächtheit der jüdischen Munzen mit hebräischen und samaritanischen Buchstaben bewiesen.* Rostock & Leipzig, 1779. [603/ 2501].

3354. —————. *Disputatio historico-philologico-critica de Pentateucho Ebraeo-Samaritano ab Ebraeo eoque Masorethico Descripto Examplari.* Bützow, 1765. [2300].

3355. —————. *De Numis Hebraicis diatribe, qua simul ad nuperas ill. F Perezii Bayerii obiectiones respondetur.* Rostock: typis Adlerianis, 1791. [64pp. A refutation of Bayer's views]. [603/ 2501].

3356. —————. "Refutación de los argumentos que el Sr. D. Francisco Perez Bayer ha alegado neuvamente en favor de las Monedas Samaritanas." In F. **Perez Bayer,** *Numorum Hebraeo-Samaritanorum Vindiciae.* Valentiae Edetanorum: Ex Officina Montfortiana, 1790. 18-24. [603/ 2501].

3357. **Tyrens, W.,** editor. "L'estoire de Eracles, empereur." *RHC.* Paris, 1844. 1:1. [808].

U

3358. Ugolini, Blasio, editor. *Thesaurus Antiquitatum Sacrum Complectens.* Venetis, 1795+.
[104].

3359. Uhlemann, Friederich. *Institutiones Linguae Samaritanae ex Antiquissimis monumentis 1 & 2 Chrestomathia Samaritana...et Glossaria.* Lipsiae, 1837.
[2600].

3360. Uhlhorn, G. "Dositheus." *PRE* 3 (1878): 683.
[1503/ 3004].

3361. —————. "Menander." *PRE* 9 (1881): 543f.
[1506.1].

3362. Ujvari, Péter. "Szmaritanusok." In *Magyar Zsidó Lexicon.* Budapest, 1929. 821-823.
[201].

3363. Ulrich, E. "The Biblical Scrolls from Qumran Cave 4: An Overview and a Progress Report on their Publication." *RQ* 14 (1989): 207-228.
[2307].

3364. —————. "Double Literary Editions of Biblical Narratives and Reflections on Determining the Form to be Translated." In J. Grenshaw, editor, *Perspectives on the Hebrew Bible: Essays in Honor of Walter J. Harrelson.* Macon: Mercer University Press, 1988. 101-116.
[2307].

3365. Uri ben Simeon. *Cippi Hebraica...ii De nummis Orientalium.* Heidelberg, 1659.
[Second ed. 1662].
[603].

3366. Uri, J. *Bibliothecae Bodleianae codicum manuscriptorum orientalium...catalogus. Pt.1.* Oxonii, 1787.
[101].

3367. Urmann, G. Y. Reviewer. J. Macdonald, "Memar Marqah." (Hebrew) *QS* 39.no. 2647 (1963-4): 376-377.
[107/ 1803].

3368. Ussher, James Bishop of Armagh. "Samaritanorum." In *Annales Veteris et Novi Testamenti.* London, 1654. Reprinted Paris, 1673.
[105/ 200].

3369. Uzzi, Jacob ben. Abraham b. Zebulun, translator, *The Celebration of the Passover by the Samaritans.* Jerusalem, 1934.
[1404].

V

3370. **Vaccari, A.** "Due Codici del Pentateucho Samaritano." *Biblica* 21 (1940): 242-246.
[103/ 2300].

3371. **Vailhe, S.** "Samaria." In *The Catholic Encyclopaedia.* New York, 1912. 13: 416.
[410].

3372. **Vajda, G.** Reviewer. **J. S. Isser,** "The Dositheans." *REJ* 138 (1979): 165.
[107/ 1503].

3373. —————. Reviewer. **H. Pohl,** "Kitab al Mirat." *REJ* 135 (1976): 249-250.
[107/ 2200].

3374. —————. Reviewer. **Z. Ben-Hayyim,** "Literary and Oral Tradition." *REJ* 127 (1968): 262f.
[107/ 1550/ 2600].

3375. —————. Reviewer. **J. Macdonald,** "Memar Marqah." *REJ* 123 (1964):
[107/ 1803].

3376. —————. Reviewer. **S. Lowy,** "The Principles of Samaritan Bible Exegesis."
REJ 138 (1979): 438-440.
[107/ 2305].

3377. —————. Reviewer. **J. Macdonald,** "Samaritan Chronicle II." *REJ* 130 (1971):
376.
[107/ 1603].

3378. —————. Reviewer. **J. Bowman,** "Samaritanische Probleme." *REJ* 127 (1968):
270-272.
[107/ 1500].

3379. —————. Reviewer. **M. Gaster,** "Studies and Texts." (Reprint edn.) *REJ* 131 (1972): 209.
[107/ 200].

3380. **Van Beek, G.** "Samaria." *IDB* (1962): 182-188.
[410].

3381. **Van Cangh, J. M.** "Nouveaux fragments hexaplaires." *RB* 78 (1971): 384-390.
[2300].

3382. **Van Den Born, A.** "Samarie", "Samaritaines." In *Dictionnaire encyclopédique de la Bible.* Louvain, 1960. 1672-1675.
[201/ 410].

3383. **Van den Eynde, P.** "Le bon samaritain." *BVC* 70 (1966): 27-35.
[1502.3].

3384. **Van der Woude, A. S.** Reviewer. H. **Kippenberg,** "Garizim und Synagoge." *JSJ* 2 (1971): 188-190.
[107/ 200/ 805].

3385. **Van Gelderen, C.** "Samaritanen en Joden aan de Zuidgrens van Egypte." *Stemmen des Tijds* 1&2 (1912): 1126-1153.
[300/ 505/ 803].

3386. —————. "Samaritaner und Juden in Elephantine Syene." *OLZ* 15 (1912): 337-344.
[300/ 505/ 803/ 1003.4].

3387. **Van Goudoever, J.** *Biblical Calendars.* Leiden: Brill, 1961. [Revised and expanded edn.1967].
[1400].

3388. **Van Selms, A.** "Ein boek-religie: de vereering van der rol van Abisha door de Samaritanen." *NTT* 1 (1947): 193-203.
[2301].

3389. **Van Stockum, Th C.** "Viif variaties op sen thema: Schiller en de gelijkenis van de barmartige Samaritaan." *NTT* 17 (1962-3): 338-347.
[1502.3].

3390. **Van Unnik, W. C.** "A Greek Characteristic of Prophecy in the Fourth Gospel." In E. **Best & R. McL.Wilson,** editors, *Text and Interpretation: Studies in the New Testament Presented to Matthew Black.* London, Melbourne andNew York: CUP, 1979. 211-229.
[1107/ 1502.1].

3391. **Van Vloten, W. and S. F. J. Ravio.** *Specimen philologicum quod continet descriptionem cod. MS Bibliothecae Lugduno-Batavae partemque inde excerptam versionis Samaritano-Arabicae Pentateuchi Mosaici.* Leyden, 1803. [94 pp.].
[2300/ 2302].

3392. **Vanderhoff, B.** Reviewer. A. **Merx,** "Der Messias oder Taeb der Samaritaner." *TR* (1910): 175.
[107/ 1107].

3393. **Vassie, Roderic.** *The Bible in Arabic: An Exhibition at the British Library.* London: British Library Board, 23 November 1990 to May 1991. [The single sheet guide to the exhibition includes some notes on the Samaritan Pentateuch].
[100/ 103].

3394. **Vattioni, F.** Reviewer. R. **Macuch,** "Grammatik des samaritanischen Hebräisch." *Augustinianum* 12 (1972): 196-197.
[107/ 2602].

3395. —————. "Saggio di Bibliografia semitica 1985-1986." *AION* 46.4 (1986): 563-624. [Pp. 613-614 deal with the Samaritans].
[100].

3396. **Veenhof, K. R.** "De Samaria Papyri II." *Phoenix* 10.1 (1964): 137-140.
[303.3].

3397. **Veith, Johann Emanuel.** *Die Samaritin.* Wien, 1840.
Sermons.
[200].

3398. **Verschuir, Joannes Henricus.** *Dissertationes philologico-exegeticae quibus S. Codicis loca illustrantur...Addita est oratio eiusdem inauguralis.* Leovardiae et Franquerae, 1773.
[2600].

3399. **Vigouroux, F.** "Les samaritains au temps de Jésus Christ." In *Mélanges bibliques.* Paris, 1882.
[807/ 1003.1].

3400. **Vilar Hueso, V.** "Samaria","Samaritanos." In *Gran Enciclopedia Rialp.* Madrid, 1974.
[201].

3401. **Vilmar, Eduard.** *Abulfathi Annales Samaritani.* Gotha, 1865.
[1601].

3402. ——————. "Notizen zum Briefwechsel der Samaritaner." *ZDMG* 17 (1863): 375-376.
[1700].

3403. **Vilnai, Z.** (Hebrew) *Judah and Samaria.* Tel Aviv, 1968.
[1800].

3404. ——————. *Legends of Palestine.* Philadelphia, 1932. 259-270. [Hebrew edn. *Legends of Israel*, Jerusalem, 1949].
[1800].

3405. **Vilsker, Leib H..** "Samaritânskoe brakorazvodnoe pishmo." In **Maria Macuch, Christa Müller-Kessler and Bert G. Fragner,** editors, *Studia Semitica necnon iranica. Rudolpho Macuch septuagenario ab amicis et discipulis dedicata.* Wiesbaden: Harrassowitz, 1989. 353-365.
[2100].

3406. ——————. "Antdekte Oistres." (Yiddish) *Sovietisch Heimland* 51.3 (1985): 3-63. Available separatum.
[800].

3407. ——————. "Evrejsko-arabskie slovari v samaritjanskom sobranii Gosudarstvennoj Publicnoj biblioteki im M.E. Saltykova-Scedrina." *Semitistkie Jazkyi* 1 (1969): 148-153.
[103/ 2603/ 2700].

3408. ——————. *Issledovanie Samaritjanskojgo Jazyka.* Moscow, 1970.
[200].

3409. —————. Jean Margain, translator, *Manuel d'Araméen samaritain*. Paris: CNRS, 1981.
[2600/ 2800].

3410. —————. "Ob odnom samaritjanskom izobrazitel' nom pamjatnike v Gosudarstvennnoj biblioteke SSSR imeni V.I.Lenina." *Zapiski Otdela rukopisei* 32 (1971): 73-80.
[103].

3411. —————. "The Samaritan Documents in the MSS Collection of the M. E. Saltykov Tschedrin State Public Library in Leningrad." In *Historica Philologicae Investigatia.* 1971. 9-18.
[101/ 103].

3412. —————. "A Samaritan Inscription on Silk." *PS* 27.90 (1981).
[2500].

3413. —————. "A Samaritan Translation of Saadyah's 'Bakasha'." (Yiddish) *Sovietish Heimland* 6 (1981): 139-144.
[1003.4/ 1004].

3414. —————. "Samaritjanskie nadpisi." *Voprosy filologii stran Azii i Afriki.* Leningrad, 1971. 152-160.
[2600/ 2800].

3415. —————. "Samaritjanskie rukopisi v bibliotekakh Sovetskogo Sojuza." *Narody Azii i Afriki* 4 (1979): 152-157.
[103].

3416. —————. *Samaritjanskij Jazyk.* Moscow, 1974.
[2600].

3417. —————. "Unknown Samaritan Inscriptions in the Public Library in Leningrad." (Hebrew) *A–B* 348 (1983): 6-10. [A Yiddish version appeared in *Sovietish Heimland* 9 (1983) 109-116].
[2301/ 2500].

3418. **Vincent, L.-H.** "Le culte d'Hélène à Samarie I. Hélène et les Dioscures II. Hélène et Simon le magicien." *RB* 45 (1936): 221-232. Plate 6.
[1110/ 1506].

3419. —————. "Fouilles allemandes à Balatah-Sichem." *RB* 36 (1927): 419-425.
[Plates 11 & 12].
[412/ 600].

3420. —————. "Un hypogée antique à Naplouse, nouvelles diverses." *RB* 29 (1920): 126-135.
[600].

3421. —————. "Notes d'épigraphie palestinienne." *RB* 12 (1903): 605-617.
[2500].

3422. —————. "Puits de Jacob ou de la Samaritaine." *RB* 65 (1958): 547-567.
[407].

3423. —————. Reviewer. M. Gaster, "Samaritains (=review of *Samaritan Eschatology)*." *RB* 42 (1933): 452-453.
[107/ 200/ 1105].

3424. Vink, J. G. "The Samaritan Schism." *OTS* 15 (1969): 51-57.
[801.1].

3425. Vinnikov, I. N. "'Samaritjanskoe Pjatiknizie' i ustnaja palestinskaja tradicija." *PS* 15.78 (1966): 74-90.
[2300].

3426. Vitray/Vitré, Anton. *Linguarum Orientalium Alphabeta*. Paris, 1636. [Bodleian Library].
[105/ 2501].

3427. Viviano, P. A. "2 Kings 17: A Rhetorical and Form Critical Analysis." *CBQ* 49 (1987): 548-559.
[801/ 801.1].

3428. Vogel, E. K. "Bibliography of Holy Land Sites." *HUCA* 42 (1971). [See entries for Gerizim and Shechem].
[100].

3429. Vogliano, P. Mil. *Papiri della Univers la Degli Studi de Milano*. Milano, 1967.
[Volume 4].
[303.2].

3430. Voigt, W. *Verseichnis der orientalischen Handschriften in Deutschland*. Wiesbaden, 1965. [Bd.VI. 2].
[101/ 103].

3431. Vollers, K. Reviewer. M. Heidenheim, "Bibliotheca Samaritana I." *Lo.Ph.* (1885): 91-95.
[107/ 2401].

3432. —————. *Katalog der islamischen, christlich-orientalischen, jüdischen und samaritanischen Handschriften der Universitätsbiblitek zu Leipzig= Katalog der Handschriften der Universitätsbiblitek zu Leipzig, II*. Leipzig: Harrasowitz, 1906. [Reprinted Osnabrück, 1975].
[101/ 103].

3433. Volz, P. "Vom Tabor nach Jerusalem." *PJB* 7 (1905): 110-125. [A good section on Nablus].
[408/ 412].

3434. Von Gall, August Frh. "Ankündigung einer neuen Ausgabe des hebräischen Pentateuchs der Samaritaner." *ZAW* 26 (1906): 293-305.
[2300].

3435. —————. *Der hebräische Pentateuchs der Samaritaner.* Giessen: Töpelmann, 1914-1918. [Reprinted, 1966].
[2300].

3436. **Von Murr, C. G.** "Von syrischen, samaritanischen und kotptischen Typen." *Literarische Blätter* 17 (1805): 266-271.
[105].

3437. **Von Schreiber, T.** "Die Dreiflussbasic von Nablus." *ZDPV* 7 (1884): 136-139.
[400.4].

3438. **Von Weisl, W.** "Das Kamf um das heilige Land." In *Palästina von Heute.* Berlin, 1925.
[400].

3439. —————. "Das Passah opfer auf dem Berg Garizim." *Beilage zur Vossichen Zeitung.* 11 May (1924):
[1404].

3440. —————. "The Last of the Samaritans." *Menorah Journal* April (1926): 177-182.
[200].

W

3441. **W., H. B. S.** "The Samaritan Temple." *PEFQS* 19 (1885): 139.
[1305].

3442. **Wacholder, Ben-Zion.** *Eupolemus—A Study of Judaeo-Greek Literature.* Cincinati, 1974.
[2000/ 2004].

3443. **Wacholder, Ben-Zion.** "'Pseudo-Eupolemus'. Two Greek Fragments on the Life of Abraham." *HUCA* 34 (1963): 83-113.
[2004].

3444. —————. "A Qumranic Polemic Against a Divergent Reading of Ex. 6:20." *JANES* 16-17 (1984-1985): 225-228.
[2300/ 2305].

3445. **Wachsmuth, K.** *Einleitung in das Studium der alten Geschichte.* Leipzig, 1895.
[3010.1].

3446. **Wächter, Ludwig.** "Das Baumheiligtum bei Sichem." *Folia Orientalia* 17 (1976): 71-86.
[401].

3447. —————. "Salem bei Sichem." *ZDPV* 84 (1968): 63-72. Plates 12-13.
[410.1/ 412].

3448. **Wachter, Ludwig.** "Zur Lokalisierung das sichemitischen Baumheiligtums." *ZDPV* 103 (1987): 1-2.
[401].

3449. **Wagner, M.** Reviewer. R. Macuch, "Grammatik des samaritanischen Hebräisch." *TZ* 29 (1973): 135-137.
[107/ 2602].

3450. **Waitz, H.** "Simon Magus in der altchristlichen Literatur." *ZNW* 5 (1904): 121-143.
[1506.2].

3451. **Walker, R.** "Jüngerwort und Herrenwort. Zur Auslegung von Joh. 4:39-42." *ZNW* 57.1-2 (1966): 49-54. [*NTAb* (1966).11 no.291].
[1502.1].

3452. **Wallenstein, M.** Reviewer. A. Murtonen, "Materials for a Non-Masoretic Grammar I." *VT* 10 (1960): 234-239.
[107/ 2300/ 2600].

3453. **Walter, N.** "Zu Pseudo-Eupolemos." *Klio* 43-45 (1965): 282-290.
[2004].

3454. **Waltke, Bruce Kenneth.** "Prolegomena to the Samaritan Pentateuch." *HTR* 57 (1965): 434-464.
[2300].

3455. —————. Prolegomena to the Samaritan Pentateuch. (Ph.D.) Cambridge, Mass.: Harvard University, 1965. University Microfilms.
[2300].

3456. —————. "The Samaritan Pentateuch and the Old Testament." In **J. B. Payne**, editor, *New Perspectives on the Old Testament.* Waco, Texas: Word Press, 1970. 212-239.
[2300].

3457. **Walton, Brian.** *Dissertatio in qua de linguis orientalibus...Samaritana.* Daventriae: Johannis Colombii, 1658.
[2300/ 2600].

3458. —————. *Introductio ad Lectionem Linguarum Orientalium.* London: Thomas Roycroft, 1655.
[2300/ 2600].

3459. **Walton, Brian, Edmund Castell and John Lightfoot.** "Animadversiones Samariticae.Textum hebraeum et samaritanum." In *Biblia Polyglotta Complectentia Textus Originales: Hebraicum cum Pentateucho Samaritano etc.* London, 1653-1657. Vol.6 (1657).
[2300].

3460. **Wankowicz, M. K.** "Passover on the Mountain: The Samaritans Celebrate the Festival." *Commentary* 15 (1953): 396-400.
[1404].

3461. **Wansbrough, J.** Reviewer. **J. S. Isser,** "The Dositheans." *BSOAS* 40 (1977): 604-605.
[107/ 1503].

3462. —————. Reviewer. **S. Lowy,** "Principles of Samaritan Bible Exegesis." *BSOAS* 42 (1979): 142.
[107/ 2305].

3463. **Warren, Charles.** *Underground Jerusalem.* London, 1876. Chapter 10: 206-235. [Warren had considerable contact with the Samaritans and is mentioned in their modern chronicles].
[308/ 801].

3464. **Watson, W. Scott.** "A Samaritan Manuscript of the Hebrew Pentateuch Written in AH 35." *JAOS* 20 (1899): 173-179.
[103/ 2300].

3465. —————. "A Critical Copy of the Samaritan Pentateuch Written in AD 1232." *Hebraica* 9-10 (1893-1894). 9:216-225, 10:122-158. [Also printed in the *Presbyterian and Reformed Review* (1893) 656-662].
[103/ 2300].

3466. **Wattenbach, W.** "Fausse correspondance du Sultan avec Clement 1." *AOL* 2 (1884): 297-303.
[810].

3467. **Waylen, Hector.** "The Samaritans." *New Church Magazine* (January, 1927): 47-53.
[200].

3468. **Wedel, Gerhard.** "Aspekte der Etablierung des Arabischen als Literatursprache bei den Samaritern." In **Maria Macuch, Christa Müller-Kessler and Bert G. Fragner,** editors, *Studia Semitica necnon iranica. Rudolpho Macuch septuagenario ab amicis et discipulis dedicata.* Wiesbaden: Harrassowitz, 1989. 397-407.
[2700].

3469. ————. "Das Kitâb at-Tabbah (KT) des Samaritaners Abu l-Hasan as-Suri." In **F. Dexinger and R. Pummer,** eds., *Die Samaritaner.* Darmstadt: Wissenschaftliche Buchgesellschaft, 1992. 428-430.
[2202].

3470. ————. "Ehehindernisse bei den Samaritern. Ergebnisse aus der Arbeit an der Edition des Kitab at-Tabbah von Abu'l-Hasan as-Suri (AH)." In **Einer von Schuler,** editor, *XXIII Deutscher Orientalistentag vom 16 bis 20 September 1985 in Würzburg. Ausgewählte Vorträge.* ZDMG Supplement VII. Stuttgart: Franz Steiner Verlag, Wiesbaden AG, 1989. 28-37.
[2202].

3471. ————. *Kitab at Tabbah des Samaritaners Abu'l-Hasan as-Suri ; Kritische Edition und Kommentierte Übersetzung der ersten Teils.* Berlin: Fachbereich Altertumswissenschaften der Freien Universität Berlin, 1987.
[2202].

3472. ————. "Kitab at-Tabbah of Abu'l-Hasan as-Suri." In **A. D. Crown,** editor, *The Samaritans.* Tübingen: Mohr, 1989. 468-480.
[2202].

3473. ————. "Samaritanische Uminterpretation der Anthropomorphismen im Pentateuch." In **Werner Diem and Abdoldjavad Falaturi,** editors, *XXIV Deutscher Orientalistentag vom 26 bis 30 September 1985 in Koln Ausgewählte Vorträge.* ZDMG Supplement VIII. Stuttgart: Franz Steiner Verlag, 1990. 46-54.
[2305].

3474. ————. "Abu l-Hasan as-Suri's Kitab at-Tabbah." In **A. Tal & M. Florentin,** editors, *Proceedings of the First International Congress of the Société d'Études Samaritaines.* Tel Aviv: Chaim Rosenberg School for Jewish Studies, University of Tel Aviv, 1991. 305-314.
[2202].

3475. **Weemes, John.** *The Christian Synagogue with the Customs of the Hebrews and Proselytes and of all those Nations with Whom They Were Conversant.* London, 1623. [Other editions].
[1502].

3476. —————. *Exercitations Divine...out of the Scriptures...Samaritaine...copies.* London, 1632. [Other editions]. [2300].

3477. **Wegenest, K.** "Simon (8)." *Der Kleine Pauly.* Munich, 1975. 5: 203-204. [1506.2].

3478. **Wehr, H.** *Verzeichnis der arabischen Handschriften in der Bibliothek der deutschen Morgenländischen Gesellschaft.* Leipzig: AKM, 1940. [Reprinted, Lichtenstein 1966=AKM 25]. [101/ 103].

3479. **Weijers, H. E. and P. De Jong.** *Catalogus Codicum Orientalium Bibliothecae Academiae Regiae Scientiarum (Lugdunum Batavorum).* Leiden: Brill, 1862. 48-68. [101/ 103].

3480. **Weile, L. G.** *De Religione et Templo Samaritanorum in Monte Garizim.* København, 1735. [1100/ 1305].

3481. **Weill, J.** Reviewer. **J. A. Montgomery,** "The Samaritans." *REJ* 54 (1907): 294-295. [107/ 200].

3482. **Weinfeld, Moshe.** Reviewer. "On J. Blenkinsopp, Gibeon and Israel; the Rôle of Gibeon and the Gibeonites in the Political and Religious History of Early Israel, 1972." *IEJ* 26 (1976): 126-132. [801].

3483. **Weingarten, Samuel Hacohen.** "'That Man'(Jesus) was a Samaritan." (Hebrew) *Sinai* 72 (1973): 378-388. [Identifies Jesus as a Samaritan]. [1002/ 1502.1].

3484. **Weingreen, Jacob.** "Rabbinic Type Glosses in the Old Testament." *JSS* 11 (1957): 149-162. [Reprinted in *From Bible to Mishna*, Manchester, 1976]. [2300].

3485. **Weis, P. R.** "Abu'l Hasan al-Suri's Discourse on the Calendar in the Kitab al-Tabbakh, Rylands Samaritan Codex IX." *BJRL* 30 (1946-47): 146-156. [1400/ 2202].

3486. —————. "Abu'l Hasan al-Suri's Discourse on the Rules of Leprosy in the Kitab al-Tabbakh, Rylands Samaritan Codex IX." *BJRL* 33 (1950-51): 131-137. [1109/ 2202].

3487. —————. "Some Samaritanisms of Justin Martyr." *JTS* 45 (1944): 199-205. [1003.1/ 1502].

3488. **Weiss, H. F.** Reviewer. **J. Macdonald,** "Memar Marqah." *OLZ* 61 (1966): 468-472. [107/ 1803].

3489. **Weiss, J.** *The History of Primitive Christianity.* New York, 1937. [Completed by R.Knopf].
[807].

3490. **Weiss, M.** (Hebrew) *Hamiqra Kidmuto.* Jerusalem, 1962.
[2300].

3491. **Weiss, Raphael.** "Concerning one Type of Revision in the Samaritan Pentateuch." In **M. E. Stone,** editor, *Armenian and Biblical Studies.* Jerusalem: St James Press, 1976. 157-164.
[2300].

3492. —————. Reviewer. "L. A. Mayer's Bibliography of the Samaritans." (Hebrew) *Tarbiz* 35 (1965-66): 400-403.
[100/ 107].

3493. —————. "Mt. Gerizim v. Jerusalem." (Hebrew) *Yediot Aharonot* (29/3/63): 12.
[406/ 2205].

3494. —————. "The Samaritan Pentateuch." In *Problems of the Pentateuch: Study Aids on the Samaritan Pentateuch.* Jerusalem: Academon, 1972. 15-37.
[2300].

3495. —————. "The Samaritan Pentateuch." (Hebrew) in *Mishut Bemiqra.* Jerusalem: Rabinowitz, 1976. 317-331.
[2300].

3496. —————. "Samaritan Publications." (Hebrew) *Lamerhav* (14/2/65): 2.
[105/ 106].

3497. —————. "The Samaritan Torah." (Hebrew) *Herut* (16/2/62): 6f.
[2300].

3498. —————. Reviewer. "The Samaritan Version." (Hebrew) *Lamerhav* (18/6/65): 10. [A review of the work of the Tsedaka brothers].
[107/ 2300].

3499. —————. "The Samaritan Version of the Pentateuch." (Hebrew) *Ha'aretz* (7/8/64): 10,13.
[2300].

3500. —————. Reviewer. "The Samaritan Version of Exodus." (Hebrew) *Haboker* (10/7/64): 10. [A review of the edition by the Tsedaka brothers].
[107/ 2300].

3501. —————. (Hebrew) *A Selected Bibliography of the Samaritans.* 28pp. Jerusalem: Academon, Hebrew University, 1969. [2nd edn. 1970, 3rd edn. 1973-4].
[100].

3502. —————. (Hebrew) *Studies in the Text and Language of the Bible.* Jerusalem, 1981.
[2300/ 2600].

3503. —————. "Supplements to the Samaritan Bibliography." *AION* 35 (1975): 265-273.
[100].

3504. —————. "Variants in the Barberini MS of the Samaritan Pentateuch." (Hebrew) *Leshonenu* 39 (1975): 41-51.
[103/ 2300].

3505. **Weiss, Raphael (under the pen name of Avi-Ailat.)** Reviewer. "The Pentateuch from Mt. Gerizim." (Hebrew) *Yediot Aharonot* (8/1/65): [A review of the edition of Leviticus by the Tsedaka brothers].
[107/ 2300].

3506. **Weiss, Raphael (Under the pen name R.E.)** Reviewer. "The Tsedaka Edition of the Samaritan Pentateuch." (Hebrew) *Herut* (19/11/65): 5.
[107/ 2300].

3507. **Weissenberg, J.** "Die autochthone Bevölkerung Palästinas anthropologischer Beziehung (Fellachen, Juden, Samaritaner)." *Zeitschrift für Demographie und Statistik der Jüden* 5 (1909): 129-139.
[2901].

3508. —————. "Die Samaritaner." *Ost und West* 13 (1913): 679-690. [Illustrated].
[102/ 200].

3509. —————. "Die syrischen Juden in anthropologischer betrachtet." *Zeitschrift für Ethnologie* 43 (1911): 80-90.
[2901].

3510. **Wellhausen, J.** Reviewer. L. Wreschner, "Samaritanische Traditionen." *DL* 9 (1888): 50.
[107/ 1100/ 1200].

3511. **Wenning, Robert and Erich Zenger.** "Ein bäuerliches Baal-Heiligtum im samarischen Gebirge aus der Zeit der Anfänge Israel, Erwägungen zu dem von A. Mazar zwischen Dotan und Tirza entdeckten 'Bull Site'." *ZDPV* 102 (1986): 75-86.
[801].

3512. **Wernberg-Møller, Prében.** Reviewer. H.Kippenberg, "Garizim und Synagoge." *JJS* 23 (1972): 90-92.
[107/ 805/ 1003.1].

3513. —————. Reviewer. **R. J. Coggins,** "Samaritans and Jews." *JJS* 28.20 (1977): 203.
[107/ 801].

3514. —————. Reviewer. **F. Pérez-Castro,** "Sefer Abisa." *JSS* 6-7 (1961): 130-137.
[107/ 2301].

3515. **Westergaard, Niels L.** *Codices orientales Bibliothecae Regiae Havniensis.* Havniae, 1846. Part 3.
[101].

3516. **Weston, Stephen.** "Description of a Very Rare Samaritan Coin Struck at Acoth
Segol." *Archaeologia* 16 (1812): 276f. [Plate 14.4.Coin of Antigonus *Kohen
Gadol*, misread].
[603].

3517. **Weymar, Daniel.** *Decalogus ex fonte Hebraeo et rivulo Samaritano cum versione
Latina...translatus.* Jenae, 1680.
[1103].

3518. **Whaley, Ernest B.** Samaria and the Samaritans in Josephus'Antiquities 1-11.
(Ph.D. thesis) Emory University, 1989.
[303.5].

3519. **Whiston, William.** *An essay...the Text of the Old Testament to which is Subjoined a
Large Appendix containing 1, the variations of the Samaritan Pentateuch from
the Hebrew.* London, 1722.
[2300].

3520. **White, L. M.** "The Delos Synagogue Revisited: Recent Fieldwork in the Greco-
Roman Diaspora." *HTR* 80.2 (1987): 133-160.
[504/ 2507].

3521. **White, Richard.** Reviewer. **Alan D. Crown,** "Bibliography of the Samaritans."
JJS 36.1 (1985): 141.
[100/ 107].

3522. ————. Reviewer. **J. Cohen,** "A Samaritan Chronicle." *JJS* 36.1 (1985): 124-
125.
[107/ 1603/ 3003].

3523. ————. Reviewer. **A. Broadie,** "A Samaritan Philosophy." *JJS* 36.1 (1985):
125-126.
[107/ 1803].

3524. **White, Sidnie Ann.** A Critical Edition of Seven Manuscripts of Deuteronomy:
4QDT (A, C, D, F, G, I & N) Dead Sea Scrolls. (Ph.D.) Harvard: Harvard
University, 1988.
[2307/ 2501.1].

3525. **Whiting, J. D.** "The Last Israelitish Blood Sacrifice. How the Vanishing
Samaritans Celebrate the Passover on Sacred Mount Gerizim." *National
Geographic Magazine* 37 (January, 1920): 1-46. [Illustrated].
[102/ 1404].

3526. ————. *Samaritanernas påskfest i ord och bild. Bibliska blodsofer i våra dagar.*
Stockholm, 1917.
[102/ 1404].

3527. **Wichmannshausen, Joannes C.** *Diatribe Philologia de Nergal Cuthaeorum.*
Wittenberg, 1707.
[801.1/ 1110].

3528. —————. *Dissertatio de Portu Kittureorum*. Wittenberg, 1708.
[801.1].

3529. **Wickersheimer, C. A. Ernest.** *Catalogue général des manuscrits des bibliothèques publiques de France.Départements, vol. 47, Strasbourg.* Paris, 1923.
[101/ 103].

3530. **Widengren, Geo.** "The Ascension of the Apostle and the Heavenly King." In *King and Saviour*. Uppsala Universitets Årsskrift 7. Uppsala-Leipzig: Harrassowitz, 1950. 3:
[1506.2/ 3004].

3531. —————. "The Samaritan Schism and the Construction of the Samaritan Temple." In J. H. Hayes and J. Maxwell Miller, eds., *Israelite and Judaean History*. Philadelphia: SCM Press, 1977. 511-514.
[801.1/ 802.1/ 1305].

3532. **Wiener, Harold M.** "Samaritan Septuagint Massoretic Text." *The Expositor* 9.8th series (1911): 200-219.
[2309/ 2400].

3533. **Wiet, Gaston,** editor. *Ya'kubi, Les pays*. Cairo, 1937. 180-183.
[307/ 307.1].

3534. **Wiet, Gaston and J. H. Kramers,** editors. *Ibn Hauqal; Kitab Surat al Ard (=Configuration of the earth)*. Paris, 1964. 1.
[307/ 307.1].

3535. **Wilkinson, Frank H.** "Oded: The Prototype of the Good Samaritan." *ET* 69 (1957): 94f.
[1502.3].

3536. **Wilkinson, John.** *Jerusalem Pilgrims Before the Crusades*. Warminster: Aris and Phillips, 1977.
[306.2].

3537. **Willemerus, J. A.** *Positiones Philologicae de Creatione Mundi Samaritanum Pentateuchi Textum*. Wittenberg: Mattaei Henckeli, 1677.
[105/ 2300/ 2305].

3538. **Williams, M. A.** Reviewer. J. Fossum, "Name of God and the Angel of the Lord." *JBL* 107.1 (1988): 153-156.
[107/ 1101].

3539. **Williams, R. B.** Reviewer. J. Macdonald, "Theology of the Samaritans." *Journal of Religion* 46 (1966): 404.
[107/ 1100].

3540. **Williamson, G. A.,** translator. *Procopius, The Secret History*. London: Pelican Books, 1966.
[305.4].

3541. **Williamson, H. G. M.** "The Historical Value of Josephus' Jewish Antiquities XI, 297-301." *JTS* 28.New series (1977): 49-66.
[303.5].

3542. —————. "Samaritans." In *Illustrated Bible Dictionary.* Leicester, Illinois and Sydney, 1980. 3: 1378-1381.
[201].

3543. **Wilson, C. W.** "Ebal and Gerizim, 1866." *PEFQS* (1873): 66-71.
[1404].

3544. —————. "Samaria." In **J. D. Hastings,** *A Dictionary of the Bible.* Edinburgh: T. & T. Clark, 1902. 4: [Various impressions].
[201/ 410].

3545. **Wilson, Col.** *Picturesque Palestine, Sinai and Egypt.* London, 1820. [Vol. 1 pp. 233-238].
[308].

3546. **Wilson, John.** *The Lands of the Bible Visited and Described.* Edinburgh, 1847. 2: 45-79; 687-701.
[308/ 401].

3547. **Wilson, R. McL.** Reviewer. J. Fossum, "The Name of God and the Angel of the Lord." *ET* 97.7 (April, 1986): 214b-215a.
[107/ 1101].

3548. —————. "Simon, Dositheus and the Dead Sea Scrolls." *ZRGG* 9 (1957): 21-30.
[1005/ 1506.2/ 3004].

3549. **Wilson, Robert D.** Reviewer. J. H. Petermann & K. Vollers, "Pentateuchus Samaritanus." *Presbyterian and Reform Review* (1892): 199.
[107/ 2300].

3550. **Wilson, W. D.** "The Date of the Samaritan Pentateuch." *Thinker* 1.5 (1892): 385.
[2300].

3551. **Winckler, H.** "Nehemiah's Reform." *Altorientalische Forschungen* 2 (1898-1901): 228-236.
[802.1].

3552. **Winer, Georg Benedict.** "Samaritaner." In *Biblisches realwörterbuch zum Handgebrauch für Studierende.* 3rd edn. Leipzig: F.C.Vogel, 1847-8.
[201].

3553. —————. *De versionis Pentateuchi Samaritanae indole dissertatio critico-exegetica.* Leipzig, 1817.
[2300].

3554. **Winkler, Sabine.** Die Samaritaner unter Justinian.Humboldt University: 1973.
[808/ 808.1].

3555. —————. "Die Samariter in den Jahren 520-530." *Klio* 43-45 (1965): 435-457.
[808.1].

3556. **Wintner, I., R. Felix and H. Bar Joseph.** "A Psychological Comparative Study of
the Samaritan Community Shechem (Nablus) and Holon." *IAP* 9 (1971): 117-
131. [Part II. See 937 in the first edition of the bibliography].
[903/ 2900].

3557. **Wirth, Albrecht.** *Aus orientalischen Chroniken.* Frankfurt, 1894.
[700].

3558. **Wise, Michael.** Reviewer. **Judith E. Sanderson,** "An Exodus Scroll from
Qumran: 4Qpaleo-Exod^m and the Samaritan Tradition." *JNES* 49.2 (1990):
195-196.
[107/2307].

3559. **Wits, Hermann.** *Aegyptica.* Amsterdam, 1671.
[2300].

3560. **Wokenius, Francis.** *Disputatio philologico-critica de utilitate novae Pentateuchi
Samaritanae editionis. Quam defendet Ioh. Godofr. Mullerus.* Wittenberg, 1728.
[2300].

3561. —————. *Dissertatio Critica de Samaritanismo et Hebraismo justinim Quam
preside Francisco Wokenio...disputationi subjiciet Johannes Rehlingius.*
Wittenberg, 1729.
[2300/ 2600].

3562. **Wolf, J. C.** *Bibliotheca Hebraea.* Hamburg, 1715-1733. 4 vols.
[2300].

3563. **Wood, L. E.** "A Samaritan Passover Manuscript." *JBL* 40 (1921): 159-161. [Forbes
Library, Northampton, Mass. A manuscript of 1735, now missing].
[103].

3564. **Wowern, Johann von,** editor. "Symmacho Samaritano." In *Syntagma der Graeca
et Latina Bibliorum interpretatione.* Chapter 11, Hamburg, 1618. [Reprinted,
1658].
[2309/ 2400].

3565. **Wreschner, Leopold.** Samaritanische Traditionen.(Ph.D.) Berlin: University of
Halle, 1888. [Reprinted, Berlin, 1888 as *Samaritanische Traditionen, mitgeteilt
und nach ihrer geschichtlichen Entwickelung untersucht*].
[1000/ 1100].

3566. **Wright, G. E.** "1600 Years of Shechem and Its Pillars of the Covenant." *ILN*
August 10 (1963): 204-207. [Figs. 1-27].
[412/ 600/ 801].

3567. —————. "The First Campaign at Tell Balâtah (Shechem)." *BASOR* 144
(1956): 9-20. Figs. 1-6.
[412/ 600].

3568. ——————. "The 'Granary' at Shechem and the Underlying Storage Pits." *ZAW*
82 (1970): 275-278.
[412/ 600].

3569. ——————. "Israelite Samaria and Iron Age Chronology." *BASOR* (1959): 13-19.
[410].

3570. ——————. "The Place Name Balatah and the Excavations at Shechem." *ZDPV*
83 (1967): 199-202.
[412/ 600].

3571. ——————. "Samaria." *BA* (1959): 67-78.
[410].

3572. ——————. "The Samaritans at Shechem." *HTR* 55 (1962): 357-366.
[Reprinted in Dexinger and Pummer, *Die Samaritaner*, 263-273].
[412/ 801].

3573. ——————. "The Second Campaign at Tell Balâtah (Shechem)." *BASOR* 148
(1957): 11-28. Figs. 1-5.
[412/ 600].

3574. ——————. "Selected Seals from the Excavations at Tell Balatâh (Shechem)."
BASOR 167 (1962): 5-13.
[412/ 607].

3575. ——————. "Shechem." *BA* 20 (1957): 2-32. Figs. 1-10.
[412/ 600].

3576. ——————. "Shechem." In **D. Winton-Thomas,** *Archaeology and Old Testament
Study.* Oxford: OUP, 1967. 335-337.
[412/ 600/ 801].

3577. ——————. "Shechem." (Hebrew) *EAEHL* (1975): 539-545. English version
1978 edn., vol.4. 1083-1094.
[412].

3578. ——————. "Shechem (Tell Balatah)." In **C. F. Pfeiffer,** editor, *The Biblical
World. A Dictionary of Biblical Archaeology.* Grand Rapids, Michigan: Baker
Book House, 1966. 518-522.
[412/ 600/ 801].

3579. ——————. *Shechem: The Biography of a Biblical City.* New York and Toronto:
McGraw-Hill, 1965.
[412/ 600/ 801].

3580. **Wright, G. R. H.** "Another Fluted Column Fragment from Bronze-Age
Shechem." *PEQ* (1969): 34-36.
[412/ 600].

3581. ——————. "The Architectural Recording of the Shechem Excavation." *BA* 23
(1960): 120-126.
[412/ 600].

3582. —————. "The City Gates at Shechem; Simple Reconstruction Drawings." *ZDPV* 10.1 (1985): 1-8.
[412/ 600].

3583. —————. "An Egyptian God at Shechem." *ZDPV* 99 (1983): 99-109.
[412/ 600].

3584. —————. "Fluted Columns in the Bronze-Age Temple of Baal-Berith at Shechem." *PEQ* (1965): 66-84.
[412/ 600].

3585. —————. "Temples at Shechem." *ZAW* 80.1 (1968): 1-35.
[412/ 600/ 1305].

3586. Wright, Thomas, editor. "The Journeys of Henry Maundrell from Aleppo to Jerusalem." In *Early Travels in Palestine*. London: Henry Bohn, 1848. 383-506.
[306.3].

3587. —————. "The Travels of Bertrandon de la Brocquière." In *Early Travels in Palestine*. London: Henry Bohn, 1848. 282-382.
[306.3].

3588. Wright, William Aldiss. "Untitled note concerning a fragment of the Samaritan Targum." *JA* 15.6th series (1870): 525-526.
[2401].

3589. —————. "Untitled note concerning a Samaritan tablet at Leeds—from Nablus." *PSBA* 6 (1883-4): 25-26. 1 plate.
[2504].

3590. Wright, William Aldiss and S. M. Schiller-Szinessy. *A Descriptive List of the Arabic, Persian and Turkish Manuscripts in the Library of Trinity College, Cambridge, with an Appendix Containing a Catalogue of the Hebrew and Samaritan Manuscripts in the Same Library*. Cambridge: Cambridge University, 1872.
[101/ 103].

3591. Würthwein, Ernst. *The Text of the Old Testament*. Oxford: Blackwell, 1957. [Various German editions and printings; English version reprinted, 1980].
[2300].

3592. Würzburg, John of. Aubrey Stewart, editor, *Description of the Holy Land*. London, 1896.
[306.2].

Y

3593. **Yaʻari, Abraham.** *Igrot Eretz Yisrael.* Tel Aviv: Gazit, 1953.
[300].

3594. ———. *Masaʼot Eretz Yisrael.* Ramat Gan: Massada Press, 1976.
[300].

3595. **Yadin, Yigal.** "Ancient Jewish Weights and the Date of the Samaria Ostraca."
Scripta Hierosolymitana (1961): 25-29.
[600].

3596. **Yafet Hassanin, the Priest.** *Hashomronim Vehageihem* (= *The Samaritans and Their
Festivals.* Nablus, 1968.
[1400].

3597. **Yahuda, Abraham S.** "Eine Bemerkung über das Alter der Thorarolle des
Abischa." *SPAW* 39 (1908): 913-914.
[2301].

3598. ———. "Über die Unechtheit des samaritanischen Josua-buches." *SPAW* 39
(1908): 887-914. [Reprinted in *Die Welt* 45 (1908)].
[1604/ 1605].

3599. ———. "Zum samaritanischen Josua. Eine Erklärung." *ZDMG* 62 (1908):
754.
[1604/ 1605].

3600. **Yahya, Gedaliah ibn.** (Hebrew) *Sefer Shalshelet Haqabalah.* Warsaw, 1877. [Other
editions].
[801/ 1305].

3601. **Yamauchi, E. M.** *Pre-Christian Gnosticism. A Survey of Proposed Evidences.* Grand
Rapids, Michigan: Eerdmans, 1973. 58-65.
[1506].

3602. **Yaron, Joseph.** Samuel Cohen's Contribution to Samaritan Lexicography.
(Hebrew) Jerusalem: Hebrew University, 1976. Doctoral thesis.
[2603].

3603. **Yehoshua, Sh et al.** *Pesach in Beit El.* Holon, 1972. 44pp.
[1404].

3604. **Yehudi, Adv Prem Doss Swami Doss.** *The Samaritans of Israel.* 99 pp.+ v Kerala:
Sachethana, 1991.
[200].

3605. **Yeivin (Yevin), Z.** "Archaeological Activities in Samaria." (Hebrew) in *Eretz
Shomron.* Jerusalem: IES, 1973. 147-162. [Sebastiyeh, Askar].
[410/ 600].

3606. ———. "Kh. Askar (communication)." *RB* 81 (1974): 97-98.
[413].

3607. **Yellin, David.** "Ein Sabbath im Hause des samaritanischen Hohenpriesters."
Hashiloah 25 (1911): 507-515.
[903/ 1405].

3608. ———. (Hebrew) *Hashomronim: Heker Divre Yemeihem, Sifrutam,
Emunatam, Minhageihem, Umatzaveihem Beyameinu Eileh (= The Samaritans
etc).* Jerusalem: Private publication, 1908. [20 pp. The Annenberg Research
Center copy is bound with idem, *Midivrei Yemei Hashomronim*, 11 pp.].
[200].

3609. ———. "Letters." (Hebrew) in **I. Klausner,** editor, *The Writings of David
Yellin.* Jerusalem: Reuben Mass, 1975-1976. 4: 219-373, 5: 353-372:
[411/ 903].

3610. **Yerushalmi, Moses.** "The Travels of Moses Yerushalmi." (Hebrew) in **A. Ya'ari,**
editor, *Travellers to the Holy Land.* Ramat Gan, 1976. 424-458.
[304.4].

3611. **Yonick, Stephen.** "The Samaritan Inscription from Siyagha: A Reconstruction and
Restudy." *Liber Annuus* 17 (1967): 162-221.
[2511].

3612. **Young, Norman H.** "The Commandment to Love Your Neighbour as Yourself
and the Parable of the Good Samaritan (Luke 10:25-37)." *Andrews University
Seminary Studies* 21.3 (1983): 265-272.
[1502.3].

3613. ———. "Once Again 'Now, Who Is My Neighbour?' (A Comment)." *EQ* 49
(1977): 178-179.
[1502.4].

3614. **Young, Robert.** *Complete Paradigms of the Samaritan Verbs, Regular and Irregular.*
Edinburgh, 1855.
[2602].

3615. ———. *Samaritan Wordbook or the Principal Words in the Samaritan Version
of the Pentateuch in Alphabetical Order, with English Explanations.* Edinburgh,
1855. 34 pp.
[2300/ 2603].

3616. ———. *Song of a Finlandian Country Girl in the Original Finnish, with Literal
Translations into the Hebrew-Samaritan and Chaldee-Samaritan languages.*
Edinburgh, 1854.
[2600].

3617. ———. *Toledot 'Adam. The Hexaglot Pentateuch with the Corresponding
Samaritan, Chaldaic, Syriac and Arabic.* Edinburgh, 1852.
[2300].

3618. **Younovitch, R.** "Étude sérologique des juifs samaritains." *Comptes Rendus de la Société de Biologie* 112 (1933): 970-971.
[2901/ 3500].

3619. **Youtie, Herbert C. et al.** *Tax Rolls from Karanis.* (Michigan Papyri, vol. 4) Ann Arbor: University of Michigan, 1936. [Nos. 223, 224].
[303.2].

Z

3620. **Zachariae, Just Friederich W.** *Sive de Samaritanis eorumque templo in monte Garizim aedificato...dissertatio.* Jenae, 1723.
[1305].

3621. **Zacharias Scholasticus, Bishop of Mitylene. F. J. Hamilton,** translator, *Ecclesiastical History of Zacharias Rhetor...translated from the Syriac.* London?: Private publication, 1892. [British Library].
[305.6].

3622. **Zacuto, A.** (Hebrew) *Sefer Yuchasin.* Zhitomir, 1861. [Other editions. Knows of and quotes the Arabic Book of Joshua].
[1604].

3623. **Zadok, R.** "Samaritan Notes." *BO* 5-6 (1985): 567-572.
[200].

3624. **Zafrani, Haïm.** "Langues juives du Maroc et traductions judéo-arabes de la Bible." In **Rothschild and Sixdenier,** editors, *Études samaritaines.* Louvain-Paris, 1988. 219-234.
[2600/ 2700].

3625. **Zayadine, F.** "Early Hellenistic Pottery from the Theatre Excavations at Samaria." *ADAJ* 11 (1966): 53-64. [Fig.1. Plates 27-31].
[410/ 600/ 606.1].

3626. —————. "Samaria—Sebaste, Clearance and Excavations (October 1965-June 1967)." *ADAJ* 12-13 (1967-68): 70-80. [Plates 50-53].
[410/ 600].

3627. —————. "La Samarie, héllenistique et romaine. Samarie." *BTS* 121 (1970): 3-14.
[410/ 600/ 804].

3628. —————. "Une tombe du Fer II à Samaria—Sébaste." *RB* 75 (1968): 562-585. [9 figs. Plates 55-63].
[410/ 600].

3629. **Zedler, Johann H.** "Samaria." In *Grosser Vollständiges Universal Lexicon.* Leipzig & Halle, 1742. 33: 1630-1644. [Reprinted, Gräz, 1961 with the name changed to *Grosses...*].
[201/ 410].

3630. **Zeitlin, Solomon.** *The Rise and Fall of the Judaean State.* Philadelphia: JPSA, 1962. 1-33.
[801.1].

3631. —————. "The Tobias Family and the Hasmonaeans." *AAJR* 4 (1933): 169-223. [Especially the appendix, "Sanballat and the Samaritans?"].
[802.1].

3632. **Zeligman, Y. A.** "Researches in the History of the Bible Versions." (Hebrew) *Tarbiz* 25 (1956): 118-139.
[2300].

3633. **Zeron, A.** "Einige Bemerkungen zu M. F. Collins, 'The Hidden Vessels in Samaritan Tradition'." *JSJ* 4.2 (1973): 165-168.
[806/ 1800].

3634. **Zertal, Adam.** "Ayin Kushi and the Cities of the Route." *A-B* 212 (1977): 14-21.
[400].

3635. —————. "Eight Seasons of Excavation at Mt. Ebal." *Qadmoniot* 23.1-2 (1990): 42-50.
[600].

3636. —————. "Mount Ebal." *IEJ* 34.1 (1984): 55.
[404].

3637. —————. "Relationships Between the Samaritans and the Jews in the Byzantine Period." (Hebrew) *A–B* 249-250 (1979): 49-52.
[808/ 1003.4].

3638. —————. "A Samaritan Ring and the Identification of 'Ain Kushi'." (Hebrew) *Qadmoniyot* 10.2-3 (1977): 84-86. [See Loewenstamm].
[601/ 606.1].

3639. —————. "The Samaritans in the District of Caesarea." *Ariel* 48 (1979): 98-116. [Reprinted in the *Israel Yearbook* (1980) 173-183].
[403.1].

3640. —————. "The Wedge Decorated Bowl and the Origin of the Cutheans." (Hebrew) *Eretz Israel* 20 (1989): 181-187. English summary p. 200*.
[606.1/801.1].

3641. —————. "The Wedge-shape Decorated Bowl and the Origin of the Samaritans." *BASOR* 276 (1989): 77-84.
[606.1/801.1].

3642. **Zetterstéen, Karl V.** "Die arabischen, persischen und türkischen Handschriften der universitätsbibliothek zu Uppsala. Katalog nebst einem Anhang, hebräische, syrische und samaritanische Handschriften enthaltend." *Le Monde Oriental.* Uppsala: Acta Bibliothecae R. Universitatis Upsaliensis, 1928. 22: I-XVIII, 1-498. [Various printings after 1930].
[101].

3643. **Ziegler, J.** "Pentateuch, Samaritanischer." *Lexicon.* 8: 265-266.
[2300].

3644. **Zimmerman, H.** "Das Gleichnis vom barmherzigen Samariter; Lk.10, 25-37." In **G. Bornkamm and K. Rahner,** editors, *Die Zeit Jesus. Festschrift für Heinrich Schlier.* Freiburg, 1970. 58-69.
[1502.3].

3645. **Zimmerman, J.** "The Samaritan Passover." *Records of the Past* 9 (May, 1910): 130-153.
[1404].

3646. **Zimmerman, J. D.** Reviewer. **J. Macdonald,** "The Theology of the Samaritans." *ATR* 47 (1965): 299-302.
[107/ 1100].

3647. **Zonaras, John.** "Annals." *PG.* 134: 107-110, 203-206, 211-214, 319-330, 500-506.
[305.4].

3648. **Zorell, F.** "De 'Psalterio Samaritano'." *Biblica* 5 (1924): 205-206.
[2100].

3649. —————. "De quodam psalterio samaritano nuper invento." *Biblica* 5 (1924): 73-76.
[2100].

3650. **Zori /Zimbalist, Nehemiah.** "The Ancient Synagogue at Beth-Shean." *EI* 8 (1967): 149-167.
[1304].

3651. —————. "A Lamp with a Samaritan Inscription." *Yediot* 18 (1953): 270-271.
[605/ 2500].

3652. **Zorn, Walter D.** Mark and the Samaritans. (Ph.D.) East Lansing: Michigan State University, 1983.
[1003.1/1502].

3653. **Zotenberg, Hermann.** *Manuscrits orientaux. Catalogue des manuscrits hébreux et samaritains de la Bibliothèque Impériale.* Paris, 1866.
[101].

KEY TO THE SUBJECT INDEX

The reader is advised to consult this key to note
the general area of concern before using the
detailed index. Each broad heading is sub-
classified in the index itself.

2003	-Kleodemus Malchos
2004	-Pseudo-Eupolemos
2005	-Theodotus
2006	-Melchizedek
2007	-Other works
2100	Liturgy, poetry and belles lettres
2101	-Belles lettres
2102	Daily prayers, Sabbath and festival prayers
2102.1	-Defter
2102.2	-Durran
2103	-Rites of passage
2104	-Sabbath Prayers
2200	Religious writings and codes: general
2201	-Hillukh
2202	-Kitab at-Tabbakh
2203	-Kitab al-Kafi
2203.1	-Kitab al-Khilaf
2204	-Kitab al-Mirath
2205	-Polemics and apologetics
2206	-Malef
2207	-Sefer Hayerushot
2300	PENTATEUCH VERSIONS , COMMENTARIES AND EXEGESIS
2301	-Abisha scroll
2302	Arabic versions
2304	Commentaries
2305	Exegesis
2306.1	Massorah
2307	Proto-Samaritan texts -Qumran
2308	Reading of the Pentateuch
2309	Samariticon
2309.1	Pentateuch scrolls
2400	Septuagint
2400.1	Origen's Hexapla
2401	Targum
2500	INSCRIPTIONS AND PALAEOGRAPHY
2501	Epigraphy and script
2501.1	Palaeography
2502	-Amwas/Emmaus
2503	-Beit el-Ma
2503.1	-Beth Shean
2504	-Decalogue
2505	-es Sindiane
2506	-Damascus
2507	-Delos
2508	-Gaza
2508.1	-Gerizim
2509	-Kfar Bilu
2510	-Kafr Khalil

SUBJECT INDEX

<u>**100   BIBLIOGRAPHY**</u>

94, 112, 167, 209, 306, 571, 573, 724, 747, 796, 1386, 1397, 1398, 1477,
1576, 1583, 1641, 1814, 1879, 1887, 1897, 1912, 1913, 2139, 2140, 2141,
2144, 2159, 2172, 2217, 2321, 2326, 2425, 2514, 2796, 2856, 2875, 3016,
3349, 3393, 3395, 3428, 3492, 3501, 3503, 3521

101   Catalogues

2, 24, 39, 41, 42, 43, 44, 84, 161, 162, 183, 307, 308, 420, 426, 464, 584, 585,
672, 674, 675, 682, 703, 872, 873, 903, 981, 983, 994, 1092, 1128, 1326,
1360, 1402, 1529, 1530, 1583, 1647, 1708, 1762, 1767, 1830, 2003, 2005,
2086, 2114, 2142, 2184, 2241, 2244, 2251, 2297, 2318, 2350, 2394, 2395,
2399, 2415, 2416, 2493, 2498, 2512, 2513, 2526, 2538, 2576, 2656, 2657,
2681, 2722, 2724, 2725, 2727, 2741, 2744, 2762, 2768, 2783, 2786, 2789,
2793, 2794, 2795, 2796, 2851, 2852, 2916, 2926, 2976, 2996, 3076, 3191,
3270, 3366, 3411, 3430, 3432, 3478, 3479, 3515, 3529, 3590, 3642, 3653

102   Illustrations (pictures)

1192, 1225, 1868, 1927, 1947, 1993, 2021, 2038, 2126, 2629, 2755, 2761,
2763, 2874, 2973, 3032, 3135, 3508, 3525, 3526

103   Manuscripts

2, 24, 39, 41, 42, 43, 44, 68, 69, 70, 75, 76, 77, 78, 84, 119, 133, 161, 162,
183, 185, 215, 223, 226, 228, 232, 250, 274, 307, 308, 319, 367, 375, 383,
397, 407, 420, 421, 426, 451, 463, 464, 505, 506, 531, 576, 584, 585, 674,
675, 683, 802, 803, 852, 857, 861, 862, 870, 872, 873, 883, 884, 885, 886,
887, 891, 893, 943, 967, 969, 972, 981, 986, 994, 1021, 1077, 1092, 1128,
1226, 1227, 1228, 1229, 1231, 1232, 1233, 1234, 1241, 1268, 1303, 1326,
1360, 1391, 1404, 1413, 1501, 1529, 1530, 1715, 1731, 1738, 1753, 1760,
1761, 1767, 1781, 1998, 1999, 2003, 2023, 2076, 2086, 2114, 2181, 2183,
2185, 2208, 2210, 2211, 2212, 2241, 2244, 2247, 2248, 2250, 2251, 2297,
2319, 2350, 2394, 2395, 2399, 2403, 2409, 2415, 2416, 2432, 2444, 2451,
2483, 2493, 2498, 2512, 2513, 2526, 2538, 2563, 2564, 2621, 2622, 2623,
2656, 2681, 2722, 2724, 2725, 2727, 2734, 2741, 2762, 2781, 2783, 2789,
2793, 2796, 2818, 2852, 2916, 2926, 2938, 2964, 2965, 2976, 2985, 2996,
3012, 3076, 3144, 3145, 3156, 3158, 3238, 3294, 3298, 3349, 3370, 3393,
3407, 3410, 3411, 3415, 3430, 3432, 3464, 3465, 3478, 3479, 3504, 3529,
3563, 3590

104   Periodicals

1117, 1120, 2187, 3291, 3313, 3328, 3329, 3358

105   Printing, publishing, typography

22, 59, 60, 89, 90, 91, 112, 143, 146, 161, 162, 194, 199, 200, 241, 258, 261,

420, 422, 423, 424, 576, 594, 624, 633, 634, 680, 711, 724, 774, 927, 937, 964, 965, 966, 1062, 1065, 1081, 1085, 1104, 1217, 1230, 1251, 1286, 1460, 1561, 1943, 1944, 1972, 2205, 2252, 2329, 2330, 2331, 2332, 2333, 2397, 2489, 2497, 2500, 2573, 2574, 2594, 2637, 2854, 2855, 2903, 2907, 2950, 2951, 3028, 3039, 3265, 3368, 3426, 3436, 3496, 3537

106   Research (as a subject)
        72, 83, 311, 312, 316, 329, 342, 350, 362, 529, 730, 958, 1579, 1738, 1897, 1912, 2057, 2427, 2431, 2440, 2557, 2608, 2611, 2617, 2618, 2657, 2752, 2787, 2796, 2814, 3496

107   Reviews
        7, 94, 95, 96, 106, 115, 119, 126, 129, 166, 183, 185, 187, 189, 190, 208, 210, 212, 216, 217, 221, 222, 227, 229, 230, 231, 243, 262, 266, 269, 270, 302, 307, 308, 317, 318, 325, 328, 338, 347, 416, 417, 418, 456, 473, 517, 562, 574, 579, 629, 642, 725, 745, 747, 748, 749, 750, 751, 753, 754, 755, 770, 776, 780, 793, 800, 803, 853, 859, 860, 873, 876, 877, 890, 918, 919, 943, 944, 959, 961, 962, 983, 984, 987, 988, 1000, 1013, 1022, 1033, 1058, 1059, 1083, 1099, 1100, 1129, 1132, 1153, 1202, 1205, 1219, 1244, 1271, 1282, 1291, 1306, 1326, 1327, 1336, 1359, 1398, 1400, 1431, 1432, 1433, 1440, 1448, 1453, 1458, 1471, 1534, 1536, 1565, 1579, 1604, 1627, 1631, 1640, 1684, 1687, 1689, 1690, 1691, 1692, 1705, 1731, 1762, 1774, 1775, 1777, 1782, 1783, 1784, 1785, 1824, 1840, 1845, 1853, 1863, 1874, 1879, 1884, 1887, 1896, 1906, 1910, 1928, 1948, 1950, 1951, 1960, 1964, 1980, 1990, 1991, 1996, 2009, 2010, 2018, 2058, 2060, 2067, 2078, 2079, 2081, 2086, 2087, 2094, 2095, 2096, 2097, 2115, 2116, 2141, 2142, 2145, 2151, 2152, 2167, 2168, 2170, 2173, 2199, 2207, 2209, 2227, 2233, 2237, 2238, 2239, 2242, 2270, 2271, 2272, 2273, 2274, 2285, 2308, 2309, 2311, 2312, 2340, 2348, 2354, 2356, 2358, 2359, 2365, 2371, 2395, 2402, 2405, 2422, 2434, 2436, 2437, 2438, 2439, 2474, 2496, 2505, 2511, 2516, 2522, 2523, 2547, 2552, 2559, 2560, 2561, 2565, 2567, 2576, 2585, 2587, 2610, 2614, 2619, 2628, 2630, 2639, 2643, 2647, 2654, 2656, 2658, 2698, 2723, 2727, 2728, 2729, 2730, 2732, 2734, 2736, 2748, 2785, 2788, 2790, 2791, 2792, 2793, 2797, 2801, 2802, 2808, 2809, 2831, 2836, 2857, 2865, 2876, 2882, 2896, 2898, 2917, 2936, 2937, 2983, 2984, 2989, 3002, 3010, 3015, 3020, 3021, 3022, 3023, 3029, 3034, 3071, 3072, 3077, 3078, 3090, 3099, 3100, 3110, 3113, 3180, 3183, 3197, 3204, 3219, 3220, 3222, 3236, 3237, 3249, 3250, 3252, 3308, 3309, 3367, 3372, 3373, 3374, 3375, 3376, 3377, 3378, 3379, 3384, 3392, 3394, 3423, 3431, 3449, 3452, 3461, 3462, 3481, 3488, 3492, 3498, 3500, 3505, 3506, 3510, 3512, 3513, 3514, 3521, 3522, 3523, 3538, 3539, 3547, 3549, 3558, 3646

108   Abstracts
        785, 838

200   GENERAL AND POPULAR WORKS
        23, 37, 54, 64, 74, 81, 82, 88, 106, 114, 116, 117, 121, 122, 123, 124, 125, 128, 134, 135, 136, 137, 138, 144, 147, 193, 209, 219, 220, 237, 239, 244, 249, 258, 259, 266, 267, 269, 270, 271, 290, 366, 373, 378, 405, 410, 411, 435, 444, 452, 466, 467, 474, 475, 476, 541, 544, 548, 549, 564, 566, 567, 596, 639, 641, 659, 685, 688, 693, 748, 755, 757, 768, 769, 778, 787, 792,

796, 799, 801, 804, 810, 836, 850, 876, 877, 878, 892, 938, 951, 962, 989,
990, 991, 996, 1000, 1013, 1033, 1038, 1042, 1043, 1044, 1068, 1087, 1172,
1192, 1197, 1205, 1221, 1262, 1263, 1271, 1288, 1312, 1314, 1316, 1318,
1324, 1328, 1340, 1344, 1346, 1377, 1392, 1405, 1419, 1431, 1433, 1434,
1448, 1449, 1450, 1454, 1456, 1473, 1492, 1497, 1532, 1534, 1556, 1563,
1567, 1573, 1594, 1597, 1602, 1610, 1626, 1627, 1640, 1646, 1663, 1684,
1694, 1696, 1701, 1703, 1716, 1719, 1733, 1738, 1754, 1755, 1756, 1776,
1788, 1804, 1805, 1824, 1826, 1846, 1851, 1879, 1883, 1891, 1892, 1896,
1938, 1939, 1952, 1965, 1979, 1990, 1991, 2006, 2021, 2022, 2046, 2080,
2096, 2097, 2119, 2125, 2126, 2163, 2170, 2179, 2239, 2245, 2275, 2278,
2279, 2282, 2292, 2310, 2312, 2313, 2314, 2317, 2339, 2343, 2352, 2359,
2373, 2389, 2393, 2405, 2406, 2412, 2414, 2428, 2430, 2447, 2450, 2453,
2481, 2523, 2536, 2547, 2566, 2567, 2604, 2615, 2631, 2633, 2641, 2666,
2702, 2706, 2719, 2723, 2763, 2775, 2777, 2792, 2814, 2817, 2829, 2838,
2891, 2894, 2898, 2913, 2941, 2949, 2993, 2998, 3021, 3022, 3056, 3065,
3082, 3100, 3117, 3135, 3168, 3169, 3174, 3175, 3176, 3179, 3182, 3197,
3229, 3230, 3265, 3266, 3278, 3279, 3281, 3314, 3368, 3379, 3384, 3397,
3408, 3423, 3440, 3467, 3481, 3508, 3604, 3608, 3623

201 Encyclopaedias
81, 82, 121, 122, 123, 124, 125, 128, 134, 135, 136, 138, 147, 290, 321, 452,
474, 550, 566, 592, 639, 643, 712, 804, 809, 810, 836, 942, 1020, 1044, 1240,
1313, 1324, 1325, 1328, 1463, 1487, 1511, 1517, 1626, 1814, 1815, 1816,
1823, 1859, 1938, 1939, 1952, 1968, 2196, 2201, 2202, 2300, 2343, 2374,
2375, 2390, 2420, 2501, 2530, 2532, 2545, 2550, 2583, 2650, 2692, 2879,
2904, 3013, 3026, 3027, 3115, 3118, 3305, 3362, 3382, 3400, 3542, 3544,
3552, 3629

202 Other surveys
81, 82, 152, 405, 558, 561, 643, 703, 755, 769, 1287, 1296, 1314, 1454, 1463,
1487, 1511, 1517, 2196, 2529, 2635

300 SOURCES

General
608, 1375, 3095, 3311, 3385, 3386, 3593, 3594

301 Biblical sources
62, 2956

302.1 Apocryphal sources
706, 1071

302.2 Pseudepigraphical sources
706

303 Hellenistic sources
1168, 1171, 3088, 3095

303.1 -Jewish sources
835, 1009, 1168, 1171, 1630, 2287

303.2   -Greek papyri
             292, 1889, 2972, 3429, 3619

303.3   -Wadi Daliyeh papyri
             826, 827, 828, 830, 831, 834, 1240, 1441, 1442, 1443, 1852, 1931, 1934,
             1935, 1936, 1937, 1962, 3396

303.4   -Latin
             10, 1018

303.5   -Josephus
             13, 20, 73, 126, 166, 178, 434, 438, 580, 603, 746, 1110, 1111, 1169, 1170,
             1400, 1484, 2131, 2132, 2214, 2422, 2614, 2919, 2920, 3088, 3094, 3518,
             3541

304   Early Jewish and Rabbinic sources
             155, 186, 398, 601, 1009, 1012, 1249, 1264, 1379, 1562, 1585, 1586, 2260,
             2262, 2263, 2264

304.1   -Mishna
             47, 155, 664

304.2   -Talmud
             155, 186, 260, 941, 1461, 1599, 1846, 1847, 1982, 1983, 1984, 2024, 2046,
             2259, 2261, 2404, 3151

304.3   -Karaite
             188, 1480

304.4   -Jewish Travellers
             25, 26, 144, 279, 360, 384, 427, 1521, 3346, 3610

305   Early Christian and Patristic sources
             86, 276, 609, 684, 700, 714, 715, 716, 717, 718, 719, 720, 726, 905, 906, 907,
             908, 909, 910, 1127, 1139, 1140, 1150, 1375, 1502, 1509, 2275, 2276, 2335,
             2381

305.1   -Arabic
             821, 900

305.2   -Armenian
             38

305.3   -Coptic
             14, 280, 609, 797, 1741

305.4   -Greek
             86, 276, 684, 713, 714, 715, 716, 717, 718, 719, 720, 773, 924, 1010, 1011,
             1025, 1060, 1138, 1140, 1147, 1148, 1177, 1403, 1610, 1681, 1740, 1749,
             1803, 1833, 2120, 2216, 2384, 2389, 2412, 2417, 2419, 2445, 2467, 2468,

2469, 2470, 2471, 2472, 2473, 2539, 2597, 3052, 3209, 3214, 3215, 3216, 3217, 3218, 3540, 3647

305.5   -Latin
700, 726, 773, 1102, 1103, 1750, 2540, 2542, 2543, 3095, 3192, 3196, 3210, 3211, 3212

305.6   -Syriac
14, 699, 1459, 2380, 2380, 2868, 3621

306   Later Christian sources
197, 198, 295, 1174, 1357, 2381, 2909, 2914

306.1   -Missionaries
2909, 2914

306.2   -Pilgrims
98, 109, 120, 148, 149, 156, 159, 184, 198, 238, 249, 289, 733, 739, 784, 1004, 1464, 1871, 2077, 2193, 2231, 2276, 2408, 2411, 2466, 2541, 2569, 2764, 2909, 2914, 3101, 3102, 3103, 3104, 3105, 3106, 3107, 3108, 3536, 3592

306.3   -Travellers to 1800CE
145, 295, 1005, 1006, 1130, 1186, 1466, 1479, 1554, 1613, 1679, 1680, 2197, 2215, 2718, 2846, 3060, 3101, 3102, 3103, 3104, 3105, 3106, 3107, 3108, 3586, 3587

307   Islamic sources
29, 1007, 1008, 1220, 1344, 1401, 1483, 1563, 2864, 3109, 3533, 3534

307.1   -Muslim geographers
15, 33, 1665, 1666, 1890, 2195, 2485, 3533, 3534

307.2   -Muslim historians
16, 970, 1401, 1476, 1612, 2001, 2119, 2195, 2393, 2906

307.3   -Muslim theologians
2195

308   Modern travellers
54, 605, 657, 731, 785, 928, 978, 979, 982, 1164, 1215, 1225, 1546, 1584, 1609, 1822, 1953, 2048, 2301, 2349, 2529, 2572, 2590, 2595, 2600, 2699, 2753, 2782, 2869, 3064, 3130, 3225, 3266, 3463, 3545, 3546

309   Modern Jewish travellers
1224, 1607, 2257, 2453, 2461, 2839

309.1   Samaritan sources
1114, 1143, 3112

309.2   Samaritan pilgrims
1308

3419, 3433, 3447, 3566, 3567, 3568, 3570, 3572, 3573, 3574, 3575, 3576, 3577, 3578, 3579, 3580, 3581, 3582, 3583, 3584, 3585

413   -Sychar
921, 922, 1001, 1447, 1838, 2867, 3606

414   -Tel Qasile
1793, 3275, 3276

415   -Tell er-Ras
614, 615, 618, 620, 621, 1272, 1820, 2113

416   -Yavneh
735

500   DIASPORA
244, 388, 403, 404, 783, 792, 868, 869, 1638, 1639, 1723, 2043, 2615, 3326

500.1   -Armenia
1803

501   -Arabia
1612

502   -Byzantium
280, 1417

503   -Damascus
477, 1004, 1228, 1920

504   -Delos
590, 1888, 3520

505   -Egypt
14, 427, 1414, 1844, 2123, 2372, 3385, 3386

506   -Greece
154, 1417, 1833

507   -Lebanon
2029

508   -Jordan
399, 1576, 2832

512   -Thessalonica
1986, 2733, 2870

600   ARCHAEOLOGY AND MATERIAL REMAINS
8, 92, 158, 159, 168, 171, 177, 178, 182, 195, 196, 234, 245, 251, 252, 253, 254, 255, 256, 265, 289, 310, 359, 363, 380, 385, 406, 462, 479, 488, 489,

612, 613, 615, 619, 621, 622, 623, 644, 647, 649, 650, 651, 652, 653, 655,
723, 730, 731, 735, 736, 740, 786, 788, 822, 833, 841, 842, 843, 844, 845,
846, 847, 921, 922, 932, 933, 935, 936, 1023, 1024, 1179, 1187, 1240, 1272,
1536, 1574, 1576, 1722, 1738, 1739, 1792, 1830, 1986, 2102, 2104, 2105,
2106, 2107, 2293, 2398, 2459, 2605, 2625, 2700, 2701, 2733, 2778, 2779,
2780, 2883, 2942, 2943, 2944, 2946, 2947, 3089, 3093, 3147, 3194, 3243,
3244, 3245, 3419, 3420, 3566, 3567, 3568, 3570, 3573, 3575, 3576, 3578,
3579, 3580, 3581, 3582, 3583, 3584, 3585, 3595, 3605, 3625, 3626, 3627,
3628, 3635

601   Amulets
       503, 606, 607, 846, 1307, 1510, 1796, 1798, 1799, 1800, 2025, 2029, 2137,
       2158, 2315, 2548, 2605, 2620, 2669, 2695, 2899, 2900, 2901, 3208, 3638

602   Architecture
       11, 63, 1115, 1515, 1659, 2112, 2593

603   Coinage and numismatics
       246, 265, 277, 284, 285, 740, 798, 846, 1255, 1266, 1267, 1527, 1528, 1531,
       1543, 1577, 1864, 1865, 2033, 2100, 2101, 2253, 2254, 2256, 2307, 2484,
       2680, 2703, 2704, 2707, 2708, 2709, 2711, 2830, 2881, 2942, 3000, 3038,
       3136, 3137, 3352, 3353, 3355, 3356, 3365, 3516

604   Cult symbols
       71, 85, 246, 2944, 2946, 3131

605   Lamps
       310, 377, 396, 406, 934, 1370, 2219, 2385, 2386, 3131, 3132, 3133, 3651

606   Miqvaot
       2108, 2694

606.1 Objects, Ivories, glass pottery
       845, 847, 1135, 1187, 1633, 1635, 1707, 1830, 1831, 1932, 1933, 2016, 2047,
       2218, 2672, 2673, 2850, 3057, 3092, 3093, 3124, 3625, 3638, 3640, 3641

607   Seals and scarabs
       299, 846, 1634, 2927, 3574

700   CHRONOLOGY
       374, 375, 512, 524, 581, 1102, 1103, 1185, 1277, 1413, 1940, 2535, 2578,
       2579, 2580, 2758, 2906, 2981, 3083, 3086, 3557

800   HISTORY BY PERIOD AND TOPIC
       6, 64, 66, 71, 85, 100, 103, 106, 126, 193, 235, 259, 278, 378, 411, 417, 418,
       425, 435, 440, 470, 487, 527, 541, 567, 589, 633, 645, 685, 687, 688, 689,
       743, 745, 750, 752, 757, 778, 792, 797, 850, 851, 935, 951, 989, 1113, 1150,
       1163, 1193, 1316, 1348, 1434, 1482, 1573, 1667, 1694, 1696, 1703, 1704,
       1733, 1751, 1754, 1755, 1837, 1845, 1846, 1861, 1914, 1947, 2065, 2078,
       2119, 2283, 2293, 2450, 2451, 2461, 2559, 2560, 2644, 2654, 2706, 2731,
       2817, 2853, 2908, 2986, 3083, 3099, 3100, 3142, 3175, 3297, 3299, 3406

801   Biblical period
           20, 35, 52, 55, 57, 100, 127, 150, 153, 157, 235, 288, 439, 478, 480, 487, 489,
           511, 611, 616, 618, 644, 647, 648, 649, 651, 652, 654, 673, 709, 744, 913,
           933, 1098, 1105, 1106, 1198, 1240, 1482, 1514, 1646, 1691, 1825, 1866,
           1867, 1903, 2067, 2182, 2282, 2418, 2421, 2499, 2644, 2653, 2670, 2930,
           3019, 3023, 3035, 3148, 3149, 3150, 3178, 3187, 3241, 3242, 3251, 3252,
           3427, 3463, 3482, 3511, 3513, 3566, 3572, 3576, 3578, 3579, 3600

801.1   -Samaritan origins
           47, 164, 235, 288, 382, 409, 569, 702, 722, 725, 741, 743, 744, 752, 867, 999,
           1026, 1068, 1091, 1106, 1126, 1152, 1260, 1383, 1519, 1544, 1720, 1805,
           1812, 1853, 2022, 2043, 2044, 2060, 2067, 2069, 2078, 2128, 2273, 2317,
           2418, 2527, 2570, 2630, 2645, 2648, 2655, 2670, 2717, 2736, 2745, 2746,
           2755, 2798, 2872, 3014, 3019, 3020, 3023, 3099, 3142, 3151, 3173, 3202,
           3248, 3424, 3427, 3527, 3528, 3531, 3630, 3640, 3641

801.2   -Ten lost tribes
           400, 913, 1397, 2407

802   Post-exilic period
           20, 157, 511, 568, 722, 742, 823, 832, 999, 1491, 1721, 1812, 1866, 2295,
           2322, 2323, 2798, 2859, 3019, 3178, 3187, 3246

802.1   -Sanballat
           823, 832, 1240, 1997, 2803, 2804, 2805, 2807, 2859, 2919, 2933, 2974, 3246,
           3247, 3531, 3551, 3631

803   Persian period
           611, 823, 1155, 1625, 1630, 1717, 2295, 2320, 2322, 2323, 2379, 3089, 3091,
           3093, 3143, 3147, 3385, 3386

804   The Hellenistic period
           4, 6, 154, 313, 434, 438, 513, 603, 645, 823, 828, 830, 933, 1001, 1018, 1420,
           1482, 1570, 1625, 1691, 1734, 1806, 1842, 2102, 2104, 2106, 2132, 2200,
           2322, 2323, 2324, 2421, 2442, 2638, 2676, 2919, 2920, 3627

805   The Hasmonaean period
           155, 457, 513, 1010, 1011, 1071, 1420, 1547, 1842, 2009, 2045, 2115, 2132,
           2242, 2322, 2323, 2324, 2325, 2422, 2655, 2820, 3098, 3384, 3512

806   The Herodian period
           154, 172, 461, 602, 645, 933, 960, 1035, 1135, 1471, 1482, 1503, 1504, 1734,
           1842, 1843, 1977, 2192, 2228, 2242, 2655, 2808, 2809, 2821, 2951, 3633

807   The period of the Procurators
           13, 46, 151, 173, 174, 180, 645, 1179, 1264, 1471, 1854, 1977, 2192, 2226,
           2559, 2560, 2649, 3094, 3399, 3489

808   Romano-Byzantine period
           8, 30, 172, 173, 174, 176, 180, 181, 404, 564, 600, 604, 666, 726, 851, 869,
           875, 880, 923, 925, 933, 956, 1025, 1046, 1060, 1074, 1138, 1147, 1264,

1678, 1710, 1718, 1742, 1797, 1817, 1854, 1977, 1982, 1983, 1984, 2075,
2105, 2109, 2115, 2120, 2338, 2378, 2417, 2463, 2539, 2597, 2620, 2664,
2665, 2689, 2806, 2808, 2809, 2822, 2823, 2824, 2825, 2883, 2885, 2953,
2954, 3077, 3078, 3116, 3131, 3274, 3308, 3357, 3554, 3637

808.1   -Rebellions against Byzantium
             10, 179, 564, 924, 932, 956, 1046, 2120, 2221, 2664, 2954, 3554, 3555

809   Islamic Rule to 900 CE
             6, 16, 19, 33, 635, 699, 820, 851, 1373, 1459, 1665, 1666, 1941, 2119, 2691,
             2954

810   Crusading period
             16, 19, 156, 365, 430, 977, 1357, 1373, 1665, 1666, 1818, 1819, 1941, 2305,
             2589, 2848, 3466

811   The Mediaeval period
             87, 427, 1435, 1818, 2910, 3305

812   The Renaissance period
             79

813   The modern period
             372, 389, 460, 778, 799, 973, 974, 975, 990, 1084, 1131, 1184, 1269, 1662,
             1769, 2049, 2245, 2246, 2290, 2292, 2760, 2877, 2910, 2911, 2912, 2993,
             3118, 3175, 3305

813.1   Under the Ottomans
             275, 389, 1596, 1662, 2911, 2915

813.2   In World War II
             300, 1315, 2860, 2911, 3097

900   SOCIAL AND ECONOMIC CONDITIONS
             General
             1683

902   Mediaeval period
             295, 384

903   Modern period
             23, 104, 107, 139, 140, 141, 275, 297, 372, 658, 661, 670, 758, 973, 974,
             975, 980, 990, 1043, 1076, 1084, 1131, 1172, 1182, 1192, 1193, 1224, 1262,
             1263, 1269, 1315, 1629, 1682, 1726, 1769, 1788, 1822, 1953, 2021, 2040,
             2048, 2049, 2245, 2246, 2290, 2292, 2298, 2340, 2675, 2744, 2759, 2760,
             2769, 2773, 2827, 2860, 2877, 2910, 2911, 2912, 3097, 3294, 3314, 3556,
             3607, 3609

1000   HISTORY OF RELIGION BY TOPIC AND PERIOD
             64, 138, 415, 685, 687, 688, 750, 757, 811, 875, 1033, 1121, 1318, 1367,
             1492, 3013, 3565

1001   Biblical period
            138, 551, 577, 654, 721, 795, 1035, 1284, 1297, 1526, 1687, 2606

1002   New Testament Period
            151, 197, 287, 296, 507, 662, 899, 947, 1035, 1213, 1216, 1436, 1570, 1571,
            1580, 1581, 1587, 1606, 1687, 1842, 1843, 1987, 1989, 1994, 1995, 2009,
            2242, 2255, 2284, 2338, 2655, 2791, 2928, 2999, 3223, 3483

1003   Relations with non-Samaritans
            67, 85, 167, 449, 513, 1161, 1260, 2424, 3109

1003.1   -Relations with Christianity
            67, 160, 207, 236, 240, 257, 286, 441, 450, 455, 461, 471, 502, 507, 509, 514,
            515, 520, 540, 545, 554, 591, 612, 613, 628, 656, 713, 714, 717, 719, 734,
            866, 896, 897, 898, 902, 912, 960, 1017, 1025, 1159, 1160, 1161, 1181, 1189,
            1207, 1248, 1387, 1399, 1416, 1417, 1422, 1435, 1503, 1504, 1516, 1570,
            1571, 1580, 1581, 1600, 1605, 1615, 1616, 1652, 1676, 1688, 1789, 1790,
            1791, 1810, 1834, 1835, 1836, 1838, 1855, 1856, 1862, 1923, 1959, 2007,
            2198, 2203, 2321, 2327, 2370, 2433, 2452, 2454, 2469, 2539, 2554, 2598,
            2616, 2626, 2634, 2885, 2975, 3069, 3114, 3193, 3399, 3487, 3512, 3652

1003.2   -Relations with Falashas
            1142, 1180

1003.3   -Relations with Islam
            282, 450, 516, 635, 821, 900, 902, 1119, 1220, 1331, 1344, 1347, 1380, 1483,
            1612, 1728, 1907, 2051, 2056, 2068, 2073, 2099, 2294, 2471, 2473, 2506,
            3109

1003.4   -Relations with Judaism
            47, 48, 186, 202, 282, 297, 450, 453, 454, 602, 603, 808, 854, 914, 925, 1031,
            1035, 1093, 1122, 1131, 1181, 1208, 1242, 1261, 1264, 1339, 1342, 1387,
            1498, 1500, 1503, 1504, 1524, 1525, 1562, 1567, 1611, 1920, 1976, 2004,
            2011, 2012, 2013, 2014, 2287, 2289, 2306, 2328, 2424, 2606, 2609, 2642,
            2791, 2863, 2873, 3248, 3302, 3386, 3413, 3637

1004   -Relations with Karaites
            87, 331, 351, 402, 1390, 1477, 1480, 1494, 1525, 1712, 1875, 2011, 2012,
            2013, 2014, 2122, 2124, 2173, 2586, 3413

1005   -Relations with Qumran
            40, 232, 234, 355, 362, 363, 446, 447, 518, 519, 824, 829, 833, 866, 1082,
            1129, 1145, 1206, 1380, 1478, 1860, 2203, 2286, 2506, 2690, 2905, 3172,
            3255, 3263, 3548

1100   THEOLOGY AND BELIEFS
            201, 211, 470, 482, 541, 559, 561, 567, 606, 751, 789, 811, 882, 889, 1022,
            1029, 1030, 1040, 1160, 1295, 1318, 1319, 1331, 1339, 1342, 1345, 1363,
            1500, 1694, 1696, 1719, 1754, 1755, 1757, 1805, 1811, 1832, 1844, 1869,
            1880, 1901, 2055, 2056, 2066, 2071, 2072, 2079, 2227, 2274, 2354, 2396,
            2658, 2743, 2984, 3029, 3068, 3222, 3480, 3510, 3539, 3565, 3646

1403   New Year
         202, 3304

1404   Passover
         54, 118, 130, 196, 205, 224, 225, 273, 379, 539, 664, 817, 901, 914, 957,
         1019, 1182, 1202, 1270, 1282, 1305, 1329, 1412, 1518, 1582, 1588, 1590,
         1591, 1697, 1702, 1732, 1735, 1746, 1809, 1849, 1908, 1909, 1960, 1967,
         1973, 1974, 1992, 1993, 2041, 2074, 2159, 2188, 2190, 2224, 2309, 2341,
         2342, 2345, 2346, 2347, 2446, 2456, 2529, 2549, 2551, 2600, 2760, 2893,
         2932, 2973, 2982, 3032, 3063, 3064, 3228, 3272, 3277, 3280, 3284, 3300,
         3318, 3322, 3323, 3351, 3369, 3439, 3460, 3525, 3526, 3543, 3603, 3645

1405   Sabbath
         1332, 1700, 3289, 3290, 3315, 3317, 3320, 3321, 3325, 3337, 3607

1406   Seven Sabbaths
         3316

1407   Shavuot/Weeks
         539, 560, 1330, 1418, 2495, 3310, 3319, 3337

1408   Simhat Torah
         2189

1409   Succoth/Tabernacles
         113, 539, 1429, 3312, 3321, 3324

1500 SECTS AND MOVEMENTS
         188, 214, 518, 541, 543, 547, 638, 710, 726, 750, 754, 879, 900, 1031, 1083,
         1087, 1122, 1141, 1214, 1602, 1713, 1748, 1964, 1989, 2039, 2393, 2462,
         2540, 2542, 2543, 2584, 2802, 2879, 3378

1501   Athinganoi-Touch me not
         820, 1406

1502   Christian Samaritans
         197, 207, 286, 432, 436, 437, 448, 461, 507, 540, 628, 698, 782, 837, 839,
         840, 896, 897, 912, 939, 940, 946, 960, 1061, 1078, 1137, 1248, 1493, 1618,
         1657, 1658, 1862, 2203, 2316, 2370, 2433, 2470, 2476, 2502, 2503, 2554,
         2565, 2616, 2634, 2693, 2712, 2732, 2826, 2922, 2923, 2975, 3069, 3114,
         3193, 3240, 3268, 3271, 3475, 3487, 3652

1502.1   -John's Gospel
         36, 160, 207, 236, 240, 264, 286, 471, 472, 485, 486, 502, 509, 510, 515, 528,
         545, 554, 565, 598, 612, 613, 637, 662, 667, 704, 705, 715, 782, 837, 839,
         894, 895, 896, 897, 898, 905, 909, 912, 939, 940, 948, 949, 950, 993, 1015,
         1016, 1066, 1156, 1183, 1235, 1236, 1237, 1238, 1247, 1352, 1354, 1368,
         1381, 1421, 1426, 1439, 1470, 1472, 1488, 1505, 1615, 1622, 1652, 1657,
         1658, 1743, 1801, 1837, 1838, 1869, 1912, 1913, 1959, 1966, 1987, 2020,
         2232, 2233, 2234, 2235, 2249, 2296, 2299, 2353, 2410, 2445, 2454, 2455,
         2458, 2460, 2465, 2468, 2494, 2510, 2553, 2558, 2568, 2575, 2591, 2592,
         2640, 2750, 2800, 2815, 2816, 2867, 2878, 2895, 2935, 2995, 3037, 3066,
         3067, 3070, 3198, 3390, 3451, 3483

1502.2   -Stephen-Acts
           257, 263, 436, 437, 756, 837, 839, 896, 897, 1070, 1074, 1094, 1161, 1203,
           1396, 1418, 1605, 1657, 1658, 1736, 1834, 1835, 1836, 1857, 2133, 2243,
           2487, 2720, 2721, 2861, 2884, 2924, 2990, 2991, 3045, 3055, 3079, 3138,
           3264

1502.3   -Good Samaritan
           431, 441, 448, 449, 536, 681, 814, 815, 816, 838, 926, 929, 1014, 1088, 1089,
           1116, 1124, 1256, 1353, 1369, 1409, 1410, 1493, 1578, 1580, 1595, 1730,
           1787, 1855, 1925, 1926, 1955, 1956, 1994, 1995, 2206, 2213, 2302, 2502,
           2503, 2504, 2603, 2674, 2696, 2720, 2842, 2948, 2987, 3024, 3025, 3044,
           3051, 3207, 3383, 3389, 3535, 3612, 3644

1502.4   -Luke
           514, 591, 1136, 1146, 1207, 1257, 1258, 1259, 1395, 1411, 1736, 1856, 2302,
           2452, 2472, 2603, 2674, 2918, 3613

1502.5   -Barnabas
           525

1503   Dositheans
           101, 188, 296, 465, 543, 547, 601, 638, 776, 858, 1141, 1214, 1481, 1489,
           1631, 1685, 1686, 1840, 1872, 1873, 1894, 1895, 1920, 1989, 2130, 2238,
           2303, 2356, 2371, 2540, 2542, 2543, 2610, 2639, 2732, 3360, 3372, 3461

1504   Dustan Sect
           638, 1214, 1872, 1873, 1894, 1895, 2008, 2615

1505   Essenes
           214

1506   Gnostic Samaritans
           36, 296, 432, 433, 1183, 1201, 1208, 1209, 1211, 1246, 1427, 1485, 1744,
           1923, 1961, 2031, 2249, 2662, 2925, 3045, 3268, 3269, 3418, 3601

1506.1   -Menander
           1201, 1427, 2540, 3361

1506.2   -Simon Magus
           36, 280, 432, 433, 631, 632, 669, 671, 687, 696, 697, 1078, 1201, 1245, 1246,
           1252, 1427, 1486, 1506, 1535, 1602, 1961, 1985, 2031, 2032, 2229, 2240,
           2300, 2475, 2477, 2479, 2540, 2599, 2663, 2810, 2834, 2835, 2849, 2892,
           3017, 3045, 3059, 3450, 3477, 3530, 3548

1507   Sabbeans
           2304

1550   LITERATURE

           84, 124, 189, 190, 340, 417, 418, 589, 685, 811, 870, 970, 1175, 1302, 1316,
           1550, 1555, 1647, 1880, 1971, 2015, 2051, 2094, 2285, 2588, 2755, 2904,
           3073, 3160, 3267, 3340, 3374

1600   Chronicles-general
        28, 66, 129, 409, 737, 777, 853, 863, 970, 1185, 1244, 1318, 1432, 1552,
        1899, 2076, 2436, 2482, 2505, 2555, 2556, 2601, 3085, 3087

1601   -Abu l-Fath's chronicle
        17, 18, 66, 421, 602, 1678, 2306, 2375, 2482, 2505, 2509, 2823, 2886, 2888,
        3080, 3081, 3083, 3401

1602   -Adler and Seligsohn's chronicle/New Chronicle
        28, 737, 1678, 2601, 2795

1603   -Chronicle II
        230, 231, 318, 762, 961, 1204, 1359, 1469, 1600, 1705, 1950, 2062, 2237,
        2348, 2436, 2516, 2788, 2831, 3010, 3377, 3522

1604   -Joshua, Book of (Arabic version)
        27, 129, 165, 370, 371, 813, 855, 882, 917, 918, 919, 920, 1158, 1219, 1278,
        1279, 1293, 1301, 1322, 1325, 1423, 1624, 1745, 1747, 1752, 1782, 1783,
        1784, 1785, 2602, 2668, 2698, 2917, 3598, 3599, 3622

1605   -Joshua, Book of (Hebrew version)
        27, 191, 370, 371, 387, 786, 793, 855, 856, 882, 917, 918, 919, 920, 1219,
        1283, 1285, 1293, 1298, 1299, 1301, 1322, 1325, 1423, 1624, 1745, 1747,
        1777, 1778, 1782, 1783, 1784, 1785, 2042, 2602, 2668, 2698, 2917, 3598,
        3599

1607   -Tulida
        553, 737, 1552, 2400, 2401

1700   Correspondence with western scholars
        45, 62, 83, 167, 958, 969, 997, 1598, 1946, 2006, 2034, 2246, 2331, 2828,
        2890, 3402

1701   -De Sacy
        969, 1598

1702   -Huntington
        1655, 1656

1703   -Ludolph
        595, 686, 2034

1704   -Pietro della Valle
        1005, 1006

1705   -Scaliger
        971, 1508, 2331, 2334, 2464

1800   Folklore and legends
        291, 409, 777, 779, 1056, 1191, 1317, 1379, 1564, 2449, 2524, 2581, 2642,
        2651, 2744, 3022, 3301, 3341, 3403, 3404, 3633

2102.1   -Defter
            583, 1226, 1231, 1761, 1771, 1841, 2183, 2186, 3143

2102.2   -Durran
            340, 2071

2103   Rites of passage
            97, 854, 881, 889, 1321, 3134, 3288

2104   Sabbath Prayers
            542, 3289, 3290, 3315, 3317, 3320, 3321, 3325, 3337

2200   Religious writings and codes: general
            3, 481, 482, 484, 1858, 2151, 2166, 2392, 2587, 2715, 2716, 3002, 3373

2201   -Hillukh
            3087

2202   -Kitab at-Tabbakh
            482, 2423, 3469, 3470, 3471, 3472, 3474, 3485, 3486

2203   -Kitab al-Kafi
            3, 482, 2429, 2561, 2729

2203.1   -Kitab al-Khilaf
            1495

2204   -Kitab al-Mirath
            217, 325, 482, 1863, 2354, 2392, 2562

2205   -Polemics and apologetics
            83, 260, 570, 1495, 1498, 1500, 1875, 1976, 2122, 2328, 2606, 2908, 3054,
            3074, 3493

2206   -Malef
            534, 546

2207   -Sefer Hayerushot
            3282, 3283

2300   PENTATEUCH VERSIONS , COMMENTARIES AND EXEGESIS
            General
            1, 22, 39, 62, 68, 70, 72, 76, 77, 78, 80, 83, 84, 93, 95, 96, 102, 114, 119, 124,
            125, 133, 142, 163, 199, 200, 209, 212, 215, 218, 221, 223, 226, 227, 228,
            229, 232, 250, 267, 274, 283, 314, 324, 327, 338, 362, 363, 367, 375, 383,
            397, 407, 451, 458, 459, 463, 469, 483, 508, 586, 610, 625, 626, 627, 636,
            640, 642, 660, 668, 673, 678, 689, 692, 724, 725, 727, 749, 753, 765, 774,
            808, 810, 812, 819, 822, 829, 836, 911, 937, 952, 953, 954, 955, 967, 968,
            995, 1003, 1020, 1021, 1050, 1067, 1077, 1079, 1090, 1096, 1100, 1107,
            1118, 1123, 1151, 1153, 1154, 1173, 1190, 1222, 1223, 1229, 1232, 1233,
            1234, 1240, 1273, 1274, 1306, 1310, 1334, 1337, 1339, 1341, 1342, 1343,
            1345, 1355, 1362, 1364, 1374, 1376, 1382, 1383, 1384, 1388, 1389, 1391,
            1393, 1419, 1430, 1438, 1458, 1507, 1512, 1538, 1541, 1542, 1545, 1548,

1551, 1566, 1568, 1572, 1593, 1614, 1636, 1642, 1643, 1645, 1648, 1649, 1650, 1651, 1653, 1654, 1706, 1737, 1738, 1759, 1760, 1761, 1773, 1779, 1780, 1821, 1826, 1827, 1828, 1829, 1850, 1874, 1876, 1878, 1881, 1882, 1885, 1898, 1905, 1921, 1942, 1943, 1944, 1946, 1951, 1954, 1969, 1970, 1988, 1990, 1991, 1998, 1999, 2035, 2036, 2160, 2169, 2180, 2185, 2191, 2194, 2199, 2201, 2204, 2209, 2220, 2223, 2225, 2258, 2259, 2260, 2261, 2262, 2263, 2264, 2265, 2266, 2267, 2270, 2285, 2291, 2319, 2329, 2330, 2332, 2333, 2337, 2355, 2360, 2361, 2363, 2367, 2377, 2391, 2409, 2418, 2420, 2447, 2480, 2481, 2488, 2490, 2507, 2531, 2533, 2534, 2544, 2570, 2626, 2647, 2648, 2652, 2660, 2685, 2686, 2690, 2735, 2736, 2737, 2738, 2744, 2758, 2768, 2782, 2796, 2797, 2811, 2812, 2813, 2840, 2841, 2847, 2866, 2921, 2931, 2934, 2945, 2957, 2970, 2977, 2992, 2994, 3012, 3020, 3046, 3047, 3048, 3050, 3113, 3129, 3146, 3165, 3171, 3180, 3181, 3183, 3184, 3185, 3186, 3221, 3226, 3227, 3233, 3234, 3235, 3236, 3237, 3238, 3249, 3250, 3255, 3256, 3259, 3260, 3261, 3262, 3263, 3309, 3327, 3331, 3342, 3354, 3370, 3381, 3391, 3425, 3434, 3435, 3444, 3452, 3454, 3455, 3456, 3457, 3458, 3459, 3464, 3465, 3476, 3484, 3490, 3491, 3494, 3495, 3497, 3498, 3499, 3500, 3502, 3504, 3505, 3506, 3519, 3537, 3549, 3550, 3553, 3559, 3560, 3561, 3562, 3591, 3615, 3617, 3632, 3643

2301   Abisha scroll
        367, 800, 848, 849, 1309, 1311, 1371, 1372, 1759, 1760, 2318, 2517, 2518, 2519, 2520, 2521, 2739, 2744, 2748, 3015, 3062, 3170, 3183, 3195, 3388, 3417, 3514, 3597

2302   Arabic versions
        208, 218, 451, 463, 937, 969, 972, 976, 1050, 1075, 1096, 1501, 1661, 1664, 1714, 1753, 1761, 1765, 1900, 1902, 2092, 2138, 2507, 2508, 2688, 2747, 2887, 2958, 2959, 2960, 2961, 2962, 2963, 2964, 2965, 2966, 2967, 2969, 3331, 3391

2304   Commentaries
        1496, 1520, 1858, 2000, 2011, 2012, 2013, 2191, 2401, 2612, 2889

2305   Exegesis
        227, 262, 483, 522, 761, 959, 1208, 1222, 1223, 1338, 1689, 1690, 1758, 2017, 2026, 2027, 2028, 2084, 2085, 2088, 2434, 2448, 2585, 2619, 2679, 2771, 3054, 3156, 3376, 3444, 3462, 3473, 3537

2306.1 Massorah
        327, 763, 764, 1290, 1304, 1382, 1761, 1764, 1773, 2525

2307   Proto-Samaritan texts -Qumran
        40, 209, 446, 579, 586, 626, 627, 640, 749, 945, 1129, 1132, 1241, 1343, 1430, 1542, 1648, 2208, 2210, 2211, 2212, 2496, 2843, 2844, 2845, 2882, 3005, 3006, 3007, 3008, 3009, 3011, 3050, 3120, 3172, 3253, 3255, 3257, 3259, 3260, 3261, 3262, 3263, 3363, 3364, 3524, 3558

2308   Reading of the Pentateuch
        229, 327, 542, 660, 807, 1276, 1619, 2052, 3043

2309   Samariticon
            218, 1010, 1011, 1157, 1241, 1393, 1394, 1877, 2435, 2496, 2671, 3258,
            3532, 3564

2309.1   Pentateuch scrolls
            640, 891, 1310, 1996, 2134, 2208, 2209, 2210, 2211, 2212, 3057, 3293

2400   Septuagint
            32, 218, 636, 774, 1010, 1011, 1157, 1177, 1222, 1223, 1299, 1355, 1541,
            1566, 1614, 1729, 1877, 2265, 2266, 2267, 2671, 2931, 3049, 3162, 3258,
            3532, 3564

2400.1   Origen's Hexapla
            1177

2401   Targum
            218, 248, 451, 574, 588, 959, 986, 988, 1048, 1049, 1051, 1053, 1058, 1059,
            1104, 1337, 1404, 1772, 1781, 1845, 2035, 2084, 2095, 2147, 2149, 2150,
            2152, 2157, 2167, 2168, 2174, 2176, 2285, 2310, 2439, 2451, 2480, 2628,
            2876, 3001, 3004, 3155, 3158, 3161, 3163, 3164, 3165, 3166, 3167, 3189,
            3331, 3431, 3588

2500   INSCRIPTIONS AND PALAEOGRAPHY

            12, 34, 51, 56, 58, 132, 213, 233, 336, 369, 376, 377, 390, 391, 392, 393, 394,
            395, 406, 408, 413, 414, 428, 429, 468, 469, 624, 634, 677, 679, 680, 701,
            728, 729, 1178, 1424, 1637, 2202, 2368, 2369, 2382, 2383, 2384, 2387, 2388,
            2515, 2605, 2613, 2756, 2770, 2956, 3058, 3119, 3192, 3199, 3200, 3350,
            3412, 3417, 3421, 3651

2501   Epigraphy and script
            45, 84, 90, 91, 99, 103, 111, 233, 277, 284, 285, 396, 398, 412, 414, 422, 423,
            424, 445, 447, 594, 624, 627, 630, 633, 676, 692, 694, 740, 798, 825, 864,
            865, 871, 874, 904, 915, 1062, 1063, 1065, 1085, 1101, 1104, 1144, 1251,
            1266, 1267, 1361, 1617, 1632, 1886, 1917, 1971, 1981, 2033, 2437, 2489,
            2500, 2548, 2637, 2703, 2711, 2830, 2903, 2988, 2997, 3036, 3039, 3136,
            3137, 3200, 3347, 3352, 3353, 3355, 3356, 3426

2501.1   Palaeography
            930, 1097, 1303, 1335, 1915, 2646, 3003, 3524

2502   -Amwas/Emmaus
            84, 393, 428, 738, 985, 1149, 1356, 1490, 1916, 1918, 1919, 2885, 3126

2503   -Beit el-Ma
            34, 132, 369, 392, 408

2503.1   -Beth Shean
            396, 1795

2504   -Decalogue
            56, 58, 213, 396, 457, 533, 556, 3121, 3589

2505   -es Sindiane
            2902

2506   -Damascus
            414, 2369, 2767, 3030

2507   -Delos
            3520

2508   -Gaza
            10, 12, 51, 131, 728, 729, 732, 2546, 2596, 2939, 3199, 3200, 3201

2508.1   -Gerizim
            391

2509   -Kfar Bilu
            111, 395

2510   -Kafr Khalil
            213, 390

2510.1   -Nablus
            2050, 2100, 2515, 2770, 3123

2510.2   -Salbit
            3127, 3128

2511   -Siyagha
            3611

2512   -Tell Qasile
            2090, 2486, 3275

2513   -Thessalonica
            1637, 2646, 3254

2514   -Ustinov collection
            132, 336

2515   -Yavneh and Lydda
            337, 376, 394, 735, 1794

2600   **SAMARITAN LANGUAGES**

Hebrew-general
22, 59, 124, 242, 247, 301, 305, 312, 322, 327, 329, 330, 332, 334, 335, 341,
343, 344, 345, 347, 349, 350, 354, 355, 356, 357, 358, 361, 364, 429, 456,
468, 469, 575, 578, 599, 676, 677, 678, 679, 680, 691, 694, 759, 818, 819,
984, 1054, 1095, 1144, 1199, 1200, 1242, 1253, 1361, 1385, 1415, 1432,
1441, 1443, 1522, 1537, 1539, 1540, 1555, 1608, 1623, 1632, 1641, 1644,
1648, 1693, 1724, 1763, 1766, 1774, 1786, 1880, 1910, 1911, 1928, 1970,

1971, 2002, 2015, 2030, 2036, 2058, 2083, 2088, 2093, 2117, 2118, 2121,
2129, 2146, 2151, 2164, 2165, 2171, 2205, 2268, 2269, 2270, 2285, 2333,
2337, 2355, 2361, 2362, 2363, 2383, 2384, 2413, 2443, 2444, 2492, 2500,
2531, 2661, 2682, 2683, 2684, 2728, 2749, 2772, 2796, 2836, 2897, 2904,
2907, 2937, 2950, 2955, 3036, 3110, 3111, 3152, 3153, 3154, 3177, 3206,
3224, 3348, 3359, 3374, 3398, 3409, 3414, 3416, 3452, 3457, 3458, 3502,
3561, 3616, 3624

2600.1   -Accent systems
343, 355

2601   Samaritan Hebrew and Qumran
344, 663, 1884

2602   -Grammar
221, 305, 327, 347, 357, 691, 759, 1336, 1365, 1924, 2061, 2089, 2098, 2148,
2149, 2150, 2176, 2268, 2364, 2528, 2571, 2659, 2661, 2730, 2749, 3048,
3219, 3220, 3394, 3449, 3614

2603   -Lexicography
323, 332, 689, 1195, 1365, 1644, 1779, 1878, 2152, 2153, 2155, 2156, 2285,
3048, 3159, 3340, 3407, 3602, 3615

2603.1   -Morphology and orthography
345, 763, 764, 765, 766, 2136, 2164, 2366

2604   -pronunciation
322, 333, 1620, 1668, 1766, 1770, 1786, 2367, 3046, 3047, 3048

2605   -tetragrammaton
333, 1558, 1692, 2070

2606   -speech
1945

2607   -vocalisation
327, 341, 344, 358, 1668, 1669, 1671, 1768, 2135, 2136, 2154, 2165, 2364,
2367

2700   Arabic
2015, 2962, 2968, 2971, 3084, 3407, 3468, 3624

2800   Aramaic
216, 222, 242, 326, 332, 334, 346, 348, 473, 860, 916, 1047, 1052, 1055,
1057, 1165, 1194, 1196, 1442, 1608, 2015, 2058, 2082, 2084, 2093, 2129,
2134, 2145, 2147, 2155, 2156, 2157, 2162, 2174, 2177, 2491, 2776, 2785,
2855, 2936, 2971, 3001, 3004, 3018, 3034, 3153, 3154, 3157, 3190, 3345,
3409, 3414

2900   SAMARITAN ETHNOLOGY AND ETHNOGRAPHY
138, 490, 491, 492, 493, 494, 495, 496, 497, 498, 499, 500, 501, 541, 1349,
1350, 1351, 1788, 2344, 3556

2901   Anthropology
        490, 491, 492, 493, 494, 495, 496, 497, 498, 499, 500, 501, 629, 1349, 1350,
        1351, 1378, 1462, 1660, 2340, 2819, 2862, 2949, 3139, 3140, 3141, 3507,
        3509, 3618

2902   Clans and families
        382

2904   Demography and statistics
        382, 460, 544, 670, 758, 1172, 1629

3000 SAMARITAN INDIVIDUALS
        366, 368, 886, 2744, 2952

3000.1 Aaron
        1411

3001   Abu l-Fath
        2375

3002   Abu l-Hassan as-Suri
        3, 1496, 2423

3002.2 Abraham Qabassa
        1499

3003   Baba Rabba
        231, 762, 2823, 3522

3004   Dositheus
        1489, 1987, 2130, 3360, 3530, 3548

3005   Ibrahim ibn al-'Ayyah
        2524, 2742

3006   Jacob es Shelaby
        1738, 2760

3006.1 Joshua
        858

3006.2 Joseph
        1145, 2905

3007   Marinus
        2837

3008   Moses
        7, 293, 963, 1036, 1167, 1191, 1212, 1327, 1411, 1474, 2064, 2235, 2236,
        2651, 2774, 2832, 2945, 3203, 3287

3008.1   Muslim ibn Murjan
         2771

3009   Munnaja
         1022, 2984

3009.1   Pinhas
         1408

3010   Proculus
         2837

3010.1   Thallus
         2726, 3445

3011   Tsedaka family
         658, 3313

3100   SAMARITAN ART
         70, 3293

3300   SAMARITAN MUSIC
         760, 767, 1358, 1366, 1592, 1593, 1620, 1621, 1670, 1671, 1807, 1808, 2051,
         3031, 3040, 3041, 3042

3301   Accent systems in music
         3041

3302   Cantillation
         1619, 3043

3303   Organum
         2687

3500   SAMARITAN MEDICINE AND SCIENCE
         1080, 1239, 1758, 2344, 2819, 2862, 3075, 3618

3600   SAMARITAN COOKING
         1893

SHORT TITLE INDEX

ABOUT THE AUTHOR

Alan David Crown (M.A., University of Leeds, Ph.D., University of Sydney) is currently Head of the Department of Semitic Studies at the University of Sydney. The holder of a personal chair in Semitic Studies, he is also a Senior Associate Fellow of the Oxford Centre for Postgraduate Hebrew Studies and a Director of the Archive of Australian Judaica at the University of Sydney. He is active in the Société d'Études Samaritaines, of which he was a founding member. In 1989 he was elected to join the Advisory Council of the World Union of Jewish Studies, and in 1991 he became an Honorary Member of the Society for the Study of Ethiopian Jewry, which he had helped to establish.

His long-term interest in the Samaritans is reflected in his numerous articles on the subject, the book *The Samaritans* (J. C. B. Mohr, Tübingen) which he edited in 1989, his conjoint editorship of *A Companion to Samaritan Studies* (J. C. B. Mohr, Tübingen, 1993) and this second edition of *A Bibliography of the Samaritans* (Scarecrow, 1993).